THE FIFTH DISCIPLINE

THE FIFTH DISCIPLINE

THE ART AND PRACTICE OF THE
LEARNING ORGANIZATION

PETER M. SENGE

CENTURY
BUSINESS

The right of Peter M. Senge to be identified as the author of this work has been
asserted by him in accordance with the Copyright, Designs and Patents Act, 1988

First trade edition published in the USA by Doubleday

First published in Great Britain (by arrangement with Doubleday, a division of
Bantam Doubleday Dell Publishing Group, Inc,) in 1992
by Century Business

Reprinted 1992, 1993, 1994, 1995, 1996, 1997, 1998

This paperback edition first published in Great Britain in 1993
by Century Business
An imprint of Random House UK Ltd
20 Vauxhall Bridge Road, London SW1V 2SA

Random House Australia (Pty) Ltd
20 Alfred Street, Milsons Point
Sydney, NSW 2061, Australia

Random House New Zealand Ltd
18 Poland Road, Glenfield
Auckland 10, New Zealand

Random House, South Africa (Pty) Ltd
Endulini, 5a Jubilee Road,
Parktown 2193, South Africa

Printed and bound in Great Britain by
Athenæum Press Ltd, Gateshead, Tyne & Wear

A catalogue record for this book is available from the British Library

ISBN 0–7126–5687–1

TO DIANE

CONTENTS

P A R T   I V

PROTOTYPES

P A R T   V

CODA

PART I

How Our Actions
Create Our Reality . . .
and How We Can
Change It

1

"GIVE ME A LEVER LONG ENOUGH...AND SINGLE-HANDED I CAN MOVE THE WORLD"

From a very early age, we are taught to break apart problems, to fragment the world. This apparently makes complex tasks and subjects more manageable, but we pay a hidden, enormous price. We can no longer see the consequences of our actions; we lose our intrinsic sense of connection to a larger whole. When we then try to "see the big picture," we try to reassemble the fragments in our minds, to list and organize all the pieces. But, as physicist David Bohm says, the task is futile—similar to trying to reassemble the fragments of a broken mirror to see a true reflection. Thus, after a while we give up trying to see the whole altogether.

The tools and ideas presented in this book are for destroying the illusion that the world is created of separate, unrelated forces. When we give up this illusion—we can then build "learning organizations," organizations where people continually expand their capacity to create the results they truly desire, where new and expansive patterns of thinking are nurtured, where collective aspiration is set free, and where people are continually learning how to learn together.

As *Fortune* magazine recently said, "Forget your tired old ideas about leadership. The most successful corporation of the 1990s will be something called a learning organization." "The ability to learn faster than your competitors," said Arie De Geus, head of planning for Royal Dutch/Shell, "may be the only sustainable competitive advantage." As the world becomes more interconnected and business becomes more complex and dynamic, work must become more "learningful." It is no longer sufficient to have one person learning for the organization, a Ford or a Sloan or a Watson. It's just not possible any longer to "figure it out" from the top, and have everyone else following the orders of the "grand strategist." The organizations that will truly excel in the future will be the organizations that discover how to tap people's commitment and capacity to learn at *all* levels in an organization.

Learning organizations are possible because, deep down, we are all learners. No one has to teach an infant to learn. In fact, no one has to teach infants anything. They are intrinsically inquisitive, masterful learners who learn to walk, speak, and pretty much run their households all on their own. Learning organizations are possible because not only is it our nature to learn but we love to learn. Most of us at one time or another have been part of a great "team," a group of people who functioned together in an extraordinary way—who trusted one another, who complemented each others' strengths and compensated for each others' limitations, who had common goals that were larger than individual goals, and who produced extraordinary results. I have met many people who have experienced this sort of profound teamwork—in sports, or in the performing arts, or in business. Many say that they have spent much of their life looking for that experience again. What they experienced was a learning organization. The team that became great didn't start off great—it *learned* how to produce extraordinary results.

One could argue that the entire global business community is learning to learn together, becoming a learning community. Whereas once many industries were dominated by a single, undisputed leader —one IBM, one Kodak, one Procter & Gamble, one Xerox—today industries, especially in manufacturing, have dozens of excellent companies. American and European corporations are pulled forward by the example of the Japanese; the Japanese, in turn, are pulled by the Koreans and Europeans. Dramatic improvements take place in corporations in Italy, Australia, Singapore—and quickly become influential around the world.

There is also another, in some ways deeper, movement toward learning organizations, part of the evolution of industrial society. Material affluence for the majority has gradually shifted people's orientation toward work—from what Daniel Yankelovich called an "instrumental" view of work, where work was a means to an end, to a more "sacred" view, where people seek the "intrinsic" benefits of work.[1] "Our grandfathers worked six days a week to earn what most of us now earn by Tuesday afternoon," says Bill O'Brien, CEO of Hanover Insurance. "The ferment in management will continue until we build organizations that are more consistent with man's higher aspirations beyond food, shelter and belonging."

Moreover, many who share these values are now in leadership positions. I find a growing number of organizational leaders who, while still a minority, feel they are part of a profound evolution in the nature of work as a social institution. "Why can't we do good works at work?" asked Edward Simon, president of Herman Miller, recently. "Business is the only institution that has a chance, as far as I can see, to fundamentally improve the injustice that exists in the world. But first, we will have to move through the barriers that are keeping us from being truly vision-led and capable of learning."

Perhaps the most salient reason for building learning organizations is that we are only now starting to understand the capabilities such organizations must possess. For a long time, efforts to build learning organizations were like groping in the dark until the skills, areas of knowledge, and paths for development of such organizations became known. What fundamentally will distinguish learning organizations from traditional authoritarian "controlling organizations" will be the mastery of certain basic disciplines. That is why the "disciplines of the learning organization" are vital.

DISCIPLINES OF
THE LEARNING ORGANIZATION

On a cold, clear morning in December 1903, at Kitty Hawk, North Carolina, the fragile aircraft of Wilbur and Orville Wright proved that powered flight was possible. Thus was the airplane invented; but it would take more than thirty years before commercial aviation could serve the general public.

Engineers say that a new idea has been "invented" when it is proven to work in the laboratory. The idea becomes an "innovation" only when it can be replicated reliably on a meaningful scale at practical costs. If the idea is sufficiently important, such as the telephone, the digital computer, or commercial aircraft, it is called a "basic innovation," and it creates a new industry or transforms an existing industry. In these terms, learning organizations have been invented, but they have not yet been innovated.

In engineering, when an idea moves from an invention to an innovation, diverse "component technologies" come together. Emerging from isolated developments in separate fields of research, these components gradually form an "ensemble of technologies that are critical to each others' success. Until this ensemble forms, the idea, though possible in the laboratory, does not achieve its potential in practice.[2]

The Wright Brothers proved that powered flight was possible, but the McDonnell Douglas DC-3, introduced in 1935, ushered in the era of commercial air travel. The DC-3 was the first plane that supported itself economically as well as aerodynamically. During those intervening thirty years (a typical time period for incubating basic innovations), myriad experiments with commercial flight had failed. Like early experiments with learning organizations, the early planes were not reliable and cost effective on an appropriate scale.

The DC-3, for the first time, brought together five critical component technologies that formed a successful ensemble. They were: the variable-pitch propeller, retractable landing gear, a type of lightweight molded body construction called "monocque," radial air-cooled engine, and wing flaps. To succeed, the DC-3 needed all five; four were not enough. One year earlier, the Boeing 247 was introduced with all of them except wing flaps. Lacking wing flaps, Boeing's engineers found that the plane was unstable on take-off and landing and had to downsize the engine.

Today, I believe, five new "component technologies" are gradually converging to innovate learning organizations. Though developed separately, each will, I believe, prove critical to the others' success, just as occurs with any ensemble. Each provides a vital dimension in building organizations that can truly "learn," that can continually enhance their capacity to realize their highest aspirations:

Systems Thinking. A cloud masses, the sky darkens, leaves twist upward, and we know that it will rain. We also know that after the storm, the runoff will feed into groundwater miles away, and the sky will grow clear by tomorrow. All these events are distant in time and space, and yet they are all connected within the same pattern. Each has an influence on the rest, an influence that is usually hidden from view. You can only understand the system of a rainstorm by contemplating the whole, not any individual part of the pattern.

Business and other human endeavors are also systems. They, too, are bound by invisible fabrics of interrelated actions, which often take years to fully play out their effects on each other. Since we are part of that lacework ourselves, it's doubly hard to see the whole pattern of change. Instead, we tend to focus on snapshots of isolated parts of the system, and wonder why our deepest problems never seem to get solved. Systems thinking is a conceptual framework, a body of knowledge and tools that has been developed over the past fifty years, to make the full patterns clearer, and to help us see how to change them effectively.

Though the tools are new, the underlying worldview is extremely intuitive; experiments with young children show that they learn systems thinking very quickly.

Personal Mastery. Mastery might suggest gaining dominance over people or things. But mastery can also mean a special level of proficiency. A master craftsman doesn't dominate pottery or weaving. People with a high level of personal mastery are able to consistently realize the results that matter most deeply to them— in effect, they approach their life as an artist would approach a work of art. They do that by becoming committed to their own lifelong learning.

Personal mastery is the discipline of continually clarifying and deepening our personal vision, of focusing our energies, of developing patience, and of seeing reality objectively. As such, it is an essential cornerstone of the learning organization—the learning organization's spiritual foundation. An organization's commitment to and capacity for learning can be no greater than that of its members. The roots of this discipline lie in both Eastern and Western spiritual traditions, and in secular traditions as well.

But surprisingly few organizations encourage the growth of their people in this manner. This results in vast untapped resources: "People enter business as bright, well-educated, high-energy people, full of energy and desire to make a difference," says Hanover's O'Brien. "By the time they are 30, a few are on the "fast track" and the rest 'put in their time' to do what matters to them on the weekend. They lose the commitment, the sense of mission, and the excitement with which they started their careers. We get damn little of their energy and almost none of their spirit."

And surprisingly few adults work to rigorously develop their own personal mastery. When you ask most adults what they want from their lives, they often talk first about what they'd like to get rid of: "I'd like my mother-in-law to move out," they say, or "I'd like my back problems to clear up." The discipline of personal mastery, by contrast, starts with clarifying the things that really matter to us, of living our lives in the service of our highest aspirations.

Here, I am most interested in the connections between personal learning and organizational learning, in the reciprocal commitments between individual and organization, and in the special spirit of an enterprise made up of learners.

Mental Models. "Mental models" are deeply ingrained assumptions, generalizations, or even pictures or images that influence how we understand the world and how we take action. Very often, we are not consciously aware of our mental models or the effects they have on our behavior. For example, we may notice that a co-worker dresses elegantly, and say to ourselves, "She's a country club person." About someone who dresses shabbily, we may feel, "He doesn't care about what others think." Mental models of what can or cannot be done in different management settings are no less deeply entrenched. Many insights into new markets or outmoded organizational practices fail to get put into practice because they conflict with powerful, tacit mental models.

Royal Dutch/Shell, one of the first large organizations to understand the advantages of accelerating organizational learning came to this realization when they discovered how pervasive was the influence of hidden mental models, especially those that become widely shared. Shell's extraordinary success in managing through the dramatic changes and unpredictability of the world oil business in the 1970s and 1980s came in large measure from learning how to surface and challenge manager's mental models. (In the early 1970s Shell was the weakest of the big seven oil companies; by the late 1980s it was the strongest.) Arie de Geus, Shell's recently retired Coordinator of Group Planning, says that continuous adaptation and growth in a changing business environment depends on "institutional learning, which is the process whereby management teams change their shared mental models of the company, their markets, and their competitors. For this reason, we think of planning as learning and of corporate planning as institutional learning."[3]

The discipline of working with mental models starts with turning the mirror inward; learning to unearth our internal pictures of the world, to bring them to the surface and hold them rigorously to scrutiny. It also includes the ability to carry on "learningful" conversations that balance inquiry and advocacy, where people expose their own thinking effectively and make that thinking open to the influence of others.

Building Shared Vision. If any one idea about leadership has inspired organizations for thousands of years, it's the capacity to hold a shared picture of the future we seek to create. One is hard pressed to think of any organization that has sustained some measure of greatness in the absence of goals, values, and missions that become deeply shared throughout the organization. IBM had "service"; Polaroid had instant photography; Ford had public transportation for the masses and Apple had computing power for the masses. Though radically different in content and kind, all these organizations managed to bind people together around a common identity and sense of destiny.

When there is a genuine vision (as opposed to the all-too-familiar "vision statement"), people excel and learn, not because they are told told to, but because they want to. But many leaders have personal visions that never get translated into shared visions that galvanize an organization. All too often, a company's shared vision has revolved around the charisma of a leader, or around a crisis that galvanizes everyone temporarily. But, given a choice, most people opt for pursuing a lofty goal, not only in times of crisis but at all times. What has been lacking is a discipline for translating individual vision into shared vision—not a "cookbook" but a set of principles and guiding practices.

The practice of shared vision involves the skills of unearthing shared "pictures of the future" that foster genuine commitment and enrollment rather than compliance. In mastering this discipline, leaders learn the counterproductiveness of trying to dictate a vision, no matter how heartfelt.

Team Learning. How can a team of committed managers with individual IQs above 120 have a collective IQ of 63? The discipline of team learning confronts this paradox. We know that teams can learn; in sports, in the performing arts, in science, and even, occasionally, in business, there are striking examples where the intelligence of the team exceeds the intelligence of the individuals in the team, and where teams develop extraordinary capacities for coordinated action. When teams are truly learning, not only are they producing extraordinary results but the individual members are growing more rapidly than could have occurred otherwise.

The discipline of team learning starts with "dialogue," the capacity of members of a team to suspend assumptions and enter into a genuine "thinking together." To the Greeks *dia-logos* meant a free-flowing of meaning through a group, allowing the group to discover insights not attainable individually. Interestingly, the practice of dialogue has been preserved in many "primitive" cultures, such as that of the American Indian, but it has been almost completely lost to modern society. Today, the principles and practices of dialogue are being rediscovered and put into a contemporary context. (Dialogue differs from the more common "discussion," which has its roots with "percussion" and "concussion," literally a heaving of ideas back and forth in a winner-takes-all competition.)

The discipline of dialogue also involves learning how to recognize the patterns of interaction in teams that undermine learning. The patterns of defensiveness are often deeply engrained in how a team operates. If unrecognized, they undermine learning. If recognized and surfaced creatively, they can actually accelerate learning.

Team learning is vital because teams, not individuals, are the fundamental learning unit in modern organizations. This where "the rubber meets the road"; unless teams can learn, the organization cannot learn.

If a learning organization were an engineering innovation, such as the airplane or the personal computer, the components would be called "technologies." For an innovation in human behavior, the components need to be seen as *disciplines*. By "discipline," I do not mean an "enforced order" or "means of punishment," but a body of theory and technique that must be studied and mastered to be put into practice. A discipline is a developmental path for acquiring certain skills or competencies. As with any discipline, from playing the piano to electrical engineering, some people have an innate "gift," but anyone can develop proficiency through practice.

To practice a discipline is to be a lifelong learner. You "never arrive"; you spend your life mastering disciplines. You can never say, "We are a learning organization," any more than you can say, "I am an enlightened person." The more you learn, the more acutely aware you become of your ignorance. Thus, a corporation cannot be "excellent" in the sense of having arrived at a permanent excellence; it is always in the state of practicing the disciplines of learning, of becoming better or worse.

That organizations can benefit from disciplines is not a totally new idea. After all, management disciplines such as accounting have been around for a long time. But the five learning disciplines differ from more familiar management disciplines in that they are "personal" disciplines. Each has to do with how we think, what we truly want, and how we interact and learn with one another. In this sense, they are more like artistic disciplines than traditional management disciplines. Moreover, while accounting is good for "keeping score," we have never approached the subtler tasks of building organizations, of enhancing their capabilities for innovation and creativity, of crafting strategy and designing policy and structure through assimilating new disciplines. Perhaps this is why, all too often, great organizations are fleeting, enjoying their moment in the sun, then passing quietly back to the ranks of the mediocre.

Practicing a discipline is different from emulating "a model." All too often, new management innovations are described in terms of the "best practices" of so-called leading firms. While interesting, I believe such descriptions can often do more harm than good, leading to piecemeal copying and playing catch-up. I do not believe great organizations have ever been built by trying to emulate another, any more than individual greatness is achieved by trying to copy another "great person."

When the five component technologies converged to create the DC-3 the commercial airline industry began. But the DC-3 was not the end of the process. Rather, it was the precursor of a new industry. Similarly, as the five component learning disciplines converge they will not create *the* learning organization but rather a new wave of experimentation and advancement.

THE FIFTH DISCIPLINE

It is vital that the five disciplines develop as an ensemble. This is challenging because it is much harder to integrate new tools than simply apply them separately. But the payoffs are immense.

This is why systems thinking is the fifth discipline. It is the discipline that integrates the disciplines, fusing them into a coherent body of theory and practice. It keeps them from being separate gimmicks or the latest organization change fads. Without a systemic orientation, there is no motivation to look at how the disciplines interrelate. By enhancing each of the other disciplines, it continually reminds us that the whole can exceed the sum of its parts.

For example, vision without systems thinking ends up painting lovely pictures of the future with no deep understanding of the forces that must be mastered to move from here to there. This is one of the reasons why many firms that have jumped on the "vision band-wagon" in recent years have found that lofty vision alone fails to turn around a firm's fortunes. Without systems thinking, the seed of vision falls on harsh soil. If nonsystemic thinking predominates, the first condition for nurturing vision is not met: a genuine belief that we can make our vision real in the future. We may say "We can achieve our vision" (most American managers are conditioned to this belief), but our tacit view of current reality as a set of conditions created by somebody else betrays us.

But systems thinking also needs the disciplines of building shared vision, mental models, team learning, and personal mastery to realize its potential. Building shared vision fosters a commitment to the long term. Mental models focus on the openness needed to unearth shortcomings in our present ways of seeing the world. Team learning develops the skills of groups of people to look for the larger picture that lies beyond individual perspectives. And personal mastery fosters the personal motivation to continually learn how our actions affect our world. Without personal mastery, people are so steeped in the reactive mindset ("someone/something else is creating my problems") that they are deeply threatened by the systems perspective.

Lastly, systems thinking makes understandable the subtlest aspect of the learning organization—the new way individuals perceive themselves and their world. At the heart of a learning organization is a shift of mind—from seeing ourselves as separate from the world to connected to the world, from seeing problems as caused by someone or something "out there" to seeing how our own actions create the problems we experience. A learning organization is a place where people are continually discovering how they create their reality. And how they can change it. As Archimedes has said, "Give me a lever long enough . . . and single-handed I can move the world."

METANOIA—A SHIFT OF MIND

When you ask people about what it is like being part of a great team, what is most striking is the meaningfulness of the experience. People talk about being part of something larger than themselves, of being connected, of being generative. It becomes quite clear that, for many, their experiences as part of truly great teams stand out as singular periods of life lived to the fullest. Some spend the rest of their lives looking for ways to recapture that spirit.

The most accurate word in Western culture to describe what happens in a learning organization is one that hasn't had much currency for the past several hundred years. It is a word we have used in our work with organizations for some ten years, but we always caution them, and ourselves, to use it sparingly in public. The word is "metanoia" and it means a shift of mind. The word has a rich history. For the Greeks, it meant a fundamental shift or change, or more literally transcendence (*"meta"*—above or beyond, as in "metaphysics") of mind ("noia," from the root *"nous,"* of mind). In the early (Gnostic) Christian tradition, it took on a special meaning of awakening shared intuition and direct knowing of the highest, of God. "Metanoia" was probably the key term of such early Christians as John the Baptist. In the Catholic corpus the word metanoia was eventually translated as "repent."

To grasp the meaning of "metanoia" is to grasp the deeper meaning of "learning," for learning also involves a fundamental shift or movement of mind. The problem with talking about "learning organizations" is that the "learning" has lost its central meaning in contemporary usage. Most people's eyes glaze over if you talk to them about "learning" or "learning organizations." Little wonder—for, in everyday use, learning has come to be synonymous with "taking in information." "Yes, I learned all about that at the course yesterday." Yet, taking in information is only distantly related to real learning. It would be nonsensical to say, "I just read a great book about bicycle riding—I've now learned that."

Real learning gets to the heart of what it means to be human. Through learning we re-create ourselves. Through learning we become able to do something we never were able to do. Through learning we reperceive the world and our relationship to it. Through learning we extend our capacity to create, to be part of the generative process of life. There is within each of us a deep hunger for this type of learning. It is, as Bill O'Brien of Hanover Insurance says, "as fundamental to human beings as the sex drive."

This, then, is the basic meaning of a "learning organization"—an organization that is continually expanding its capacity to create its future. For such an organization, it is not enough merely to survive. "Survival learning" or what is more often termed "adaptive learning" is important—indeed it is necessary. But for a learning organization, "adaptive learning" must be joined by "generative learning," learning that enhances our capacity to create.

A few brave organizational pioneers are pointing the way, but the territory of building learning organizations is still largely unexplored. It is my fondest hope that this book can accelerate that exploration.

PUTTING THE IDEAS INTO PRACTICE

I take no credit for inventing the five major disciplines of this book. The five disciplines described below represent the experimentation, research, writing, and invention of hundreds of people. But I have worked with all of the disciplines for years, refining ideas about them, collaborating on research, and introducing them to organizations throughout the world.

When I entered graduate school at the Massachusetts Institute of Technology in 1970, I was already convinced that most of the problems faced by humankind concerned our inability to grasp and manage the increasingly complex systems of our world. Little has happened since to change my view. Today, the arms race, the environmental crisis, the international drug trade, the stagnation in the Third World, and the persisting U.S. budget and trade deficits all attest to a world where problems are becoming increasingly complex and interconnected. From the start at MIT I was drawn to the work of Jay Forrester, a computer pioneer who had shifted fields to develop what he called "system dynamics." Jay maintained that the causes of many pressing public issues, from urban decay to global ecological threat, lay in the very well-intentioned policies designed to alleviate them. These problems were "actually systems" that lured policymakers into interventions that focused on obvious symptoms not underlying causes, which produced short-term benefit but long-term malaise, and fostered the need for still more symptomatic interventions.

As I began my doctoral work, I had little interest in business management. I felt that the solutions to the Big Issues lay in the public sector. But I began to meet business leaders who came to visit our MIT group to learn about systems thinking. These were thoughtful people, deeply aware of the inadequacies of prevailing ways of managing. They were engaged in building new types of organizations —decentralized, nonhierarchical organizations dedicated to the wellbeing and growth of employees as well as to success. Some had crafted radical corporate philosophies based on core values of freedom and responsibility. Others had developed innovative organization designs. All shared a commitment and a capacity to innovate that was lacking in the public sector. Gradually, I came to realize why business is the locus of innovation in an open society. Despite whatever hold past thinking may have on the business mind, business has a freedom to experiment missing in the public sector and, often, in nonprofit organizations. It also has a clear "bottom line," so that experiments can be evaluated, at least in principle, by objective criteria.

By why were they interested in systems thinking? Too often, the most daring organizational experiments were foundering. Local autonomy produced business decisions that were disastrous for the organization as a whole. "Team building" exercises sent colleagues white-water rafting together, but when they returned home they still disagreed fundamentally about business problems. Companies pulled together during crises, and then lost all their inspiration when business improved. Organizations which started out as booming successes, with the best possible intentions toward customers and employees, found themselves trapped in downward spirals that got worse the harder they tried to fix them.

Then, we all believed that the tools of systems thinking could make a difference in these companies. As I worked with different companies, I came to see why systems thinking was not enough by itself. It needed a new type of management practitioner to really make the most of it. At that time, in the mid-1970s, there was a nascent sense of what such a management practitioner could be. But it had not yet crystallized. It is crystallizing now with leaders of our MIT group: William O'Brien of Hanover Insurance; Edward Simon from Herman Miller, and Ray Stata, CEO of Analog Devices. All three of these men are involved in innovative, influential companies. All three have been involved in our research program for several years, along with leaders from Apple, Ford, Polaroid, Royal Dutch/ Shell, and Trammell Crow.

For eleven years I have also been involved in developing and conducting Innovation Associates' Leadership and Mastery workshops, which have introduced people from all walks of life to the fifth discipline ideas that have grown out of our work at MIT, combined with IA's path-breaking work on building shared vision and personal mastery. Over four thousand managers have attended. We started out with a particular focus on corporate senior executives, but soon found that the basic disciplines such as systems thinking, personal mastery, and shared vision were relevant for teachers, public administrators and elected officials, students, and parents. All were in leadership positions of importance. All were in "organizations" that had still untapped potential for creating their future. All felt that to tap that potential required developing their own capacities, that is, learning.

So, this book is for the learners, especially those of us interested in the art and practice of collective learning.

For managers, this book should help in identifying the specific practices, skills, and disciplines that can make building learning organizations less of an occult art (though an art nonetheless).

For parents, this book should help in letting our children be our teachers, as well as we theirs—for they have much to teach us about learning as a way of life.

For citizens, the dialogue about why contemporary organizations are not especially good learners and about what is required to build learning organizations reveals some of the tools needed by communities and societies if they are to become more adept learners.

2

DOES YOUR ORGANIZATION HAVE A LEARNING DISABILITY?

Few large corporations live even half as long as a person. In 1983, a Royal Dutch/Shell survey found that one third of the firms in the Fortune "500" in 1970 had vanished.[1] Shell estimated that the average lifetime of the largest industrial enterprises is less than forty years, roughly half the lifetime of a human being! The chances are fifty-fifty that readers of this book will see their present firm disappear during their working career.

In most companies that fail, there is abundant evidence in advance that the firm is in trouble. This evidence goes unheeded, however, even when individual managers are aware of it. The organization as a whole cannot recognize impending threats, understand the implications of those threats, or come up with alternatives.

Perhaps under the laws of "survival of the fittest," this continual death of firms is fine for society. Painful though it may be for the employees and owners, it is simply a turnover of the economic soil, redistributing the resources of production to new companies and new cultures. But what if the high corporate mortality rate is only a symptom of deeper problems that afflict *all* companies, not just the ones that die? What if even the most successful companies are poor learners—they survive but never live up to their potential? What if, in light of what organizations *could* be, "excellence" is actually "mediocrity"?

It is no accident that most organizations learn poorly. The way they are designed and managed, the way people's jobs are defined, and, most importantly, the way we have all been taught to think and interact (not only in organizations but more broadly) create fundamental learning disabilities. These disabilities operate despite the best efforts of bright, committed people. Often the harder they try to solve problems, the worse the results. What learning does occur takes place despite these learning disabilities—for they pervade all organizations to some degree.

Learning disabilities are tragic in children, especially when they go undetected. They are no less tragic in organizations, where they also go largely undetected. The first step in curing them is to begin to identify the seven learning disabilities:

1. "I AM MY POSITION"

We are trained to be loyal to our jobs—so much so that we confuse them with our own identities. When a large American steel company began closing plants in the early 1980s, it offered to train the displaced steelworkers for new jobs. But the training never "took"; the workers drifted into unemployment and odd jobs instead. Psychologists came in to find out why, and found the steelworkers suffering from acute identity crises. "How could I do anything else?" asked the workers. "I *am* a lathe operator."

When asked what they do for a living, most people describe the tasks they perform every day, not the *purpose* of the greater enterprise in which they take part. Most see themselves within a "system" over which they have little or no influence. They "do their job," put in their time, and try to cope with the forces outside of their control. Consequently, they tend to see their responsibilities as limited to the boundaries of their position.

Recently, managers from a Detroit auto maker told me of stripping down a Japanese import to understand why the Japanese were able to achieve extraordinary precision and reliability at lower cost on a particular assembly process. They found the same standard type of bolt used three times on the engine block. Each time it mounted a different type of component. On the American car, the same assembly required three different bolts, which required three different wrenches and three different inventories of bolts—making the car much slower and more costly to assemble. Why did the Americans use three separate bolts? Because the design organization in Detroit had three groups of engineers, each responsible for "their component only." The Japanese had one designer responsible for the entire engine mounting, and probably much more. The irony is that each of the three groups of American engineers considered their work successful because *their* bolt and assembly worked just fine.

When people in organizations focus only on their position, they have little sense of responsibility for the results produced when all positions interact. Moreover, when results are disappointing, it can be very difficult to know why. All you can do is assume that "someone screwed up."

2. "THE ENEMY IS OUT THERE"

A friend once told the story of a boy he coached in Little League, who after dropping three fly balls in right field, threw down his glove and marched into the dugout. "No one can catch a ball in that darn field," he said.

There is in each of us a propensity to find someone or something outside ourselves to blame when things go wrong. Some organizations elevate this propensity to a commandment: "Thou shalt always find an external agent to blame." Marketing blames manufacturing: "The reason we keep missing sales targets is that our quality is not competitive." Manufacturing blames engineering. Engineering blames marketing: "If they'd only quit screwing up our designs and let us design the products we are capable of, we'd be an industry leader."

The "enemy is out there" syndrome is actually a by-product of "I am my position," and the nonsystemic ways of looking at the world that it fosters. When we focus only on our position, we do not see how our own actions extend beyond the boundary of that position. When those actions have consequences that come back to hurt us, we misperceive these new problems as externally caused. Like the person being chased by his own shadow, we cannot seem to shake them.

The "Enemy Is Out There" syndrome is not limited to assigning blame *within* the organization. During its last years of operation, the once highly successful People Express Airlines slashed prices, boosted marketing, and bought Frontier Airlines—all in a frantic attempt to fight back against the perceived cause of its demise: increasingly aggressive competitors. Yet, none of these moves arrested the company's mounting losses or corrected its core problem, service quality that had declined so far that low fares were its only remaining pull on customers.

For many American companies, "the enemy" has become Japanese competition, labor unions, government regulators, or customers who "betrayed us" by buying products from someone else. "The enemy is out there," however, is almost always an incomplete story. "Out there" and "in here" are usually part of a single system. This learning disability makes it almost impossible to detect the leverage which we can use "in here" on problems that straddle the boundary between us and "out there."

3. THE ILLUSION OF TAKING CHARGE

Being "proactive" is in vogue. Managers frequently proclaim the need for taking charge in facing difficult problems. What is typically meant by this is that we should face up to difficult issues, stop waiting for someone else to do something, and solve problems before they grow into crises. In particular, being proactive is frequently seen as an antidote to being "reactive"—waiting until a situation gets out of hand before taking a step. But is taking aggressive action against an external enemy really synonymous with being proactive?

Not too long ago, a management team in a leading property and liability insurance company with whom we were working got bitten by the proactiveness bug. The head of the team, a talented vice president for claims, was about to give a speech proclaiming that the company wasn't going to get pushed around anymore by lawyers litigating more and more claims settlements. The firm would beef up its own legal staff so that it could take more cases through to trial by verdict, instead of settling them out of court.

Then we and some members of the team began to look more systemically at the probable effects of the idea: the likely fraction of cases that might be won in court, the likely size of cases lost, the monthly direct and overhead costs regardless of who won or lost, and how long cases would probably stay in litigation. (The tool we used is discussed in Chapter 17, "Microworlds.") Interestingly, the team's scenarios pointed to *increasing* total costs because, given the quality of investigation done initially on most claims, the firm simply could not win enough of its cases to offset the costs of increased litigation. The vice president tore up his speech.

All too often, "proactiveness" is reactiveness in disguise. If we simply become more aggressive fighting the "enemy out there," we are reacting—regardless of what we call it. *True proactiveness comes from seeing how we contribute to our own problems.* It is a product of our way of thinking, not our emotional state.

4. THE FIXATION ON EVENTS

Two children get into a scrap on the playground and you come over to untangle them. Lucy says, "I hit him because he took my ball." Tommy says, "I took her ball because she won't let me play with her airplane." Lucy says, "He can't play with my airplane because he broke the propeller." Wise adults that we are, we say, "Now, now, children—just get along with each other." But are we really any different in the way we explain the entanglements we find ourselves caught in? We are conditioned to see life as a series of events, and for every event, we think there is one obvious cause.

Conversations in organizations are dominated by concern with events: last month's sales, the new budget cuts, last quarter's earnings, who just got promoted or fired, the new product our competitors just announced, the delay that just was announced in our new product, and so on. The media reinforces an emphasis on short-term events—after all, if it's more than two days' old it's no longer "news." Focusing on events leads to "event" explanations: "The Dow Jones average dropped sixteen points today," announces the newspaper, "because low fourth-quarter profits were announced yesterday." Such explanations may be true as far as they go, but they distract us from seeing the longer-term patterns of change that lie behind the events and from understanding the causes of those patterns.

Our fixation on events is actually part of our evolutionary programming. If you wanted to design a cave person for survival, ability to contemplate the cosmos would not be a high-ranking design criterion. What *is* important is the ability to see the saber-toothed tiger over your left shoulder and react quickly. The irony is that, *today,*

*the primary threats to our survival, both of our organizations and of
our societies, come not from sudden events but from slow, gradual
processes;* the arms race, environmental decay, the erosion of a
society's public education system, increasingly obsolete physical
capital, and decline in design or product quality (at least relative to
competitors' quality) are all slow, gradual processes.

Generative learning cannot be sustained in an organization if people's thinking is dominated by short-term events. If we focus on
events, the best we can ever do is predict an event before it happens
so that we can react optimally. But we cannot learn to create.

5. THE PARABLE OF THE BOILED FROG

Maladaptation to gradually building threats to survival is so pervasive in systems studies of corporate failure that it has given rise to
the parable of the "boiled frog." If you place a frog in a pot of boiling
water, it will immediately try to scramble out. But if you place the
frog in room temperature water, and don't scare him, he'll stay put.
Now, if the pot sits on a heat source, and if you gradually turn up
the temperature, something very interesting happens. As the temperature rises from 70 to 80 degrees F., the frog will do nothing. In fact,
he will show every sign of enjoying himself. As the temperature
gradually increases, the frog will become groggier and groggier, until
he is unable to climb out of the pot. Though there is nothing restraining him, the frog will sit there and boil. Why? Because the frog's
internal apparatus for sensing threats to survival is geared to sudden
changes in his environment, not to slow, gradual changes.

Something similar happened to the American automobile industry.
In the 1960s, it dominated North American production. That began
to change very gradually. Certainly, Detroit's Big Three did not see
Japan as a threat to their survival in 1962, when the Japanese share
of the U.S. market was below 4 percent. Nor in 1967, when it was
less than 10 percent. Nor in 1974, when it was under 15 percent. By
the time the Big Three began to look critically at its own practices
and core assumptions, it was the early 1980s, and the Japanese share
of the American market had risen to 21.3 percent. By 1989, the
Japanese share was approaching 30 percent, and the American auto
industry could account for only about 60 percent of the cars sold in
the U.S.[2] It is still not clear whether this particular frog will have the
strength to pull itself out of the hot water.

Learning to see slow, gradual processes requires slowing down our frenetic pace and paying attention to the subtle as well as the dramatic. If you sit and look into a tidepool, initially you won't see much of anything going on. However, if you watch long enough, after about ten minutes the tidepool will suddenly come to life. The world of beautiful creatures is always there, but moving a bit too slowly to be seen at first. The problem is our minds are so locked in one frequency, it's as if we can only see at 78 rpm; we can't see anything at 33⅓. We will not avoid the fate of the frog until we learn to slow down and see the gradual processes that often pose the greatest threats.

6. THE DELUSION OF LEARNING FROM EXPERIENCE

The most powerful learning comes from direct experience. Indeed, we learn eating, crawling, walking, and communicating through direct trial and error—through taking an action and seeing the consequences of that action; then taking a new and different action. But what happens when we can no longer observe the consequences of our actions? What happens if the primary consequences of our actions are in the distant future or in a distant part of the larger system within which we operate? We each have a "learning horizon," a breadth of vision in time and space within which we assess our effectiveness. When our actions have consequences beyond our learning horizon, it becomes impossible to learn from direct experience.

Herein lies the core *learning dilemma* that confronts organizations: *we learn best from experience but we never directly experience the consequences of many of our most important decisions*. The most critical decisions made in organizations have systemwide consequences that stretch over years or decades. Decisions in R&D have first-order consequences in marketing and manufacturing. Investing in new manufacturing facilities and processes influences quality and delivery reliability for a decade or more. Promoting the right people into leadership positions shapes strategy and organizational climate for years. These are exactly the types of decisions where there is the least opportunity for trial and error learning.

Cycles are particularly hard to see, and thus learn from, if they last longer than a year or two. As systems-thinking writer Draper Kauffman, Jr., points out, most people have short memories. "When a temporary oversupply of workers develops in a particular field," he wrote, "everyone talks about the big surplus and young people are steered away from the field. Within a few years, this creates a shortage, jobs go begging, and young people are frantically urged into the field—which creates a surplus. Obviously, the best time to start training for a job is when people have been talking about a surplus for several years and few others are entering it. That way, you finish your training just as the shortage develops." [3]

Traditionally, organizations attempt to surmount the difficulty of coping with the breadth of impact from decisions by breaking themselves up into components. They institute functional hierarchies that are easier for people to "get their hands around." But, functional divisions grow into fiefdoms, and what was once a convenient division of labor mutates into the "stovepipes" that all but cut off contact between functions. The result: analysis of the most important problems in a company, the complex issues that cross functional lines, becomes a perilous or nonexistent exercise.

7. THE MYTH OF THE MANAGEMENT TEAM

Standing forward to do battle with these dilemmas and disabilities is "the management team," the collection of savvy, experienced managers who represent the organization's different functions and areas of expertise. Together, they are supposed to sort out the complex cross-functional issues that are critical to the organization. What confidence do we have, really, that typical management teams can surmount these learning disabilities?

All too often, teams in business tend to spend their time fighting for turf, avoiding anything that will make them look bad personally, and pretending that everyone is behind the team's collective strategy—maintaining the *appearance* of a cohesive team. To keep up the image, they seek to squelch disagreement; people with serious reservations avoid stating them publicly, and joint decisions are watered-down compromises reflecting what everyone can live with, or else reflecting one person's view foisted on the group. If there is disagreement, it's usually expressed in a manner that lays blame, polarizes opinion, and fails to reveal the underlying differences in assumptions and experience in a way that the team as a whole could learn.

"Most management teams break down under pressure," writes

THE FIFTH DISCIPLINE

THE FIFTH DISCIPLINE

DISCIPLINE

Copyright © Peter M. Senge 1990

Harvard's Chris Argyris—a longtime student of learning in management teams. "The team may function quite well with routine issues. But when they confront complex issues that may be embarrassing or threatening, the 'teamness' seems to go to pot."[4]

Argyris argues that most managers find collective inquiry inherently threatening. School trains us never to admit that we do not know the answer, and most corporations reinforce that lesson by rewarding the people who excel in advocating their views, not inquiring into complex issues. (When was the last time someone was rewarded in your organization for raising difficult questions about the company's current policies rather than solving urgent problems?) Even if we feel uncertain or ignorant, we learn to protect ourselves from the pain of appearing uncertain or ignorant. That very process blocks out any new understandings which might threaten us. The consequence is what Argyris calls "skilled incompetence"—teams full of people who are incredibly proficient at keeping themselves from learning.

DISABILITIES AND DISCIPLINES

These learning disabilities have been with us for a long time. In *The March of Folly*, Barbara Tuchman traces the history of devastating large-scale policies "pursued contrary to ultimate self-interest,"[5] from the fall of the Trojans through the U.S. involvement in Vietnam. In story after story, leaders could not see the consequences of their own policies, even when they were warned in advance that their own survival was at stake. Reading between the lines of Tuchman's writing, you can see that the fourteenth-century Valois monarchs of France suffered from "I am my position" disabilities—when they devalued currency, they literally didn't realize they were driving the new French middle class toward insurrection.

In the mid-1700s Britain had a bad case of boiled frog. The British went through "a full decade," wrote Tuchman, "of mounting conflict with the [American] colonies without any [British official] sending a representative, much less a minister, across the Atlantic . . . to find out what was endangering the relationship . . ."[6] By 1776, the start of the American Revolution, the relationship was irrevocably endangered. Elsewhere, Tuchman describes the Roman Catholic cardinals of the fifteenth and sixteenth centuries, a tragic management "team" in which piety demanded that they present an appearance of agreement. However, behind-the-scenes backstabbing (in some cases, literal backstabbing) brought in opportunistic popes whose abuses of office provoked the Protestant Reformation.

We live in no less perilous times today, and the same learning disabilities persist, along with their consequences. The five disciplines of the learning organization can, I believe, act as antidotes to these learning disabilities. But first, we must see the disabilities more clearly—for they are often lost amid the bluster of day-to-day events.

3

PRISONERS OF
THE SYSTEM, OR
PRISONERS OF OUR
OWN THINKING?

In order to see the learning disabilities in action, it helps to start with a laboratory experiment—a microcosm of how real organizations function, where you can see the consequences of your decisions play out more clearly than is possible in real organizations. For this reason, we often invite people to take part in a simulation called the "beer game," first developed in the 1960s at the Massachusetts Institute of Technology's Sloan School of Management. Because it is a "laboratory replica" of a real setting, rather than reality itself, we can isolate the disabilities and their causes more sharply than is possible in real organizations. This reveals that the problems originate in basic ways of thinking and interacting, more than in peculiarities of organization structure and policy.

The beer game does this by immersing us in a type of organization which is rarely noticed but widely prevalent: a production/distribution system, the kind responsible for producing and shipping consumer and commercial goods in all industrial countries. In this case, it's a system for producing and distributing a single brand of beer. The players at each position are completely free to make any decision that seems prudent. Their only goal is to manage their position as best they can to maximize their profits.[1]

As with many games, the "playing" of a single session of the beer game can be told as a story. There are three main characters in the story—a retailer, a wholesaler, and the marketing director of a brewery.[2] This story is told, in turn, through each of the players' eyes.

THE RETAILER

Imagine that you're a retail merchant. Perhaps you're the franchise manager of a brightly lit twenty-four-hour chain store at a suburban intersection. Or maybe you own a mom-and-pop grocery on a street of Victorian-era brownstones. Or a discount beverage outlet on a remote highway.

No matter what your store looks like, or whatever else you sell, beer is a cornerstone of your business. Not only do you make a profit on it, but it draws customers in to buy, perhaps, popcorn and potato chips. You stock at least a dozen different brands of beer, and keep a rough tally of how many cases of each are in your back room, which is where you keep your inventory.

Once each week, a trucker arrives at the rear entrance of your store. You hand him a form on which you've filled in that week's order. How many cases of each brand do you want delivered? The trucker, after he makes his other rounds, returns your order to your beer wholesaler, who then processes it, arranges outgoing orders in a proper sequence, and ships the resulting order to your store. Because of all that processing, you're used to a four-week delay on average on your orders; in other words, a delivery of beer generally arrives in your store about four weeks after you order it.

You and your beer wholesaler never speak to each other directly. You communicate only through those check marks on a piece of paper. You probably have never even met him; you know only the truck driver. And that's for good reason: you have hundreds of products in your store. Dozens of wholesalers dole them out to you. Meanwhile, your beer wholesaler handles deliveries to several hundred stores, in a dozen different cities. Between your steady deluge of customers and his order-shuffling, who has time for chit-chat? That single number is the only thing you need to say to each other.

One of your steadiest beer brands is called Lover's Beer. You are dimly aware that it's made by a small but efficient brewery located about three hundred miles away from you. It's not a super-popular brand; in fact, the brewery doesn't advertise at all. But every week, as regularly as your morning newspaper deliveries, four cases of Lover's Beer sell from the shelves. Sure, the customers are young—most are in their twenties—and fickle; but somehow, for every one who graduates to Miller or Bud, there's a younger sister or brother to replace him.

To make sure you always have enough Lover's Beer, you try to keep twelve cases in the store at any time. That means ordering four cases each Monday, when the beer truck comes. Week after week after week. By now, you take that four-case turnover for granted; it's inextricably wedded to the image in your mind of the beer's performance. You don't even articulate it to yourself when placing the order: "Oh, yeah," runs the automatic litany. "Lover's Beer. Four cases."

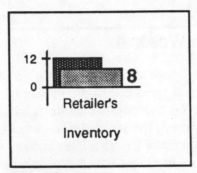

Week 2

Week 2: Without warning, one week in October (let's call it Week 2), sales of the beer double. They jump from four cases to eight. That's all right, you figure; you have an eight-case surplus in your store. You don't know why they've sold so much more suddenly. Maybe someone is having a party. But to replace those extra cases, you raise your order to eight. That will bring your inventory back to normal.

Week 3: Strangely enough, you also sell eight cases of Lover's Beer the *next* week. And it's not even spring break. Every once in a while, in those rare moments between sales, you briefly ponder the reason why. There's no advertising campaign for the beer; you would have received a mailing about it. Unless the mailing got lost, or you accidentally threw it out. Or maybe there's another reason . . . but a customer comes in, and you lose your train of thought.

At the moment the deliveryman comes, you're still not thinking much about Lover's Beer, but you look down at your sheet and see that he's brought only four cases this time. (It's from the order you placed four weeks ago.) You only have four cases left in stock, which means—unless there's a drop-back in sales—you're going to sell out all your Lover's Beer this week. Prudence dictates an order of at least eight cases to keep up with sales. Just to be on the safe side, you order twelve so you can rebuild your inventory.

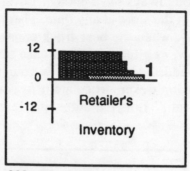

Week 4

Week 4: You find time on Tuesday to quiz one or two of your younger customers. It turns out that a new music video appeared a month or so back on the popular cable television channels. The video's recording group, the Iconoclasts, closes their song with the line, "I take one last sip of Lover's Beer and run into the sun." You don't know why they used that line, but your wholesaler would have told you if there was any new merchandising deal. You think of calling the wholesaler, but a delivery of potato chips arrives and the subject of Lover's Beer slips your mind.

When your next delivery of beer comes in, only five cases of beer arrive. You're chagrined now because you have only one case in stock. You're almost sold out. And thanks to this video, demand might go up even *further*. Still, you know that you have some extra cases on order, but you're not sure exactly how many. Better order at least sixteen more.

Week 5: Your one case sells out Monday morning. Fortunately, you receive a shipment for seven more cases of Lover's (apparently your wholesaler is starting to respond to your higher orders). But all are sold by the end of the week, leaving you with absolutely zero inventory. Glumly, you stare at the empty shelf. Better order another sixteen. You don't want to get a reputation for being out of stock of popular beers.

Week 6: Sure enough, customers start coming in at the beginning of the week, looking for Lover's. Two are loyal enough to wait for your backlog. "Let us know as soon as it comes in," they say, "and we'll be back to buy it." You note their names and phone numbers: they've promised to buy one case each.

Only six cases arrive in the next shipment. You call your two "backlogged" customers. They stop in and buy their shares; and the rest of the beer sells out before the end of the week. Again, two customers give you their names to call as soon as your next shipment arrives. You wonder how many more you could have sold had your shelves not been empty at the end of the week. Seems there's been a run on the beer: none of the stores in the area have it. This beer is hot, and it's apparently getting more popular all the time.

After two days of staring at the parched, empty shelf, it doesn't feel right to order any less than another sixteen cases. You're tempted to order more, but you restrain yourself because you know the big orders you've been placing will start to arrive soon. But when . . . ?

Week 7: The delivery truck brings only five cases this week, which means that you're facing another week of empty shelves. As soon as you fill your back orders, Lover's Beer is sold out again, this time within two days. This week, amazingly, five customers give you their names. You order another sixteen and silently pray that your big orders will start arriving. You think of all the lost potato chip sales.

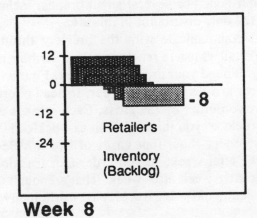

Week 8

Week 8: By now, you're watching Lover's Beer more closely than any other product you sell. The suspense is palpable: every time a customer buys a six-pack of that quiet beer, you notice it. People seem to be talking about the beer. Eagerly, you wait for the trucker to roll in the sixteen cases you expect . . .

But he brings only five. "What do you mean, five?" you say. "Gee, I don't know anything about it," the deliveryman tells you. "I guess they're backlogged. You'll get them in a couple of weeks." A couple of *weeks!?!* By the time you call your backlogged customers, you'll be sold out before you can sell a single new case. You'll be without a bottle of Lover's on your shelf all week. What will this do to your reputation?

You place an order for twenty-four more cases—twice as much as you had planned to order. What is that wholesaler *doing* to me, you wonder? Doesn't he know what a ravenous market we have down here? What's going through his mind, anyway?

THE WHOLESALER

As the manager of a wholesale distributing firm, beer is your life. You spend your days at a steel desk in a small warehouse stacked high with beer of every conceivable brand: Miller, Bud, Coors, Rolling Rock, a passel of imported beers—and, of course, regional beers such as Lover's Beer. The region you serve includes one large city, several smaller satellite cities, a web of suburbs, and some outlying rural areas. You're not the only beer wholesaler here, but you're very well established. For several small brands, including Lover's Beer, you are the only distributor in this area.

Mostly, you communicate with the brewery through the same method which retailers use to reach you. You scribble numbers onto a form which you hand your driver each week. Four weeks later, on average, the beer arrives to fill that order. Instead of ordering by the case, however, you order by the gross. Each gross is about enough to fill a small truck, so you think of them as truckloads. Just as your typical retailer orders about four cases of Lover's Beer from you, week after week after week, so you order four truckloads from the brewery, week after week after week. That's enough to give you a typical accumulation of twelve truckloads' worth in inventory at any given time.

By Week 8, you had become almost as frustrated and angry as your retailers. Lover's Beer had always been a reliably steady brand. But a few weeks ago—in Week 4, actually—those orders had abruptly started rising sharply. The next week, orders from retailers had risen still further. By Week 8, most stores were ordering three or four times their regular amount of beer.

At first, you had easily filled the extra orders from your inventory in the warehouse. And you had been prescient; noting that there was a trend, you had immediately raised the amount of Lover's Beer you ordered from the brewery. In Week 6, after seeing an article in *Beer Distribution News* about the rock video, you had raised your brewery order still further, to a dramatic twenty truckloads per week. That was five times as much beer as your regular order. But you had needed that much; the beer's popularity was doubling, tripling, and even quadrupling, to judge from the stores' demand.

By Week 6, you had shipped out all the beer you had in inventory and entered the hellishness of backlog. Each week you sent out what you could, and sent the stores paperwork equivalents of I.O.U.s to cover the rest. A few of the larger chain stores called you and got what preferential treatment you could offer, but the Lover's Beer in your inventory was gone. At least you knew it would be only a couple of weeks more before the extra beer you ordered would begin to arrive.

In Week 8, when you had called the brewery to ask if there was any way to speed up their deliveries (and to let them know that you were upping your order to thirty truckloads), you were dismayed to find out that they had only just stepped up production two weeks before. They were just learning of the increase in demand. How could they be so slow?

Now it's **Week 9.** You're getting orders for twenty truckloads'

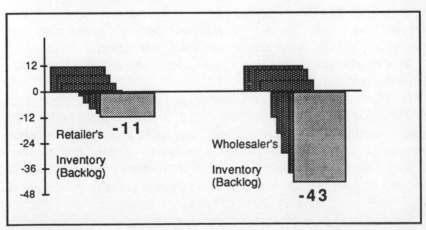

Week 9

worth of Lover's Beer per week, and you still don't have it. By the end of last week, you had backlogged orders of another twenty-nine truckloads. Your staff is so used to fielding calls that they've asked you to install an answering machine devoted to an explanation about Lover's Beer. But you're confident that, this week, the twenty truckloads you ordered a month ago will finally arrive.

However, only six truckloads arrive. Apparently the brewery is still backlogged, and the larger production runs are only now starting to get shipped out. You call some of your larger chains and assure them that the beer they ordered will be coming shortly.

Week 10 is infuriating. The extra beer you were expecting—at least twenty truckloads' worth—doesn't show. The brewery simply couldn't ramp up production that fast. Or so you guess. They only send you eight truckloads. It's impossible to reach anybody on the phone down there—they're apparently all on the factory floor, manning the brewery apparatus.

The stores, meanwhile, are apparently selling the beer wildly. You're getting unprecedented orders—for twenty-six truckloads this week. Or maybe they're ordering so much because *they* can't get any of the beer from you. Either way, you have to keep up. What if you can't get any of the beer and they go to one of your competitors?

You order forty truckloads from the brewery.

In **Week 11**, you find yourself tempted to take extra-long lunches at the bar around the corner from your warehouse. Only *twelve* truckloads of Lover's Beer arrive. You still can't reach anybody at the brewery. And you have over *a hundred* truckloads' worth of orders to fill: seventy-seven truckloads in backlog, and another twenty-eight truckloads' worth of orders from the stores which you receive this week. Some of those backlog costs come due, and you're afraid to tell your accountant what you expect.

You've got to get that beer: you order *another* forty truckloads from the brewery.

By **Week 12**, it's clear. This new demand for Lover's Beer is a far more major change than you expected. You sigh with resignation when you think of how much money you could make if you only had enough in stock. How could the brewery have *done* this to you? Why did demand have to rise so *quickly?* How are you ever expected to keep up? All you know is that you're never going to get caught in this situation again. You order sixty more truckloads.

For the next four weeks, the demand continues to outstrip your supply. In fact, you can't reduce your backlog at all in **Week 13**.

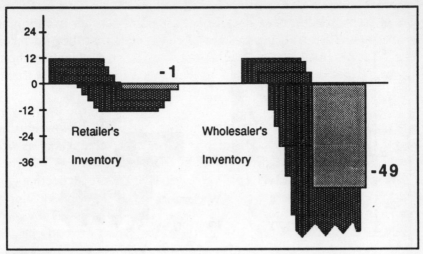

Week 14

You finally start receiving larger shipments from the brewery in **Weeks 14 and 15.** At the same time, orders from your stores drop off a bit. Maybe in the previous weeks, you figure, they overordered a bit. At this point, anything that helps work off your backlog is a welcome reprieve.

And now, in **Week 16,** you finally get almost *all* the beer you asked for weeks ago: fifty-five truckloads. It arrives early in the week, and you stroll back to that section of the warehouse to take a look at it, stacked on pallets. It's as much beer as you keep for any major brand. And it will be moving out soon.

Throughout the week, you wait expectantly for the stores' orders to roll in. You even stop by the intake desk to see the individual forms. But on form after form, you see the same number written: zero. Zero. Zero. Zero. Zero. What's wrong with these people? Four weeks ago, they were screaming at you for the beer, now, they don't even want any.

Suddenly, you feel a chill. Just as your trucker leaves for the run that includes the brewery, you catch up with him. You initial the form, and cross out the twenty-four truckloads you had ordered, replacing it with a zero of your own.

Week 17: The next week, sixty more truckloads of Lover's Beer arrive. The stores still ask for—zero. You still ask for—zero. One hundred and nine truckloads of the stuff sit in your warehouse. You could bathe in the stuff every day, and it wouldn't make a dent.

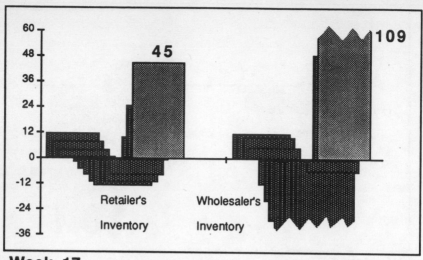

Week 17

Surely the stores will want more *this* week. After all, that video is still running. In your brooding thoughts, you consign every retailer to the deepest corner of hell; the corner reserved for people who don't keep their promises.

And, in fact, the retailers once again order zero cases of Lover's Beer from you. You, in turn, order zero truckloads from the brewery. And yet, the brewery continues to deliver beer. Sixty more truckloads appear on your dock this week. Why does that brewery have it in for you? When will it ever end?

THE BREWERY

Imagine that you were hired four months ago to manage distribution and marketing at the brewery, where Lover's Beer is only one of several primary products. Yours is a small brewery, known for its quality, not its marketing savvy. That's why you were hired.

Now, clearly, you have been doing something right. Because in only your second month (Week Six of this game), new orders had begun to rise dramatically. By the end of your third month on the job, you felt the satisfaction of getting orders for forty gross worth of beer per *week*, up dramatically from the four when you started. And you shipped out . . . well, you shipped out thirty.

Because breweries get backlogs too. It takes (in your brewery, at least) two weeks from the time you decide to brew a bottle of beer until the moment when that beer is ready for shipment. Admittedly, you kept a few weeks' worth of beer in your warehouse, but those stocks were exhausted by Week 7, only two weeks after the rising orders came in. The next week, while you had back orders for nine gross and another twenty-four gross in new orders, you could send out only twenty-two gross. By that time you were a hero within your company. The plant manager had given everyone incentives to work double-time, and was feverishly interviewing for new factory help.

You had lucked out with that Iconoclasts' video mentioning the beer. You had learned about the video in Week 3—from letters written by teenagers to the brewery. But it had taken until Week 6 to see that video translate into higher orders.

Even by Week 14, the factory had *still* not caught up with its backlogged orders. You had regularly requested brew batches of seventy gross or more. You had wondered how large your bonus would be that year. Maybe you could ask for a percentage of the profits, at least once you caught up with back orders. You had even idly pictured yourself on the cover of *Marketing Week*.

Finally, you *had* caught up with the backlog in Week 16. But the next week, your distributors had asked for only nineteen gross. And last week, **Week 18,** they had not asked for any more beer at all. Some of the order slips actually had orders crossed out on them.

Now, it's **Week 19.** You have a hundred gross of beer in inventory. And the orders, once again, ask for virtually no new deliveries. Zero beer. Meanwhile the beer you've been brewing keeps rolling in. You place the phone call you've dreaded making to your boss. "Better hold off on production for a week or two," you say. "We've got"—

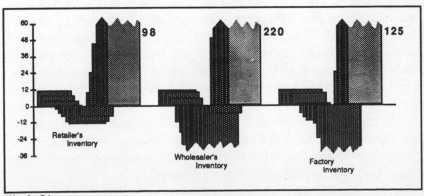

Week 21

and you use a word you've picked up in business school—"a discontinuity." There is silence on the other end of the phone. "But I'm sure it's only temporary," you say.

The same pattern continues for four more weeks: **Weeks 20, 21, 22, and 23.** Gradually your hopes of a resurgence slide, and your excuses come to sound flimsier and flimsier. Those distributors screwed us, you say. The retailers didn't buy enough beer. The press and that rock video hyped up the beer and got everybody sick of it. At root, it's the fickle kids—they have no loyalty whatsoever. How could they buy hundreds of cases one month, and nothing at all the next?

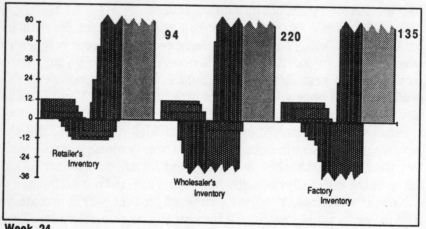

Week 24

Nobody misses you when you borrow the company car at the beginning of **Week 24.** Your first stop is the wholesaler's office. Not only is it the first time you have ever met face to face, but it is only the second time you have ever spoken. There has never been anything to say until this crisis. You greet each other glumly, and then the wholesaler takes you out to the back warehouse. "We haven't gotten an order for your brand in two months," says the wholesaler. "I feel completely jerked around. Look! We still have 220 truckloads here."

What must have happened, you decide together, is that demand rose rapidly, and then fell dramatically. Another example of the fickleness of the public. If the retailers had stayed on top of it and warned you, this would never have happened.

You are working over the phrasing of a marketing strategy report in your mind on the way home when, on a whim, you decide to stop at the store of a retailer you pass along the way. Fortuitously, the owner of the store is in. You introduce yourself and the retailer's face breaks into a sardonic grin. Leaving an assistant in charge of the shop, the two of you walk next door to a luncheonette for a cup of coffee.

The retailer has brought along the shop's inventory tally note-books, and spreads them open across the table. "You don't know how much I wanted to strangle you a few months ago."

"Why?" you ask.

"Look—we're stuck with ninety-three cases in our back room. At this rate, it's going to be another six weeks before we order any more."

Six weeks, you think to yourself. And then you pull out a pocket calculator. If *every* retailer in this area waits six weeks before order-ing any more beer, and then only orders a few cases a week, it's going to be a year or more before they put a dent in those 220 truckloads sitting at the wholesaler's. "This is a tragedy," you say.

"Who let it happen—I mean, how can we keep it from happening again?"

"Well, it's not *our* fault," says the retailer, after sipping some coffee. "We were selling four cases of beer when that music video came out. Then, in Week 2, we sold eight cases."

"And then it mushroomed," you say. "But then why did it die down?"

"No, you don't understand," says the retailer. "The demand never mushroomed. And it never died out. We *still* sell eight cases of beer—week after week after week. But *you* didn't send us the beer we wanted. So we had to keep ordering, just to make sure we had enough to keep up with our customers."

"But we got the beer out as soon as it was necessary."

"Then maybe the wholesaler screwed up somehow," says the retailer. "I've been wondering if I should switch suppliers. Anyway, I wish you'd do a coupon promotion or something, so I could make back some of my costs. I'd like to unload some of those ninety-three cases."

You pick up the tab for coffee. Then, on your trip back, you plan the wording of your resignation notice. Obviously, you'll be blamed for any layoffs or plant closings that come out of this crisis—just as the wholesaler blamed the retailer, and the retailer blamed the wholesaler, and both of them wanted to blame you. At least it's early enough in the process that you can quit with some dignity. If only you could come up with some explanation to show that it wasn't your fault—to show that you were the victim, instead of the culprit . . .

LESSONS OF THE BEER GAME

1. *Structure Influences Behavior*
Different people in the same structure tend to produce qualitatively similar results. When there are problems, or performance fails to live up to what is intended, it is easy to find someone or something to blame. *But, more often than we realize, systems cause their own crises, not external forces or individuals' mistakes.*

2. *Structure in Human Systems is Subtle*
We tend to think of "structure" as external constraints on the individual. But, *structure* in complex living systems, such as the "structure" of the multiple "systems" in a human body (for example, the cardiovascular and neuromuscular) *means the basic interrelationships that control behavior.* In human systems, structure includes how people make decisions—the "operating policies" whereby we translate perceptions, goals, rules, and norms into actions.

3. *Leverage Often Comes from New Ways of Thinking*
In human systems, people often have potential leverage that they do not exercise because they focus only on their own decisions and ignore how their decisions affect others. In the beer game, players have it in their power to eliminate the extreme instabilities that invariably occur, but they fail to do so because they do not understand how they are creating the instability in the first place.

People in the business world love heroes. We lavish praise and promotion on those who achieve visible results. But if something goes wrong, we feel intuitively that somebody must have screwed up.

In the beer game, there are no such culprits. There is no one to blame. Each of the three players in our story had the best possible intentions: to serve his customers well, to keep the product moving smoothly through the system, and to avoid penalties. Each participant made well-motivated, clearly defensible judgments based on reasonable guesses about what might happen. There were no villains, but there was a crisis nonetheless—built into the structure of the system.

In the last twenty years, the beer game has been played thousands of times in classes and management training seminars. It has been played on five continents, among people of all ages, nationalities, cultural origins, and vastly varied business backgrounds. Some players had never heard of a production/distribution system before; others had spent a good portion of their lives working in such businesses. Yet every time the game is played the same crises ensue. First, there is growing demand that can't be met. Orders build throughout the system. Inventories are depleted. Backlogs grow. Then the beer arrives en masse while incoming orders suddenly decline. By the end of the experiment, almost all players are sitting with large inventories they cannot unload—for example, it is not unusual to find brewery inventory levels in the hundreds overhanging orders from wholesalers for eight, ten, or twelve cases per week.[3]

If literally thousands of players, from enormously diverse backgrounds, all generate the same qualitative behavior patterns, the causes of the behavior must lie beyond the individuals. The causes of the behavior must lie in the structure of the game itself.

Moreover "beer game"-type structures create similar crises in real-life production-distribution systems. For instance, in 1985, personal computer memory chips were cheap and readily available; sales went down by 18 percent and American producers suffered 25 to 60 percent losses.[4] But in late 1986 a sudden shortage developed and was then exacerbated by panic and overordering. The result was a 100 to 300 percent increase in prices for the same chips.[5] A similar surge and collapse in demand occurred in the semiconductor industry in 1973 to 1975. After a huge order buildup and increases in delivery delays throughout the industry, demand collapsed and you could have virtually any product you wanted off any supplier's shelf overnight. Within a few years, Siemens, Signetics, Northern Telecom, Honeywell, and Schlumberger all entered the business by buying weakened semiconductor manufacturers.[6]

In mid-1989, General Motors, Ford, and Chrysler, as the May 30

Wall Street Journal put it, "were simply producing far more cars than they were selling, and dealer inventories were piling up . . . The companies already are idling plants and laying off workers at rates not seen for years."[7] Entire national economies undergo the same sorts of surges in demand and inventory overadjustments, due to what economists call the "inventory accelerator" theory of business cycles.

Similar boom and bust cycles continue to recur in diverse service businesses. For example, real estate is notoriously cyclic, often fueled by speculators who drive up prices to attract investors to new projects. "The phone would ring," Massachusetts condominium developer Paul Quinn told the *"MacNeil-Lehrer Newshour"* in 1989, "in our offices, and we said 'How are we going to handle this? We'll tell everybody to send in a $5,000 check with their name and we'll put them on the list.' The next thing we knew, we had over 150 checks sitting on the desk." The glut followed quickly on the boom: "It was a slow, sinking feeling," Quinn said, interviewed in a seaside town full of unsold developments. "Now's the time to start building for the next boom. Unfortunately, the people in the real estate industry are too busy trying to address the problems they have left over from the last one."[8]

In fact, reality in production-distribution systems is often worse than the beer game. A real retailer can order from three or four wholesalers at once, wait for the first group of deliveries to arrive, and cancel the other orders. Real producers often run up against production capacity limits not present in the game, thereby exacerbating panic throughout the distribution system. In turn, producers invest in additional capacity because they believe that current demand levels will continue into the future, then find themselves strapped with excess capacity once demand collapses.

The dynamics of production-distribution systems such as the beer game illustrate the first principle of systems thinking:

STRUCTURE INFLUENCES BEHAVIOR

When placed in the same system, people, however different, tend to produce similar results.

The systems perspective tells us that we must look beyond individual mistakes or bad luck to understand important problems. We must

look beyond personalities and events. We must look into the underlying structures which shape individual actions and create the conditions where types of events become likely. As Donella Meadows
expresses it:

> A truly profound and different insight is the way you begin to see
> that the system causes its own behavior.[9]

This same sentiment was expressed over a hundred years ago by
a systems thinker of an earlier vintage. Two thirds of the way
through *War and Peace,* Leo Tolstoy breaks off from his narrative
about the history of Napoleon and czarist Russia to contemplate why
historians, in general, are unable to explain very much:

> The first fifteen years of the nineteenth century present the spec-
> tacle of an extraordinary movement of millions of men. Men leave
> their habitual pursuits; rush from one side of Europe to the other;
> plunder, slaughter one another, triumph and despair; and the
> whole current of life is transformed and presents a quickened ac-
> tivity, first moving at a growing speed, and then slowly slackening
> again. What was the cause of that activity, or from what laws did
> it arise? asked the human intellect.
>
> The historians, in reply to that inquiry, lay before us the sayings
> and doings of some dozens of men in one of the buildings in the
> city of Paris, summing up those doings and sayings by one word
> —revolution. Then they give us a detailed biography of Napoleon,
> and of certain persons favorably or hostilely disposed to him; talk
> of the influence of some of these persons upon others; and then
> say that this it is to which the activity is due; and these are its
> laws.
>
> But, the human intellect not only refuses to believe in that ex-
> planation, but flatly declares that the method of explanation is not
> a correct one . . . The sum of men's individual wills produced
> both the revolution and Napoleon; and only the sum of those wills
> endured them and then destroyed them.
>
> "But whenever there have been wars, there have been great
> military leaders; whenever there have been revolutions in states,
> there have been great men," says history. "Whenever there have
> been great military leaders there have, indeed, been wars," replies
> the human reason; "but that does not prove that the generals were
> the cause of the wars, and that the factors leading to warfare can
> be found in the personal activity of one man. . . ."[10]

Tolstoy argues that only in trying to understand underlying "laws of history," his own synonym for what we now call systemic structures, lies any hope for deeper understanding:

For the investigation of the laws of history, we must completely change the subject of observations, must let kings and ministers and generals alone, and study the homogeneous, infinitesimal elements by which the masses are led. No one can say how far it has been given to man to advance in that direction in understanding the laws of history. But it is obvious that only in that direction lies any possibility of discovering historical laws; and that the human intellect has hitherto not devoted to that method of research one millionth part of the energy that historians have put into the description of the doings of various kings, ministers, and generals . . ."

The term "structure," as used here, does not mean the "logical structure" of a carefully developed argument or the reporting "structure" as shown by an organization chart. Rather, "systemic structure" is concerned with the key interrelationships that influence behavior over time. These are not interrelationships between people, but among key variables, such as population, natural resources, and food production in a developing country; or engineers' product ideas and technical and managerial know-how in a high-tech company.

In the beer game, the structure that caused wild swings in orders and inventories involved the multiple-stage supply chain and the delays intervening between different stages, the limited information available at each stage in the system, and the goals, costs, perceptions, and fears that influenced individuals' orders for beer. But it is very important to understand that when we use the term "systemic structure" we do not just mean structure outside the individual. The nature of structure in human systems is subtle because *we* are part of the structure. This means that we often have the power to alter structures within which we are operating.

However, more often than not, we do not perceive that power. In fact, we usually don't see the structures at play much at all. Rather, *we just find ourselves feeling compelled to act in certain ways.*

In 1973, psychologist Philip Zimbardo performed an experiment in which college students were placed in the roles of prisoners and guards in a mock prison set up in the basement of the psychology building at Stanford. What started as mild resistance by the "prisoners" and assertiveness by the "guards," steadily escalated into increasing rebelliousness and abusiveness, until the "guards" began to physically abuse the "prisoners" and the experimenters felt the situation was dangerously out of control. The experiment was ended prematurely, after six days, when students began to suffer from depression, uncontrollable crying, and psychosomatic illnesses.[12]

I'll never forget one particularly chilling illustration of the power of structure in international politics. It occurred in a private meeting with a high-ranking member of the Soviet embassy, a few months after the Soviets had sent troops into Afghanistan. The official talked, eloquently and with great sincerity, about how the U.S.S.R. had been the first to recognize the country after its founding. The U.S.S.R. had been the first to come to its aid, repeatedly, when there was internal strife or instability. Beginning in the late 1970s, as threats from guerrilla factions increased, the ruling government asked for increasing Soviet assistance. Modest assistance led to greater needs for broader help. It came to a point, the official explained, where "We really had no choice but to intervene militarily."

As I listened to this tale, I couldn't help but think of how retailers or wholesalers in the beer game will explain, when the game is over, that they really had no choice but to keep increasing their orders. It also brought to mind similar stories of American officials, ten or fifteen years earlier, trying to explain how the United States became entangled in Vietnam.

What, exactly, does it mean to say that structures generate particular patterns of behavior? How can such controlling structures be recognized? How would such knowledge help us to be more successful in a complex system?

The beer game provides a laboratory for exploring how structure influences behavior. Each player—retailer, wholesaler, and brewery—made only one decision per week: how much beer to order. The retailer is the first to boost orders significantly, with orders peaking around Week 12. At that point, the expected beer fails to arrive on time—because of backlogs at the wholesale and brewery levels. But the retailer, not thinking of those backlogs, dramatically increased orders to get beer at any cost. That sudden jump in orders is then amplified through the whole system—first by the wholesaler, and then by the brewery. Wholesaler orders peak at about 40, and brewery production peaks at about 80.

The result is a characteristic pattern of buildup and decline in orders at each position, amplified in intensity as you move "upstream," from retailers to breweries. In other words, the further from the ultimate consumer, the higher the orders, and the more dramatic the collapse. In fact, virtually all brewery players go through major crises, ending with near-zero production rates only weeks after having produced 40, 60, 100 or more gross per week.[13]

The other characteristic pattern of behavior in the game can be seen in the inventories and backlogs. The retailer's inventory begins to drop below zero at around Week 5. The retailer's backlog continues to increase for several weeks and the retailer doesn't get back to a positive inventory until around Weeks 12 to 15. Similarly, the wholesaler is in backlog from around Week 7 through around Weeks 15 to 18, and the brewery from Week 9 through Weeks 18 to 20. Once inventories begin to accumulate, they reach large values (about 40 for the retailer, 80 to 120 for the wholesaler, and 60 to 80 for the brewery by Week 30)—much larger than intended. So each position goes through an inventory-backlog cycle: first there is insufficient inventory, then there is too much inventory.

These characterisic patterns of overshoot and collapse in ordering and inventory-backlog cycles occur *despite stable consumer demand*. The actual consumer orders experienced only one change. In Week 2, consumer orders doubled—going from four cases of beer per week to eight. They remained at eight cases per week for the rest of the game.

In other words, after a one-time increase, consumer demand, for the rest of the simulation, was perfectly flat! Of course, none of the players other than the retailer knew consumer demand, and even the retailers saw demand only week by week, with no clue about what would come next.

After the beer game, we ask the people who played wholesalers and brewers to draw what they think the consumer orders were. Most draw a curve which rises and falls, just as their orders rose and fell.[14] In other words, the players assume that if orders in the game rose and collapsed, this must have been due to a surge and collapse in consumer orders. Such assumptions of an "external cause" are characteristic of nonsystemic thinking.

Players' guesses regarding consumer demand shed light on our deeply felt need to find someone or something to blame when there are problems. Initially, after the game is over, many believe that the culprits are the players in the other positions. This belief is shattered by seeing that the same problems arise in all plays of the game, regardless of who is manning the different positions. Many then direct their search for a scapegoat toward the consumer. "There must have been a wild buildup and collapse in consumer demand," they reason. But when their guesses are compared with the flat customer orders, this theory too is shot down.

This has a devastating impact on some players. I'll never forget the president of a large trucking firm sitting back, wide-eyed, staring at the beer game charts. At the next break, he ran to the telephones. "What happened?" I asked when he returned.

"Just before we came here," he said, "my top management team had concluded a three-day review of operations. One of our divisions had tremendously unstable fluctuations in fleet usage. It seemed pretty obvious that the division president didn't have what it took to get the job done. We automatically blamed the man, just as each of us in the experiment automatically blamed the brewery. It just hit me that the problems were probably structural, not personal. I just dashed out to call our corporate headquarters and cancel his termination process."

Once they see that they can no longer blame one another, or the customer, the players have one last recourse—*blame the system*. "It's an unmanageable system," some say. "The problem is that we couldn't communicate with each other." Yet this too turns out to be an untenable position. In fact, given the "physical system" of inventories, shipping delays, and limited information, there is substantial room for improving most team's scores.

REDEFINING YOUR SCOPE OF INFLUENCE: HOW TO IMPROVE PERFORMANCE IN THE BEER GAME

To begin to see the possibilities for improvement, consider the outcomes if each player did nothing to correct his inventory or backlog. Following the "no strategy" strategy, each player would simply place new orders equal to orders he received. This is about the simplest ordering policy possible. If you receive new incoming orders for four cases of beer, you place orders for four. If you receive incoming orders for eight, you place orders for eight. Given the pattern of consumer demand in this game, that means ordering four cases or truckloads every week—until you receive your first order of eight. Thereafter you order eight.

When this strategy is followed unswervingly by all three players, all three positions settle into a form of stability by Week 11. The retailer and wholesaler never quite catch up with their backlogs. Backlogs develop, as in the basic game, due to the delays in getting orders filled. Backlogs persist because the players make no effort to correct them—because the "no strategy" strategy precludes placing the orders in excess of orders received needed to correct backlogs.

Is the "no strategy" strategy successful? Probably, most players would say no. After all, the strategy generates persistent backlogs. This means that everyone throughout the system is kept waiting longer than necessary for his orders to be filled. In real life, such a situation would, undoubtedly, invite competitors to enter a market and provide better delivery service. Only producers/distributors with monopolies on markets would be likely to stick to such a strategy.[15]

But the strategy eliminates the buildup and collapse in ordering, and the associated wild swings in inventories. Moreover, total cost generated by all positions in the "no strategy" strategy is lower than what is achieved by 75 percent of the teams that play the game![16] In other words, the majority of players in the game, many of them experienced managers, do much worse than if they simply placed orders equal to the orders they receive. In trying to correct the imbalances that result from "doing nothing," most players make matters worse, in many cases dramatically worse.

On the other hand, about 25 percent of the players score better than the "no strategy" strategy, and about 10 percent score very much better. In other words, success is possible. But it requires a shift of view for most players. It means getting to the heart of fundamental mismatches between common ways of thinking about the game—what we will later call our "mental model" of it—and the actual reality of how the game works. Most players see their job as "managing their position" in isolation from the rest of the system. What is required is to see how their position interacts with the larger system.

Consider how you feel if you are a typical player at any position. You pay close attention to your own inventory, costs, backlog, orders, and shipments. Incoming orders come from "outside"—most wholesalers and brewers, for instance, are shocked by the implacable mystery of those latter-half orders, which *should* be high numbers, but instead appear week after week as "zero, zero, zero, zero." You respond to new orders by shipping out beer, but you have little sense of how those shipments will influence the next round of orders. Likewise, you have only a fuzzy concept of what happens to the orders you place; you simply expect them to show up as new shipments after a reasonable delay. Your perspective of the system looks something like this:

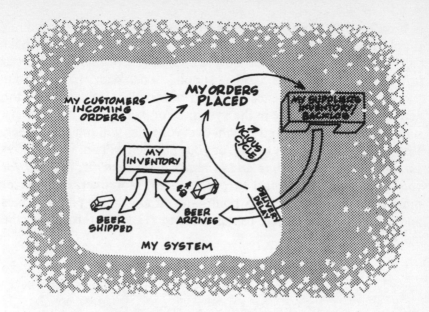

Given this picture of the situation, if you need beer it makes sense to place more orders. If your beer doesn't arrive when expected, you place still more orders. Given this picture of the situation, your job is to "manage your position," reacting to changes in the "external imputs" of incoming orders, beer arrivals, and your supplier's delivery delay.

What the typical "manage your position" view misses is the ways that your orders interact with others' orders to influence the variables you perceive as "external." The players are part of a larger system that most perceive only dimly. For example, if they place a large number of orders, they can wipe out their supplier's inventory, thereby causing their supplier's delivery delay to increase. If they, then, respond (as many do) by placing still more orders, they create a "vicious cycle" that increases problems throughout the system.

This vicious cycle can be set off by any player who panics, anywhere within the system—be he retailer, or wholesaler. Even factories can create the same effect, simply by failing to produce enough beer. Eventually, as one vicious circle influences other vicious circles, the resulting panic spreads up and down the entire production-distribution system. Once the panic builds momentum, I have seen players generate orders that are twenty to fifty times what is actually needed to correct real inventory imbalances.

To improve performance in the beer game players must redefine their scope of influence. As a player in any position, your influence is broader than simply the limits of your own position. You don't simply place orders which go off into the ether and return as beer supplies; those orders influence your supplier's behavior. Which in turn might influence yet another supplier's behavior. In turn, your success is not just influenced by your orders; it is influenced by the actions of everyone else in the system. For example, if the brewery runs out of beer, then pretty soon, everyone else will run out of beer. Either the larger system works, or your position will not work. *Interestingly, in the beer game and in many other systems, in order for you to succeed others must succeed as well.* Moreover, each player must share this systems viewpoint—for, if any single player panics and places a large order, panics tend to reinforce throughout the system.

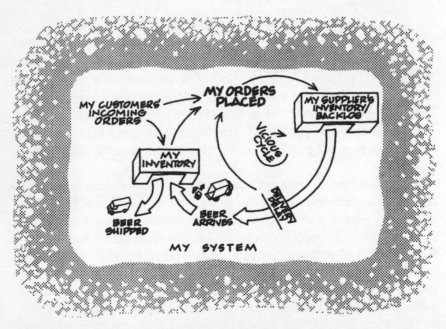

There are two key guidelines for players in the game.

First, keep in mind the beer that you have ordered but which, because of the delay, has not yet arrived. I call this the "Take two aspirin and wait" rule. If you have a headache and need to take aspirin, you don't keep taking aspirin every five minutes until your headache goes away. You wait patiently for the aspirin to take effect because you know that aspirin operates with a delay. Many players keep ordering beer every week until their inventory discrepancy goes away.

Second, don't panic. When your supplier can't get you the beer you want as quickly as normal, the worst thing you can do is order more beer. Yet, that is exactly what many players do. It takes discipline to contain the overwhelming urge to order more when backlogs are building and your customers are screaming. But, without that discipline, you and everyone else will suffer.

These guidelines are consistently missed by most players because they are evident only if you understand the interactions that cross the boundaries between different positions. The "take two aspirin and wait" guideline comes from understanding the delay embedded in the response of your supplier's shipments to changes in your orders placed. The "don't panic" guideline comes from understanding the vicious cycle created when your orders placed exacerbate your supplier's delivery delay.

How well can players do if they follow these guidelines?

It is not possible to totally eliminate all overshoots in orders and all inventory/backlog cycles. It is possible to hold these instabilities to a very modest level, a small fraction of what occurred in Lover's Beer. It is possible to achieve total costs that are one fifth of the "do nothing" strategy, or about one tenth the typical costs achieved by teams. In other words, substantial improvements are possible.

THE LEARNING DISABILITIES AND OUR WAYS OF THINKING

All of the learning disabilities described in Chapter 2 operate in the beer game:

- Because they "become their position," people do not see how their actions affect the other positions.
- Consequently, when problems arise, they quickly blame each other—"the enemy" becomes the players at the other positions, or even the customers.
- When they get "proactive" and place more orders, they make matters worse.
- Because their overordering builds up gradually, they don't realize the direness of their situation until it's too late.
- By and large, they don't learn from their experience because the most important consequences of their actions occur elsewhere in the system, eventually coming back to create the very problems they blame on others.[17]

• The "teams" running the different positions (usually there are two or three individuals at each position) become consumed with blaming the other players for their problems, precluding any opportunity to learn from each others' experience.[18]

The deepest insights in the beer game come from seeing how these learning disabilities are related to alternative ways of thinking in complex situations. For most, the overall experience of playing the game is deeply dissatisfying because it is purely reactive. Yet, most eventually realize that the source of the reactiveness lies in their own focus on week-by-week events. Most of the players in the game get overwhelmed by the shortages of inventory, surges in incoming orders, disappointing arrivals of new beer. When asked to explain their decisions, they give classic "event explanations." I ordered forty at Week 11 because my retailers ordered thirty-six and wiped out my inventory." So long as they persist in focusing on events, they are doomed to reactiveness.

The systems perspective shows that there are multiple levels of explanation in any complex situation, as suggested by the diagram below. In some sense, all are equally "true." But their usefulness is quite different. Event explanations—"who did what to whom"— doom their holders to a reactive stance. As discussed earlier, event explanations are the most common in contemporary culture, and that is exactly why reactive management prevails.

Systemic Structure (generative)

↓

Patterns of Behavior (responsive)

↓

Events (reactive)

Pattern of behavior explanations focus on seeing longer-term trends and assessing their implications. For example, in the beer game, a pattern of behavior explanation would be: "Production/distribution systems are inherently prone to cycles and instability, which become more severe the further you move from the retailer. Therefore, sooner or later, severe crises are likely at the brewery." Pattern of behavior explanations begin to break the grip of short-term reactiveness. At least they suggest how, over a longer term, we can *respond* to shifting trends.[19]

The third level of explanation, the "structural" explanation, is the least common and most powerful. It focuses on answering the question, "What causes the patterns of behavior?" In the beer game, a structural explanation must show how orders placed, shipments, and inventory interact to generate the observed patterns of instability and amplification; taking into account the effects of built-in delays in filling new orders, and the vicious cycle that arises when rising delivery delays lead to more orders placed. Though rare, structural explanations, when they are clear and widely understood, have considerable impact.

An exceptional example of a leader providing such insight was Franklin Roosevelt, when he went on the radio on March 12, 1933, to explain the four-day "banking holiday." In a time of panic, Roosevelt calmly explained how the banking system worked, structurally. "Let me state the simple fact that when you deposit money in a bank the bank does not put the money into a safe-deposit vault," he said. "It invests your money in many different forms of credit— bonds, mortgages. In other words, the bank puts your money to work to keep the wheels turning around . . ." He explained how banks were required to maintain reserves, but how those reserves were inadequate if there were widespread withdrawals; and why closing the banks for four days was necessary to restore order. In so doing, he generated public support for a radical but necessary action, and began his reputation as a master of public communication.[20]

The reason that structural explanations are so important is that only they address the underlying causes of behavior at a level that patterns of behavior *can be changed*. Structure produces behavior, and changing underlying structures can produce different patterns of behavior. In this sense, structural explanations are inherently *generative*. Moreover, since structure in human systems includes the "operating policies" of the decision makers in the system, redesigning our own decision making redesigns the system structure.[21]

For most players of the game, the deepest insight usually comes when they realize that their problems, *and* their hopes for improvement, are inextricably tied to how they think. Generative learning cannot be sustained in an organization where event thinking predominates. It requires a conceptual framework of "structural" or systemic thinking, the ability to discover structural causes of behavior. Enthusiasm for "creating our future" is not enough.

As the players in the beer game come to understand the structures that cause its behavior, they see more clearly their power to change that behavior, to adopt ordering policies that work in the larger system. They also discover a bit of timeless wisdom delivered years ago by Walt Kelly in his famous line from "Pogo": "We have met the enemy and he is us."

PART II

The Fifth Discipline: The Cornerstone of the Learning Organization

4

THE LAWS OF
THE FIFTH
DISCIPLINE[1]

1. *Today's problems come from yesterday's "solutions."*

Once there was a rug merchant who saw that his most beautiful
carpet had a large bump in its center.[2] He stepped on the bump to
flatten it out—and succeeded. But the bump reappeared in a new
spot not far away. He jumped on the bump again, and it disappeared
—for a moment, until it emerged once more in a new place. Again
and again he jumped, scuffing and mangling the rug in his frustration;
until finally he lifted one corner of the carpet and an angry snake
slithered out.

   Often we are puzzled by the causes of our problems; when we
merely need to look at our own solutions to other problems in the
past. A well-established firm may find that this quarter's sales are off
sharply. Why? Because the highly successful rebate program last
quarter led many customers to buy then rather than now. Or a new
manager attacks chronically high inventory costs and "solves" the
problem—except that the salesforce is now spending 20 percent
more time responding to angry complaints from customers who are

still waiting for late shipments, and the rest of its time trying to convince prospective customers that they can have "any color they want so long as it's black."

Police enforcement officials will recognize their own version of this law: arresting narcotics dealers on Thirtieth Street, they find that they have simply transferred the crime center to Fortieth Street. Or, even more insidiously, they learn that a new citywide outbreak of drug-related crime is the result of federal officials intercepting a large shipment of narcotics—which reduced the drug supply, drove up the price, and caused more crime by addicts desperate to maintain their habit.

Solutions that merely shift problems from one part of a system to another often go undetected because, unlike the rug merchant, those who "solved" the first problem are different from those who inherit the new problem.

2. *The harder you push, the harder the system pushes back.*

In George Orwell's *Animal Farm*, the horse Boxer always had the same answer to any difficulty: "I will work harder," he said. At first, his well-intentioned diligence inspired everyone, but gradually, his hard work began to backfire in subtle ways. The harder he worked, the more work there was to do. What he didn't know was that the pigs who managed the farm were actually manipulating them all for their own profit. Boxer's diligence actually helped to keep the other animals from seeing what the pigs were doing.[3] Systems thinking has a name for this phenomenon: "Compensating feedback": when well-intentioned interventions call forth responses from the system that offset the benefits of the intervention. We all know what it feels like to be facing compensating feedback—the harder you push, the harder the system pushes back; the more effort you expend trying to improve matters, the more effort seems to be required.

Examples of compensating feedback are legion. Many of the best intentioned government interventions fall prey to compensating feedback. In the 1960s there were massive programs to build low-income housing and improve job skills in decrepit inner cities in the United States. Many of these cities were even worse off in the 1970s despite the largesse of government aid. Why? One reason was that low-income people migrated from other cities and from rural areas to those cities with the best aid programs. Eventually, the new housing units became overcrowded and the job training programs were swamped with applicants. All the while, the city's tax base continued to erode, leaving more people trapped in economically depressed areas.

Similar compensating feedback processes have operated to thwart food and agricultural assistance to developing countries. More food available has been "compensated for" by reduced deaths due to malnutrition, higher net population growth, and eventually more malnutrition.

Similarly, efforts to correct the U.S. trade imbalance by letting the value of the dollar fall in the mid-1980s were compensated for by foreign competitors who let prices of their goods fall in parallel (for countries whose currency was "pegged to the dollar," their prices adjusted automatically). Efforts by foreign powers to suppress indigenous guerrilla fighters often lead to further legitimacy for the guerrillas' cause, thereby strengthening their resolve and support, and leading to still further resistance.

Many companies experience compensating feedback when one of their products suddenly starts to lose its attractiveness in the market. They push for more aggressive marketing; that's what always worked in the past, isn't it? They spend more on advertising, and drop the price; these methods may bring customers back temporarily, but they also draw money away from the company, so it cuts corners to compensate. The quality of its service (say, its delivery speed or care in inspection) starts to decline. In the long run, the more fervently the company markets, the more customers it loses.

Nor is compensating feedback limited to "large systems"—there are plenty of personal examples. Take the person who quits smoking only to find himself gaining weight and suffering such a loss in self-image that he takes up smoking again to relieve the stress. Or the protective mother who wants so much for her young son to get along with his schoolmates that she repeatedly steps in to resolve problems and ends up with a child who never learns to settle differences by himself. Or the enthusiastic newcomer so eager to be liked that she never responds to subtle criticisms of her work and ends up embittered and labeled "a difficult person to work with."

Pushing harder, whether through an increasingly aggressive intervention or through increasingly stressful withholding of natural instincts, is exhausting. Yet, as individuals and organizations, we not only get drawn into compensating feedback, we often glorify the suffering that ensues. When our initial efforts fail to produce lasting improvements, we "push harder"—faithful, as was Boxer, to the creed that hard work will overcome all obstacles, all the while blind-ing ourselves to how we are contributing to the obstacles ourselves.

3. *Behavior grows better before it grows worse.*

Low-leverage interventions would be much less alluring if it were not for the fact that many actually work, in the short term. New houses get built. The unemployed are trained. Starving children are spared. Lagging orders turn upward. We stop smoking, relieve our child's stress, and avoid a confrontation with a new coworker. Com-pensating feedback usually involves a "delay," a time lag between the short-term benefit and the long-term disbenefit. *The New Yorker* once published a cartoon in which a man sitting in an armchair pushes over a giant domino encroaching upon him from the left. "At last, I can relax," he's obviously telling himself in the cartoon. Of course, he doesn't see that the domino is toppling another domino, which in turn is about to topple another, and another, and that the chain of dominoes behind him will eventually circle around his chair and strike him from the right.

The better before worse response to many management interven-tions is what makes political decision making so counterproductive. By "political decision making," I mean situations where factors other than the intrinsic merits of alternative courses of action weigh in making decisions—factors such as building one's own power base, or "looking good," or "pleasing the boss." In complex human systems there are always many ways to make things look better in the short run. Only eventually does the compensating feedback come back to haunt you.

The key word is "eventually." The delay in, for example, the circle of dominoes, explains why systemic problems are so hard to recognize. A typical solution feels wonderful, when it first cures the symptoms. Now there's improvement; or maybe even the problem has gone away. It may be two, three, or four years before the prob-lem returns, or some new, worse problem arrives. By that time, given how rapidly most people move from job to job, someone new is sitting in the chair.

4. *The easy way out usually leads back in.*

In a modern version of an ancient Sufi story, a passerby encounters a drunk on his hands and knees under a street lamp. He offers to help and finds out that the drunk is looking for his house keys. After several minutes, he asks, "Where did you drop them?" The drunk replies that he dropped them outside his front door. "Then why look for them here?" asks the passerby. "Because," says the drunk, "there is no light by my doorway."

We all find comfort applying familiar solutions to problems, sticking to what we know best. Sometimes the keys are indeed under the street lamp; but very often they are off in the darkness. After all, if the solution *were* easy to see or obvious to everyone, it probably would already have been found. Pushing harder and harder on familiar solutions, while fundamental problems persist or worsen, is a reliable indicator of nonsystemic thinking—what we often call the "what we need here is a bigger hammer" syndrome.

5. *The cure can be worse than the disease*.

Sometimes the easy or familiar solution is not only ineffective; sometimes it is addictive and dangerous. Alcoholism, for instance, may start as simple social drinking—a solution to the problem of low self-esteem or work-related stress. Gradually, the cure becomes worse than the disease; among its other problems it makes self-esteem and stress even worse than they were to begin with.

The long-term, most insidious consequence of applying nonsystemic solutions is increased need for more and more of the solution. This is why ill-conceived government interventions are not just ineffective, they are "addictive" in the sense of fostering increased dependency and lessened abilities of local people to solve their own problems. The phenomenon of short-term improvements leading to long-term dependency is so common, it has its own name among systems thinkers—it's called "Shifting the Burden to the Intervenor." The intervenor may be federal assistance to cities, food relief agencies, or welfare programs. All "help" a host system, only to leave the system fundamentally weaker than before and more in need of further help.

Finding examples of shifting the burden to the intervenor, as natural resource expert and writer Donella Meadows says, "is easy and fun and sometimes horrifying"[4] and hardly limited to government intervenors. We shift the burden of doing simple math from our knowledge of arithmetic to a dependency on pocket calculators. We take away extended families, and shift the burden for care of the aged to nursing homes. In cities, we shift the burden from diverse local communities to housing projects. The Cold War shifted responsibility for peace from negotiation to armaments, thereby strengthening the military and related industries. In business, we can shift the burden to consultants or other "helpers" who make the company dependent on them, instead of training the client managers to solve problems themselves. Over time, the intervenor's power grows— whether it be a drug's power over a person, or the military budget's hold over an economy, the size and scope of foreign assistance agencies, or the budget of organizational "relief agencies."

Shifting the Burden structures show that any long-term solution must, as Meadows says, "strengthen the ability of the system to shoulder its own burdens." Sometimes that is difficult; other times it is surprisingly easy. A manager who has shifted the burden of his personnel problems onto a Human Relations Specialist may find that the hard part is deciding to take the burden back; once that happens, learning how to handle people is mainly a matter of time and commitment.

6. *Faster is slower*.

This, too, is an old story: the tortoise may be slower, but he wins the race. For most American business people the best rate of growth is fast, faster, fastest. Yet, virtually all natural systems, from ecosystems to animals to organizations, have intrinsically optimal rates of growth. The optimal rate is far less than the fastest possible growth. When growth becomes excessive—as it does in cancer—the system itself will seek to compensate by slowing down; perhaps putting the organization's survival at risk in the process. In Chapter 8, the story of People Express airlines offers a good example of how faster can lead to slower—or even full stop—in the long run.

Observing these characteristics of complex systems, noted biologist and essayist Lewis Thomas has observed, "When you are dealing with a complex social system, such as an urban center or a hamster, with things about it that you are dissatisfied with and eager to fix, you cannot just step in and set about fixing with much hope of helping. This realization is one of the sore discouragements of our century."[5]

When managers first start to appreciate how these systems principles have operated to thwart many of their own favorite interventions, they can be discouraged and disheartened. The systems principles can even become excuses for inaction—for doing nothing rather than possibly taking actions that might backfire, or even make matters worse. This is a classic case of "a little knowledge being a dangerous thing." For the real implications of the systems perspective are not inaction but a new type of action rooted in a new way of thinking—systems thinking is both more challenging *and* more promising than our normal ways of dealing with problems.

7. *Cause and effect are not closely related in time and space.*

Underlying all of the above problems is a fundamental characteristic of complex human systems: "cause" and "effect" are not close in time and space. By "effects," I mean the obvious symptoms that indicate that there are problems—drug abuse, unemployment, starving children, falling orders, and sagging profits. By "cause" I mean the interaction of the underlying system that is most responsible for generating the symptoms, and which, if recognized, could lead to changes producing lasting improvement. Why is this a problem? Because most of us assume they *are*—most of us assume, most of the time, that cause and effect *are* close in time and space.

When we play as children, problems are never far away from their solutions—as long, at least, as we confine our play to one group of toys. Years later, as managers, we tend to believe that the world works the same way. If there is a problem on the manufacturing line, we look for a cause in manufacturing. If salespeople can't meet targets, we think we need new sales incentives or promotions. If there is inadequate housing, we build more houses. If there is inadequate food, the solution must be more food.

As the players in the beer game described in Chapter 3 eventually discover, the root of our difficulties is neither recalcitrant problems nor evil adversaries—but ourselves. There is a fundamental mismatch between the nature of reality in complex systems and our predominant ways of thinking about that reality. The first step in correcting that mismatch is to let go of the notion that cause and effect are close in time and space.

8. *Small changes can produce big results—but the areas of highest leverage are often the least obvious.*

Some have called systems thinking the "new dismal science" because it teaches that most obvious solutions don't work—at best, they improve matters in the short run, only to make things worse in the long run. But there is another side to the story. For systems thinking also shows that small, well-focused actions can sometimes produce significant, enduring improvements, if they're in the right place. Systems thinkers refer to this principle as "leverage."

Tackling a difficult problem is often a matter of seeing where the high leverage lies, a change which—with a minimum of effort—would lead to lasting, significant improvement.

The only problem is that high-leverage changes are usually highly *nonobvious* to most participants in the system. They are not "close in time and space" to obvious problem symptoms. This is what makes life interesting.

Buckminster Fuller had a wonderful illustration of leverage that also served as his metaphor for the principle of leverage—the "trim tab." A trim tab is a small "rudder on the rudder" of a ship. It is only a fraction the size of the rudder. Its function is to make it easier to turn the rudder, which, then, makes it easier to turn the ship. The larger the ship, the more important is the trim tab because a large volume of water flowing around the rudder can make it difficult to turn.

But what makes the trim tab such a marvelous metaphor for leverage is not just its effectiveness, but its nonobviousness. If you knew absolutely nothing about hydrodynamics and you saw a large oil tanker plowing through the high seas, where would you push if you wanted the tanker to turn left? You would probably go to the bow and try to push it to the left. Do you have any idea how much force it requires to turn an oil tanker going fifteen knots by pushing on its bow? The leverage lies in going to the stern and pushing the tail end of the tanker to the right, in order to turn the front to the left. This, of course, is the job of the rudder. But in what direction does the rudder turn in order to get the ship's stern to turn to the right? Why to the left, of course.

You see, ships turn because their rear end is "sucked around." The rudder, by being turned into the oncoming water, compresses the water flow and creates a pressure differential. The pressure differential pulls the stern in the opposite direction as the rudder is turned. This is exactly the same way that an airplane flies: the airplane's wing creates a pressure differential and the airplane is "sucked" upward.

The trim tab—this very small device that has an enormous effect on the huge ship—does the same for the rudder. When it is turned to one side or the other, it compresses the water flowing around the rudder and creates a small pressure differential that "sucks the rudder" in the desired direction. But, if you want the rudder to turn to the left, what direction do you turn the trim tab?—to the right, naturally.

The entire system—the ship, the rudder, and the trim tab—is marvelously engineered through the principle of leverage. Yet, its functioning is totally nonobvious if you do not understand the force of hydrodynamics.

So, too, are the high-leverage changes in human systems nonobvious *until* we understand the forces at play in those systems.

There are no simple rules for finding high-leverage changes, but there are ways of thinking that make it more likely. Learning to see underlying "structures" rather than "events" is a starting point; each of the "systems archetypes" developed below suggests areas of high- and low-leverage change.

Thinking in terms of processes of change rather than "snapshots" is another.

9. *You* can *have your cake and eat it too—but not at once*.

Sometimes, the knottiest dilemmas, when seen from the systems point of view, aren't dilemmas at all. They are artifacts of "snapshot" rather than "process" thinking, and appear in a whole new light once you think consciously of change over time.

For years, for example, American manufacturers thought they had to choose between low cost and high quality. "Higher quality products cost more to manufacture," they thought. "They take longer to assemble, require more expensive materials and components, and entail more extensive quality controls." What they didn't consider was all the ways the increasing quality and lowering costs could go hand in hand, over time. What they didn't consider was how basic improvements in work processes could eliminate rework, eliminate quality inspectors, reduce customer complaints, lower warranty costs, increase customer loyalty, and reduce advertising and sales promotion costs. They didn't realize that they could have both goals, if they were willing to wait for one while they focused on the other. Investing time and money to develop new skills and methods of assembly, including new methods for involving everyone responsible for improving quality, is an up front "cost." Quality and costs may *both* go up in the ensuing months; although some cost savings (like reduced rework) may be achieved fairly quickly, the full range of cost savings may take several years to harvest.

Many apparent dilemmas, such as central versus local control, and happy committed employees versus competitive labor costs, and rewarding individual achievement versus having everyone feel valued are by-products of static thinking. They only appear as rigid "either-or" choices, because we think of what is possible at a fixed point in time. Next month, it may be true that we must choose one or the other, but the real leverage lies in seeing how both can improve over time.[6]

10. *Dividing an elephant in half does not produce two small elephants.*

Living systems have integrity. Their character depends on the whole. The same is true for organizations; to understand the most challenging managerial issues requires seeing the whole system that generates the issues.

Another Sufi tale illustrates the point of this law. As three blind men encountered an elephant, each exclaimed aloud. "It is a large rough thing, wide and broad, like a rug," said the first, grasping an ear. The second, holding the trunk, said, "I have the real facts. It is a straight and hollow pipe." And the third, holding a front leg, said, "It is mighty and firm, like a pillar." Are the three blind men any different from the heads of manufacturing, marketing, and research in many companies? Each sees the firm's problems clearly, but none see how the policies of their department interact with the others. Interestingly, the Sufi story concludes by observing that "Given these men's way of knowing, they will never know an elephant."

Seeing "whole elephants" does not mean that every organizational issue can be understood only by looking at the entire organization. Some issues *can* be understood only by looking at how major functions such as manufacturing, marketing, and research interact; but there are other issues where critical systemic forces arise within a given functional area; and others where the dynamics of an entire industry must be considered. The key principle, called the "principle of the system boundary," is that the interactions that must be examined are those most important to the issue at hand, *regardless* of parochial organizational boundaries.

What makes this principle difficult to practice is the way organizations are designed to keep people from seeing important interactions. One obvious way is by enforcing rigid internal divisions that inhibit inquiry across divisional boundaries, such as those that grow up between marketing, manufacturing, and research. Another is by "leaving" problems behind us, for someone else to clean up. Many European cities have avoided the problems of crime, entrenched poverty, and helplessness that afflict so many American inner cities because they have forced themselves to face the balances that a healthy urban area must maintain. One way they have done this is by maintaining large "green belts" around the city that discourage the growth of suburbs and commuters who work in the city but live outside it. By contrast, many American cities have encouraged steady expansion of surrounding suburbs, continually enabling wealthier residents to move further from the city center and its problems. (Impoverished areas today, such as Harlem in New York and Roxbury in Boston were originally upper-class suburbs.) Corporations do the same thing by continually acquiring new businesses and "harvesting" what they choose to regard as "mature" businesses rather than reinvesting in them.

Incidentally, sometimes people go ahead and divide an elephant in half anyway. You don't have two small elephants then; you have a mess. By a mess, I mean a complicated problem where there is no leverage to be found because the leverage lies in interactions that cannot be seen from looking only at the piece you are holding.

11. *There is no blame.*

We tend to blame outside circumstances for our problems. "Someone else"—the competitors, the press, the changing mood of the marketplace, the government—did it to us. Systems thinking shows us that there is no outside; that you and the cause of your problems are part of a single system. The cure lies in your relationship with your "enemy."

5

A SHIFT OF MIND

SEEING THE WORLD ANEW

There is something in all of us that loves to put together a puzzle, that loves to see the image of the whole emerge. The beauty of a person, or a flower, or a poem lies in seeing all of it. It is interesting that the words "whole" and "health" come from the same root (the Old English *hal,* as in "hale and hearty"). So it should come as no surprise that the unhealthiness of our world today is in direct proportion to our inability to see it as a whole.

Systems thinking is a discipline for seeing wholes. It is a framework for seeing interrelationships rather than things, for seeing patterns of change rather than static "snapshots." It is a set of general principles—distilled over the course of the twentieth century, spanning fields as diverse as the physical and social sciences, engineering, and management. It is also a set of specific tools and techniques, originating in two threads: in "feedback" concepts of cybernetics and in "servo-mechanism" engineering theory dating back to the nineteenth century. During the last thirty years, these tools have been applied to understand a wide range of corporate, urban, regional, economic, political, ecological, and even physiological systems.[1] And systems thinking is a sensibility—for the subtle interconnectedness that gives living systems their unique character.

Today, systems thinking is needed more than ever because we are becoming overwhelmed by complexity. Perhaps for the first time in history, humankind has the capacity to create far more information than anyone can absorb, to foster far greater interdependency than anyone can manage, and to accelerate change far faster than anyone's ability to keep pace. Certainly the scale of complexity is without precedent. All around us are examples of "systemic breakdowns"—problems such as global warming, ozone depletion, the international drug trade, and the U.S. trade and budget deficits —problems that have no simple local cause. Similarly, organizations break down, despite individual brilliance and innovative products, because they are unable to pull their diverse functions and talents into a productive whole.

Complexity can easily undermine confidence and responsibility—as in the frequent refrain, "It's all too complex for me," or "There's nothing I can do. It's the system." Systems thinking is the antidote to this sense of helplessness that many feel as we enter the "age of interdependence." Systems thinking is a discipline for seeing the "structures" that underlie complex situations, and for discerning high from low leverage change. That is, by seeing wholes we learn how to foster health. To do so, systems thinking offers a language that begins by restructuring how we think.

I call systems thinking the fifth discipline because it is the conceptual cornerstone that underlies all of the five learning disciplines of this book. All are concerned with a shift of mind from seeing parts to seeing wholes, from seeing people as helpless reactors to seeing them as active participants in shaping their reality, from reacting to the present to creating the future. Without systems thinking, there is neither the incentive nor the means to integrate the learning disciplines once they have come into practice. As the fifth discipline, systems thinking is the cornerstone of how learning organizations think about their world.

There is no more poignant example of the need for systems thinking than the U.S.-U.S.S.R. arms race. While the world has stood and watched for the past forty years, the two mightiest political powers have engaged in a race to see who could get fastest to where no one wanted to go. I have not yet met a person who is in favor of the arms race. Even those who regard it as absolutely necessary, or who profit from it, will, in their quieter moments, confess that they wish it were not necessary. It has drained the U.S. economy and devastated the Soviet economy. It has ensnared successive administrations of political leaders, and terrified two generations of the world's citizens.

The roots of the arms race lie not in rival political ideologies, nor in nuclear arms, but in a way of thinking both sides have shared. The United States establishment, for example, has had a viewpoint of the arms race that essentially resembled the following:

U.S.S.R. ARMS ⟶ THREAT TO AMERICANS ⟶ NEED TO BUILD U.S. ARMS

At the same time, the Soviet leaders have had a view of the arms race somewhat resembling this:

U.S. ARMS ⟶ THREAT TO SOVIETS ⟶ NEED TO BUILD U.S.S.R. ARMS

From the American viewpoint, the Soviets have been the aggressor, and U.S. expansion of nuclear arms has been a defensive response to the threats posed by the Soviets. From the Soviet viewpoint, the United States has been the aggressor, and Soviet expansion of nuclear arms has been a defensive response to the threat posed by the Americans.

But the two straight lines form a circle. The two nations' individual, "linear," or nonsystemic viewpoints interact to create a "system," a set of variables that influence one another:

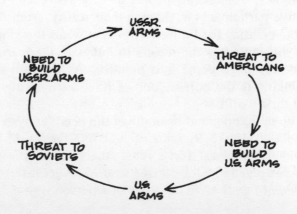

The systems view of the arms race shows a perpetual cycle of aggression. The United States responds to a perceived Threat to Americans by increasing U.S. arms, which increases the Threat to the Soviets, which leads to more Soviet arms, which increases the Threat to the United States, which leads to more U.S. arms, which increases the Threat to the Soviets, which . . . and so on, and so on. From their individual viewpoints, each side achieves its short-term goal. Both sides respond to a perceived threat. But their actions end up creating the opposite outcome, increased threat, in the long run. Here, as in many systems, *doing the obvious thing does not produce the obvious, desired outcome*. The long-term result of each side's efforts to be more secure is heightened insecurity for all, with a combined nuclear stockpile of ten thousand times the total firepower of world War II.

Interestingly, both sides failed for years to adopt a true systems view, despite an abundance of "systems analysts," sophisticated analyses of each others' nuclear arsenals, and complex computer simulations of attack and counterattack war scenarios.[2] Why then have these supposed tools for dealing with complexity not empowered us to escape the illogic of the arms race?

The answer lies in the same reason that sophisticated tools of forecasting and business analysis, as well as elegant strategic plans, usually fail to produce dramatic breakthroughs in managing a business. They are all designed to handle the sort of complexity in which there are many variables: *detail complexity. But there are two types of complexity*. The second type is *dynamic complexity*, situations where cause and effect are subtle, and where the effects over time of interventions are not obvious. Conventional forecasting, planning, and analysis methods are not equipped to deal with dynamic complexity. Mixing many ingredients in a stew involves detail complexity, as does following a complex set of instructions to assemble a machine, or taking inventory in a discount retail store. But none of these situations is especially complex dynamically.

When the same action has dramatically different effects in the short run and the long, there is dynamic complexity. When an action has one set of consequences locally and a very different set of consequences in another part of the system, there is dynamic complexity. When obvious interventions produce nonobvious consequences, there is dynamic complexity. A gyroscope is a dynamically complex machine: If you push downward on one edge, it moves to the left; if you push another edge to the left, it moves upward. Yet, how trivially simple is a gyroscope when compared with the complex dynamics of an enterprise, where it takes days to produce something, weeks to develop a new marketing promotion, months to hire and train new people, and years to develop new products, nurture management talent, and build a reputation for quality—and all of these processes interact continually.

The real leverage in most management situations lies in understanding dynamic complexity, not detail complexity. Balancing market growth and capacity expansion is a dynamic problem. Developing a profitable mix of price, product (or service) quality, design, and availability that make a strong market position is a dynamic problem. Improving quality, lowering total costs, and satisfying customers in a sustainable manner is a dynamic problem.

Unfortunately, most "systems analyses" focus on detail complexity not dynamic complexity. Simulations with thousands of variables and complex arrays of details can actually distract us from seeing patterns and major interrelationships. In fact, sadly, for most people "systems thinking" means "fighting complexity with complexity," devising increasingly "complex" (we should really say "detailed") solutions to increasingly "complex" problems. In fact, this is the antithesis of real systems thinking.

The arms race is, most fundamentally, a problem of dynamic complexity. Insight into the causes and possible cures requires seeing the interrelationships, such as between our actions to become more secure and the threats they create for the Soviets. It requires seeing the delays between action and consequence, such as the delay between a U.S. decision to build up arms and a consequent Soviet counter-buildup. And it requires seeing patterns of change, not just snapshots, such as continuing escalation.

Seeing the major interrelationships underlying a problem leads to new insight into what might be done. In the case of the arms race, as in any escalation dynamic, the obvious question is, "Can the vicious cycle be run in reverse?" "Can the arms race be run backward?"

This may be just what is happening today. Soviet General Secretary Mikhail Gorbachev's initiatives in arms reduction have started a new "peace race" with both sides eager to keep pace with the other's reductions in nuclear arsenals. It is too early to tell whether the shifts in policy initiated by the Soviets in 1988 and 1989 will initiate a sustained unwinding of the U.S.-U.S.S.R. arms race. There are many other factors in the global geopolitical system beyond the pure U.S.-U.S.S.R. interaction. But we appear to be witnessing the first glimmer of a genuinely systemic approach.[3]

The essence of the discipline of systems thinking lies in a shift of mind:

- seeing interrelationships rather than linear cause-effect chains, and
- seeing processes of change rather than snapshots

The practice of systems thinking starts with understanding a simple concept called "feedback" that shows how actions can reinforce or counteract (balance) each other. *It builds to learning to recognize types of "structures" that recur again and again:* the arms race is a generic or archetypal pattern of escalation, at its heart no different from turf warfare between two street gangs, the demise of a marriage, or the advertising battles of two consumer goods companies fighting for market share. Eventually, systems thinking forms a rich language for describing a vast array of interrelationships and patterns of change. Ultimately, *it simplifies life* by helping us see the deeper patterns lying behind the events and the details.

Learning any new language is difficult at first. But as you start to master the basics, it gets easier. Research with young children has shown that many learn systems thinking remarkably quickly.[4] It appears that we have latent skills as systems thinkers that are undeveloped, even repressed by formal education in linear thinking. Hopefully, what follows will help rediscover some of those latent skills and bring to the surface the systems thinker that is within each of us.

SEEING CIRCLES OF CAUSALITY[5]

Reality is made up of circles but we see straight lines. Herein lie the beginnings of our limitation as systems thinkers.

One of the reasons for this fragmentation in our thinking stems from our language. Language shapes perception. What we *see* depends on what we are prepared to see. Western languages, with their subject-verb-object structure, are biased toward a linear view.[6] If we want to see systemwide interrelationships, we need a language of interrelationships, a language made up of circles. Without such a language, our habitual ways of seeing the world produce fragmented views and counterproductive actions—as it has done for decision makers in the arms race. Such a language is important in facing dynamically complex issues and strategic choices, especially when individuals, teams, and organizations need to see beyond events and into the forces that shape change.

To illustrate the rudiments of the new language, consider a very simple system—filling a glass of water. You might think, "That's not a system—it's too simple." But think again.

From the linear viewpoint, we say, "I am filling a glass of water." What most of us have in mind looks pretty much like the following picture:

But, in fact, as we fill the glass, we are watching the water level rise. We monitor the "gap" between the level and our goal, the "desired water level." As the water approaches the desired level, we adjust the faucet position to slow the flow of water, until it is turned off when the glass is full. In fact, when we fill a glass of water we operate in a "water-regulation" system involving five variables: our desired water level, the glass's current water level, the gap between the two, the faucet position, and the water flow. These variables are organized in a circle or loop of cause-effect relationships which is called a "feedback process." The process operates continuously to bring the water level to its desired level:

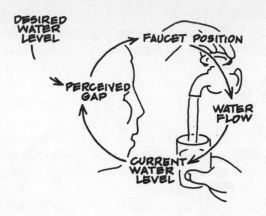

People get confused about "feedback" because we often use the word in a somewhat different way—to gather opinions about an act we have undertaken. "Give me some feedback on the brewery decision," you might say. "What did you think of the way I handled it?" In that context, "positive feedback" means encouraging remarks and "negative feedback" means bad news. But in systems thinking, feedback is a broader concept. It means any reciprocal flow of influence. In systems thinking it is an axiom that every influence is both *cause* and *effect*. Nothing is ever influenced in just one direction.

HOW TO READ A SYSTEMS DIAGRAM

The key to seeing reality systemically is seeing circles of influence rather than straight lines. This is the first step to breaking out of the reactive mindset that comes inevitably from "linear" thinking. Every circle tells a story. By tracing the flows of influence, you can see patterns that repeat themselves, time after time, making situations better or worse.

From any element in a situation, you can trace arrows that represent influence on another element:

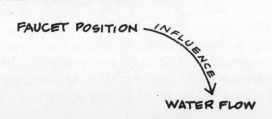

Above, the faucet position arrow points to water flow. Any change made to the faucet position will alter the flow of water. But arrows never exist in isolation:

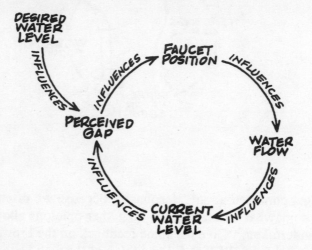

To follow the story, start at any element and watch the action ensue, circling as the train in a toy railroad does through its recurring journey. A good place to start is with the action being taken by the decision maker:

I set the faucet position, which adjusts the water flow, which changes the water level. As the water level changes, the perceived gap (between the current and desired water levels) changes. As the gap changes, my hand's position on the faucet changes again. And so on . . .

When reading a feedback circle diagram, the main skill is to see the "story" that the diagram tells: how the structure creates a particular pattern of behavior (or, in a complex structure, several patterns of behavior) and how that pattern might be influenced. Here the story is filling the water glass and gradually closing down the faucet as the glass fills.

Though simple in concept, the feedback loop overturns deeply ingrained ideas—such as causality. In everyday English we say, "I am filling the glass of water" without thinking very deeply about the real meaning of the statement. It implies a one-way causality—"I am causing the water level to rise." More precisely, "My hand on the faucet is controlling the rate of flow of water into the glass." Clearly, this statement describes only half of the feedback process: the linkages from "faucet position" to "flow of water" to "water level."

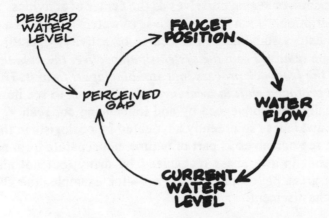

But it would be just as true to describe only the other "half" of the process: "The level of water in the glass is controlling my hand."

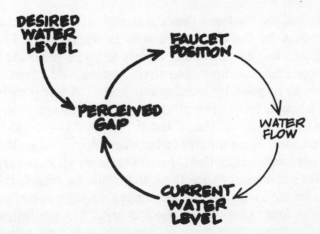

Both statements are equally incomplete. The more complete statement of causality is that my intent to fill a glass of water creates a system that causes water to flow in when the level is low, then shuts the flow off when the glass is full. In other words, the structure causes the behavior. This distinction is important because seeing only individual actions and missing the structure underlying the actions, as we saw in the beer game in Chapter 3, lies at the root of our powerlessness in complex situations.

In fact, all causal attributions made in everyday English are highly suspect! Most are embedded in linear ways of seeing. They are at best partially accurate, inherently biased toward describing portions of reciprocal processes, not the entire processes.

Another idea overturned by the feedback perspective is anthropocentrism—or seeing ourselves as the center of activities. The simple description, "I am filling the glass of water," suggests a world of human actors standing at the center of activity, operating on an inanimate reality. *From the systems perspective, the human actor is part of the feedback process, not standing apart from it. This represents a profound shift in awareness.* It allows us to see how we are continually both influenced by and influencing our reality. It is the shift in awareness so ardently advocated by ecologists in their cries that we see ourselves as part of nature, not separate from nature. It is the shift in awareness recognized by many (but not all) of the world's great philosophical systems—for example, the *Bhagavad Gita*'s chastisement:

> All actions are wrought by the qualities of nature only. The self, deluded by egoism, thinketh: "I am the doer."[7]

In addition, the feedback concept complicates the ethical issue of responsibility. In the arms race, who is responsible? From each side's linear view, responsibility clearly lies with the other side: "It is their aggressive actions, and their nationalistic intent, that are causing us to respond by building our arms." A linear view always suggests a simple locus of responsibility. When things go wrong, this is seen as blame—"he, she, it did it"—or guilt—"I did it." At a deep level, there is no difference between blame and guilt, for both spring from linear perceptions. From the linear view, we are always looking for someone or something that must be responsible—they can even be directed toward hidden agents within ourselves. When my son was four years old, he used to say, "My stomach won't let me eat it," when turning down his vegetables. We may chuckle, but is his assignment of responsibility really different from the adult who says, "My neuroses keep me from trusting people."

In mastering systems thinking, we give up the assumption that there must be an individual, or individual agent, responsible. The feedback perspective suggests that *everyone shares responsibility for problems generated by a system.* That doesn't necessarily imply that everyone involved can exert equal leverage in changing the system.

But it does imply that the search for scapegoats—a particularly alluring pastime in individualistic cultures such as ours in the United States—is a blind alley.

Finally, the feedback concept illuminates the limitations of our language. When we try to describe in words even a very simple system, such as filling the water glass, it gets very awkward: "When I fill a glass of water, there is a feedback process that causes me to adjust the faucet position, which adjusts the water flow and feeds back to alter the water position. The goal of the process is to make the water level rise to my desired level." This is precisely why a new language for describing systems is needed. If it is this awkward to describe a system as simple as filling a water glass, *imagine our difficulties using everyday English to describe the multiple feedback processes in an organization.*

All this takes some getting used to. We are steeped in a linear language for describing our experience. We find simple statements about causality and responsibility familiar and comfortable. It is not that they must be given up, anymore than you give up English to learn French. There are many situations where simple linear descriptions suffice and looking for feedback processes would be a waste of time. But not when dealing with problems of dynamic complexity.

REINFORCING AND BALANCING FEEDBACK AND DELAYS: THE BUILDING BLOCKS OF SYSTEMS THINKING

There are two distinct types of feedback processes: reinforcing and balancing. *Reinforcing* (or amplifying) feedback processes are the engines of growth. Whenever you are in a situation where things are growing, you can be sure that reinforcing feedback is at work. Reinforcing feedback can also generate accelerating decline—a pattern of decline where small drops amplify themselves into larger and larger drops, such as the decline in bank assets when there is a financial panic.

Balancing (or stabilizing) feedback operates whenever there is a goal-oriented behavior. If the goal is to be not moving, then balancing feedback will act the way the brakes in a car do. If the goal is to be moving at sixty miles per hour, then balancing feedback will cause you to accelerate to sixty but no faster. The "goal" can be an explicit target, as when a firm seeks a desired market share, or it can be implicit, such as a bad habit, which despite disavowing, we stick to nevertheless.

In addition, many feedback processes contain *"delays,"* interruptions in the flow of influence which make the consequences of actions occur gradually.

All ideas in the language of systems thinking are built up from these elements, just as English sentences are built up from nouns and verbs. Once we have learned the building blocks, we can begin constructing stories: the systems archetypes of the next chapter.

REINFORCING FEEDBACK: DISCOVERING HOW SMALL CHANGES CAN GROW

If you are in a reinforcing feedback system, you may be blind to how small actions can grow into large consequences—for better or for worse. Seeing the system often allows you to influence how it works.

For example, managers frequently fail to appreciate the extent to which their own expectations influence subordinates' performance. If I see a person as having high potential, I give him special attention to develop that potential. When he flowers, I feel that my original assessment was correct and I help him still further. Conversely, those I regard as having lower potential languish in disregard and inattention, perform in a disinterested manner, and further justify, in my mind, the lack of attention I give them.

Psychologist Robert Merton first identified this phenomenon as the "self-fulfilling prophecy."[8] It is also known as the "Pygmalion effect," after the famous George Bernard Shaw play (later to become *My Fair Lady*). Shaw in turn had taken his title from Pygmalion, a character in Greek and Roman mythology, who believed so strongly in the beauty of the statue he had carved that it came to life.

Pygmalion effects have been shown to operate in countless situations.[9] An example occurs in schools, where a teacher's opinion of a student influences the behavior of that student. Jane is shy and does particularly poorly in her first semester at a new school (because her parents were fighting constantly). This leads her teacher to form an opinion that she is unmotivated. Next semester, the teacher pays less attention to Jane and she does poorly again, withdrawing further. Over time, Jane gets caught in an ever-worsening spiral of withdrawal, poor performance, "labeling" by her teachers, inattention, and further withdrawing. Thus, students are unintentionally "tracked" into a high self-image of their abilities, where they get personal attention, or a low self-image, where their poor class work is reinforced in an ever-worsening spiral.

In *reinforcing processes* such as the Pygmalion effect, a small change builds on itself. Whatever movement occurs is amplifed, producing more movement in the same direction. A small action snowballs, with more and more and still more of the same, resembling compounding interest. Some reinforcing (amplifying) processes are "vicious cycles," in which things start off badly and grow worse. The "gas crisis" was a classic example. Word that gasoline was becoming scarce set off a spate of trips to the local service station, to fill up. Once people started seeing lines of cars, they were convinced that the crisis was here. Panic and hoarding then set in. Before long, everyone was "topping off" their tanks when they were only one-quarter empty, lest they be caught when the pumps went dry. A run on a bank is another example, as are escalation structures such as the arms race or price wars.

But there's nothing inherently bad about reinforcing loops. There are also "virtuous cycles"—processes that reinforce in desired directions. For instance, physical exercise can lead to a reinforcing spiral; you feel better, thus you exercise more, thus you're rewarded by feeling better and exercise still more. The arms race run in reverse, if it can be sustained, makes another virtuous circle. The growth of any new product involves reinforcing spirals. For example, many products grow from "word of mouth." Word of mouth about a product can reinforce a snowballing sense of good feeling (as occurred with the Volkswagen Beetle and more recent Japanese imports) as satisfied customers tell others who then become satisfied customers, who tell still others.

Here is how you might diagram such a process:

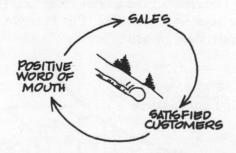

HOW TO READ A REINFORCING CIRCLE DIAGRAM

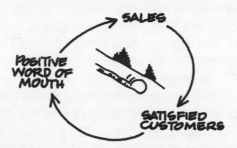

Reinforcing Sales Process Caused by Customers Talking to Each Other About Your Product

This diagram shows a reinforcing feedback process wherein actions *snowball*. Again, you can follow the process by walking yourself around the circle:

If the product is a good product, more sales means more satisfied customers, which means more positive word of mouth. That will lead to still more sales, which means even more widespread word of mouth . . . and so on. On the other hand, if the product is defective, the virtuous cycle becomes a vicious cycle: sales lead to less satisfied customers, less positive word of mouth, and less sales; which leads to still less positive word of mouth and less sales.

The behavior that results from a reinforcing loop is either accelerating growth or accelerating decline. For example, the arms race produces an accelerating growth of arms stockpiles:

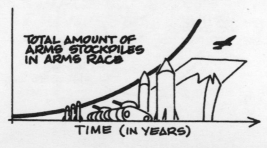

Positive word of mouth produced rapidly rising sales of Volkswagens during the 1950s, and videocassette recorders during the 1980s. A bank run produces an accelerating decline in a bank's deposits.

Folk wisdom speaks of reinforcing loops in terms such as "snowball effect," "bandwagon effect," or "vicious circle," and in phrases describing particular systems: "the rich get richer and the poor get poorer." In business, we know that "momentum is everything," in building confidence in a new product or within a fledgling organization. We also know about reinforcing spirals running the wrong way. "The rats are jumping ship" suggests a situation where, as soon as a few people lose confidence, their defection will cause others to defect in a vicious spiral of eroding confidence. Word of mouth can easily work in reverse, and (as occurred with contaminated over-the-counter drugs) produce marketplace disaster.

Both good news and bad news reinforcing loops accelerate so quickly that they often take people by surprise. A French schoolchildren's jingle illustrates the process. First there is just one lily pad in a corner of a pond. But every day the number of lily pads doubles. It takes thirty days to fill the pond, but for the first twenty-eight days, no one even notices. Suddenly, on the twenty-ninth day, the pond is half full of lily pads and the villagers become concerned. But by this time there is little that can be done. The next day their worst fears come true. That's why environmental dangers are so worrisome, especially those that follow reinforcing patterns (as many environmentalists fear occurs with such pollutants as CFCs). By the time the problem is noticed, it may be too late. Extinctions of species often follow patterns of slow, gradually accelerating decline over long time periods, then rapid demise. So do extinctions of corporations.

But pure accelerating growth or decline rarely continues unchecked in nature, because reinforcing processes rarely occur in isolation. Eventually, limits are encountered—which can slow growth, stop it, divert it, or even reverse it. Even the lily pads stop growing when the limit of the pond's perimeter is encountered. These limits are one form of *balancing feedback,* which, after reinforcing processes, is the second basic element of systems thinking.

BALANCING PROCESSES:
DISCOVERING THE SOURCES OF STABILITY
AND RESISTANCE

If you are in a balancing system, you are in a system that is seeking stability. If the system's goal is one you like, you will be happy. If it is not, you will find all your efforts to change matters frustrated— until you can either change the goal or weaken its influence.

Nature loves a balance—but many times, human decision makers act contrary to these balances, and pay the price. For example, managers under budget pressure often cut back staff to lower costs, but eventually discover that their remaining staff is now overworked, and their costs have not gone down at all—because the remaining work has been farmed out to consultants, or because overtime has made up the difference. The reason that costs don't stay down is that *the system has its own agenda*. There is an implicit goal, unspoken but very real—the amount of work that is expected to get done.

In a balancing (stabilizing) system, there is a self-correction that attempts to maintain some goal or target. Filling the glass of water is a balancing process with the goal of a full glass. Hiring new employees is a balancing process with the goal of having a target work force size or rate of growth. Steering a car and staying upright on a bicycle are also examples of balancing processes, where the goal is heading in a desired direction.

Balancing feedback processes are everywhere. They underlie all goal-oriented behavior. Complex organisms such as the human body contain thousands of balancing feedback processes that maintain temperature and balance, heal our wounds, adjust our eyesight to the amount of light, and alert us to threat. A biologist would say that all of these processes are the mechanisms by which our body achieves *homeostasis*—its ability to maintain conditions for survival

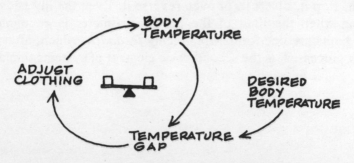

in a changing environment. Balancing feedback prompts us to eat when we need food, and to sleep when we need rest, or—as shown in the diagram above—to put on a sweater when we are cold.

As in all balancing processes, the crucial element—our body temperature—gradually adjusts itself toward its desired level:

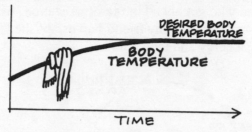

Organizations and societies resemble complex organisms because they too have myriad balancing feedback processes. In corporations, the production and materials ordering process is constantly adjusting in response to changes in incoming orders; short-term (discounts) and long-term (list) prices adjust in response to changes in demand or competitors' prices; and borrowing adjusts with changes in cash balances or financing needs.

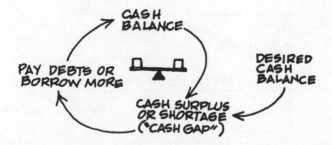

Planning creates longer-term balancing processes. A human resource plan might establish long-term growth targets in head count and in skill profile of the work force to match anticipated needs. Market research and R&D plans shape new product development and investments in people, technologies, and capital plant to build competitive advantage.

What makes balancing processes so difficult in management is that the goals are often implicit, and no one recognizes that the balancing process exists at all. I recall a good friend who tried, fruitlessly, to reduce burnout among professionals in his rapidly growing training business. He wrote memos, shortened working hours, even closed

and locked offices earlier—all attempts to get people to stop over-
working. But all these actions were offset—people ignored the
memos, disobeyed the shortened hours, and took their work home
with them when the offices were locked. Why? Because an unwritten
norm in the organization stated that the *real* heros, the people who
really cared and who got ahead in the organization, worked seventy
hours a week—a norm that my friend had established himself by his
own prodigious energy and long hours.

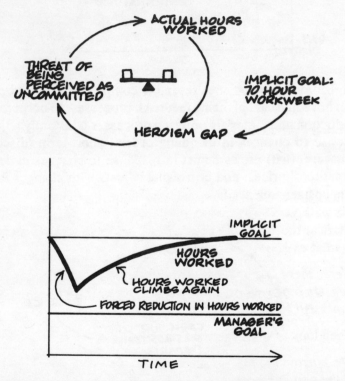

To understand how an organism works we must understand its
balancing processes—those that are explicit *and* implicit. We could
master long lists of body parts, organs, bones, veins, and blood
vessels and yet we would not understand how the body functions—
until we understand how the neuromuscular system maintains balance, or how the cardiovascular system maintains blood pressure
and oxygen levels. This is why many attempts to redesign social
systems fail. The state-controlled economy fails because it severs
the multiple self-correcting processes that operate in a free market
system.[10] This is why corporate mergers often fail. When two hospitals in Boston, both with outstanding traditions of patient care, were

HOW TO READ A
BALANCING CIRCLE DIAGRAM

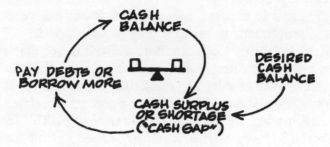

Balancing Process for Adjusting Cash Balance to Cash Surplus or Shortage

This diagram shows a balancing feedback process.

To walk yourself through the process, it's generally easiest to start at the gap—the discrepancy between what is desired and what exists:

Here, there is a shortfall in cash on hand for our cash flow needs. (In other words, there's a gap between our desired and actual cash balances.)

Then look at the actions being taken to correct the gap:

We borrow money, which makes our cash balance larger, and the gap decreases.

The chart shows that a balancing process is always operating to reduce a gap between what is desired and what exists. Moreover, such goals as desired cash balances change over time with growth or decline in the business. Regardless, the balancing process will continue to work to adjust actual cash balances to what is needed, even if the target is moving.

merged several years ago, the new larger hospital had state-of-the-art facilities but lost the spirit of personal care and employee loyalty that had characterized the original institutions. In the merged hospital, subtle balancing processes in the older hospitals that monitored quality, paid attention to employee needs, and maintained friendly relationships with patients were disrupted by new administrative structures and procedures.

Though simple in concept, balancing processes can generate surprising and problematic behavior if they go undetected.

In general, balancing loops are more difficult to see than reinforcing loops because it often *looks* like nothing is happening. There's no dramatic growth of sales and marketing expenditures, or nuclear arms, or lily pads. Instead, the balancing process maintains the status quo, even when all participants want change. The feeling, as Lewis Carroll's Queen of Hearts put it, of needing "all the running you can do to keep in the same place," is a clue that a balancing loop may exist nearby.

Leaders who attempt organizational change often find themselves unwittingly caught in balancing processes. To the leaders, it looks as though their efforts are clashing with sudden resistance that seems to come from nowhere. In fact, as my friend found when he tried to reduce burnout, the resistance is a response by the system, trying to maintain an implicit system goal. Until this goal is recognized, the change effort is doomed to failure. So long as the leader continues to be the "model," his work habits will set the norm. Either he must change his habits, or establish new and different models.

Whenever there is "resistance to change," you can count on there being one or more "hidden" balancing processes. Resistance to change is neither capricious nor mysterious. It almost always arises from threats to traditional norms and ways of doing things. Often these norms are woven into the fabric of established power relationships. The norm is entrenched because the distribution of authority and control is entrenched. Rather than pushing harder to overcome resistance to change, artful leaders discern the source of the resistance. They focus directly on the implicit norms and power relationships within which the norms are embedded.

DELAYS: WHEN THINGS HAPPEN . . . EVENTUALLY

As we've seen, systems seem to have minds of their own. Nowhere is this more evident than in delays—interruptions between your actions and their consequences. Delays can make you badly overshoot your mark, or they can have a positive effect if you recognize them and work with them.

"One of the highest leverage points for improving system performance," says Ray Stata, CEO of Analog Devices, "is the minimization of system delays." Stata is referring to an increasing awareness on the part of American manufacturers that while they have worked traditionally to control tightly the amount of inventory in warehouses, their Japanese counterparts have concentrated on reducing delays—a much more successful effort. "The way leading companies manage time," says George Stalk, vice president of the Boston Consulting Group, "—in production, in new product development, in sales and distribution—represents the most powerful new source of competitive disadvantage."

Delays between actions and consequences are everywhere in human systems. We invest now to reap a benefit in the distant future; we hire a person today but it may be months before he or she is fully productive; we commit resources to a new project knowing that it will be years before it will pay off. But delays are often unappreciated and lead to instability. For example, the decision makers in the beer game consistently misjudged the delays that kept them from getting orders filled when they thought they would.

Delays, when the effect of one variable on another takes time, constitute the third basic building block for a systems language. Virtually all feedback processes have some form of delay. But often the delays are either unrecognized or not well understood. This can result in "overshoot," going further than needed to achieve a desired result. The delay between eating and feeling full has been the nemesis of many a happy diner; we don't yet feel full when we should stop eating, so we keep going until we are overstuffed. The delay between starting a new construction project and its completion results in overbuilding real estate markets and an eventual shakeout. In the beer game, the delay between placing and receiving orders for beer regularly results in overordering.

Unrecognized delays can also lead to instability and breakdown, especially when they are long. Adjusting the shower temperature,

HOW TO READ A DELAY

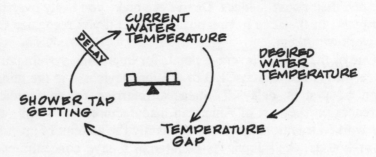

Balancing Process with a Delay: A Sluggish Shower

Here's our earlier "water faucet" feedback diagram again —but this time, with antiquated plumbing. Now there's a significant delay between the time you turn the faucet, and the time you see change in the water flow. Those two cross-hatch lines represent the delay.

Arrows with cross-hatch lines don't tell you how many seconds (or years) the delay will last. You only know it's long enough to make a difference.

When you follow an arrow with a delay, add the word "eventually" to the story you tell in your mind. "I moved the faucet handle, which eventually changed the water flow." Or, "I began a new construction project and, eventually, the houses were ready." You may even want to skip a beat— "one, two"—as you talk through the process.

for instance, is far more difficult when there is a ten-second delay before the water temperature adjusts, then when the delay takes only a second or two.

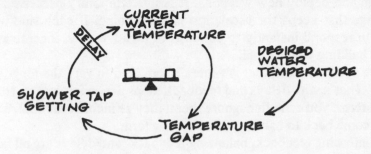

During that ten seconds after you turn up the heat, the water remains cold. You receive no response to your action; so you *perceive* that your act has had no effect. You respond by continuing to turn up the heat. When the hot water finally arrives, a 190-degree water gusher erupts from the faucet. You jump out and turn it back; and, after another delay, it's frigid again. On and on you go, through the balancing loop process. Each cycle of adjustments compensates somewhat for the cycle before. A diagram would look like this:

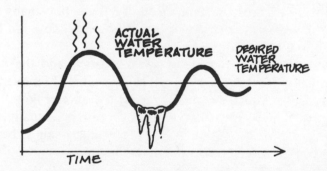

The more aggressive you are in your behavior—the more drastically you turn the knobs—the longer it will take to reach the right temperature. That's one of the lessons of balancing loops with delays: that aggressive action often produces exactly the opposite of what is intended. It produces instability and oscillation, instead of moving you more quickly toward your goal.

Delays are no less problematic in reinforcing loops. In the arms race example, each side perceives itself as gaining advantage from expanding its arsenal because of the delay in the other side's response. This delay can be as long as five years because of the time required to gather intelligence on the other side's weaponry, and to design and deploy new weapons. It is this temporary perceived advantage that keeps the escalation process going. If each side were able to respond instantly to buildups of its adversary, incentives to keep building would be nil.

The systems viewpoint is generally oriented toward the long-term view. That's why delays and feedback loops are so important. In the short term, you can often ignore them; they're inconsequential. They only come back to haunt you in the long term.

Reinforcing feedback, balancing feedback, and delays are all fairly simple. They come into their own as building blocks for the "systems archetypes"—more elaborate structures that recur in our personal and work lives again and again.

6

NATURE'S
TEMPLATES:
IDENTIFYING THE
PATTERNS THAT
CONTROL EVENTS

Some years ago, I witnessed a tragic accident while on an early spring canoe trip in Maine. We had come to a small dam, and put in to shore to portage around the obstacle. A second group arrived, and a young man who had been drinking decided to take his rubber raft over the dam. When the raft overturned after going over the dam, he was dumped into the freezing water. Unable to reach him, we watched in horror as he struggled desperately to swim downstream against the backwash at the base of the dam. His struggle lasted only a few minutes; then he died of hypothermia. Immediately, his limp body was sucked down into the swirling water. Seconds later, it popped up, ten yards downstream, free of the maelstrom at the base of the dam. What he had tried in vain to achieve in the last moments of his life, the currents accomplished for him within seconds after his death. Ironically, it was his very struggle against the forces at the base of the dam that killed him. He didn't know that the only way out was "counterintuitive. If he hadn't tried to keep his head above water, but instead dived down to where the current flowed downstream, he would have survived.

This tragic story illustrates the essence of the systems perspective, first shown in the beer game in Chapter 3, and again in the arms race at the beginning of Chapter 5. *Structures of which we are unaware hold us prisoner.* Conversely, learning to see the structures within which we operate begins a process of freeing ourselves from previously unseen forces and ultimately mastering the ability to work with them and change them.

One of the most important, and potentially most empowering, insights to come from the young field of systems thinking is that certain patterns of structure recur again and again. These "systems archetypes" or "generic structures" embody the key to learning to see structures in our personal and organizational lives. The systems archetypes—of which there are only a relatively small number [1]—suggest that not all management problems are unique, something that experienced managers know intuitively.

If reinforcing and balancing feedback and delays are like the nouns and verbs of systems thinking, then the systems archetypes are analogous to basic sentences or simple stories that get retold again and again. Just as in literature there are common themes and recurring plot lines that get recast with different characters and settings, a relatively small number of these archetypes are common to a very large variety of management situations.

The systems archetypes reveal an elegant simplicity underlying the complexity of management issues. As we learn to recognize more and more of these archetypes, it becomes possible to see more and more places where there is leverage in facing difficult challenges, *and* to explain these opportunities to others.

As we learn more about the systems archetypes, they will no doubt contribute toward one of our most vexing problems, a problem against which managers and leaders struggle incessantly—specialization and the fractionation of knowledge. In many ways, the greatest promise of the systems perspective is the unification of knowledge across all fields—for these same archetypes recur in biology, psychology, and family therapy; in economics, political science, and ecology; as well as in management. [2]

Because they are subtle, when the archetypes arise in a family, an ecosystem, a news story, or a corporation, you often don't see them so much as feel them. Sometimes they produce a sense of *déjà vu,* a hunch that you've seen this pattern of forces before. "There it is again," you say to yourself. Though experienced managers already know many of these recurring plot lines intuitively, they often don't know how to explain them. The systems archetypes provide that language. They can make explicit much of what otherwise is simply "management judgment."

Mastering the systems archetypes starts an organization on the path of putting the systems perspective into practice. It is not enough to espouse systems thinking, to say, "We must look at the big picture and take the long-term view." It is not enough to appreciate basic systems principles, as expressed in the laws of the fifth discipline (Chapter 4) or as revealed in simulations such as the beer game (Chapter 3). It is not even enough to see a particular structure underlying a particular problem (perhaps with the help of a consultant). *This can lead to solving a problem, but it will not change the thinking that produced the problem in the first place.* For learning organizations, only when managers start thinking in terms of the systems archetypes, does systems thinking become an active daily agent, continually revealing how we create our reality.

The purpose of the systems archetypes is to recondition our perceptions, so as to be more able to *see* structures at play, and to see the leverage in those structures. Once a systems archetype is identified, it will always suggest areas of high- and low-leverage change. Presently, researchers have identified about a dozen systems archetypes, nine of which are presented and used in this book (Appendix 2 contains a summary of the archetypes used here). All of the archetypes are made up of the systems building blocks: reinforcing processes, balancing processes, and delays. Below are two that recur frequently, and which are steppingstones to understanding other archetypes and more complex situations.

ARCHETYPE 1: LIMITS TO GROWTH

DEFINITION

A reinforcing (amplifying) process is set in motion to produce a desired result. It creates a spiral of success but also creates inadvertent secondary effects (manifested in a balancing process) which eventually slow down the success.

MANAGEMENT PRINCIPLE

Don't push growth; remove the factors limiting growth.

WHERE IT IS FOUND

The limits to growth structure is useful for understanding all situations where growth bumps up against limits. For example, organizations grow for a while, but then stop growing. Working groups get better for a while, but stop getting better. Individuals improve themselves for a period of time, then plateau.

Many sudden but well-intentioned efforts for improvement bump up against limits to growth. A farmer increases his yield by adding fertilizer, until the crop grows larger than the rainfall of the region can sustain. A crash diet works at first to shave off a few pounds of fat, but then the dieter loses his or her resolve. We might "solve" sudden deadline pressures by working longer hours; eventually, however, the added stress and fatigue slow down our work speed and quality, compensating for the longer hours.

People who try to break a bad habit such as criticizing others frequently come up against limits to growth. At first, their efforts to stop criticizing pay off. They criticize less. The people around them feel more supported. The others reciprocate with positive feelings, which makes the person feel better and criticize less. This is a reinforcing spiral of improved behavior, positive feelings, and further improvement. But, then, their resolve weakens. Perhaps they start to find themselves facing the aspects in others' behavior that really gives them the most trouble: it was easy to overlook a few little things, but *this* is another matter. Perhaps, they just become complacent and stop paying as close attention to their knee-jerk criticisms. For whatever reason, before long, they are back to their old habits.

Once, in one of our seminars, a participant said, "Why, that's just like falling in love." Cautiously, I asked, "How so?" She responded, "Well, first, you meet. You spend a little time together and it's wonderful. So you spend more time together. And it's more wonderful. Before long, you're spending all your free time together. Then you get to know each other better. He doesn't always open the door for you, or isn't willing to give up bowling with his buddies— every other night. He discovers that you have a jealous streak, or a bad temper, or aren't very neat. Whatever it is, you start to see each other's shortcomings." As you learn each other's flaws, she reminded the rest of us, the dramatic growth in feelings comes to a sudden halt—and may even reverse itself, so that you feel worse about each other than you did when you first met.

STRUCTURE

In each case of limits to growth, there is a reinforcing (amplifying) process of growth or improvement that operates on its own for a period of time. Then it runs up against a balancing (or stabilizing) process, which operates to limit the growth. When that happens, the rate of improvement slows down, or even comes to a standstill.

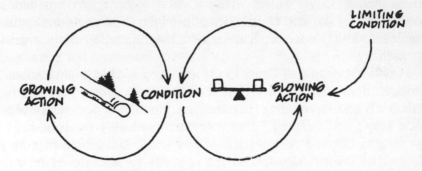

UNDERSTANDING AND USING THE STRUCTURE

Limits to growth structures operate in organizations at many levels. For example, a high-tech organization grows rapidly because of its ability to introduce new products. As new products grow, revenues grow, the R&D budget grows, and the engineering and research staff grows. Eventually, this burgeoning technical staff becomes increasingly complex and difficult to manage. The management burden often falls on senior engineers, who in turn have less time to spend on engineering. Diverting the most experienced engineers from engineering to management results in longer product development times, which slow down the introduction of new products.[3]

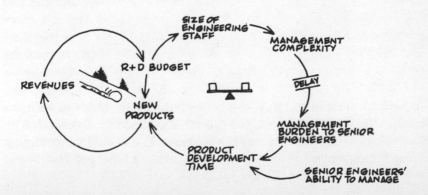

To read any "limits to growth" structure diagram, for example, start with the reinforcing circle of growth. That circle provides the structure with its initial momentum. Walk yourself around the circle: remind yourself how new product growth might generate revenues, which in turn can be reinvested to generate more new products. At some point, however, the forces will shift—here, for example, the growth in R&D budget eventually leads to complexity beyond the senior engineers' ability to manage without diverting precious time from product development. After a delay (whose length depends on the rate of growth, complexity of products, and engineers' management skills), new product introductions slow, slowing overall growth.

Another example of limits to growth occurs when a professional organization, such as a law firm or consultancy, grows very rapidly when it is small, providing outstanding promotion opportunities. Morale grows and talented junior members are highly motivated, expecting to become partners within ten years. But as the firm gets larger, its growth slows. Perhaps it starts to saturate its market niche. Or it might reach a size where the founding partners are no longer interested in sustaining rapid growth. However the growth rate slows, this means less promotion opportunities, more in-fighting among junior members, and an overall decline in morale. The limits to growth structure can be diagrammed as follows:[4]

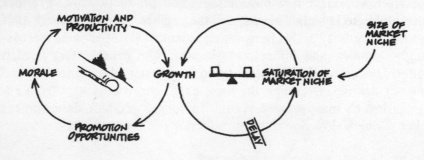

PATTERN OF BEHAVIOR

In each of these structures, the limit gradually becomes more powerful. After its initial boom, the growth mysteriously levels off. The technology company may never recapture its capabilities for developing breakthrough new products or generating rapid growth.

Eventually, growth may slow so much that the reinforcing spiral may turn around and run in reverse. The law firm or consulting firm loses its dominance in its market niche. Before long, morale in the firm has actually started on a downward spiral, caused by the reinforcing circle running in reverse.

Limits to growth structures often frustrate organizational changes that seem to be gaining ground at first, then run out of steam. For example, many initial attempts to establish "quality circles" fail ultimately in U.S. firms, despite making some initial progress. Quality circle activity begins to lead to more open communication and collaborative problem solving, which builds enthusiasm for more quality circle activity. But the more successful the quality circles become, the more threatening they become to the traditional distribution of political power in the firm. Union leaders begin to fear that the new openness will break down traditional adversarial relations between workers and management, thereby undermining union leaders' ability to influence workers. They begin to undermine the quality

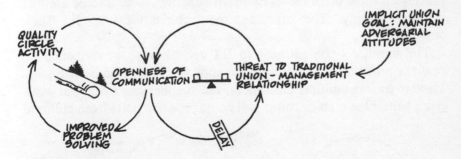

circle activity by playing on workers' apprehensions about being manipulated and "snowed" by managers: "Be careful; if you keep coming up with cost saving improvements on the production line, your job will be the next to go."[5]

Managers, on the other hand, are often unprepared to share control with workers whom they have mistrusted in the past. They end up participating in quality circle activities but only going through the motions. They graciously acknowledge workers' suggestions but fail to implement them.

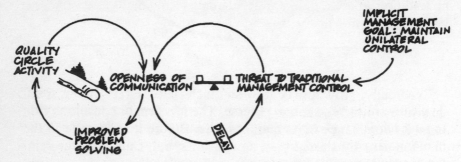

Rather than achieving steady acceptance, quality circle activity rises for a time—then plateaus or declines. Often, the response of the leader to disappointing results from the quality circle simply feeds fuel to the flame. The more aggressively the leader promotes the quality circle, the more people feel threatened and the more stonewalling takes place.

You see similar dynamics with "Just in Time" inventory systems, which depend on new relationships of trust between suppliers and manufacturers. Initial improvements in production flexibility and cost are not sustained. Often, the supplier in a JIT system eventually demands to be a sole source to offset the risk in supplying the manufacturer overnight. This threatens the manufacturer, who is used to placing multiple orders with different suppliers to guarantee control of parts supply. The manufacturer's commitment to JIT then wavers.

The supplier's commitment to JIT can likewise waver, once he realizes that the manufacturer demands to be his prime customer. Used to having multiple customers, the supplier can't help but wonder whether the manufacturer will go on ordering parts from multiple

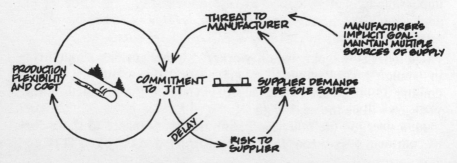

suppliers and then suddenly cancel orders. The more aggressively you try to change the process, the more aware both sides are of their risks. Thus, the more likely they are to hedge those risks by sticking to traditional practices of multiple suppliers and multiple customers, thereby undermining the trust a JIT system requires.[6]

HOW TO ACHIEVE LEVERAGE

Typically, most people react to limits to growth situations by trying to push hard: if you can't break your bad habit, become more diligent in monitoring your own behavior; if your relationship is having problems, spend more time together or work harder to make the relationship work; if staff are unhappy, keep promoting junior staff to make them happy; if the flow of new products is slowing down, start more new product initiatives to offset the problems with the ones that are bogged down; or advocate quality circle more strongly.

It's an understandable response. In the early stages when you can see improvement, you want to do more of the same—after all, it's working so well. When the rate of improvement slows down, you want to compensate by striving even harder. Unfortunately, the more vigorously you push the familiar levers, the more strongly the balancing process resists, and the more futile your efforts become. Sometimes, people just give up their original goal—lowering their goal to stop criticizing others, or giving up on their relationship, or giving up on quality circle or JIT improvements.

But there is another way to deal with limits to growth situations. *In each of them, leverage lies in the balancing loop—not the reinforcing loop. To change the behavior of the system, you must identify and change the limiting factor.* This may require actions you may not yet have considered, choices you never noticed, or difficult changes in rewards and norms. To reach your desired weight may be impossible by dieting alone—you need to speed up the body's metabolic rate, which may require aerobic exercise. Sustaining loving relationships requires giving up the ideal of the "perfect partner"— the implicit goal that limits the continued improvement of any relationship. Maintaining morale and productivity as a professional firm matures requires a different set of norms and rewards that salute work well done, not a person's place in the hierarchy. It may also require distributing challenging work assignments equitably and not to "partners only." Maintaining effective product development processes as a firm grows requires dealing with the management burden brought on by an increasingly complex research and engineering organization. Some firms do this by decentralizing, some by bringing in professionals skilled in managing creative engineers (which is not easy), and some by management development for engineers who want to manage.

Not surprisingly, where quality circles have succeeded they have been part of a broader change in managerial-employee relationships. In particular, successes have involved genuine efforts to redistribute control, thereby dealing with the union and management concerns over loss of control. Likewise, successful Just in Time systems have taken root as part of "Total Quality" programs that focus on meeting customer needs, stablilizing production rates, and sharing benefits with valued suppliers. These changes were necessary to overcome the distrust that lay behind traditional goals of maintaining multiple sources of supply and multiple customers. In successful cases, managers had to ignore temptations to think that quality circle failures were due to individual troublemakers; or that JIT problems came from a recalcitrant supplier. [7]

But there is another lesson from the limits to growth structure as well. There will always be more limiting processes. When one source of limitation is removed or made weaker, growth returns until a new source of limitation is encountered. In some settings, like the growth of a biological population, the fundamental lesson is that growth eventually *will* stop. Efforts to extend the growth by removing limits can actually be counterproductive, forestalling the eventual day of reckoning, which given the pace of change that reinforcing processes can create (remember the French lily pads) may be sooner than we think.

HOW TO CREATE YOUR OWN "LIMITS TO GROWTH" STORY

The best way to understand an archetype is to diagram your own version of it. The more actively you work with the archetypes, the better you will become at recognizing them and finding leverage.

Most people have many limits to growth structures in their lives. The easiest way to recognize them is through the pattern of behavior. Is there a situation in which things get better and better at first, and then mysteriously stop improving? Once you have such a situation in mind, see if you can identify the appropriate elements of the reinforcing and balancing loops:[8]

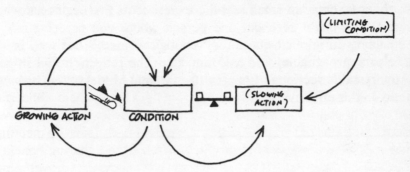

First, identify the reinforcing process—what is getting better and what is the action of activity leading to improvement? (There may be other elements of the reinforcing process, but there are always at least a condition which is improving, and an action leading to the improvement.) It might, for instance, be the story of an organizational improvement: an equal opportunity hiring program, for example. The "growing action" is the equal opportunity program itself; and the condition is the percentage of women and minorities on staff. For example, as the percentage of women in management increases, confidence in or commitment to the program increases, leading to still further increase in women in management.

There is, however, bound to be a limiting factor, typically an implicit goal, or norm, or a limiting resource. The second step is to identify the limiting factor and the balancing process it creates. What "slowing action" or resisting force starts to come into play to keep the condition from continually improving? In this case, some managers might have an idea in their minds of how many women or minority executives are "too much." That unspoken number is the limiting factor; as soon as that threshold is approached, the slowing action—manager's resistance—will kick in. Not only will they resist more equal opportunity hires, but they may make life exceptionally difficult for the new people already in place.

Once you've mapped out your situation, look for the leverage. It won't involve pushing harder; that will just make the resistance stronger. More likely, it will require weakening or removing the limiting condition.

For the best results, test your limits to growth story in real life. Talk to others about your perception. Test your ideas about leverage in small real-life experiments first. For example, you might seek out one person whom you perceive as holding an implicit quota for "enough women," but who is also approachable, and ask him. (See the reflection and inquiry skills section in Chapter 10, "Mental Models," for how to do this effectively.)

ARCHETYPE 2:
SHIFTING THE BURDEN

DEFINITION

An underlying problem generates symptoms that demand attention. But the underlying problem is difficult for people to address, either because it is obscure or costly to confront. So people "shift the burden" of their problem to other solutions—well-intentioned, easy fixes which seem extremely efficient. Unfortunately, the easier "solutions" only ameliorate the symptoms; they leave the underlying problem unaltered. The underlying problem grows worse, unnoticed because the symptoms apparently clear up, and the system loses whatever abilities it had to solve the underlying problem.

MANAGEMENT PRINCIPLE

Beware the symptomatic solution. Solutions that address only the symptoms of a problem, not fundamental causes, tend to have short-term benefits at best. In the long term, the problem resurfaces and there is increased pressure for symptomatic response. Meanwhile, the capability for fundamental solutions can atrophy.

WHERE IT IS FOUND

Shifting the burden structures are common in our personal as well as organizational lives. They come into play when there are obvious "symptoms of problems" that cry out for attention, and quick and ready "fixes" that can make these symptoms go away, at least for a while.

Consider the problem of stress that comes when our personal workload increases beyond our capabilities to deal with it effectively. We juggle work, family, and community in a never-ending blur of activity. If the workload increases beyond our capacity (which tends to happen for us all) the only fundamental solution is to limit the workload. This can be tough—it may mean passing up a promotion that will entail more travel. Or it may mean declining a position on the local school board. It means prioritizing and making choices. Instead, people are often tempted to juggle faster, relieving the stress with alcohol, drugs, or a more benign form of "stress reduction" (such as exercise or meditation). But, of course, drinking doesn't really solve the problem of overwork—it only masks the problem by temporarily relieving the stress. The problem comes back, and so does the need for drinking. Insidiously, the shifting the burden structure, if not interrupted, generates forces that are all-too-familiar in contemporary society. These are the dynamics of avoidance, the result of which is increasing dependency, and ultimately addiction.

A shifting the burden structure lurks behind many "solutions" which seem to work effectively, but nonetheless leave you with an uneasy feeling that they haven't quite taken care of the problem. Managers may believe in delegating work to subordinates but still rely too much on their own ability to step in and "handle things" at the first sign of difficulty, so that the subordinate never gets the necessary experience to do the job. Businesses losing market share to foreign competitors may seek tariff protection and find themselves unable to operate without it. A Third World nation, unable to face difficult choices in limiting government expenditures in line with its tax revenues, finds itself generating deficits that are "financed" through printing money and inflation. Over time, inflation becomes a way of life, more and more government assistance is needed, and chronic deficits become accepted as inevitable. Shifting the burden structures also include food relief programs that "save" farmers from having to grow crops, and pesticides that temporarily remove vermin, but also eliminate natural controls, making it easier for the pest to surge back in the future.

STRUCTURE

The shifting the burden is composed of two balancing (stabilizing) processes. Both are trying to adjust or correct the same problem symptom. The top circle represents the symptomatic intervention; the "quick fix." It solves the problem symptom quickly, but only temporarily. The bottom circle has a delay. It represents a more fundamental response to the problem, one whose effects take longer to become evident. However, the fundamental solution works far more effectively—it may be the only enduring way to deal with the problem.

Often (but not always), in shifting the burden structures there is also an additional reinforcing (amplifying) process created by "side effects" of the symptomatic solution. When this happens, the side effects often make it even more difficult to invoke the fundamental solution—for example, the side effects of drugs administered to correct a health problem. If the problem was caused originally by an unhealthy lifestyle (smoking, drinking, poor eating habits, lack of exercise), then the only fundamental solution lies in a change in lifestyle. The drugs (the symptomatic solution) make the symptom better, and remove pressure to make difficult personal changes. But they also have side effects that lead to still more health problems, making it even more difficult to develop a healthy lifestyle.

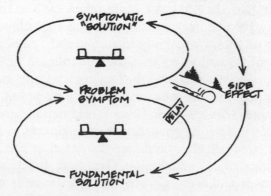

UNDERSTANDING AND USING THE STRUCTURE

The shifting the burden structure explains a wide range of behaviors where well-intended "solutions" actually make matters worse over the long term. Opting for "symptomatic solutions" is enticing. Apparent improvement is achieved. Pressures, either external or internal, to "do something" about a vexing problem are relieved. But easing a problem symptom also reduces any perceived need to find more fundamental solutions. Meanwhile, the underlying problem remains unaddressed and may worsen, and the side effects of the symptomatic solution make it still harder to apply the fundamental solution. Over time, people rely more and more on the symptomatic solution, which is becoming increasingly the only solution. Without anyone making a conscious decision, people have "shifted the burden" to increasing reliance on symptomatic solutions.

Interactions between corporate staff and line managers are fraught with shifting the burden structures. For example, busy managers are often tempted to bring in human resource specialists to sort out personnel problems. The HR expert may solve the problem, but the manager's ability to solve other related problems has not improved. Eventually, other personnel issues will arise and the manager will be just as dependent on the HR expert as before. The very fact that the outside expert was used successfully before makes it even easier to turn to the expert again. "We had a new batch of difficulties, so we brought in the personnel specialists again. They are getting to know our people and our situation well, so they are very efficient." Over time, HR experts become increasingly in demand, staff costs soar, and managers' development (and respect) declines.

Shifting the burden structures often underlie unintended drifts in strategic direction and erosion in competitive position. A recent group of executives in a high-tech firm were deeply concerned that their company was "losing its edge" by not bringing dramatic new products to market. It was less risky to improve existing products. However, they feared that a culture of "incrementalism" rather than "breakthrough" was being fostered. The safer, more predictable, easier-to-plan-for-and-organize processes of improvement innovation were becoming so entrenched that the managers wondered if the company was still capable of basic innovation.

As I listened, I recalled a similar strategic drift described by managers of a leading consumer goods producer, which had become

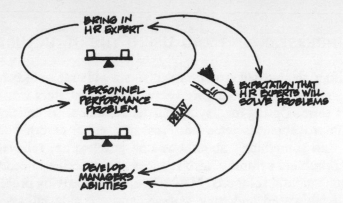

more and more dependent on advertising versus new product development. Whenever business sagged for one of its many products, the tendency was to run a new advertising promotion. The advertising culture had become so entrenched, that the last three CEOs were all ex-advertising executives, who frequently wrote ad copy personally. Meanwhile, the flow of major new products had dwindled to a trickle under their leadership.

A special case of shifting the burden, which recurs with alarming frequency, is "eroding goals." Whenever there is a gap between our goals and our current situation there are two sets of pressures: to improve the situation and to lower our goals. How these pressures are dealt with is central to the discipline of personal mastery, as will be shown in Chapter 9.

Societies collude in eroding goals all the time: witness the lowered standards for "full employment" in the United States. The federal full-employment target slid from 4 percent in the 1960s to 6 to 7 percent by the early 1980s. (In other words, we were willing to tolerate 50 to 75 percent more unemployment as "natural.") Likewise, 3 to 4 percent inflation was considered severe in the early 1960s, but a victory for anti-inflation policies by the early 1980s. In 1984, the U.S. Congress passed the "Gramm-Rudman-Hollings" deficit reduction bill. The original bill called for reaching a balanced budget by 1991. Shortly thereafter, it was clear that the budget reduction was not proceeding on pace, so the target was shifted to 1993. This eroding goal structure can be diagrammed as follows:

As we will see in the next two chapters, similar eroding goal dynamics play out in organizations around goals for quality, goals for innovation, goals for personal growth of employees, and goals for organizational improvement. In effect, we all can become "addicted" to lowering our goals. Or, as a bumper sticker I saw recently said, "If all else fails, lower your goals."

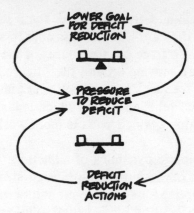

PATTERN OF BEHAVIOR

Regardless of the choice of symptomatic solution, it works—in a way. Drinking, for example, lifts some tension, at least for a while. It relieves the problem symptom. If it didn't, people wouldn't drink. But it also gives the person the feeling of having "solved the problem," thereby diverting attention from the fundamental problem—controlling the workload. Failing to take a stand may well cause the workload to gradually increase further, since most of us are continually besieged by more demands on our time than we can possibly respond to. Over time, the workload continues to build, the stress returns, and the pressure to drink increases.

What makes the shifting the burden structure insidious is the subtle reinforcing cycle it fosters, increasing dependence on the symptomatic solution. Alcoholics eventually find themselves physically

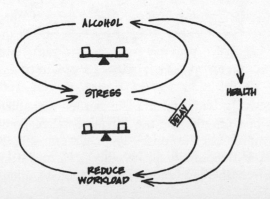

addicted. Their health deteriorates. As their self-confidence and judgment atrophy, they are less and less able to solve their original workload problem. To trace out the causes of the reinforcing cycle, just imagine you are moving around the "figure eight" created by the two interacting feedback processes: stress builds, which leads to more alcohol, which relieves stress, which leads to less perceived need to adjust workload, which leads to more workload, which leads to more stress.

These are the generic dynamics of addiction. In fact, almost all forms of addiction have shifting the burden structures underlying them. All involve opting for symptomatic solutions, the gradual atrophy of the ability to focus on fundamental solutions, and the increasing reliance on symptomatic solutions. By this definition, organizations and entire societies are subject to addiction as much as are individuals.

Shifting the burden structures tend to produce periodic crises, when the symptoms of stress surface. The crises are usually resolved with more of the symptomatic solution, causing the symptoms to temporarily improve. What is often less evident is a slow, long-term drift to lower levels of health: financial health for the corporation or physical health for the individual. The problem symptom grows worse and worse. The longer the deterioration goes unnoticed, or the longer people wait to confront the fundamental causes, the more difficult it can be to reverse the situation. While the fundamental response loses power, the symptomatic response grows stronger and stronger.

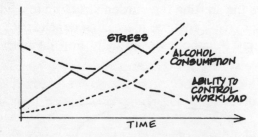

HOW TO ACHIEVE LEVERAGE

Dealing effectively with shifting the burden structures requires a combination of strengthening the fundamental response and weakening the symptomatic response. The character of organizations is often revealed in their ability (or inability) to face shifting-the-burden structures. Strengthening fundamental responses almost always requires a long-term orientation and a sense of shared vision. Without a vision of succeeding through new product innovation, pressures to divert investment into short-term problem-solving will be overwhelming. Without a vision of skilled "people-oriented" managers, the time and energy to develop those skills will not be forthcoming. Without a shared vision of the role government can and should play, and for which people will provide tax revenues to support, there can be no long-term solution to balance government spending and income.

Weakening the symptomatic response requires willingness to tell the truth about palliatives and "looking good" solutions. Managers might acknowledge, for example, that heavy advertising "steals" market share from competitors, but doesn't expand the market in any significant way. And politicians must admit that the resistance they face to raising taxes comes from the perception that the government is corrupt. Until they deal credibly with perceived corruption, they will neither be able to raise taxes nor reduce spending.

A splendid illustration of the principles of leverage in shifting the burden structures can be found in the approach of some of the most effective alcoholism and drug treatment programs. They insist that people face their addiction on one hand, while offering support groups and training to help them rehabilitate on the other. For example, the highly successful Alcoholics Anonymous creates powerful peer support to help people revitalize their ability to face whatever problems were driving them to drink, with a sense of vision that those problems can be solved. They also force individuals to acknowledge that "I am addicted to alcohol and will be for my entire life," so that the symptomatic solution can no longer function in secret.[9]

In the business example of managers becoming more and more dependent on HR consultants, the managers' own abilities must be developed more strongly, even though that may mean a larger initial investment. The HR experts must become coaches and mentors, not problem solvers, helping managers develop their own personal skills.

Sometimes symptomatic solutions *are* needed—for example, in treating a person suffering from a disease created by smoking or drinking. But symptomatic solutions must always be acknowledged as such, *and* combined with strategies for rehabilitating the capacity for fundamental solution, if the shifting the burden dynamic is to be interrupted. If symptomatic solutions are employed *as if* they are fundamental solutions, the search for fundamental solutions stops and shifting the burden sets in.

HOW TO CREATE YOUR OWN "SHIFTING THE BURDEN" STORY

There are three clues to the presence of a shifting the burden structure. First, there's a problem that gets gradually worse over the long term—although every so often it seems to get better for a while. Second, the overall health of the system gradually worsens. Third, there's a growing feeling of help-lessness. People start out feeling euphoric—they've solved their problem!—but end up feeling as if they are victims.

In particular, look for situations of dependency, in which you have a sense that the real issues, the deeper issues, are never quite dealt with effectively. Again, once you have such a situation in mind, see if you can identify the appropriate elements of the reinforcing and balancing loops.

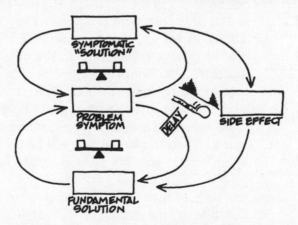

Start by identifying the "problem symptom." This will be the "squeaky wheel" that demands attention—such as stress, subordinates' inabilities to solve pressing problems, falling market share. Then identify a "fundamental solution" (there may be more than one)—a course of action that would, you believe, lead to enduring improvement. Then, identify one or several "symptomatic solutions" that might ameliorate symp-toms for a time.

In fact, "fundamental solutions" and "symptomatic solu-tions" are relative terms, and what is most valuable is recognizing the multiple ways in which a problem can be addressed, from the most fundamental to the most superficial.

Then identify the possible negative "side effects" of the symptomatic solution.

The primary insights in shifting the burden will come from (1) distinguishing different types of solutions; (2) seeing how reliance on symptomatic solutions can reinforce further reliance. The leverage will always involve strengthening the bottom circle, and/or weakening the top circle. Just as with limits to growth, it's best to test your conclusions here with small actions—and to give the tests time to come to fruition. In particular, strengthening an atrophied ability will most likely take a long period of time.

Limits to growth and shifting the burden are but two of the basic systems archetypes. Several others are introduced in the following chapters. (Appendix 2 summarizes all the archetypes used in this book.) As the archetypes are mastered, they become combined into more elaborate systemic descriptions. The basic "sentences" become parts of paragraphs. The simple stories become integrated into more involved stories, with multiple themes, many characters, and more complex plots.

But the archetypes start the process of mastering systems thinking. By using the archetypes, we start to *see* more and more of the circles of causality that surround our daily activity. Over time, this leads naturally to thinking and acting more systemically.

To see how the archetypes get put into practice, the next chapter examines one way in which limits to growth and shifting the burden have proven useful—in understanding the ways a company with great growth potential can fail to realize that potential.

7

THE PRINCIPLE OF
LEVERAGE

The bottom line of systems thinking is leverage—seeing where actions and changes in structures can lead to significant, enduring improvements. Often, leverage, follows the principle of economy of means: where the best results come not from large-scale efforts but from small well-focused actions. Our nonsystemic ways of thinking are so damaging specifically because they consistently lead us to focus on low-leverage changes: we focus on symptoms where the stress is greatest. We repair or ameliorate the symptoms. But such efforts only make matters better in the short run, at best, and worse in the long run.

It's hard to disagree with the *principle* of leverage. But the leverage in most real-life systems, such as most organizations, is not obvious to most of the actors in those systems. They don't see the "structures" underlying their actions. The purpose of the systems archetypes, such as limits to growth and shifting the burden, is to help see those structures and thus find the leverage, especially amid the pressures and crosscurrents of real-life business situations.

For example, let's look at a real story that we have seen again and again. In fact, the following case is a mosaic pieced together from several specific instances where the same story unfolded.[1]

WHEN WE CREATE OUR OWN "MARKET LIMITATIONS"

In the mid-1960s a new electronics company was founded with a unique high-tech product—a new type of computer. Thanks to its engineering know-how, WonderTech had a virtual lock on its market niche. There was enormous demand for its products, and there were enough investors to guarantee no financial constraints.

Yet the company, which began with meteoric growth, never sustained its rapid growth after its first three years. Eventually it declined into bankruptcy.

That fate would have seemed unthinkable during WonderTech's first three years, when sales doubled annually. In fact, sales were so good that backlogs of orders began to pile up midway through their second year. Even with steadily increasing manufacturing capacity (more factories, more shifts, more advanced technology), the demand grew so fast that delivery times slipped a bit. Originally they had promised to deliver machines within eight weeks, and they intended to return to that standard; but with some pride, the top management told investors, "Our computers are so good that some customers are willing to wait fourteen weeks for them. We know it's a problem, and we're working to fix it, but nonetheless they're *still* glad to get the machines, and they love 'em when they get 'em."

The top management knew that they had to add production capacity. After six months of study, while manufacturing changed from a one-shift to a two-shift operation, they decided to borrow the money to build a new factory. To make sure the growth kept up, they pumped much of the incoming revenue directly back into sales and marketing. Since the company sold its products only through a direct sales force, that meant hiring and training more sales people. During the company's third year, the sales force doubled.

But despite this, sales started to slump at the end of the third year.

By the middle of the fourth year, sales had dropped off to crisis levels. The curve of sales, so far, looked like this:

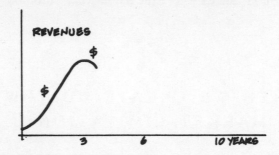

At this point, the new factory came on-line. "We've hired all these people," said the vice president of manufacturing. "What are we going to do with them?" The top management began to panic about what to tell their investors, after they had spent all this money on a new manufacturing facility. It was as if everyone in the company simultaneously turned and looked at one person: the marketing and sales vice president.

Not surprisingly, the marketing and sales VP had become a rising star in the company. His force had done so well during the initial boom that he had anticipated a promotion. Now there was a slump, and he was under heat to turn sales around. So he took the most likely course of action. He held high-powered sales meetings with a single message: "Sell! Sell! Sell!" He fired the low performers. He increased sales incentives, added special discounts, and ran new advertising promotions describing the machine in an exciting new way.

And indeed, sales rose again. The sales and marketing VP found himself once more hailed as a hero, a born-again motivator who could take charge of a tough situation. Once again, WonderTech was in the happy position of having rapidly rising orders. Eventually, backlogs began to grow again. And after a year, delivery times began to rise again—first to ten weeks, then to twelve, and eventually to sixteen. The debate over adding capacity started anew. But this time, having been stung on the last occasion, the top management was still more cautious. Eventually, approval of a new facility was granted, but no sooner had the papers been signed than a new sales crisis started. The slump was so bad that the sales and marketing vice president lost his job.

Over the next several years, and through a succession of marketing managers, the same situation recurred. High sales growth occurred in spurts, always followed by periods of low or no growth. The pattern looked like this:

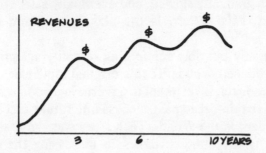

The company prospered modestly, but never came close to fulfilling its original potential. Gradually, the top managers began to fear that other firms would learn how to produce competing products. They frantically introduced ill-conceived improvements in the product. They continued to push hard on marketing. But sales never returned to the original rate of growth. The "wonder" went out of WonderTech. Eventually, the company collapsed.

In his final statement to the lingering members of his executive team, the CEO said, "We did great under the circumstances, but the demand just isn't there. Clearly it was a limited market—a niche which we have effectively filled."

The tale of WonderTech is hardly a novel one. Of every ten start-up companies, one half will disappear within their first five years, only four survive into their tenth year, and only three into their fifteenth year.[2] Whenever a company fails, people always point to specific events to explain the "causes" of the failure: product problems, inept managers, loss of key people, unexpectedly aggressive competition, or business downturns. Yet, the deeper systemic causes for unsustained growth are not recognized. With the aid of the systems archetypes, these causes often can be understood and, in many cases, successful policies can be formulated. The irony of WonderTech is that, given its product and its market potential, it could have grown vigorously for many years, not just two or three.

WonderTech's managers could not see the reasons for their own decline. This was not for lack of information. They had all the significant facts—the same facts that you have after reading this story. But they could not see the structures implicit in those facts.

As a systems thinker trying to diagnose WonderTech's problem, you would look for clues—anything that might suggest an archetype.

You'd begin with the most obvious pattern of behavior: growth leaped up at first, amplifying itself to grow stronger and stronger. But the growth gradually slowed, and eventually sales stopped growing altogether. This pattern is the classic symptom of limits to growth.

There are many possible reinforcing (amplifying) processes that could have produced WonderTech's original rapid sales growth. Investment in products, investment in advertising, good word of mouth —all could have reinforced past success into future success. But one especially evident in the WonderTech story was the reinforcing process created by investing revenues in increasing the sales force: more sales meant more revenues, which meant hiring salespeople, which meant more sales.

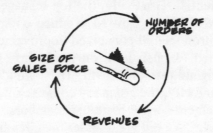

The other part of any limits to growth structure, of course, is a balancing (stabilizing) process. Something had to make the sales slow down. But sales only slow down when a market is saturated, when competition grows, or when customers grow disenchanted. In this case, the need for the WonderTech computer was still strong, and there was no significant competition. There was one factor which turned customers off: long delivery times. As backlogs rise relative to production capacity, delivery times increase. A reputation for poor delivery service builds, eventually making it harder for WonderTech's salespeople to make more sales. The limits to growth structure, then, looks like this:

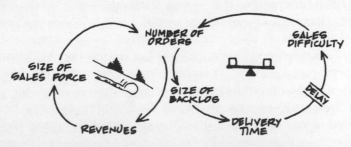

In a limits to growth structure, the worst thing you can do is push hard on the reinforcing process. But that's exactly what Wonder-Tech's managers did. They tried to reignite the "engine of growth" through sales incentives, marketing promotions, and minor product improvements—none of which had any leverage. The leverage would lie with the balancing process.

Why wasn't that balancing process noticed? First, WonderTech's financially oriented top management did not pay much attention to their delivery service. They mainly tracked sales, profits, return on investment, and market share. So long as these were healthy, delivery times were the least of their concerns. When financial performance weakened, pressures shifted to boost orders. Usually, by this time, delivery times were already starting to come down because orders were falling. Thus, whether times were good, or times were bad, the top management paid little attention to the time customers had to wait to get their computers.

Even if they had, they would not necessarily have seen delivery time as a key factor affecting sales. Delivery times had been getting longer and longer, for more than a year and a half, before the first sales crisis hit. This reinforced an attitude among top management: "Customers don't care about late shipments." But that complacency was misplaced; customers *were* concerned, but their concern was obscured, to WonderTech's management, by a built-in delay in the system. A customer would say, "I want the machine delivered in eight weeks." The salesperson would say fine. But after nine, ten, or twelve weeks, there would still be no machine. After several more months, gossip would filter out. However, the number of potential customers was vast. And the gossip had little effect until it eventually mushroomed into a widespread reputation for poor deliveries. In the chart above, this delay falls in the arrow between Delivery Time and Sales Difficulty.

WonderTech's managers had fallen prey to the classic learning disability of being unable to detect cause and effect which were separated in time. In general, if you wait until demand falls off, and *then* get concerned about delivery time, it's way too late. The slow delivery time has already begun to correct itself—temporarily. At WonderTech, delivery times grew worse during the third year, the last year of rapid growth. Then they improved during the downturn that followed; but then they grew worse again.

Over the entire ten-year history of the firm, there was an unfortunate trend of rising delivery times, interrupted by periodic improvements. Alongside that was a gradual decline in the overall health of the system—as seen in slowing growth and declining profits. The company made money in spurts, but lost money like mad in every downturn. The euphoria of the early growth period gave way to discouragement and, eventually, despair. People felt, at the end, as if they were victims. While the CEO said publicly that they had done great under the circumstances, privately he acknowledged that they had been misled by initial marketing projections that forecast a huge potential market that was never realized.

What no one realized was that the situation at WonderTech described a classic shifting the burden structure. There was a problem symptom (delivery time) that worsened steadily, albeit with periodic improvements. The overall health of the enterprise was also steadily worsening, and there was a growing feeling of victimization. As a systems thinker, you would first identify that key problem symptom, and then the symptomatic and fundamental responses to it. In this case, the fundamental response (the lower circle in the diagram below) is to expand production capacity to control delivery time. Delivery times above WonderTech's standard indicate the need for more capacity, which once it eventually arrives on-line, will correct long delivery times. But if this fundamental response is slow in coming, the burden shifts to the symptomatic response (the upper circle) of customer dissatisfaction in declining orders. Since WonderTech's managers didn't solve the problem of long delivery times by adding manufacturing capacity rapidly enough, disgruntled would-be customers "solved" the problem by walking away.

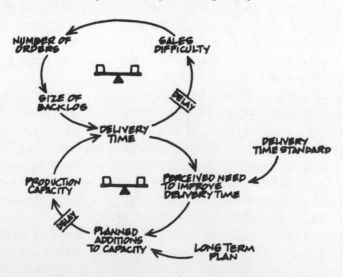

Moreover, as WonderTech allowed the "disgruntled customer" process to operate, the symptomatic response tended to get stronger and stronger—just as you'd expect from a shifting the burden structure. This occurred as WonderTech's reputation for poor delivery service spread through its market; whenever WonderTech entered a new period of rising delivery times, word spread more and more rapidly. Meanwhile, the fundamental response grew weaker. "Having been stung" when they added capacity that was left idle by falling orders, WonderTech's top management grew increasingly cautious in committing to new capacity additions. That meant that new capacity took longer and longer to come on-line—or never came on-line at all. By the time WonderTech's managers were finally ready to add capacity, the symptomatic response had already relieved the pressure, and delivery times had started to fall. Thus their long-term plan for building capacity apparently failed them each time. "Let's wait a little longer before building," they said, "to make sure the demand is there."

In effect, there was a horserace going on between the two responses. Over time, the symptomatic response became more rapid, while the fundamental response became more sluggish. The net effect was that gradually the "disgruntled customer" response assumed more and more of the burden for controlling delivery times.

As delivery times steadily worsened, WonderTech's customer base evolved toward customers who were less sensitive to poor delivery service. That meant they were more sensitive to price. Such customers are less loyal and easily lured away by competitors offering lower prices. WonderTech was drifting into the vulnerable position of being a low-quality, low-price supplier, in a market which they had pioneered.

WonderTech's fate could have been reversed. There was a point of leverage in the structure: the firms' original commitment to an eight-week delivery time. In the shifting the burden structure, the first thing a systems thinker looks for is what might be weakening the fundamental response. In this case, the firm had a *delivery time standard*—eight weeks—that obviously never meant a great deal to the financially preoccupied top managers.

After three years, the actual operating standard to which manufacturing had become accustomed was about ten weeks. Over time, as delivery problems returned, the standard continued to drift. No one thought much about it, least of all top management. When they wanted to know if additional capacity was needed, they would check with manufacturing, which reinforced the eroding standard throughout the organization.

As it happened, the *second* marketing and sales vice president periodically relayed his customers' dissatisfaction with poor deliveries to the management team. His counterpart in manufacturing acknowledged that they occasionally got behind their backlogs, but only when their capacity was inadequate. But the top managers said, "Yes, we know it's a problem, but we can't rush into major investments unless we're certain demand will be sustained." They didn't realize that demand would never be sustained until they made the investment.

We will never know for certain what might have happened if the company had held tight to its original goal and continued to invest aggressively in manufacturing capacity. But simulations based on this structure (combining limits to growth and shifting the burden) and on actual sales figures have been conducted in which the delivery time standard is not allowed to erode. In these simulations, sales continue to grow rapidly throughout the ten years, although there are still periodic plateaus. Delivery time fluctuates, but does not drift upward and the delivery time standard is constant at eight weeks. WonderTech now realizes its growth potential. At the end of the ten years, sales are many times higher than in the original case.[3]

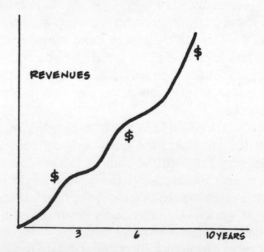

The original sales and marketing vice president had grasped these problems intuitively. He argued from the outset that WonderTech was assessing its factory capacity all wrong. "We only compare capacity to the number of orders we *have*," he said, "instead of the potential volume of orders that we *would* have if we were operating at our best." Unfortunately, the VP's arguments were interpreted as excuses for poor sales performance, and his insights went unheeded. It didn't help that he had no way, conceptually, to explain his thinking. Had he been able to describe the systems archetypes, perhaps more people would have grasped what seemed intuitive to him.

In fact, the subtle dynamics of WonderTech confirm an intuition of many experienced managers: that it is vital to hold to critical performance standards "through thick and thin," and to do whatever it takes to meet those standards. The standards that are most important are those that matter the most to the customer. They usually include product quality (design and manufacture), delivery service, service reliability and quality, and friendliness and concern of service personnel. The systemic structure at WonderTech converts this management intuition into an explicit theory, which shows how eroding standards and sluggish capacity expansion can undermine the growth of an entire enterprise. The complete structure comes from integrating limits to growth and shifting the burden:

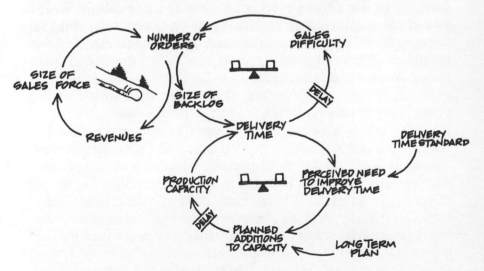

As shown here, the two structures overlap, sharing one balancing process—where disgruntled customers reduce their orders due to long delivery times. The same balancing circle that diverts attention from adding capacity (in shifting the burden) also keeps sales from expanding (in limits to growth). Whether the "disgruntled customer"

circle becomes dominant depends on how the firm responds when delivery times are long. If standards are allowed to drift, the firm's response is weakened and "the burden shifts" to the disgruntled customers. In other words, the company unwittingly becomes addicted to the limiting of its own growth.

CHOOSING BETWEEN SELF-LIMITING OR SELF-SUSTAINING GROWTH

The systemic structure underlying WonderTech explains many complex situations where companies that were once growing rapidly and were highly successful fail mysteriously. In fact, this structure is another systems archetype called growth and underinvestment, a bit more complicated than the two previous archetypes. This archetype operates whenever a company limits its own growth through underinvestment. Underinvestment means building less capacity than is really needed to serve rising customer demand. You can recognize growth and underinvestment by the failure of a firm to achieve its potential growth despite everyone's working tremendously hard (a sign of the underinvestment). Usually, there is continuing financial stress—which, ironically, is both cause and consequence of underinvestment. Financial stress makes aggressive investment difficult or impossible, but the financial stress today originates in the underinvestment of the past. If you look closely, you will also see eroding or declining standards, within the company or industry, for "quality." (By quality we mean all the things that matter to a customer, such as product quality, service quality, and delivery reliability). Standards erode, or fail to continually advance with competition, which results in a failure to invest in building capacity to serve customer needs. ("Investing" may mean adding or improving physical capacity, training personnel, improving work processes, or improving organizational structures.) Disgruntled customers then go elsewhere. Or, if there is no elsewhere, as in the case of eroding standards in an entire industry, customers stop asking for what they can't have. Reduced customer demand eliminates the symptoms of unmet demand. It also reduces financial resources to invest in more capacity.

If all this happened in a month, the whole organization or industry would be mobilized to prevent it. It is the gradualness of the eroding goals and declining growth that makes the dynamics of this structure so insidious. This is the structure that underlies the "boiled frog" syndrome discussed in the learning disabilities of Chapter 2. The frog's standards for water temperature steadily erode, and its capacity to respond to the threat of boiling atrophies.

For a single firm such as WonderTech, the result is a slow, steady decline in market share and profitability. For an entire industry, the result is increasing vulnerability to foreign competitors with higher standards, happening so slowly that it's difficult to detect, often masked by "shifting the burden" palliatives such as increased advertising, discounting, "restructuring," or lobbying for tariff protection. In my opinion, the dynamics of eroding goals and underinvestment lie at the heart of the demise, between the mid-1960s and mid-1980s, of many American manufacturing industries, such as steel autos, machine tools, and consumer electronics. In each of these industries, loss of market share to foreign competitors, which was invariably blamed on external factors, had its origins, at least in part, in weak standards for customer satisfaction, underinvestment, and unhappy customers.

There are many examples of growth and underinvestment in service industries as well. Schools which let the quality of their courses slip, until they lose accreditation. Hospitals whose reputation for patient care erodes as old facilities are not upgraded and the staff becomes increasingly overworked. Radio and television stations that cut their reporting budgets and let "happy talk" substitute for in-depth news coverage. One such prominent industry example will be examined in the next chapter—the case of People Express Airlines.

When understood, the growth and underinvestment structure can be a powerful guide for a company trying to create its own future. Jay Forrester tells an interesting story from the early days of the Digital Equipment Corporation. The company started operations in a corner of one floor of an old mill building outside Boston, with about a dozen employees. As a member of Digital's Board of Directors (Digital was founded by several of Forrester's former MIT graduate students), Forrester later persuaded the board to rent the whole football-field-sized floor as soon as the space became available. But that leap in capacity, which seemed outrageous at first, allowed Digital to grow without eroding its standards. A most dramatic experience, Forrester said later, was to come back only six months later and find the entire floor full of people, productively employed. This episode was one of the first for a company that has achieved one of the finest records of sustained growth in corporate history. For years, Digital maintained a land bank of lots all over New England, so that it had land ready when it wanted to add capacity.

The art of systems thinking lies in being able to recognize increasingly (dynamically) complex and subtle structures, such as that at WonderTech amid the wealth of details, pressures, and cross currents that attend all real management settings. In fact, the essence of mastering systems thinking as a management discipline lies in seeing patterns where others see only events and forces to react to. Seeing the forest as well as the trees is a fundamental problem that plagues all firms, as is illustrated in the next chapter.

8

THE ART OF
SEEING THE FOREST
AND THE TREES

Of all recent U.S. presidents, probably none immersed himself so deeply in the issues facing the nation than Jimmy Carter. Yet, President Carter was widely seen as a relatively ineffective leader, leaving office with a 22 percent approval rating, the lowest of any president since the end of World II, including Richard Nixon.[1]

Jimmy Carter was a victim of complexity. Carter's thirst to know about issues firsthand left him drowning in details, without a clear perspective on those details. But, in fact, was Carter really that different from most contemporary leaders, in either the public or private sector? How many CEOs today can stand and give a fifteen-minute speech that lays out a compelling explanation of the systemic causes of an important issue, and the high- and low-leverage strategies for dealing with that issue?

We all know the metaphor of being able to "step back" far enough from the details to "see the forest for the trees." But, unfortunately, for most of us when we step back we just see "lots of trees." We pick our favorite one or two and focus our attention and efforts for change on those.

Systems thinking finds it greatest benefits in helping us distinguish high- from low-leverage changes in highly complex situations. In effect, the art of systems thinking lies in seeing *through* complexity to the underlying structures generating change. Systems thinking does not mean ignoring complexity. Rather, it means organizing complexity into a coherent story that illuminates the causes of problems and how they can be remedied in enduring ways. The increasing complexity of today's world leads many managers to assume that they lack information they need to act effectively. I would suggest that the fundamental "information problem" faced by managers is not too little information but too much information. What we most need are ways to know what is important and what is not important, what variables to focus on and which to pay less attention to—and we need ways to do this which can help groups or teams develop shared understanding.

THE PERILS OF
BEING A PIONEER

One of the most spectacular and regrettable rises and falls of a prototype learning organization was People Express Airlines.[2] It is a parable of complexity that could not be disentangled in time to save the organization. Founded in 1980 to provide low-cost, high-quality airline service to travelers in the Eastern United States, People Express grew in five years to be the nation's fifth-largest carrier. Along the way, People Express established a reputation as a corporate pioneer, crafting a stirring corporate philosophy articulated by charismatic founder Don Burr. "Most organizations believe that humans are generally bad and you have to control them and watch them," said Burr in one typical statement. "At People Express, people are trusted to do a good job until they prove they definitely won't . . ."[3] The airline translated that philosophy into a host of innovative human resource policies that have since been adopted by many other firms, such as job rotation, team management, universal stock ownership, and only four levels of hierarchy (with only four pay levels in the whole company). Yet, despite its spectacular early success, in September 1986 People Express was taken over by Texas Air Corporation, having lost $133 million in the first six months of 1986 alone.

Many theories have been offered to explain People's growth and collapse. Burr and the airline had gained much public attention for unusually "soft," people-oriented management policies. Hard-headed business analysts felt that People's decline proved that "business is business." Lofty ideals and democratic workplaces conflict with profits, they said. Others blamed Burr and his management team for failing to provide ongoing strategic leadership—especially after the purchase of Denver-based Frontier Airlines in 1985, which brought in four thousand new employees who shared neither People's values nor its business strategy.

Some of People's own executives, including Burr himself, offer a different explanation. In 1984, partly in response to the success of low-cost carriers such as People Express, American Airlines introduced its Sabre seat-reservation computer system, ushering in a new era of "load management"—meaning that airlines could offer a limited number of seats at much-reduced prices, while still booking business passengers and others at full coach. It was a dramatic change in the airline business, and it brought People Express up against significant price competition for the first time.

It is no wonder that People Express poses such a puzzle. Understanding what went wrong requires sorting out an enormously complex set of factors such as:

FLEET	HUMAN RESOURCES	COMPETITIVE FACTORS
Planes	Service personnel	Market size
Capacity of aircraft	Aircraft personnel	Market segments
Routes	Maintenance personnel	Reputation
Scheduled flights	Hiring	Service quality
Competitor routes & flights	Training	Competitor service quality
Service hours per plane (per day)	Turnover	Fares
Fuel efficiency	Morale	"Load management"
	Productivity	Competitor fares
	Experience	
	Team management	
	Job rotation	
	Stock ownership	
	Temporaries	

FINANCIAL VARIABLES	"POLICY LEVERS"
	(A few of the key decisions that
Revenues	*People's management must make)*
Profit	
Cost of plane	Buying planes
operations	Hiring people
Cost of service	Pricing
operations	Marketing expenditures
Cost of marketing	"Service scope" (range of services to
Wages	offer)
Stock price	
Growth rate	
Debt	
Interest Rate	

Such "laundry lists" of important variables hint at the enormous detail complexity of realistic management problems. It's easy to get lost in the "trees" of these details and lose sight of the "forest"— mastering the dynamic complexity essential to successful strategy. Here's where the discipline of systems thinking finds its greatest advantage. By using the systems archetypes we can learn how to "structure" the details into a coherent picture of the forces at play.

A THEORY OF WHAT HAPPENED AT PEOPLE EXPRESS

Disentangling a complex story such as People Express Airlines starts with identifying the forces that shaped its evolution and the structures that may have lain behind those forces. This can lead to a very different picture of a firm's problems than suggested by just looking at the events.

People Express started with an innovative product concept, and the lowest costs in the industry. (People Express was the first airline founded after the 1978 U.S. airline deregulation.) The airline boasted a combination of deeply discounted fares and friendly, no-frills services (for example, meals and baggage handling were extra charges). Flying People Express on many of its East Coast routes was cheaper than taking a bus. This quickly attracted so many new customers that, by the third quarter of 1982, Burr announced at People Express's quarterly financial meeting: "We're now the biggest carrier, in terms of departures, at any New York airport."[4]

In its early days, with universal stock ownership, People's employees had tremendous morale buoyed by the company's rapid success and exciting vision. "I have never flown on an aircraft," wrote one journalist in 1982, "whose help is so cheerful and invested in their work."[5] As Burr said, "At People Express, attitude is as important as altitude."

But that early reputation, and those low prices, brought demand that began, by mid-1982, to outstrip the company's ability to serve. Lori Dubose, managing officer for Human Resources, was quoted as having trouble finding "enough people to staff adequately" and still "have some time for management development." By November 1982, one third of People's staff was temporary help—four hundred temporaries in all. In terms of simple head count, there were probably enough "Customer Service Managers," as People Express's service personnel were called, to keep pace. But the innovative job rotation and team management concepts meant that training and assimilation of service personnel took much longer than in more traditional airlines.

Despite these difficulties, demand for People's deep discount flights continued to grow phenomenally. Passenger seat miles more than doubled in 1982, and again in 1983. By the end of 1983, People was one of the most profitable carriers in the industry. Its stock was trading at $22 a share, up from $8.50 at startup. Despite being overworked, many of People's employees were growing wealthy. Burr preached the merits of hard work in the pursuit of a lofty vision: "People get more fatigued and stressed when they don't have a lot to do. I really believe that, and I think I have tested it. . . . It's sensational what direction can do. The beauty of the human condition is the magic people are capable of when there's direction. When there's no direction, you're not capable of much." Revenues doubled again in 1984, although profits did not rise proportionately.

Meanwhile, People Express's customers were complaining more about service problems. There were more and more ticketing and reservation delays, and canceled or overbooked flights. On-board flight attendants became less friendly and less efficient. Customers forgave all this at first, and kept returning to the airline. Thus, there was no apparent penalty for poor service. But during 1984 and 1985, increasing numbers of customers began to trickle away. Growth became entirely driven by price, and People Express's customers became increasingly price conscious, not quality conscious. Eventually, People's stock price fell, which diminished morale and service further. By its last year of operation, flying People Express had become such a dismal experience that it was nicknamed "People Distress," and its once loyal customers began to patronize other carriers.

People Express's chronic problems with service quality and having enough competent and committed service personnel suggests subtle similarities to WonderTech, with its problems of inadequate manufacturing capacity and eroding delivery service—even though the specifics at People Express differed in almost every way from the specifics at WonderTech. WonderTech was a manufacturing company. People Express was a service business. Whereas the critical capacity variable at WonderTech was production capacity, the critical capacity variable at People Express was "service capacity," the composite of personnel, experience, and morale. WonderTech drove growth through aggressive additions to its direct sales force. People Express drove growth through aggressive additions to its fleet and flight schedule. WonderTech foundered because of worsening delivery times and eroding delivery time standards. People Express foundered because of declining customer service quality and standards for service. But despite all those differences, underlying both were the dynamics of growth and underinvestment, the systems archetype that explains one of the most common ways that organizations inadvertently limit their own growth.

Below is how the growth and underinvestment structure looks, mapped onto the People Express story.

At People Express, this structure produced a pattern of rapid growth and equally rapid decline, which you can see in the following charts of behavior over the five years' time period.[6] Sales grew rapidly then slowed and then went into decline. Profits rose, then collapsed, and turned into large losses. Service quality started high then steadily eroded. Fleet size grew rapidly, as did the number of service personnel, but service capacity failed to keep pace with passenger growth.

For the managers at People Express, underinvestment was, perhaps, even harder to see than it was at WonderTech. After all, hadn't People been extremely aggressive in investing in aircraft capacity? But the *critical* underinvestment was in *service* capacity, not aircraft

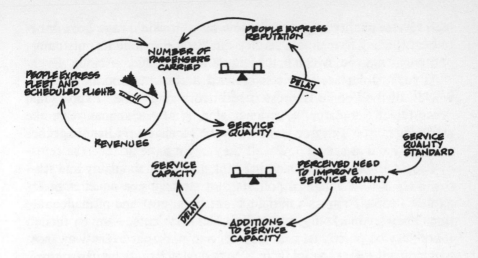

capacity. Moreover, inadequate service capacity was masked, to a degree, by tremendous growth in total head count. People didn't fail to expand the *number* of service personnel to meet its customer growth; it failed to build the composite of people, skills, and organizational infrastructure that was needed to serve customer demand at high levels of quality.[7]

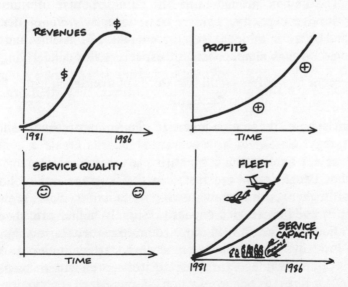

Yet, People Express *could* have been an enduring success, in the opinion of those of us who have tried to understand it systemically. It had a unique product-cost position that would have been very difficult for competitors to match. Had the firm been able to maintain high service quality to go with its low fares, it would have been hard to beat. Falling to maintain service quality made price its only competitive advantage, which in turn made it vulnerable.

At MIT, John Sterman has created a computer-based "microworld" of the People Express case history called the "People Express Flight Simulator." At the beginning of the school year, all incoming master's degree students in the Management School get to try their hand at seeing how well they might have done at the reins of People Express. As a learning tool, the flight simulator lets students try a wide range of policies and strategies in an attempt to exploit People Express's initial advantage in cost and market position. They try marketing promotions and price cuts. They try hiring more service personnel and less service personnel. They try not expanding the fleet so rapidly (e.g., not buying Frontier Airlines) and they try expanding more rapidly. They try redefining the "scope" of People's services to include more or fewer services for the basic fare. As they come to understand the growth and underinvestment dynamics, they come around to strategies that succeed in sustaining growth in revenues and profits, maintaining high service quality, and expanding service capacity at a pace in balance with passengers carried. The key is strengthening the "fundamental solution" of building service capacity. This is best done by *limiting* demand growth and by a commitment to service quality. Both objectives can be achieved through simple changes, especially through:

- 25 percent higher fares (still two thirds of average industry fares)
- Sustained, high service standards

Though simple, these high-leverage changes represent a shift in basic strategy. Sustained high service standards create a commitment to service quality as a competitive advantage. Many have suggested that People grew too fast, but the leverage lies in pricing somewhat higher, both to slow down growth *and* to increase profits to invest in building service capacity. Slightly higher prices would have left People Express with more room to maneuver (say by temporarily lowering price) when competitors started to chip away at the firm's price advantage. (In the simulator—even with a sharp drop in competitor fares, as occurred when computerized reservation systems were introduced—People Express still remains successful with the above strategy.)

In the end, People Express's executives' belief that the enemy was "out there" kept them from seeing the contradictions in their own policies and strategies. The company sought to innovate with dramatically new ideas in human resource policies, yet it also tried to become a major national player in the airline industry within a few years. The two goals were internally contradictory. For example, to sustain 100 percent per year growth, you need "cookie cutter" jobs for which people can be trained in weeks, rather than the sophisticated human resource system requiring many months for people to master many different types of skills.

Consequently, the airline slipped into a vicious cycle of underinvestment and eroding quality (for both customers and employees) that belied all of the executives' original worthy ideals about employee management and customer service. It is impossible to say with certainty what would have happened if they had kept high service quality as an unshakable goal and priced their product so they could build adequate service capacity. With the right mix of policies, People Express's innovative human-resource policies and timely entry into the deregulated airline industry might have produced an enduring success story. One thing is certain, People Express had a unique industry position that would have been very difficult for major carriers to match if it had been able to sustain the enthusiasm and commitment of its people.

Mastering such basic archetypes as growth and underinvestment is the first step in developing the capability of seeing the forest *and* the trees—of seeing information in terms of broad and detailed patterns. Only by seeing both can you respond powerfully to the challenge of complexity and change.

But, ultimately, mastering the language of systems thinking also requires the other complementary learning disciplines. Each contributes important principles and tools that make individuals, teams, and organizations more able to make the shift from seeing the world primarily from a linear perspective to seeing and acting systemically.

PART III

The Core Disciplines: Building the Learning Organization

9

PERSONAL MASTERY

THE SPIRIT OF THE
LEARNING ORGANIZATION

Organizations learn only through individuals who learn. Individual learning does not guarantee organizational learning. But without it no organizational learning occurs.

A small number of organizational leaders are recognizing the radical rethinking of corporate philosophy which a commitment to individual learning requires. Kazuo Inamori, founder and president of Kyocera (a world leader in advanced ceramics technology used in electronic components, medical materials, and its own line of office automation and communications equipment), says this:

Whether it is research and development, company management, or any other aspect of business, the active force is "people." And people have their own will, their own mind, and their own way of thinking. If the employees themselves are not sufficiently motivated to challenge the goals of growth and technological development . . . there will simply be no growth, no gain in productivity, and no technological development.[1]

Tapping the potential of people, Inamori believes, will require new understanding of the "subconscious mind," "willpower," and "action of the heart . . . sincere desire to serve the world." He teaches Kyocera employees to look inward as they continually strive for "perfection," guided by the corporate motto, "Respect Heaven and Love People." In turn, he believes that his duty as a manager starts with "providing for both the material good and spiritual welfare of my employees."

Half a world away in a totally different industry, Bill O'Brien, president of Hanover Insurance, strives for

> . . . organizational models that are more congruent with human nature. When the industrial age began, people worked 6 days a week to earn enough for food and shelter. Today, most of us have these handled by Tuesday afternoon. Our traditional hierarchical organizations are not designed to provide for people's higher order needs, self-respect and self-actualization. The ferment in management will continue until organizations begin to address these needs, for all employees.

Also like Inamori, O'Brien argues that managers must redefine their job. They must give up "the old dogma of planning, organizing and controlling," and realize "the almost sacredness of their responsibility for the lives of so many people." Managers' fundamental task, according to O'Brien, is "providing the enabling conditions for people to lead the most enriching lives they can."

Lest these sentiments seem overly romantic for building a business, let me point out that Kyocera has gone from startup to $2 billion in sales in thirty years, borrowing almost no money and achieving profit levels that are the envy of even Japanese firms. Hanover was at the rock bottom of the property and liability industry in 1969 when O'Brien's predecessor, Jack Adam, began its reconstruction around a core set of values and beliefs about people. Today, the company stands consistently in the upper quarter of its industry in profits and has grown 50 percent faster than the industry over the past ten years.

No less a source of business acumen than Henry Ford observed,

> The smallest indivisible reality is, to my mind, intelligent and is waiting there to be used by human spirits if we reach out and call them in. We rush too much with nervous hands and worried

minds. We are impatient for results. What we need . . . is reinforcement of the soul by the invisible power waiting to be used
. . . I know there are reservoirs of spiritual strength from which
we human beings thoughtlessly cut ourselves off . . . I believe we
shall someday be able to know enough about the source of power,
and the realm of the spirit to create something ourselves . . .

I firmly believe that mankind was once wiser about spiritual
things than we are today. What we now only believe, they knew.[2]

"Personal mastery" is the phrase my colleagues and I use for the
discipline of personal growth and learning. People with high levels of
personal mastery are continually expanding their ability to create the
results in life they truly seek. From their quest for continual learning
comes the spirit of the learning organization.

MASTERY AND PROFICIENCY

Personal mastery goes beyond competence and skills, though it is
grounded in competence and skills. It goes beyond spiritual unfold-
ing or opening, although it requires spiritual growth. It means approaching one's life as a creative work, living life from a creative as
opposed to reactive viewpoint. As my long-time colleague Robert
Fritz puts it:

Throughout history, almost every culture has had art, music,
dance, architecture, poetry, storytelling, pottery, and sculpture.
The desire to create is not limited by beliefs, nationality, creed,
educational background, or era. The urge resides in all of us . . .
[it] is not limited to the arts, but can encompass all of life, from
the mundane to the profound.[3]

When personal mastery becomes a discipline—an activity we integrate into our lives—it embodies two underlying movements. The
first is continually clarifying what is important to us. We often spend
too much time coping with problems along our path that we forget
why we are on that path in the first place. The result is that we only
have a dim, or even inaccurate, view of what's really important to
us.

The second is continually learning how to see current reality more
clearly. We've all known people entangled in counterproductive relationships, who remain stuck because they keep pretending everything is all right. Or we have been in business meetings where

everyone says, "We're on course relative to our plan," yet an honest look at current reality would show otherwise. In moving toward a desired destination, it is vital to know where you are now.

The juxtaposition of vision (what we want) and a clear picture of current reality (where we are relative to what we want) generates what we call "creative tension": a force to bring them together, caused by the natural tendency of tension to seek resolution. The essence of personal mastery is learning how to generate and sustain creative tension in our lives.

"Learning" in this context does not mean acquiring more information, but expanding the ability to produce the results we truly want in life. It is lifelong generative learning. And learning organizations are not possible unless they have people at every level who practice it.

Sadly, the term "mastery" suggests gaining dominance over people or things. But mastery can also mean a special level of proficiency. A "master" craftsperson, for instance, doesn't *dominate* pottery or weaving. But the craftsperson's skill allows the best pots or fabrics to emerge from the workshop. Similarly, personal mastery suggests a special level of proficiency in every aspect of life—personal and professional.

People with a high level of personal mastery share several basic characteristics. They have a special sense of purpose that lies behind their visions and goals. *For such a person, a vision is a calling rather than simply a good idea*. They see "current reality" as an ally, not an enemy. They have learned how to perceive and work with forces of change rather than resist those forces. They are deeply inquisitive, committed to continually seeing reality more and more accurately. They feel connected to others and to life itself. Yet they sacrifice none of their uniqueness. They feel as if they are part of a larger creative process, which they can influence but cannot unilaterally control.

People with a high level of personal mastery live in a continual learning mode. They never "arrive." Sometimes, language, such as the term "personal mastery," creates a misleading sense of definiteness, of black and white. But personal mastery is not something you possess. It is a process. It is a lifelong discipline. People with a high level of personal mastery are acutely aware of their ignorance, their incompetence, their growth areas. And they are deeply self-confident. Paradoxical? Only for those who do not see that "the journey is the reward."

At Hanover, where the quest is for "advanced maturity," O'Brien has written of truly mature people as building and holding deep values, making commitments to goals larger than themselves, being open, exercising free will, and continually striving for an accurate picture of reality. They also, he asserts, have a capacity for delayed gratification, which makes it possible for them to aspire to objectives which others would disregard, even considering "the impact of their choices on succeeding generations." O'Brien points to a deficiency in modern society's commitment to human development:

> Whatever the reasons, we do not pursue emotional development with the same intensity with which we pursue physical and intellectual development. This is all the more unfortunate because full emotional development offers the greatest degree of leverage in attaining our full potential.[4]

"WHY WE WANT IT"

"The total development of our people," O'Brien adds, "is essential to achieving our goal of corporate excellence." Whereas once the "morals of the marketplace" seemed to require a level of morality in business that was lower than in other activities, "We believe there is no fundamental tradeoff between the higher virtues in life and economic success. We believe we can have both. In fact, we believe that, over the long term, the more we practice the higher virtues of life, the more economic success we will have."

In essence, O'Brien is articulating his own version of the most common rationale whereby organizations come to support "personal mastery"—or whatever words they use to express their commitment to the growth of their people. People with high levels of personal mastery are more committed. They take more initiative. They have a broader and deeper sense of responsibility in their work. They learn faster. For all these reasons, a great many organizations espouse a commitment to fostering personal growth among their employees because they believe it will make the organization stronger.

But O'Brien has another reason for pursuing personal mastery, one closer to his own heart:

> Another and equally important reason why we encourage our people in this quest is the impact which full personal development can have on individual happiness. To seek personal fulfillment only

outside of work and to ignore the significant portion of our lives which we spend working, would be to limit our opportunities to be happy and complete human beings.

Herman Miller's president Ed Simon said recently, "Why can't work be one of those wonderful things in life? Why can't we cherish and praise it, versus seeing work as a necessity? Why can't it be a cornerstone in people's lifelong process of developing ethics, values, and in expressing the humanities and the arts? Why can't people learn through the process that there's something about the beauties of design, of building something to last, something of value? I believe that this potential is inherent in work, more so than in many other places."

In other words, why do we want personal mastery? We want it because we want it.

It is a pivotal moment in the evolution of an organization when leaders take this stand. It means that the organization has absolutely, fully, intrinsically committed itself to the well-being of its people. Traditionally, there was a contract: an honest day's pay for an honest day's labor. Now, there is a different relationship between employee and institution.

Pollster Daniel Yankelovich has been taking the pulse of the American public for forty years. As noted in Chapter One, Yankelovich has pointed to a "basic shift in attitude in the workplace" from an "instrumental" to a "sacred" view of work. The instrumental view implies that we work in order to earn the income to do what we really want when we are not working. This is the classic consumer orientation toward work—work is an instrument for generating income. Yankelovich uses the word "sacred" in the sociological not religious sense: "People or objects are sacred in the sociological sense when, apart from what instrumental use they serve, they are valued for themselves."[5]

Traditionally, organizations have supported people's development instrumentally—if people grew and developed, then the organization would be more effective. O'Brien goes one step further: "In the type of organization we seek to build, the fullest development of people is on an equal plane with financial success. This goes along with our most basic premise: that practicing the virtues of life and business success are not only compatible but enrich one another. This is a far cry from the traditional 'morals of the marketplace.' "

To see people's development as a means toward the organization's ends devalues the relationship that can exist between individual and organization. Max de Pree, retired CEO of Herman Miller, speaks of a "covenant" between organization and individual, in contrast to the traditional "contract" ("an honest day's pay in exchange for an honest day's work"). "Contracts," says De Pree, "are a small part of a relationship. A complete relationship needs a covenant . . . a covenantal relationship rests on a shared commitment to ideas, to issues, to values, to goals, and to management processes . . . Covenantal relationships reflect unity and grace and poise. They are expressions of the sacred nature of relationships."[6]

In Japan, a *Christian Science Monitor* reporter visiting the Matsushita corporation observed that "There is an almost religious atmosphere about the place, as if work itself were considered something sacred." Inamori of Kyocera says that his commitment to personal mastery simply evolved from the traditional Japanese commitment to lifetime employment. "Our employees agreed to live in a community in which they would not exploit each other, but rather help each other so that we may each live our life fully."

"You know the system is working," O'Brien said recently, "when you see a person who came to work for the company ten years ago who was unsure of him/herself and had a narrow view of the world and their opportunities. Now that person is in charge of a department of a dozen people. He or she feels comfortable with responsibility, digests complex ideas, weighs different positions, and develops solid reasoning behind choices. Other people listen with care to what this person says. The person has larger aspirations for family, company, industry, and society."

There is an unconditional commitment, an unequivocating courage, in the stand that an organization truly committed to personal mastery takes. We want it because we want it.

RESISTANCE

Who could resist the benefits of personal mastery? Yet, many people and organizations do. Taking a stand for the full development of your people is a radical departure from the traditional contract between employee and institution. In some ways, it is the most radical departure from traditional business practices in the learning organization.

There are obvious reasons why companies resist encouraging personal mastery. It is "soft," based in part on unquantifiable concepts such as intuition and personal vision. No one will ever be able to measure to three decimal places how much personal mastery contributes to productivity and the bottom line. In a materialistic culture such as ours, it is difficult even to discuss some of the premises of personal mastery. "Why do people need to talk about this stuff?" someone may ask. "Isn't it obvious? Don't we already know it?"

A more daunting form of resistance is cynicism. The human potential movement, and along with it much of "humanistic management," overpromised itself to corporations during the 1970s and 1980s. It prompted executives to idealize each other and expect grand, instant, human character transformations, which can never happen.

In combating cynicism, it helps to know its source. Scratch the surface of most cynics and you find a frustrated idealist—someone who made the mistake of converting his ideals into expectations. For example, many of those cynical about personal mastery once held high ideals about people. Then they found themselves disappointed, hurt, and eventually embittered because people fell short of their ideals. Hanover's Bill O'Brien points out that "burnout" comes from causes other than simply working too hard. "There are teachers, social workers, and clergy," says O'Brien, "who work incredibly hard until they are 80 years old and never suffer "burnout"— because they have an accurate view of human nature. They don't over-romanticize people, so they don't feel the great psychological stress when people let them down."

Finally, some fear that personal mastery will threaten the established order of a well-managed company. This is a valid fear. *To empower people in an unaligned organization can be counterproductive*. If people do not share a common vision, and do not share common "mental models" about the business reality within which they operate, empowering people will only increase organizational stress and the burden of management to maintain coherence and direction. This is why the discipline of personal mastery must always be seen as one among the set of disciplines of a learning organization. An organizational commitment to personal mastery would be naive and foolish if leaders in the organization lacked the capabilities of building shared vision and shared mental models to guide local decision makers.

THE DISCIPLINE
OF PERSONAL MASTERY

The way to begin developing a sense of personal mastery is to approach it as a *discipline*, as a series of practices and principles that must be applied to be useful. Just as one becomes a master artist by continual practice, so the following principles and practices lay the groundwork for continually expanding personal mastery.

PERSONAL VISION

Personal vision comes from within. Several years ago I was talking with a young woman about her vision for the planet. She said many lovely things about peace and harmony, about living in balance with nature. As beautiful as these ideas were, she spoke about them unemotionally, as if these were things that she *should* want. I asked her if there was anything else. After a pause, she said, "I want to live on a green planet," and started to cry. As far as I know, she had never said this before. The words just leaped from her, almost with a will of their own. Yet, the image they conveyed clearly had deep meaning to her—perhaps even levels of meaning that she didn't understand.

Most adults have little sense of real vision. We have goals and objectives, but these are not visions. When asked what they want, many adults will say what they want to get rid of. They'd like a better job—that is, they'd like to get rid of the boring job they have. They'd like to live in a better neighborhood, or not have to worry about crime, or about putting their kids through school. They'd like it if their mother-in-law returned to her own house, or if their back stopped hurting. Such litanies of "negative visions" are sadly commonplace, even among very successful people. They are the by-product of a lifetime of fitting in, of coping, of problem solving. As a teenager in one of our programs once said, "We shouldn't call them 'grown ups' we should call them 'given ups.' "

A subtler form of diminished vision is "focusing on the means not the result." Many senior executives, for example, choose "high market share" as part of their vision. But why? "Because I want our company to be profitable." Now, you might think that high profits is an intrinsic result in and of itself, and indeed it is for some. But for surprisingly many other leaders, profits too are a means toward a still more important result. Why choose high annual profits? "Because I want us to remain an independent company, to keep from being taken over." Why do you want that? "Because I want to keep our integrity and our capacity to be true to our purpose in starting the organization." While all the goals mentioned are legitimate, the last—being true to our purpose—has the greatest intrinsic significance to this executive. All the rest are means to the end, means which might change in particular circumstances. *The ability to focus on ultimate intrinsic desires, not only on secondary goals, is a cornerstone of personal mastery.*

Real vision cannot be understood in isolation from the idea of purpose. By purpose, I mean an individual's sense of why he is alive. No one could prove or disprove the statement that human beings have purpose. It would be fruitless even to engage in the debate. But as a working premise, the idea has great power. One implication is that happiness may be most directly a result of living consistently with your purpose. George Bernard Shaw expressed the idea pointedly when he said:

> This is the true joy in life, the being used for a purpose recognized by yourself as a mighty one . . . the being a force of nature instead of a feverish, selfish little clod of ailments and grievances complaining that the world will not devote itself to making you happy.[7]

This same principle has been expressed in some organizations as "genuine caring." In places where people felt uncomfortable talking about personal purpose, they felt perfectly at ease talking about genuine caring. When people genuinely care, they are naturally committed. They are doing what they truly want to do. They are full of energy and enthusiasm. They persevere, even in the face of frustration and setbacks, because what they are doing is what they must do. It is *their work*.

Everyone has had experiences when work flows fluidly; when he feels in tune with a task and works with a true economy of means. Someone whose vision calls him to a foreign country, for example, may find himself learning a new language far more rapidly than he ever could before. You can often recognize your personal vision because it creates such moments; it is the goal pulling you forward that makes all the work worthwhile.

But vision is different from purpose. Purpose is similar to a direction, a general heading. Vision is a specific destination, a picture of a desired future. Purpose is abstract. Vision is concrete. Purpose is "advancing man's capability to explore the heavens." Vision is "a man on the moon by the end of the 1960s." Purpose is "being the best I can be," "excellence." Vision is breaking four minutes in the mile.

It can truly be said that nothing happens until there is vision. But it is equally true that a vision with no underlying sense of purpose, no calling, is just a good idea—all "sound and fury, signifying nothing."

Conversely, purpose without vision has no sense of appropriate scale. As O'Brien says, "You and I may be tennis fans and enjoy talking about ground strokes, our backhands, the thrill of chasing down a corner shot, of hitting a winner. We may have a great conversation, but then we find out that I am gearing up to play at my local country club and you are preparing for Wimbledon. We share the same enthusiasm and love of the game, but at totally different scales of proficiency. Until we establish the scales we have in mind, we might think we are communicating when we're not."

Vision often gets confused with competition. You might say, "My vision is to beat the other team." And indeed, competition can be a useful way of calibrating a vision, of setting scale. To beat the number-ten player at the tennis club is different from beating the number one. But to be number one of a mediocre lot may not fulfill my sense of purpose. Moreover, what is my vision after I reach number one?

Ultimately, vision is intrinsic not relative. It's something you desire for its intrinsic value, not because of where it stands you relative to another. Relative visions may be appropriate in the interim, but they will rarely lead to greatness. Nor is there anything wrong with competition. Competition is one of the best structures yet invented by humankind to allow each of us to bring out the best in each other. But after the competition is over, after the vision has (or has not) been achieved, it is one's sense of purpose that draws you further, that compels you to set a new vision. *This, again, is why personal mastery must be a discipline. It is a process of continually focusing and refocusing on what one truly wants, on one's visions.*

Vision is multifaceted. There are material facets of our visions, such as where we want to live and how much money we want to have in the bank. There are personal facets, such as health, freedom, and being true to ourselves. There are service facets, such as helping others or contributing to the state of knowledge in a field. All are part of what we truly want. Modern society tends to direct our attention to the material aspects, and simultaneously foster guilt for our material desires. Society places some emphasis on our personal desires—for example, it is almost a fetish in some circles to look trim and fit—and relatively little on our desires to serve. In fact, it is easy to feel naive or foolish by expressing a desire to make a contribution. Be that as it may, it is clear from working with thousands of people that personal visions span all these dimensions and more. It is also clear that it takes courage to hold visions that are not in the social mainstream.

But it is exactly that courage to take a stand for one's vision that distinguishes people with high levels of personal mastery. Or, as the Japanese say of the master's stand, "When there is no break, not even the thickness of a hair comes between a man's vision and his action."[8]

In some ways, clarifying vision is one of the easier aspects of personal mastery. A more difficult challenge, for many, comes in facing current reality.

HOLDING CREATIVE TENSION

People often have great difficulty talking about their visions, even when the visions are clear. Why? Because we are acutely aware of the gaps between our vision and reality. "I would like to start my own company," but "I don't have the capital." Or, "I would like to pursue the profession that I really love," but "I've got to make a living." These gaps can make a vision seem unrealistic or fanciful. They can discourage us or make us feel hopeless. But the gap between vision and current reality is also a source of energy. If there was no gap, there would be no need for any action to move toward the vision. Indeed, the gap is *the* source of creative energy. We call this gap *creative tension*.

Imagine a rubber band, stretched between your vision and current reality. When stretched, the rubber band creates tension, representing the tension between vision and current reality. What does tension seek? Resolution or release. There are only two possible ways for the tension to resolve itself: pull reality toward the vision or pull the vision toward reality. Which occurs will depend on whether we hold steady to the vision.

The principle of creative tension is the central principle of personal mastery, integrating all elements of the discipline. Yet, it is widely misunderstood. For example, the very term "tension" suggests anxiety or stress. But creative tension doesn't feel any particular way. It is the force that comes into play at the moment when we acknowledge a vision that is at odds with current reality.

Still, creative tension often leads to feelings or emotions associated with anxiety, such as sadness, discouragement, hopelessness, or worry. This happens so often that people easily confuse these emotions with creative tension. People come to think that the creative process *is all about being in a state of anxiety*. But it is important to realize that these "negative" emotions that may arise when there is creative tension are not creative tension itself. These emotions are what we call *emotional tension*.

If we fail to distinguish emotional tension from creative tension, we predispose ourselves to lowering our vision. If we feel deeply discouraged about a vision that is not happening, we may have a strong urge to lighten the load of that discouragement. There is one immediate remedy: lower the vision! "Well, it wasn't really that important to shoot seventy-five. I'm having a great time shooting in the eighties."

Or, "I don't really care about being able to play in recital. I'll have to make money as a music teacher in any case; I'll just concentrate there." The dynamics of relieving emotional tension are insidious because they can operate unnoticed. Emotional tension can always be relieved by adjusting the one pole of the creative tension that is completely under our control at all times—the vision. The feelings that we dislike go away because the creative tension that was their source is reduced. Our goals are now much closer to our current reality. Escaping emotional tension is easy—the only price we pay is abandoning what we truly want, our vision.

The dynamics of emotional tension deeply resemble the dynamics of eroding goals that so troubled WonderTech and People Express, in Chapters 7 and 8. The interaction of creative tension and emotional tension is a shifting the burden dynamic, similar to that of eroding goals, that can be represented as follows:

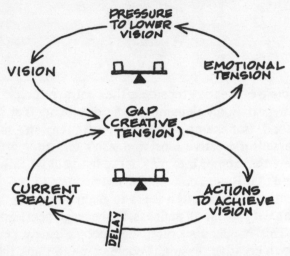

When we hold a vision that differs from current reality, a gap exists (the creative tension) which can be resolved in two ways. The lower balancing process represents the "fundamental solution": taking actions to bring reality into line with the vision. But changing reality takes time. This is what leads to the frustration and emotional tension in the upper balancing process, the "symptomatic solution" of lowering the vision to bring it into line with current reality.

But a onetime reduction in the vision usually isn't the end of the story. Sooner or later new pressures pulling reality away from the (new, lowered) vision arise, leading to still more pressures to lower the vision. The classic "shifting the burden" dynamic ensues, a subtle reinforcing spiral of failure to meet goals, frustration, lowered vision, temporary relief, and pressure anew to lower the vision still further. Gradually, the "burden" is shifting increasingly to lowering the vision.

At WonderTech and People Express relieving emotional tension took the form of decline in key operating standards that seemed impossible to meet—standards for delivery performance and for service quality. The decline was especially difficult to see because it was gradual. During each crisis at Wonder Tech delivery standards eroded just a bit relative to where they had settled after the last crisis. Likewise, managers at People Express didn't wake up one morning and declare, "We've solved our problems keeping pace with growth, we'll lower our service standards." Rather, service standards eroded quietly during repeated crises and with turnover among key leaders. So, too, do eroding personal goals go unrecognized, as we gradually surrender our dreams for the relationships we want to have, the work we want to do, and the type of world we want to live in.

In organizations, goals erode because of low tolerance for emotional tension. Nobody wants to be the messenger with bad news. The easiest path is to just pretend there is no bad news, or better yet, "declare victory"—to redefine the bad news as not so bad by lowering the standard against which it is judged.

The dynamics of emotional tension exist at all levels of human activity. They are the dynamics of compromise, the path of mediocrity. As Somerset Maugham said, "Only mediocre people are always at their best."

We allow our goals to erode when we are unwilling to live with emotional tension. On the other hand, when we understand creative tension and allow it to operate by not lowering our vision, vision becomes an active force. Robert Fritz says, "It's not what the vision is, it's what the vision does." Truly creative people use the gap between vision and current reality to generate energy for change.

For example, Alan Kay, who directed the research at Xerox Palo Alto Research Center (PARC) that led to many key features of the personal computer, actually had a vision for a different machine, which he called the "dynabook." This would be a book that was interactive. A child could test out his understanding, play games, and creatively rearrange the static presentation of ideas offered by the traditional book. Kay failed, in a sense, because the "dynabook" never became a reality. But the vision reshaped the computer industry. The prototype machines developed at PARC achieved the functionality—windows, pull-down menus, mouse control, iconic displays (images rather than words)—that was introduced commercially ten years later in the Macintosh.

Bill Russell, the legendary center for the Boston Celtics basketball team, used to keep his own personal scorecard. He graded himself after every game on scale from one to one hundred. In his career he never achieved more than sixty-five. Now, given the way most of us are taught to think about goals, we would regard Russell as an abject failure. The poor soul played in over twelve hundred basketball games and never achieved his standard! Yet, it was the striving for that standard that made him arguably the best basketball player ever.[9]

It's not what the vision is, it's what the vision does.

Mastery of creative tension transforms the way one views "failure." Failure is, simply, a shortfall, evidence of the gap between vision and current reality. Failure is an opportunity for learning—about inaccurate pictures of current reality, about strategies that didn't work as expected, about the clarity of the vision. Failures are not about our unworthiness or powerlessness. Ed Land, founder and president of Polaroid for decades and inventor of instant photography, had one plaque on his wall. It read:

A mistake is an event, the full benefit of which has not yet been turned to your advantage.

Mastery of creative tension brings out a capacity for perseverance and patience. A Japanese executive in one of our seminars once told me how, in his view, Japanese and Americans have quite different attitudes toward time. He said that, "U.S. businessmen in Japan to negotiate business deals often find the Japanese evasive and reticent to 'get down to business.' The American arrives in Japan on a tight, carefully planned five-day schedule and immediately wants to get to work. Instead, the Japanese greet them with a polite, formal tea ceremony instead, never getting down to nuts and bolts. As the days go by, the Japanese keep their slow pace, while the Americans become antsier and antsier. For the American," the executive said, "time is the enemy. For the Japanese, time is an ally."

More broadly, current reality itself is, for many of us, the enemy. We fight against what is. We are not so much drawn to what we want to create as we are repelled by what we have, from our current reality. By this logic, the deeper the fear, the more we abhor what is, the more "motivated" we are to change. "Things must get bad enough, or people will not change in any fundamental way."

This leads to the mistaken belief that fundamental change *requires* a threat to survival. This crisis theory of change is remarkably widespread. Yet, it is also a dangerous oversimplification. Often in workshops or presentations, I will ask, "How many of you believe people and organizations only change, fundamentally, when there is a crisis?'' Reliably, 75 to 90 percent of the hands go up. Then I ask people to consider a life where everything is exactly the way they would like—there are absolutely no problems of any sort in work, personally, professionally, in their relationships, or their community. Then I ask, "What is the first thing you would seek if you had a life of absolutely no problems?'' The answer, overwhelmingly, is "change —to create something new.'' So human beings are more complex than we often assume. We both fear and seek change. Or, as one seasoned organization change consultant once put it, "People don't resist change. They resist being changed.''

Mastery of creative tension leads to a fundamental shift in our whole posture toward reality. Current reality becomes the ally not the enemy. *An accurate, insightful view of current reality is as important as a clear vision.* Unfortunately, most of us are in the habit of imposing biases on our perceptions of current reality, a subject we will return to in depth in the following chapter on mental models. "We learn to rely on our concepts of reality more than on our observations,'' writes Robert Fritz. "It is more convenient to assume that reality is similar to our preconceived ideas than to freshly observe what we have before our eyes.'' [10] If the first choice in pursuing personal mastery is to be true to your own vision, the second fundamental choice in support of personal mastery is commitment to the truth.

Both are equally vital to generating creative tension. Or, as Fritz puts it, "The truly creative person knows that all creating is achieved through working with constraints. Without constraints there is no creating.''

"STRUCTURAL CONFLICT'': THE POWER OF YOUR POWERLESSNESS

Many people, even highly successful people, harbor deep beliefs contrary to their personal mastery. Very often, these beliefs are below the level of conscious awareness. To see what I mean, try the following experiment. Say out loud the following sentence: "I can create my life exactly the way I want it, in all dimensions—work, family, relationships, community, and larger world.'' Notice your internal reaction to this assertion, the "little voice'' in the back of your head. "Who's he kidding?'' "He doesn't really believe that.'' "Personally and in work, sure—but, not 'community' and 'the larger world.' " "What do I care about the 'larger world' anyhow?" All of these reactions are evidence of deep-seated beliefs.

Robert Fritz, who has worked with literally tens of thousands of people to develop their creative capacities, has concluded that practically all of us have a "dominant belief that we are not able to fulfill our desires." Where does this belief come from? Fritz argues that it is an almost inevitable by-product of growing up:

> As children we learn what our limitations are. Children are rightfully taught limitations essential to their survival. But too often this learning is generalized. We are constantly told we can't have or can't do certain things, and we may come to assume that we have an inability to have what we want.[11]

Most of us hold one of two contradictory beliefs that limit our ability to create what we really want. The more common is belief in our powerlessness—our inability to bring into being all the things we really care about. The other belief centers on unworthiness—that we do not deserve to have what we truly desire. Fritz claims that he has met only a handful of individuals who do not seem to have one or the other of these underlying beliefs. Such an assertion is difficult to prove rigorously because it is difficult to measure deep beliefs. But if we accept it as a working premise, it illuminates systemic forces that can work powerfully against creating what we really want.

Fritz uses a metaphor to describe how contradictory underlying beliefs work as a system, counter to achieving our goals. Imagine, as you move toward your goal, there is a rubber band, symbolizing creative tension, pulling you in the desired direction. But imagine also a second rubber band, anchored to the belief of powerlessness or unworthiness. Just as the first rubber band tries to pull you toward your goal, the second pulls you back toward the underlying belief that you can't (or don't deserve to) have your goal. Fritz calls the system involving both the tension pulling us toward our goal and the tension anchoring us to our underlying belief "structural conflict," because it is a structure of conflicting forces: pulling us simultaneously toward and away from what we want.

Thus, the closer we come to achieving our vision, the more the second rubber band pulls us away from our vision. This force can manifest itself in many ways. We might lose our energy. We might question whether we really wanted the vision. "Finishing the job" might become increasingly difficult. Unexpected obstacles develop in our path. People let us down. All this happens even though we are unaware of the structural conflict system, because it originates in

deep beliefs of which we are largely unaware—in fact, our unaware-
ness contributes to the power of structural conflict.

Given beliefs in our powerlessness or unworthiness, structural
conflict implies that systemic forces come into play to keep us from
succeeding *whenever* we seek a vision. Yet, we *do* succeed sometimes, and in fact many of us have become adept at identifying and
achieving goals, at least in some areas of our lives. How do we
overcome the forces of structural conflict?

Fritz has identified three generic "strategies" for coping with the
forces of structural conflict, each of which has its limitations.[12] Letting our vision erode is one such coping strategy. The second is
"conflict manipulation," in which we try to manipulate ourselves
into greater effort toward what we want by creating artificial conflict,
such as through focusing on avoiding what we don't want. Conflict
manipulation is the favored strategy of people who incessantly worry
about failure, managers who excel at "motivational chats" that point
out the highly unpleasant consequences if the company's goals are
not achieved, and of social movements that attempt to mobilize people through fear. In fact, sadly, most social movements operate
through conflict manipulation or "negative vision," focusing on getting away from what we don't want, rather than on creating what we
do want: antidrugs, antinuclear arms, antinuclear power, antismok-
ing, anti-abortion, or antigovernment corruption.

But many ask, "What's wrong with a little worry or fear if it helps
us achieve our goals?" The response of those who seek personal
mastery is the simple question: "Do you really want to live your life
in a state of fear of failure?" The tragedy is that many people who
get hooked on conflict manipulation come to believe that *only*
through being in a state of continual anxiety and fear can they be
successful. These are the people who, rather than shunning emotional tension, actually come to glorify it. For them, there is little joy
in life. Even when they achieve their goals, they immediately begin
worrying about losing what they have gained.

Fritz's third generic strategy is the strategy of "willpower," where we simply "psych ourselves up" to overpower all forms of resistance to achieving our goals. Lying behind willpower strategies, he suggests, is the simple assumption that we "motivate ourselves through heightened volition." Willpower is so common among highly successful people that many see its characteristics as synonymous with success: a maniacal focus on goals, willingness to "pay the price," ability to defeat any opposition and surmount any obstacle.

The problems with "willpower" are many, but they may hardly be noticed by the person focused narrowly on "success." First, there is little economy of means; in systems thinking terms, we act without leverage. We attain our goals, but the effort is enormous and we may find ourselves exhausted and wondering if "it was worth it" when we have succeeded. Ironically, people hooked on willpower may actually look for obstacles to overcome, dragons to slay, and enemies to vanquish—to remind themselves and others of their own prowess. Second, there are often considerable unintended consequences. Despite great success at work, the master of "willpower" will often find that he or she has gone through two marriages and has terrible relationships with his or her children. Somehow, the same dogged determination and goal orientation that "works" at work doesn't quite turn the trick at home. (Chapter 16, "Ending the War Between Work and Family," develops these ideas further.)

Worse still, just as with all of the coping strategies, "willpower" leaves the underlying system of structural conflict unaltered. In particular, the underlying belief in powerlessness has not really changed. Despite significant accomplishments, many "highly successful people" still feel a deep, usually unspoken, sense of powerlessness in critical areas of their lives—such as in their personal and family relationships, or in their ability to achieve a sense of peace and spiritual fulfillment.

These coping strategies are, to a certain extent, unavoidable. They are deeply habitual and cannot be changed overnight. We all tend to have a favorite strategy—mine has long been "willpower," as those close to me can attest.

Where then is the leverage in dealing with structural conflict? If structural conflict arises from deep underlying beliefs, then it can be changed only by changing the beliefs. But psychologists are virtually unanimous that fundamental beliefs such as powerlessness or unworthiness cannot be changed readily. They are developed early in life (remember all those "can'ts" and "don'ts" that started when you were two?). For most of us, beliefs change gradually as we accumulate new experiences—as we develop our personal mastery. But if mastery will not develop so long as we hold unempowering beliefs, and the beliefs will change only as we experience our mastery, how many we begin to alter the deeper structures of our lives?

COMMITMENT TO THE TRUTH

We may begin with a disarmingly simple yet profound strategy for dealing with structural conflict: telling the truth.

Commitment to the truth often seems to people an inadequate strategy. "What do I need to do to change my behavior?" "How do I change my underlying belief?" People often want a formula, a technique, something tangible that they can apply to solve the problem of structural conflict. But, in fact, being committed to the truth is far more powerful than any technique.

Commitment to the truth does not mean seeking the "Truth," the absolute final word or ultimate cause. Rather, it means a relentless willingness to root out the ways we limit or deceive ourselves from seeing what is, and to continually challenge our theories of why things are the way they are. It means continually broadening our awareness, just as the great athlete with extraordinary peripheral vision keeps trying to "see more of the playing field." It also means continually deepening our understanding of the structures underlying current events. Specifically, people with high levels of personal mastery see more of the structural conflicts underlying their own behavior.

Thus, the first critical task in dealing with structural conflicts is to recognize them, *and* the resulting behavior, when they are operating. It can be very difficult to recognize these coping strategies while we are playing them out, especially because of tensions and pressures that often accompany them. It helps to develop internal warning signals, such as when we find ourselves blaming something or somebody for our problems: "The reason I'm giving up is nobody appreciates me," or "The reason I'm so worried is that they'll fire me if I don't get the job done."

In my life, for example, I often felt that people let me down at critical junctures in major projects. When this happened, I would "bulldoze" through, overcoming the obstacle of their disloyalty or incompetence. It took many years before I recognized this as a recurring pattern, my own special form of the "willpower" strategy, rooted in a deep feeling of being powerless to change the way others let me down. Invariably, I ended up feeling as if "I've got to do it all myself."

Once I recognized this pattern, I began to act differently when a colleague let me down. I became angry less often. Rather, there was a twinge of recognition—"Oh, there goes my pattern." I looked more deeply at how my own actions were part of the outcome, either by creating tasks that were impossible to accomplish, or by undermining or demotivating the other person. Further, I worked to develop skills to discuss such situations with the people involved without producing defensiveness. Chapter 10, Mental Models, illustrates these skills.

I would never have developed those skills or known how to put them into practice without a shift of mind. So long as I saw the problem in terms of events, I was convinced that my problems were externally caused—"*they* let me down." Once I saw the problem as structurally caused, I began to look at what I could do, rather than at what "they had done."

Structures of which we are unaware hold us prisoner. Once we can see them and name them, they no longer have the same hold on us. This is as much true for individuals as it is for organizations. In fact, an entire field is evolving, structural family therapy, based on the assumption that individual psychological difficulties can be understood and changed only by understanding the structures of interdependencies within families and close personal relationships. Once these structures are recognized, in the words of David Kantor, a pioneer in the field, "It becomes possible to begin to alter structures to free people from previously mysterious forces that dictated their behavior." [13]

Discovering structures at play is the stock and trade of people with high levels of personal mastery. Sometimes these structures can be readily changed. Sometimes, as with structural conflict, they change only gradually. Then the need is to work more creatively within them while acknowledging their origin, rather than fighting the structures. Either way, once an operating structure is recognized, the structure itself becomes part of "current reality." The more my commitment to the truth, the more creative tension comes into play because current reality is seen more for what it really is. In the context of creative tension, commitment to the truth becomes a generative force, just as vision becomes a generative force.

One of the classic illustrations of this process is Charles Dickens's

A Christmas Carol. Through the visitations of the three ghosts on Christmas Eve, Scrooge sees more and more of the reality from which he has turned away. He sees the reality of his past, how the choices he made steadily whittled away his compassion and increased his self-centeredness. He sees the reality of his present, especially those aspects of reality that he has avoided, such as Tiny Tim's illness. And he sees the reality of his likely future, the future that will occur if he continues in his present ways. But then he wakes up. He realizes that he is not the captive of these realities. He realizes that he has a choice. He chooses to change.

Significantly, Scrooge can't make the choice to change before he becomes more aware of his current reality. In effect, Dickens says that life always avails the option of seeing the truth, no matter how blind and prejudiced we may be. And if we have the courage to respond to that option, we have the power to change ourselves profoundly. Or, to put it in more classic religious terms, only through the truth do we come to grace.

The power of the truth, seeing reality more and more as it is, cleansing the lens of perception, awakening from self-imposed distortions of reality—different expressions of a common principle in almost all the world's great philosophic and religious systems. Buddhists strive to achieve the state of "pure observation," of seeing reality directly. Hindus speak of "witnessing," observing themselves and their lives with an attitude of spiritual detachment. The Koran ends with the phrase, "What a tragedy that man must die before he wakes up." The power of the truth was no less central to early Christian thinking, although it has lost its place in Christian practice over the last two thousand years. In fact, the Hebrew symbols used to form the word *Yeheshua*, "Jesus," include the symbols for Jehovah, " ה ו ה י ," with the additional letter *shin* (ש) inserted in the middle. The symbols for Jehovah carry the meaning, "That which was, is, and will be." The inserted *shin* modifies the meaning to "that which was, is, and will be, *delivers*." This is the probable origin of the statement "The truth shall set you free."

USING THE SUBCONSCIOUS, OR, YOU DON'T REALLY NEED TO FIGURE IT ALL OUT

One of the most fascinating aspects of people with high levels of personal mastery is their ability to accomplish extraordinarily complex tasks with grace and ease. We have all marveled at the breathtakingly beautiful artistry of the championship ice skater or the prima ballerina. We know that their skills have been developed through years of diligent training, yet the ability to execute their artistry with such ease and seeming effortlessness is *still* wondrous.

Implicit in the practice of personal mastery is another dimension of the mind, the subconscious. It is through the subconscious that *all of us* deal with complexity. What distinguishes people with high levels of personal mastery is they have developed a higher level of rapport between their normal awareness and their subconscious. What most of us take for granted and exploit haphazardly, they approach as a discipline.

Is the subconscious relevant in management and organizations? Inamori of Kyocera says:

> When I am concentrating . . . I enter the subconscious mind. It is said that human beings possess both a conscious and subconscious mind, and that our subconscious mind has a capacity that is larger by a factor of ten . . ."
>
> When I talk about our "mind," I risk being called crazy. Nonetheless, I think therein may lie the hint to the secret that may determine our future.

O'Brien of Hanover likewise sees tapping mental capabilities formerly ignored as central to building the new organization:

> The greatest unexplored territory in the world is the space between our ears. Seriously, I am certain that learning organizations will find ways to nurture and focus the capabilities within us all that today we call "extraordinary."

But what is "extraordinary" is actually closely related to aspects of our lives that are so "ordinary" that we hardly notice them. Our lives are full of myriad complex tasks which we handle quite competently with almost no conscious thought. Try an experiment: touch the top of your head. Now, *how* did you do that? For most of us, the answer resembles, "Well, I just thought about my hand on my head —or, I formed a mental image of my hand on top of my head—and *voila*, it just was there." But at a neurophysiological level, raising your hand to the top of your head is an extraordinarily complex task, involving hundreds of thousands of neural firings as signals move from the brain to your arm and back again. This entire complex activity is coordinated without our conscious awareness. Likewise, if you had to think about every detail of walking, you'd be in big trouble. Walking, talking, eating, putting on your shoes, and riding a bicycle are all accomplished with almost no conscious attention—yet all are, in fact, enormously complex tasks.

These tasks are accomplished reliably because there is an aspect of our mind that is exceedingly capable of dealing with complexity. We call this dimension of mind the "subconscious," because it operates "below" or "behind" the level of conscious awareness. Others call it "unconscious" or "automatic mind." [14] Whatever it is called, without this dimension of mind it would be quite impossible to explain how human beings ever succeed in mastering any complex task. For one thing we can say confidently is that these tasks are not accomplished through our normal awareness and thinking alone.

Equally important, the subconscious is critical to how we learn. At one point in your life you were unable to carry out "mundane" tasks such as walking, talking and eating. Each had to be *learned*. The infant does not get the spoon in her mouth the first time out—it goes over the left shoulder, then the right shoulder, then the cheek. Only gradually does she learn to reliably reach her mouth. Initially, any new task requires a great deal of conscious attention and effort. As we "learn" the skills required of the task, the whole activity gradually shifts from conscious attention to subconscious control.

For example, when you first learned to drive a car, it took considerable conscious attention, especially if your were learning to drive on a standard transmission. In fact, you might have found it difficult to carry on a conversation with the person next to you. If that person had asked you to "slow down, downshift, and turn right" at the next corner, you might have given up then and there. Yet, within a few months or less, you executed the same task with little or no conscious attention. It had all become "automatic." Amazingly, before long you drove in heavy traffic while carrying on a conversation with the person sitting next to you—apparently giving almost no conscious attention to the literally hundreds of variables you had to monitor and respond to.

For example, when we first learn to play the piano or any musical instrument, we start by playing scales. Gradually, we move up to simple and then more complex compositions, leaving scales behind as a task that can be handled with little conscious attention. Even concert pianists, when sitting down to an unfamiliar piece will play that piece at half speed in order to allow concentration on the mechanics of hand and pedal positions, rhythm and tempo. But when the concert comes, the same pianist places no conscious attention on the mechanics of playing the piece. This leaves his conscious attention to focus exclusively on the aesthetics of the performance.[15]

We have all mastered a vast repertoire of skills through "training" the subconscious. Once learned, they become so taken for granted, so "subconscious," we don't even notice when we are executing them. But, for most of us, we have never given careful thought to *how* we mastered these skills and how we might continue to develop deeper and deeper *"rapport"* between our normal awareness and subconscious. Yet, these are matters of the greatest importance to the discipline of personal mastery.[16]

This is why, for instance, people committed to continually developing personal mastery practice some form of "meditation." Whether it is through contemplative prayer or other methods of simply "quieting" the conscious mind, regular meditative practice can be extremely helpful in working more productively with the subconscious mind. The subconscious appears to have no particular volition. It neither generates its own objectives nor determines its own focus. It is highly subject to direction and conditioning—what we pay attention to takes on special significance to the subconscious. In our normal highly active state of mind, the subconscious is deluged with a welter of contradictory thoughts and feelings. In a quieter state of mind, when we then focus on something of particular importance, some aspect of our vision, the subconscious is undistracted.

Moreover, there are particular ways that people with high levels of personal mastery direct their focus. As discussed earlier, they *focus on the desired result itself,* not the "process" or the means they assume necessary to achieve that result.

Focusing on the desired intrinsic result is a skill. For most of us it is not easy at first, and takes time and patience to develop. For most of us, as soon as we think of some important personal goal, almost immediately we think of all the reasons why it will be hard to achieve —the challenges we will face and the obstacles we will have to overcome. While this is very helpful for thinking through alternative strategies for achieving our goals, it is also a sign of lack of discipline when thoughts about "the process" of achieving our vision continually crowd out our focus on the outcomes we seek. We must work at learning how to separate what we truly want, from what we think we need to do in order to achieve it.

A useful starting exercise for learning how to focus more clearly on desired results is to take any particular goal or aspect of your vision. First imagine that that goal is fully realized. Then ask yourself the question, "If I actually had this, what would it get me?" What people often discover is that the answer to that question reveals "deeper" desires lying behind the goal. In fact, the goal is actually an interim step they assume is necessary to reach a more important result. For example, a person has a goal of reaching a certain level in the organizational hierarchy. When she asks herself, "What would it get me to be a senior VP?" she discovers that the answer is "respect of my peers" or "being where the action is." Though she may still aspire to the position, she now sees that there is also a deeper result she desires—a result she can start to hold as part of her vision now, independent of where she is in the organizational hierarchy. (Moreover, if she doesn't clarify "the result" she truly seeks, she may reach her stated goal and find that the more senior position is somehow still dissatisfying.)

The reason this skill is so important is precisely because of the responsiveness of the subconscious to a clear focus. When we are unclear between interim goals and more intrinsic goals, the subconscious has no way of prioritizing and focusing.

Making clear choices is also important. Only after choice are the capabilities of the subconscious brought fully into play. In fact, making choices and focusing on the results that are really important to us may be one of the highest leverage uses of our normal awareness. As Inamori puts it:

> I often tell a researcher who is lacking in dedication . . . unless [he] is motivated with determination to succeed, he will not be able to go past the obstacles . . . When his passion, his desire, becomes so strong as to rise out of his body like steam, and when the condensation of that which evaporated occurs . . . and drops back like raindrops, he will find his problem solved.

Commitment to the truth is also important for developing subconscious rapport—for the same basic reasons that lie detectors work. Lie detectors work because when most human beings do not tell the truth they create some level of internal stress, which in turn generates measurable physiological effects—blood pressure, pulse rate, and respiration. So, not only does deceiving ourselves about current reality prevent the subconscious from having accurate information about where we are relative to our vision, but it also creates distracting input to the subconscious, just as our "chatter" about why we can't achieve our vision is distracting. The principle of creative tension recognizes that the subconscious operates most effectively when it is focused clearly on our vision and our current reality.

The art of working effectively with the subconscious incorporates many techniques. An effective way to focus the subconscious is through imagery and visualization. For example, world-class swimmers have found that by imagining their hands to be twice their actual size and their feet to be webbed, they actually swim faster. "Mental rehearsal" of complex feats has become routine psychological training for diverse professional performers.

But the real effectiveness of all of this still hinges on knowing what it is that is most important to you. In the absence of knowing what truly matters to you, the specific practices and methods of working with the subconscious run the risk of becoming mechanical techniques—simply a new way of manipulating yourself into being more productive. This is not an idle concern. Almost all spiritual traditions warn against adopting the techniques of increased mental powers without diligently continuing to refine one's sense of genuine aspiration.

Ultimately, what matters most in developing the subconscious rapport characteristic of masters is the genuine caring for a desired outcome, the deep feeling of it being the "right" goal toward which to aspire. The subconscious seems especially receptive to goals in line with our deeper aspirations and values. According to some spiritual disciplines, this is because these deeper aspirations input directly to, or are part of, the subconscious mind.

A wonderful example of what can be accomplished in the pursuit of something truly important to a person is the story of Gilbert Kaplan, a highly successful publisher and editor of a leading investment periodical. Kaplan first heard Mahler's Second Symphony in a rehearsal in 1965. He "found himself unable to sleep. I went back for the performance and walked out of the hall a different person. It was the beginning of a long love affair." Despite his having had *no* formal musical training, he committed time and energy and a considerable sum of his personal finances (he had to hire an orchestra) to the pursuit of learning how to conduct the piece. Today, his performances of the symphony have received the highest praise by critics throughout the world. The *New York Times* praised his 1988 recording of the symphony with the London Symphony Orchestra as one of the five finest classical recordings of the year and the president of the New York Mahler Society called it "the outstanding recorded performance." A strict reliance on only conscious learning could never have achieved this level of artistry, even with all the "willpower" in the world. It had to depend on a high level of subconscious rapport which Kaplan could bring to bear on his new "love affair."

In many ways, the key to developing high levels of mastery in subconscious rapport comes back to the discipline of developing personal vision. This is why the concept of vision has always figured so strongly in the creative arts. Picasso once said:

It would be very interesting to record photographically, not the stages of a painting, but its metamorphoses. One would see perhaps by what course a mind finds its way toward the crystallization of its dream. But what is really very serious is to see that the picture does not change basically, that the initial vision remains almost intact in spite of appearance.[17]

PERSONAL MASTERY AND THE FIFTH DISCIPLINE

As individuals practice the discipline of personal mastery, several changes gradually take place within them. Many of these are quite subtle and often go unnoticed. In addition to clarifying the "structures" that characterize personal mastery as a discipline (such as creative tension, emotional tension, and structural conflict), the systems perspective also illuminates subtler aspects of personal mastery —especially: integrating reason and intuition; continually seeing more of our connectedness to the world; compassion; and commitment to the whole.

INTEGRATING REASON AND INTUITION

According to an ancient Sufi story, a blind man wandering lost in a forest tripped and fell. As the blind man rummaged about the forest floor he discovered that he had fallen over a cripple. The blind man and the cripple struck up a conversation, commiserating on their fate. The blind man said, "I have been wandering in this forest for as long as I can remember, and I cannot see to find my way out." The cripple said, "I have been lying on the forest floor for as long as I can remember, and I cannot get up to walk out." As they sat there talking, suddenly the cripple cried out. "I've got it," he said. "You hoist me up onto your shoulders and I will tell you where to walk. Together we can find our way out of the forest." According to the ancient storyteller, the blind man symbolized rationality. The cripple symbolized intuition. We will not find our way out of the forest until we learn how to integrate the two.

Intuition in management has recently received increasing attention and acceptance, after many decades of being officially ignored. Now numerous studies show that experienced managers and leaders rely heavily on intuition—that they do not figure out complex problems entirely rationally. They rely on hunches, recognize patterns, and draw intuitive analogies and parallels to other seemingly disparate situations.[18] There are even courses in management schools on intuition and creative problem solving. But we have a very long way to go, in our organizations and in society, toward reintegrating intuition and rationality.

People with high levels of personal mastery do not set out to integrate reason and intuition. Rather, they achieve it naturally—as a by-product of their commitment to use all resources at their disposal. They cannot afford to choose between reason and intuition, or head and heart, any more than they would choose to walk on one leg or see with one eye.

Bilateralism is a design principle underlying the evolution of advanced organisms. Nature seems to have learned to design in pairs; it not only builds in redundancy but achieves capabilities not possible otherwise. Two legs are critical for rapid, flexible locomotion. Two arms and hands are vital for climbing, lifting, and manipulating objects. Two eyes give us stereoscopic vision, and along with two ears, depth perception. Is it not possible that, following the same design principle, reason and intuition are designed to work in harmony for us to achieve our potential intelligence?

Systems thinking may hold a key to integrating reason and intuition. Intuition eludes the grasp of linear thinking, with its exclusive emphasis on cause and effect that are close in time and space. The result is that most of our intuitions don't make "sense"—that is, they can't be explained in terms of linear logic.

Very often, experienced managers have rich intuitions about complex systems, which they cannot explain. Their intuitions tell them that cause and effect are not close in time and space, that obvious solutions will produce more harm than good, and that short-term fixes produce long-term problems. But they cannot explain their ideas in simple linear cause-effect language. They end up saying, "Just do it this way. It will work."

For example, many managers sense the dangers of eroding goals or standards but cannot fully explain how they create a reinforcing tendency to underinvest and a self-fulfilling prophecy of underrealized market growth. Or, managers may feel that they are focusing on tangible, easily measured indicators of performance and masking deeper problems, and even exacerbating these problems. But they cannot explain convincingly why these are the wrong performance indicators or how alternatives might produce improved results. Both of these intuitions can be explained when the underlying systemic structures are understood.[19]

The conflict between intuition and linear, nonsystemic thinking has planted the seed that *rationality* itself is opposed to intuition. This view is demonstrably false if we consider the synergy of reason and intuition that characterizes virtually all great thinkers. Einstein said, "I never discovered anything with my rational mind." He once described how he discovered the principle of relativity by imagining himself traveling on a light beam. Yet, he could take brilliant intuitions and convert them into succinct, rationally testable propositions.

As managers gain facility with systems thinking as an alternative language, they find that many of their intuitions become explicable. Eventually, reintegrating reason and intuition may prove to be one of the primary contributions of systems thinking.

SEEING OUR CONNECTEDNESS
TO THE WORLD

My six-week-old son Ian does not yet seem to know his hands and feet. I suspect that he is aware of them, but he is clearly not aware that they are *his* hands and feet, or that he controls their actions. The other day, he got caught in a terrible reinforcing feedback loop. He had taken hold of his ear with his left hand. It was clearly agitating him, as you could tell from his pained expression and increasing flagellations. But, as a result of being agitated, he pulled harder. This increased his discomfort, which led him to get more agitated and pull still harder. The poor little guy might still be pulling if I hadn't detached his hand and quieted him down.

Not knowing that his hand was actually within his control, he perceived the source of his discomfort as an external force. Sound familiar? Ian's plight was really no different from the beer game players of Chapter 3, who reacted to suppliers' delivery times as if they were external forces, or the arms race participants in Chapter

5 ("A Shift of Mind") who reacted to each other's arms buildups as if they had no power to change them.

As I thought about Ian, I began to think that a neglected dimension of personal growth lies in "closing the loops"—in continually discovering how apparent external forces are actually interrelated with our own actions. Fairly soon, Ian will recognize his feet and hands and learn he can control their motions. Then he will discover that he can control his body position—if it is unpleasant on his back, he can roll over. Then will come internal states such as temperature, and the realization that they can be influenced by moving closer or further from a heat source such as Mommy or Daddy. Eventually comes Mommy and Daddy themselves, and the realization that their actions and emotions are subject to his influence. At each stage in this progression, there will be corresponding adjustments in his internal pictures of reality, which will steadily change to incorporate more of the feedback from his actions to the conditions in his life.

But for most of us, sometime early in life this process of closing the loops is arrested. As we get older, our rate of discovery slows down; we see fewer and fewer new links between our actions and external forces. We become locked into ways of looking at the world that are, fundamentally, no different from little Ian's.

The learning process of the young child provides a beautiful metaphor for the learning challenge faced by us all: to continually expand our awareness and understanding, to see more and more of the interdependencies between actions and our reality, to see more and more of our connectedness to the world around us. We will probably never perceive fully the multiple ways in which we influence our reality. But simply being open to the possibility is enough to free our thinking.

Einstein expressed the learning challenge when he said:

[the human being] experiences himself, his thoughts and feelings as something separated from the rest—a kind of optical delusion of our consciousness. This delusion is a kind of prison for us, restricting us to our personal desires and to affection for a few persons nearest to us. Our task must be to free ourselves from this prison by widening our circle of compassion to embrace all living creatures and the whole of nature in its beauty.

The experience of increasing connectedness which Einstein describes is one of the subtlest aspects of personal mastery, one that derives most directly from the systems perspective. His "widening . . . circle of compassion" is another.

COMPASSION

The discipline of seeing interrelationships gradually undermines older attitudes of blame and guilt. We begin to see that *all of us* are trapped in structures, structures embedded both in our ways of thinking and in the interpersonal and social milieus in which we live. Our knee-jerk tendencies to find fault with one another gradually fade, leaving a much deeper appreciation of the forces within which we all operate.

This does not imply that people are simply victims of systems that dictate their behavior. Often, the structures are of our own creation. But this has little meaning until those structures are seen. For most of us, the structures within which we operate are invisible. We are neither victims nor culprits but human beings controlled by forces we have not yet learned how to perceive.

We are used to thinking of compassion as an emotional state, based on our concern for one another. But it is also grounded in a level of awareness. In my experience, as people see more of the systems within which they operate, and as they understand more clearly the pressures influencing one another, they naturally develop more compassion and empathy.

COMMITMENT TO THE WHOLE

"Genuine commitment," according to Bill O'Brien, "is always to something larger than ourselves." Inamori talks about "action of our heart," when we are guided by "sincere desire to serve the world." Such action, he says, "is a very important issue since it has great power."

The sense of connectedness and compassion characteristic of individuals with high levels of personal mastery naturally leads to a broader vision. Without it, all the subconscious visualizing in the world is deeply self-centered—simply a way to get what I want.

Individuals committed to a vision beyond their self-interest find they have energy not available when pursuing narrower goals, as will organizations that tap this level of commitment. "I do not believe there has been a single person who has made a worthwhile discovery or invention," Inamori states, "who has not experienced a spiritual power." He describes the will of a person committed to a larger purpose as "a cry from the soul which has been shaken and awakened."

FOSTERING PERSONAL MASTERY IN AN ORGANIZATION

It must always be remembered that embarking on any path of personal growth is a matter of choice. No one can be forced to develop his or her personal mastery. It is guaranteed to backfire. Organizations can get into considerable difficulty if they become too aggressive in promoting personal mastery for their members.

Still many have attempted to do just that by creating compulsory internal personal growth training programs. However well intentioned, such programs are probably the most sure-fire way to impede the genuine spread of commitment to personal mastery in an organization. Compulsory training, or "elective" programs that people feel expected to attend if they want to advance their careers, conflict directly with freedom of choice.

For example, there have been numerous instances in recent years of overzealous managers requiring employees to participate in personal development training, which the employees regarded as contradictory to their own religious beliefs. Several of these have resulted in legal action against the organization.[20]

What then can leaders intent on fostering personal mastery do?

They can work relentlessly to foster a climate in which the principles of personal mastery are practiced in daily life. That means building an organization where it is safe for people to create visions, where inquiry and commitment to the truth are the norm, and where challenging the status quo is expected—especially when the status quo includes obscuring aspects of current reality that people seek to avoid.

Such an organizational climate will strengthen personal mastery in two ways. First, it will continually reinforce the idea that personal growth is truly valued in the organization. Second, to the extent that individuals respond to what is offered, it will provide an "on the job training" that is vital to developing personal mastery. As with any discipline, developing personal mastery must become a continual, ongoing process. There is nothing more important to an individual committed to his or her own growth than a supportive environment. An organization committed to personal mastery can provide that environment by continually encouraging personal vision, commitment to the truth, and a willingness to face honestly the gaps between the two.

Many of the practices most conducive to developing one's own personal mastery—developing a more systemic worldview, learning how to reflect on tacit assumptions, expressing one's vision and listening to others' visions, and joint inquiry into different people's views of current reality—are embedded in the disciplines for building learning organizations. So, in many ways, the most positive actions that an organization can take to foster personal mastery involve working to develop all five learning disciplines in concert.

The core leadership strategy is simple: be a model. Commit yourself to your own personal mastery. Talking about personal mastery may open people's minds somewhat, but actions always speak louder than words. There's nothing more powerful you can do to encourage others in their quest for personal mastery than to be serious in your own quest.

10

MENTAL MODELS

WHY THE BEST IDEAS FAIL

One thing all managers know is that many of the best ideas never get put into practice. Brilliant strategies fail to get translated into action. Systemic insights never find their way into operating policies. A pilot experiment may prove to everyone's satisfaction that a new approach leads to better results, but widespread adoption of the approach never occurs.

We are coming increasingly to believe that this "slip 'twixt cup and lip" stems, not from weak intentions, wavering will, or even nonsystemic understanding, but from *mental models*. More specifically, new insights fail to get put into practice because they conflict with deeply held internal images of how the world works, images that limit us to familiar ways of thinking and acting. That is why the discipline of managing mental models—surfacing, testing, and improving our internal pictures of how the world works—promises to be a major breakthrough for building learning organizations.

None of us can carry an organization in our minds—or a family, or a community. What we carry in our heads are images, assumptions, and stories. Philosophers have discussed mental models for centuries, going back at least to Plato's parable of the cave. "The Emperor's New Clothes" is a classic story, not about fatuous people, but about people bound by mental models. Their image of the monarch's dignity kept them from seeing his naked figure as it was.

In surveying the accomplishments of cognitive science in his book *The Mind's New Science,* Howard Gardner writes, "To my mind, the major accomplishment of cognitive science has been the clear demonstration of . . . a level of mental representation" active in diverse aspects of human behavior.[1] Our "mental models" determine not only how we make sense of the world, but how we take action. Harvard's Chris Argyris, who has worked with mental models and organizational learning for thirty years, puts it this way: "Although people do not [always] behave congruently with their espoused theories [what they say], they do behave congruently with their theories-in-use [their mental models]."[2]

Mental models can be simple generalizations such as "people are untrustworthy," or they can be complex theories, such as my assumptions about why members of my family interact as they do. But what is most important to grasp is that mental models are *active*—they shape how we act. If we believe people are untrustworthy, we act differently from the way we would if we believed they were trustworthy. If I believe that my son lacks self-confidence and my daughter is highly aggressive, I will continually intervene in their exchanges to prevent her from damaging his ego.

Why are mental models so powerful in affecting what we *do?* In part, because they affect what we *see.* Two people with different mental models can observe the same event and describe it differently, because they've looked at different details. When you and I walk into a crowded party, we both take in the same basic sensory data, but we pick out different faces. As psychologists say, we observe selectively. This is no less true for supposedly "objective" observers such as scientists than for people in general. As Albert Einstein once wrote, "Our theories determine what we measure." For years, physicists ran experiments that contradicted classical physics, yet no one "saw" the data that these experiments eventually provided, leading to the revolutionary theories—quantum mechanics and relativity—of twentieth-century physics.[3]

The way mental models shape our perceptions is no less important in management. For decades, the Big Three of Detroit believed that people bought automobiles on the basis of styling, not for quality or reliability. Judging by the evidence they gathered, the automakers were right. Surveys and buying habits consistently suggested that American consumers cared about styling much more than about quality. These preferences gradually changed, however, as German and Japanese automakers slowly educated American consumers in the benefits of quality and style—and increased their share of the U.S. market from near zero to 38 percent by 1986.[4] According to management consultant Ian Mitroff, these beliefs about styling were part of a pervasive set of assumptions for success at General Motors:[5]

GM is in the business of making money, not cars.

Cars are primarily status symbols. Styling is therefore more important than quality.

The American car market is isolated from the rest of the world.

Workers do not have an important impact on productivity or product quality.

Everyone connected with the system has no need for more than a fragmented, compartmentalized understanding of the business.

As Mitroff pointed out, these principles had served the industry well for many years. But the auto industry treated these principles as "a magic formula for success for all time, when all it had found was a particular set of conditions . . . that were good for a limited time."

The problems with mental models lie not in whether they are right or wrong—by definition, all models are simplifications. The problems with mental models arise when the models are tacit—when they exist below the level of awareness. The Detroit automakers didn't say, "We have a *mental model* that all people care about is styling." They said, "All people *care* about is styling." Because they remained unaware of their mental models, the models remained unexamined. Because they were unexamined, the models remained unchanged. As the world changed, a gap widened between Detroit's mental models and reality, leading to increasingly counterproductive actions.[6]

As the Detroit automakers demonstrated, entire industries can develop chronic misfits between mental models and reality. In some ways, close-knit industries are especially vulnerable because all the member companies look to each other for standards of best practice.

Such outdated reinforcement of mental models occurred in many basic U.S. manufacturing industries, not just automobiles, throughout the 1960s and 1970s. Today, similar outdated mental models dominate many service industries, which still provide mediocre quality in the name of controlling costs. (See Chapter 17, "Microworlds," for an example.)

Failure to appreciate mental models has undermined many efforts to foster systems thinking. In the late 1960s, a leading American industrial goods manufacturer—the largest in its industry—found itself losing market share. Hoping to analyze their situation, top executives sought help from an MIT team of "system dynamics" specialists. Based on computer models, the team concluded that the firm's problems stemmed from the way its executives managed inventories and production. Because it cost so much to store its bulky, expensive products, production managers held inventories as low as possible and aggressively cut back production whenever orders turned down. The result was unreliable and slow delivery, even when production capacity was adequate. In fact, the team's computer simulations predicted that deliveries would lag further during business downturns than during booms—a prediction which ran counter to conventional wisdom, but which turned out to be true.

Impressed, the firm's top executives put into effect a new policy based on the analysts' recommendations. From now on, when orders fell, they would maintain production rates and try to improve delivery performance. During the 1970 recession, the experiment worked; thanks to prompter deliveries and more repeat buying from satisfied customers, the firm's market share increased. The managers were so pleased that they set up their own systems group. But the new policies were never taken to heart, and the improvement proved temporary. During the ensuing business recovery, the managers stopped worrying about delivery service. Four years later, when the more severe OPEC-induced recession came, they went back to their original policy of dramatic production cutbacks.

Why discard such a successful experiment? The reason was the mental models deeply embedded in the firm's management traditions. Every production manager knew in his heart that there was no more sure-fire way to destroy his career than to be held responsible for stockpiling unsold goods in the warehouse. Generations of top management had preached the gospel of commitment to inventory control. Despite the new experiment, the old mental model was still alive and well.

The inertia of deeply entrenched mental models can overwhelm even the best systemic insights. This has been a bitter lesson for many a purveyor of new management tools, not only for systems thinking advocates.

But if mental models can *impede* learning—freezing companies and industries in outmoded practices—why can't they also help *accelerate* learning? As it happens, several organizations, largely operating independently, have given serious attention to this question in recent years.

INCUBATING A NEW BUSINESS WORLDVIEW

Perhaps the first large corporation to discover the potential power of mental models in learning was Royal Dutch/Shell. Managing a highly decentralized company through the turbulence of the world oil business in the 1970s, Shell discovered that, by helping managers clarify their assumptions, discover internal contradictions in those assumptions, and think through new strategies based on new assumptions they gained a unique source of competitive advantage.

Shell is unique in several ways that have made it a natural environment for experimenting with mental models. It is truly multicultural, formed originally in 1907 from a "gentleman's agreement" between Royal Dutch Petroleum and the London-based Shell Transport and Trading Company. Royal Dutch/Shell now has more than a hundred operating companies around the world, led by managers from almost as many different cultures.

The operating companies enjoy a high degree of autonomy and local independence. From its beginning, Shell managers had to learn to operate by consensus, because there was no way these "gentlemen" from different countries and cultures would be able to tell each other what to do. As Shell grew and became more global and more multicultural, its needs for building consensus across vast gulfs of style and understanding grew.

In the turbulent early 1970s, Shell's tradition of consensus management was stretched to the breaking point. What emerged was a new understanding of the underpinnings of real consensus—an understanding of shared mental models. "Unless we influenced the mental image, the picture of reality held by critical decisionmakers, our scenarios would be like water on a stone," recalled Shell's former senior planner Pierre Wack, in his seminal *Harvard Business*

Review articles about the Shell mental models work.[7] Wack had come to this realization in 1972, as he and his colleagues desperately faced their failure to convey to Shell's managers the "discontinuities" they foresaw in the world oil market.

That was the year before OPEC and the onset of the energy crisis. After analyzing long-term trends of oil production and consumption, Wack had concluded that the stable, predictable world familiar to Shell's managers was about to change. Europe, Japan, and the U.S. were becoming increasingly dependent on oil imports. Oil-exporting nations such as Iran, Iraq, Libya, and Venezuela were becoming increasingly concerned with falling reserves. Others, such as Saudi Arabia, were reaching the limits of their ability to productively invest oil revenues. These trends meant that the historical, smooth growth in oil demand and supply would eventually give way to chronic supply shortfalls, excess demand, and a "seller's market" controlled by the oil-exporting nations. While Shell's planners did not predict OPEC exactly, they foresaw the types of changes that OPEC would eventualy bring about. Yet, attempts to impress upon Shell's managers the radical shifts ahead had led "no more than a third of Shell's critical decision centers" to act on the new insights.

In principle, Shell's "Group Planning" staff were in an ideal position to disseminate insights about the changes ahead. Group Planning was the central planning department, responsible for coordinating planning activities in operating companies worldwide. At the time, Group Planning was developing a new technique called "scenario planning," a method for summarizing alternative future trends. The planners at Shell began to build in the coming discontinuities into their scenarios. But their audience of Shell managers found these new scenarios so contradictory to their years of experience with predictable growth that they paid little attention to them.

At this point, Wack and his colleagues realized that they had fundamentally misperceived their task. From that moment, Wack wrote, "We no longer saw our task as producing a documented view of the future . . . Our real target was the 'microcosms' "—Wack's word for mental models—"of our decision makers . . . We now wanted to design scenarios so that managers would question their own model of reality and change it when necessary." If the planners had once thought their job was delivering information to the decision makers, it was now clear that their task was to help managers rethink their worldview. In particular, the Group Planners developed a new set of scenarios in January–February 1973 which forced the managers to identify all of the assumptions that had to be true in order for the managers' "trouble-free" future to occur. This revealed a set of assumptions only slightly more likely to come true than a fairy tale.

Group Planning now built a new set of scenarios, carefully designed to take off from the current mental models of Shell managers. They showed how the prevailing view that "the oil business would continue as usual" was based on underlying assumptions about the nature of global geopolitics and the oil industry; then they showed that these assumptions could not possibly hold in the future that was coming. Then they helped managers begin the process of constructing a new mental model—by helping them think through how they would have to manage in this new world. For example, exploration for oil would have to expand to new countries, while refinery building would have to slow down because of higher prices and consequently slower demand growth. Also, with greater instability, nations would respond differently. Some, with free-market traditions, would let the price rise freely; others with controlled-market policies, would try to keep it low. Thus, control to Shell's locally based operating companies would have to increase to enable them to adapt to local conditions.

Although many Shell managers remained skeptical, they took the new scenarios seriously because they began to see that their present understandings were untenable. The exercise had begun to unfreeze managers' mental models and incubate a new worldview.

When the OPEC oil embargo suddenly became a reality in the winter of 1973–74, Shell responded differently from the other oil companies. They slowed down their investments in refineries, and designed refineries that could adapt to whatever type of crude oil was available. They forecast energy demand at a consistently lower level than their competitors did, and consistently more accurately. They quickly accelerated development of oil fields outside OPEC.

While competitors reined in their divisions and centralized control —a common response to crisis—Shell did the opposite. This gave their operating companies more room to maneuver while their competitors had less.

Shell's managers saw themselves entering a new era of supply shortages, lower growth, and price instability. Because they had come to expect the 1970s to be a decade of turbulence (Wack called it the decade of "the rapids"), they responded to the turbulence effectively. Shell had discovered the power of managing mental models.

The net result of Shell's efforts was nothing short of spectacular. In 1970, Shell had been considered the weakest of the seven largest oil companies. *Forbes* called it the "Ugly Sister" of the "Seven Sisters." By 1979 it was perhaps the strongest; certainly it and Exxon were in a class by themselves.[8] By the early 1980s, articulating managers' mental models was an important part of the planning process at Shell. About a half-year prior to the collapse of oil prices in 1986, Group Planning, under the direction of coordinator Arie de Geus, produced a fictitious Harvard Business School-style case study of an oil company coping with a sudden world oil glut. Managers had to critique the oil company's decisions. Thus, once again, they prepared themselves mentally for a reality which the planners suspected they *might* have to face.

OVERCOMING "THE BASIC DISEASES OF THE HIERARCHY"

"In the traditional authoritarian organization, the dogma was managing, organizing, and controlling," says Hanover's CEO Bill O'Brien. "In the learning organization, the new 'dogma' will be vision, values, and mental models. The healthy corporations will be ones which can systematize ways to bring people together to develop the best possible mental models for facing any situation at hand." O'Brien and his colleagues at Hanover have come to their interest in mental models over a journey comparable in length to Shell's, but dramatically different in almost every other way.

Hanover was originally founded in 1852. As noted earlier, it has gone from near-bankruptcy in 1969, when it was acquired by the State Mutual company, to one of the best performing companies in the property and casualty industry today. At $1.5 billion in annual premium sales, Hanover handles only one tenth of the volume of an industry giant such as Aetna, but its compound rate of return since 1980 has been 19 percent, which ranks sixteenth among sixty-eight insurance companies surveyed by *Forbes* in January 1990.

Beginning in 1969, Hanover took on a long-term mission to revamp the traditional hierarchical values that had dominated the organization for so long. "We set out," says O'Brien, "to find what would give the necessary organization and discipline to have work be more congruent with human nature. We gradually identified a set of core values that are actually principles that overcome the basic diseases of the hierarchy."

Two of these values in particular, "openness" and "merit," led Hanover to develop its approach to managing mental models. *Openness* was seen as an antidote to what O'Brien called "the disease of gamesplaying that dominated people's behavior in face-to-face meetings. Nobody described an issue at 10:00 in the morning at a business meeting the way they described the issue at 7:00 that evening, at home or over drinks with friends." *Merit*—making decisions based on the best interests of the organization—was Hanover's antidote to "decisionmaking based on bureaucratic politics, where the name of the game is getting ahead by making an impression, or, if you're already at the top, staying there." [9] As openness and merit took hold, a deep belief evolved from them: that decision-making processes could be transformed if people become more able to surface and discuss productively their different ways of looking at the world. But if this was so useful why did it seem so difficult?

In the mid-1970s, the ideas of Argyris and his colleagues were beginning to provide an answer. In "action science," they were developing a body of theory and method for reflection and inquiry on the reasoning that underlies our actions. [10] Moreover, the tools of action science are designed to be effective in organizations, and especially in dealing with organizational problems. We trap ourselves, say Argyris and his colleagues, in "defensive routines" that insulate our mental models from examination, and we consequently develop "skilled incompetence"—a marvelous oxymoron that Argyris uses to describe most adult learners, who are "highly skillful at protecting themselves from pain and threat posed by learning situations," but consequently fail to learn how to produce the results they really want.

Despite having read much of his writing, I was unprepared for what I learned when I first saw Chris Argyris practice his approach in an informal workshop with a half-dozen members of our research team at MIT. Ostensibly an academic presentation of Argyris's methods, it quickly evolved into a powerful demonstration of what action science practitioners call "reflection in action." Argyris asked each of us to recount a conflict with a client, colleague, or family member. We had to recall not only what was said, but what we were thinking and did *not* say. As Chris began to "work with these cases it became almost immediately apparent how each of us contributed to a conflict through our own thinking—how we made sweeping generalizations about the others that determined what we said and how we behaved. Yet, we never communicated the generalizations. I might think, "Joe believes I'm incompetent," but I would never ask Joe directly about it. I would simply go out of my way to try continually to make myself look respectable to Joe. Or, "Bill [my boss] is impatient and believes in quick and dirty solutions," so I go out of my way to give him simple solutions even though I don't think they will really get to the heart of difficult issues.

Within a matter of minutes, I watched the level of alertness and "presentness" of the entire group rise ten notches—thanks not so much to Argyris's personal charisma, but to his skillful practice of drawing out those generalizations. As the afternoon moved on, all of us were led to see (sometimes for the first time in our lives) subtle patterns of reasoning which underlay our behavior; and how those patterns continually got us into trouble. I had never had such a dramatic demonstration of my own mental models in action, dictating my behavior and perceptions. But even more interesting, it became clear that, with proper training, I could become much more aware of my mental models and how they operated. This was exciting.

Later I learned that O'Brien and his management team at Hanover had had a similar experience with Argyris's methods ten years earlier. This had led them to realize that, in O'Brien's words, "Despite our philosophy we had a very long way to go to being able to have the types of open, productive discussion about critical issues that we all desired. In some cases, Argyris' work revealed painfully obvious gamesplaying that we had come to accept. Chris held an incredibly high standard of real openness, of seeing our own thinking and cutting the crap. Yet, he was also not simply advocating "tell everyone everything"—he was illustrating the skills of engaging difficult issues so that everyone learned. Clearly, this was important new territory if we were really going to live our core values of openness and merit."

Working with Argyris's colleague Lee Bolman, also of Harvard, Hanover eventually developed a three-day management seminar, called "Merit, Opennness, and Localness," intended to expose all Hanover managers to the basic ideas and practices of action science. These seminars have been attended by virtually all of Hanover's middle and upper management over the past ten years. The basic purpose of the seminars is to extend the practice of these three core values by showing the skills needed to put them into practice. As Paul Stimson, the manager currently in charge of the seminar puts it, "Our first task is to get people to start to appreciate what it means to practice merit, openness, and localness in a learning organization. In traditional organizations, merit means doing what the boss wants, openness means telling the boss what he wants to hear, and localness means doing the dirty stuff that the boss doesn't want to do. So, we have a long way to go in getting people to some new understandings."

The first day is spent reviewing the basic concepts, principles, and skills of action science. Most find this enlightening but hardly earth-shaking. "Yes, of course, I agree with this. I always try very hard to be a good inquirer" is a typical response at the end of Day 1. The lights start to go on in Day 2, when Stimson and his colleagues video tape the managers attempting to apply the skills in role-playing exercises. Before their role-playing, the managers identify particular skills they want to work on. For example, a manager in a performance review role-play might want to work on "balancing inquiry and advocacy" (taking a position but also inquiring into others' views and remaining open). But within a few minutes of starting the role-play, the very same manager will be pointing his finger at the subordinate and preaching rather than listening. "When everyone watches the tapes together afterward," Stimson says, "it is often hilarious to see how much our own behavior deviates from what we say we do. People see that there is much more to putting action science skills into practice than merely nodding in agreement."

The three-days of the MOL seminar are hardly enough to become masters in the skills of action science, but the very personal exposure and initial opportunity to practice with a group of fellow learners starts a process that continues "back home." Perhaps, equally important, it shows Hanover's seriousness about approaching the mental models discipline as a set of developable skills, not as vague generalities and pieties about "thinking more effectively."

Convinced that there was a payoff in helping managers improve their basic thinking skills, Hanover later supported a second management training to, as O'Brien puts it, "expose the limitations of 'mechanistic thinking.' The problem we saw was the tendency of managers to confront complex business issues with '9-point programs,' as if the problem was fixing a flat tire. This usually results in making problems worse." This second training program, "Thinking about Thinking," was designed and delivered by a retired University of New Hampshire professor, John Beckett. Beckett leads an exhaustive, and surprisingly not exhausting, historical survey of major philosophies of thought, East and West, over five *full* days. In a process Beckett describes as "sandpaper on the brain," he shows in great detail how radically differing philosophies all have merit.

The impact of the Beckett program is striking. "Beckett shows," says O'Brien, "that if you look closely at how Eastern cultures approach basic moral, ethical, and managerial issues, they do make sense. Then he shows that Western ways of approaching these issues also make sense. But the two can lead to opposite conclusions. This leads to discovering that there is more than one way to look at complex issues. It helps enormously in breaking down the walls between the disciplines in our company, and between different ways of thinking."

The impact on managers' understanding of mental models is profound—most report that they see for the first time in their life that all we ever have are assumptions, never "truths," that we always see the world through our mental models and that the mental models are *always* incomplete, and, especially in Western culture, chronically nonsystemic. While Beckett does not provide tools for working with mental models as Argyris does, he plants a powerful seed that leaves people more open to seeing the inevitable biases in their own ways of thinking. Beckett also introduces people to basic principles of systems thinking. In particular, he emphasizes the distinction between "process thinking" and seeing only "snapshots," and poses systems thinking as a philosophical alternative to the pervasive "reductionism" in Western culture—the pursuit of simple answers to complex issues.

How has this substantial investment in developing skills and appreciation of mental models returned benefits for Hanover's management? O'Brien and others simply point to Hanover's steadily improving performance over the years: in profitability, Hanover was better than the industry average three out of five times from 1970–74, four out of five times in 1975–79, and ten out of ten years in 1980–89; in growth, Hanover bested the industry average one out of five times in 1970–74, four out of five times in 1975–79, eight out of ten times in 1980–89. From 1985–89, Hanover's average return on equity was 19.8 percent compared with 15.9 percent for the property and liability industry, and its sales growth was 21.8 percent compared with 15 percent for the industry. An essay in their 1988 annual report on "The Connection Between Learning and Competitiveness" asserts that the firm's commitment to "invest in education during good times and during bad times" has resulted in reaping benefits continuously.

Influenced by Argyris, Beckett, and others, Hanover gradually evolved its own approach to mental models—starting with building skills. Through training, frequent management bulletins, and continual practice, the firm attempts to build a foundation of basic skills in reflection, surfacing, and public examination of mental models. The audience target for these efforts is managers throughout the company, not just a small group of "mental model experts." As for the skills themselves, we will look closely at them shortly within the next section. They include:

- Recognizing "leaps of abstraction" (noticing our jumps from observation to generalization)
- Exposing the "left-hand column" (articulating what we normally do not say)
- Balancing inquiry and advocacy (skills for honest investigation)
- Facing up to distinctions between espoused theories (what we say) and theories-in-use (the implied theory in what we do)

It is interesting how personal these skills are. The skills cover not just business issues, but everyday relationships. The discipline concentrates on something which people normally take for granted: how we conduct ourselves in ordinary conversation, especially when complex and conflictual issues are on the table. Most of us believe that all we have to do is "act naturally"; yet the discipline of mental models retrains our natural inclinations so that conversations can produce genuine learning, rather than merely reinforcing prior views.

THE DISCIPLINE
OF MENTAL MODELS

Developing an organization's capacity to work with mental models involves both learning new skills and implementing institutional innovations that help bring these skills into regular practice. Though Shell and Hanover took immensely different approaches to managing mental models, their work required the same critical tasks. First, they had to bring key assumptions about important business issues to the surface. This goal, predominant at Shell, is vital to any company, because the most crucial mental models in any organization are those shared by key decision makers. Those models, if unexamined, limit an organization's range of actions to what is familiar and comfortable. Second, the two companies had to develop the face-to-face learning skills. This was of special concern at Hanover because they wanted managers throughout the company to be skillful with mental models.

Both sides of the discipline—business skills and interpersonal issues—are crucial. On the one hand, managers are inherently pragmatic (thank goodness). They are most motivated to learn what they need to learn in their business context. Training them in mental modeling or "balancing inquiry and advocacy," with no connection to pressing business issues, will often be rejected. Or, it will lead to people having "academic" skills they do not use. On the other hand, without the interpersonal skills, learning is still fundamentally adaptive, not generative. Generative learning, in my experience, requires managers with reflection and inquiry skills, not just consultants and planners. Only then will people at all levels surface and challenge their mental models before external circumstances compel rethinking.

As more companies adopt them, these two aspects of mental modeling will become increasingly integrated. In the meantime, based on the experience of Shell, Hanover, and other companies, we can begin to piece together the elements of an emerging discipline.

"PLANNING AS LEARNING" AND "INTERNAL BOARDS": MANAGING MENTAL MODELS THROUGHOUT AN ORGANIZATION

Institutionalizing reflection and surfacing mental models require mechanisms that make these practices unavoidable. Two approaches that have emerged to date involve recasting traditional planning as learning and establishing "internal boards of directors" to bring senior management and local management together regularly to challenge and expand the thinking behind local decision making.

Once Shell's planners had recognized the importance of articulating mental models, they had to develop ways to foster that articulation in over one hundred independent operating companies. That need for global reach is one factor behind Shell's unique approach to mental models, which involves developing and testing a variety of different tools in Group Planning in London, then disseminating them. Eventually, local planners master these tools for use with local company operating managers.

Scenarios, the first tool Shell adapted in pursuit of mental models, force managers to consider how they would manage under different alternative paths into the future. This offsets the tendency for managers to implicitly assume a single future. When groups of managers share a range of alternative futures in their mental models, they become more perceptive of changes in the business environment and more responsive to those changes. These are exactly the advantages that Shell enjoyed over its competitors during the post-OPEC era.

Beyond scenarios, Shell continues to experiment with a wide variety of tools for "mapping" mental models. These include the systems thinking tools presented in Chapters 4 through 8, as well as the computer simulation capabilities described in Chapter 17, "Microworlds," and numerous other "soft systems" tools—so called because they deal with important nonquantifiable variables which are usually prominent in managers' mental models.[11]

The common denominator of all these tools is that they work to expose assumptions about important business issues. Shell has institutionalized managing mental models through its planning process. Shell managers still generate traditional budget and control plans. But De Geus and his colleagues have come to rethink the role of planning in large institutions. It is less important, they have concluded, to produce perfect plans than to use planning to accelerate learning as a whole. Long-term success, according to De Geus, depends on, "the process whereby management teams change their shared mental models of their company, their markets, and their competitors. For this reason we think of planning as learning and of corporate planning as institutional learning." De Geus goes on to say that the critical question in planning is, "Can we accelerate institutional learning.?'"[12]

Hanover has its own way of institutionalizing mental models. There the process is guided by a set of operating principles, embedded in a novel organization structure. Several years ago, the firm put a network of "internal boards of directors" into place. Internal boards are composed of two to four senior managers who advise local general managers (in Hanover these are geographically determined). The internal boards bring outside perspective and breadth of view to empower local management through a mechanism much like corporate boards of directors. Their primary function is to counsel and advise, not to control local decision makers.

Through the internal boards, there are four levels of "mental modeling":

- within the team that directly reports to O'Brien
- between O'Brien's direct reports and general managers (GMs) through the internal boards
- between the GMs and their local functional managers
- between functional managers and their local workers and supervisors

At all these levels, the process is essentially the same. But what prevents Hanover's national managers from simply imposing their mental models on local managers? Superficially, the mechanism looks like that which exists between a CEO and a corporate board of directors, but the working relationships are more like those among partners who all share depth of knowledge about a business. "There are many advantages," says O'Brien, "of internal boards over more normal reporting relationships. First, when a local general manager reports to one senior manager—say, a corporate or group VP—it's pretty hard for the two of them to not get in a rut after a while. Usually, after a couple of years, each one knows the other and has found all sorts of ways to subtly manipulate their exchanges toward predetermined ends. It's rare when such a reporting relationship continues to foster penetrating inquiry over many years. That doesn't seem to happen when you've got three or four people on a board to whom you must continually present and explain your views. The internal board process tends to foster critical skills of local managers for our kind of organization: the ability to articulate your thinking on complex subjects, to assimilate diverse views, and to be both forceful and open. After their interactions with local boards, local managers find that they are much better prepared to foster learning within their divisions."

To guide the internal boards throughout the company, Hanover developed a set of operating principles for working with mental models. These principles are meant to establish a priority on inquiry, to promote a diversity of views rather than conformity, and to underscore the importance of improving mental models at all levels of the organization. This is the text of Hanover's "credo":

HANOVER'S CREDO ON MENTAL MODELS

1. The effectiveness of a leader is related to the continual improvement of the leader's mental models.

2. Don't impose a favored mental model on people. Mental models should lead to self-concluding decisions to work their best.
3. Self-concluding decisions result in deeper convictions and more effective implementation.
4. Better mental models enable owners to adjust to change in environment or circumstance.
5. Internal board members rarely need to make direct decisions. Instead, their role is to help the General Manager by testing or adding to the GMs mental model.
6. Multiple mental models bring multiple perspectives to bear.
7. Groups add dynamics and knowledge beyond what one person can do alone.
8. The goal is not congruency among the group.
9. When the process works it leads to congruency.
10. Leaders' worth is measured by their contribution to others' mental models.

"We don't have any anointed mental models," says O'Brien, "we have a philosophy of mental modeling. If we went out to the field and said, 'this is the authorized mental model for handling situation 23C,' we'd have a problem." Several points in the credo reinforce this theme. The second point, for example, cautions against imposing a favored mental model on people. "In other words," says O'Brien, "there may be a temptation for the loudest guy, or the highest-ranking guy, to assume that everyone else will swallow his mental models lock, stock, and barrel in sixty seconds. Even if his mental model is better, his role is not to inoculate everyone else with it, but to hold it up for them to consider."

Other points of the credo say that people are more effective when they develop their own models—even if mental models from more experienced people can avoid mistakes. "Sometimes I might say, 'If Billy's going to learn how to ride a bike, he's going to have to fall down.' I don't want him to scrape his knee or his elbow; but if it's necessary, I might let that happen. Because, to get through life, he's got to learn how to ride a bike."

It's important to note that the goal is not agreement or congruency. Many mental models can exist at once. Some may disagree.

All of them need to be considered and tested against situations that come up. This requires an organizational "commitment to the truth," which is an outgrowth of personal mastery. And it takes an understanding that we may never know the whole truth. Even after considering the mental models, as O'Brien says, "we might all wind up in different places. The goal is the best mental model for whoever happens to be out front on that particular issue. Everyone else focuses on helping that person (or persons) make the best possible decision by helping them to build the best mental model possible."

As O'Brien points out, the goal may not be congruency, but the process leads to congruency when it works. "We don't mind if meetings end with people pretty far apart," O'Brien said. "People put their positions out and even if you don't agree with them, you can recognize their merit because they're well considered. You can say, 'For other reasons, I'm not going in your direction.' It's amazing, in a way; people pull together better this way than they would when they are driven to come to agreement." For example, he said, there is none of the bitterness that typically wells up when people feel that they knew best, but never got a chance to make their case. "It turns out that people can live very well with the situation where they make their case and yet another view is implemented, so long as the learning process is open and everyone acts with integrity."

Many find the de-emphasis on agreement and congruency surprising. But I have often encountered statements similar to O'Brien's from members of outstanding teams. This belief that "we'll just talk it out and we'll know what to do" turns out to be a cornerstone of what David Bohm calls "dialogue," the heart of the discipline of team learning (see Chapter 12).

REFLECTION AND INQUIRY SKILLS: MANAGING MENTAL MODELS AT PERSONAL AND INTERPERSONAL LEVELS

The learning skills of "action science" practitioners such as Chris Argyris fall into two broad classes: skills of reflection and skills of inquiry. Skills of reflection concern slowing down our own thinking processes so that we can become more aware of how we form our mental models and the ways they influence our actions. Inquiry skills concern how we operate in face-to-face interactions with others, especially in dealing with complex and conflictual issues.

Argyris's longtime colleague Donald Schon of MIT has shown the importance of reflection on learning in professions including medicine, architecture, and management. While many professionals seem to stop learning as soon as they leave graduate school, those who become lifelong learners practice what he calls "reflection in action," the ability to reflect on one's thinking while acting. For Schon, reflection in action distinguishes the truly outstanding professionals:

> Phrases like "thinking on your feet," "keeping your wits about you," and "learning by doing" suggest not only that we can think about doing but that we can think about doing something while doing it. . . . When good jazz musicians improvise together . . . they feel the direction of the music that is developing out of their interwoven contributions, they make new sense of it and adjust their performance to the new sense they have made.[13]

Reflection skills start with recognizing "leaps of abstraction."

Leaps of Abstraction. Our minds literally move at lightning speed. Ironically, this often slows our learning, because we immediately "leap" to generalizations so quickly that we never think to test them. The proverbial "castles in the sky" describes our own thinking far more often than we realize.

The conscious mind is ill-equipped to deal with large numbers of concrete details. If shown photographs of a hundred individuals, most of us will have trouble remembering each face, but we will remember categories—such as tall men, or women in red, or Orientals, or the elderly. Psychologist George Miller's famous "magic number seven plus or minus two" referred to our tendency to focus on a limited number of separate variables at any one time.[14] Our rational minds are extraordinarily facile at "abstracting" from concrete particulars—substituting simple concepts for many details and then reasoning in terms of these concepts. But our very strengths in abstract conceptual reasoning also limit our learning, when we are unaware of our leaps from particulars to general concepts.

For example, have you ever heard a statement such as, "Laura doesn't care about people," and wondered about its validity? Imagine that Laura is a superior or colleague who has some particular habits that others have noted. She rarely offers generous praise. She often stares off into space when people talk to her, and then asks, "What did you say?" She sometimes cuts people off when they speak. She never comes to office parties. And in performance reviews, she mutters two or three sentences and then dismisses the person. From these particular behaviors, Laura's colleagues have concluded that she "doesn't care much about people." It's been common knowledge—except, of course, for Laura, who feels that she cares very much about people.

What has happened to Laura is that her colleagues have made a "leap of abstraction." They have substituted a generalization, "not caring about people" for many specific behaviors. More importantly, they have begun to treat this generalization as *fact*. No one questions anymore whether or not Laura cares about people. It is a given.

Leaps of abstraction occur when we move from direct observations (concrete "data") to generalization without testing. Leaps of abstraction impede learning because they become axiomatic. What was once an assumption becomes treated as a fact. Once Laura's colleagues accept as fact that she doesn't care about people, no one questions her behavior when she does things that are "noncaring," and no one notices when she does something that doesn't fit the stereotype. The general view that she doesn't care leads people to treat her with greater indifference, which takes away any opportunity she might have had to exhibit more caring. The result is that Laura and her colleagues are frozen in a state of affairs that no one desires. Moreover, untested generalizations can easily become the basis for further generalization. "Could Laura have been the one behind that office intrigue? She's probably the sort who would do that sort of thing given that she doesn't care much about people . . ."

Laura's colleagues, like most of us, are not disciplined in distinguishing what they observe directly from the generalizations they infer from their observations. There are "facts"—observable data about Laura—such as the time spent in a typical performance review or looking away during a conversation. But "Laura doesn't listen much" is a generalization not a fact, as is "Laura doesn't care much." Both may be based on facts, but they are inferences nonetheless. Failing to distinguish direct observation from generalizations inferred from observation leads us never to think to test the generalization. So no one ever asked Laura whether or not she cares. If they had, they might have found out that, in her mind, she does care very much. They also might have learned that she has a hearing impediment that she hasn't told anyone about and, largely because of that, she is painfully shy in conversations.

Leaps of abstraction are just as common with business issues. At one firm, many top managers were convinced that "Customers buy products based on price; the quality of service isn't a factor." And it's no wonder they felt that way; customers continually pressed for deeper discounts, and competitors were continually attracting away customers with price promotions. When one marketer who was new to the company urged his superiors to invest in improving service, he was turned down kindly but firmly. The senior leaders never tested the idea, because their leap of abstraction had become a "fact"—that "customers don't care about service, customers buy based on price." They sat and watched while their leading competitor steadily increased its market share by providing a level of service quality that customers had never experienced, and therefore had never asked for.

In high-tech companies, a common belief is that being first to market is the key to success. This generalization is often based on concrete experience, but it can also be misleading. The Apple III computer (an improved version of the Apple II) was an innovative product, released in 1982, but it had many bugs that turned off would-be customers, and the product turned out to be one of Apple's biggest disappointments. Yet, other computer manufacturers rushed products to market that were, if anything, less ready. Some of those products were big winners such as the Sun-3 workstation. Why does the generalization "first to market" stand up in some instances but not in others? Because the Sun-3's customers were sophisticated engineers who forgave bugs—in part because they could fix them themselves. The Apple III's largest market, consumers and business people, was much more unforgiving. They needed the new system to work the first time out and could easily be intimidated by a powerful machine that (even though the bugs were fixed within a few months after they were discovered) had the reputation of unreliability.[15]

How do you spot leaps of abstraction? First, by asking yourself what you believe about the way the world works—the nature of business, people in general, and specific individuals. Ask "What is the 'data' on which this generalization is based?" Then ask yourself, "Am I willing to consider that this generalization may be inaccurate or misleading?" It is important to ask this last question consciously, because, if the answer is no, there is no point in proceeding.

If you are willing to question a generalization, explicitly separate it from the "data" which led to it. "Paul Smith, the purchaser for Bailey's Shoes, and several other customers have told me they won't buy our product unless we lower the price 10 percent," you might say. "Thus, I conclude that our customers don't care about service quality." This puts all your cards on the table and gives you, and others, a better opportunity to consider alternative interpretations and courses of action.

Where possible, test the generalizations directly. This will often lead to inquiring into the reasons behind one another's actions. Such inquiry requires skills that will be discussed below. For example, just coming up to Laura and asking, "Don't you care very much about people?" is likely to evoke a defensive reaction. There are ways of approaching such exchanges, through owning up to our assumptions about others and citing the data upon which they are based, that reduce the chances of defensiveness.

But until we become aware of our leaps of abstraction, we are not even aware of the need for inquiry. This is precisely why practicing reflection as a discipline is so important. A second technique from action science, the "left-hand column," is especially useful both in starting and deepening this discipline.

Left-Hand Column. This is a powerful technique for beginning to "see" how our mental models operate in particular situations. It reveals ways that we manipulate situations to avoid dealing with how we actually think and feel, and thereby prevent a counterproductive situation from improving.

The left-hand column exercise can show managers that, indeed, they have mental models and those models play an active, sometimes unwelcome part in management practice. Once a group of managers have gone through the exercises, not only are they aware of the role of their mental models but they begin to see why dealing with their assumptions more forthrightly is important.

The "left-hand column" comes from a type of case presentation used by Chris Argyris and his colleagues. It starts with selecting a specific situation where I am interacting with one or several other people in a way that I feel is not working—specifically, that is not producing any apparent learning or moving ahead. I write out a sample of the exchange, in the form of a script. I write the script on the right-hand side of a page. On the left-hand side, I write what I am thinking but not saying at each stage in the exchange.

For example, imagine an exchange with a colleague, Bill, after a big presentation to our boss on a project we are doing together. I had to miss the presentation, but I've heard that it was poorly received.

ME: How did the presentation go?
BILL: Well, I don't know. It's really too early to say. Besides, we're breaking new ground here.

ME: Well, what do you think we should do? I believe that the
   issues you were raising are important.

BILL: I'm not so sure. Let's just wait and see what happens.

ME: You may be right, but I think we may need to do more than
   just wait.

Now, here is what the exchange looks like with my "left-hand
column":

WHAT I'M THINKING	WHAT IS SAID
Everyone says the presentation was a bomb.	ME: How did the presentation go?
Does he really not know how bad it was? Or is he not willing to face up to it?	BILL: Well, I don't know. It's really too early to tell. Besides, we're breaking new ground here.
	ME: Well, what do you think we should do? I believe that the issues you were raising are important.
He really is afraid to see the truth. If he only had more confidence, he could probably learn from a situation like this.	BILL: I'm not so sure. Let's just wait and see what happens.
I can't believe he doesn't realize how disastrous that presentation was to our moving ahead.	
I've got to find some way to light a fire under the guy.	ME: You may be right, but I think we may need to do more than just wait.

The left-hand column exercise always succeeds in bringing hidden
assumptions to the surface and showing how they influence behavior. In the above example, I am making two key assumptions about

Bill: he lacks confidence, especially in regard to facing up to his poor performance; and he lacks initiative. Neither may be literally true, but both are evident in my internal dialogue and both influence the way I handle the situation. My belief in his lack of confidence shows up in my skirting the fact that I have heard that the presentation was a bomb. I'm afraid that if I say it directly, he will lose what little confidence he has, or he will not be able to face the evidence. So, I bring up the subject of the presentation obliquely. My belief in Bill's lack of initiative comes up when we discuss what to do next. He gives no specific course of action despite my question. I see this as evidence of his laziness or lack of initiative: he is content to do nothing when something definitely is required, from which I conclude that I will have to manufacture some form of pressure to motivate him into action, or else I will simply have to take matters into my own hands.

The most important lesson that comes from seeing "our left-hand columns" is how we undermine opportunities for learning in conflictual situations. Rather than facing squarely our problems, Bill and I talk around the subject. Instead of determining how to move forward to resolve our problems, we end our exchange with no clear course of action—in fact, with no clear definition of a problem requiring action.

Why don't I simply tell him that I believe there is a problem? Why don't I say that we must look at steps to get our project back on track? Perhaps because I am not sure how to bring up these "delicate" issues productively. Like Laura's colleagues, I imagine that to bring them up will provoke a defensive, counterproductive exchange. I'm afraid that we'll be worse off than we are now. Perhaps I avoid the issues out of a sense of politeness or desire not to be critical. Whatever the reason, the outcome is a dissatisfying exchange and I resort to looking for a way to "manipulate" Bill into a more forceful response.

There is no one "right" way to handle difficult situations such as my exchange with Bill, but it helps enormously to see first how my own reasoning and actions can contribute to making matters worse. This is where the left-hand column technique can be useful. Once I see more clearly my own assumptions and how I may be concealing them, there are several things I might do to move the conversation forward more productively. All involve sharing my own view and the "data" upon which it is based. All require being open to the possibility that Bill may share neither the view nor the data, and that both may be wrong. (After all, my informant about the presentation may have been in error.) In effect, my task is to convert the situation into one where *both* Bill and I can learn. This requires a combination of articulating my views, and learning more about Bill's views—a process which Argyris calls "balancing inquiry and advocacy."

Balancing Inquiry and Advocacy. Most managers are trained to be advocates. In fact, in many companies, what it means to be a competent manager is to be able to solve problems—to figure out what needs to be done, and enlist whatever support is needed to get it done. Individuals became successful in part because of their abilities to debate forcefully and influence others. Inquiry skills, meanwhile, go unrecognized and unrewarded. But as managers rise to senior positions, they confront issues more complex and diverse than their personal experience. Suddenly, they need to tap insights from other people. They need to learn. Now the manager's advocacy skills become counterproductive; they can close us off from actually learning from one another. What is needed is blending advocacy and inquiry to promote collaborative learning.

Even when two advocates meet for an open, candid exchange of views, there is usually little learning. They may be genuinely interested in each other's views, but pure advocacy lends a different type of structure to the conversation:

> "I appreciate your sincerity, but my experience and judgment lead me to some different conclusions. Let me tell you why your proposal won't work . . ."

As each side reasonably and calmly advocates his viewpoint just a bit more strongly, positions become more and more rigid. Advocacy without inquiry begets more advocacy. In fact, there is a systems archetype that describes what happens next; called "escalation," it's the same structure as an arms race.

The more vehemently A argues, the greater the threat to B. Thus, B argues more fiercely. Then A counterargues even more fiercely. And so on. Managers often find escalations so grueling that, thereafter, they avoid stating any differences publicly. "It's too much grief."

The snowball effect of reinforcing advocacy can be stopped, by beginning to ask a few questions. Simple questions such as, "What is it that leads you to that position?" and "Can you illustrate your point for me?" (Can you provide some "data" or experience in support of it?) can introject an element of inquiry into a discussion.

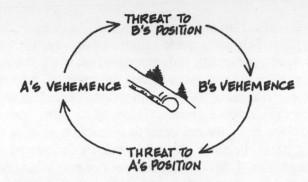

We often tape record meetings of management teams with whom we are working to develop learning skills. One indicator of a team in trouble is when in a several hour meeting there are few, if any, questions. This may seem amazing but I have seen meetings that went for three hours without a single question being asked! You don't have to be an "action science" expert to know there is not a lot of inquiry going on in such meetings.

But pure inquiry is also limited. Questioning can be crucial for breaking the spiral of reinforcing advocacy, but until a team or an individual learns to combine inquiry and advocacy, learning skills are very limited. One reason that pure inquiry is limited is that we almost always *do* have a view, regardless of whether or not we believe that our view is the only correct one. Thus, just asking lots of questions can be a way of avoiding learning—by hiding our own view behind a wall of incessant questioning.

The most productive learning usually occurs when managers combine skills in advocacy and inquiry. Another way to say this is "reciprocal inquiry." By this we mean that everyone makes his or her thinking explicit and subject to public examination. This creates an atmosphere of genuine vulnerability. No one is hiding the evidence or reasoning behind his views—advancing them without making them open to scrutiny. For example, when inquiry and advocacy are balanced, I would not only be inquiring into the reasoning behind others' views but would be stating my views in such a way as to reveal my own assumptions and reasoning and to invite others to inquire into them. I might say, "Here is my view and here is how I have arrived at it. How does it sound to you?"

When operating in pure advocacy, the goal is to win the argument. When inquiry and advocacy are combined, the goal is no longer "to win the argument" but to find the best argument. This shows in how we use data and in how we reveal the reasoning behind abstractions. For example, when we operate in pure advocacy, we tend to use data selectively, presenting only the data that confirm our position. When we explain the reasoning behind our position, we expose only enough of our reasoning to "make our case," avoiding areas where we feel our case might be weak. By contrast, when both advocacy and inquiry are high, we are open to disconfirming data as well as confirming data—because we are genuinely interested in finding flaws in our views. Likewise, we expose our reasoning and look for flaws in it, and we try to understand others' reasoning.

The ideal of combining inquiry and advocacy is challenging. It can be especially difficult if you work in a highly political organization that is not open to genuine inquiry (Chapter 13, Openness, deals with this subject further). Speaking as a veteran advocate, I can say that I have found patience and perseverance needed to move toward a more balanced approach. Progress comes in stages. For me, the first stage was learning how to inquire into others' views when I do not agree with them. My habitual response to such disagreements was to advocate my view harder. Usually, this was done without malice but in the genuine belief that I had thought things through and had a valid position. Unfortunately, it often had the consequence of polarizing or terminating discussions, and left me without the sense of partnership I truly wanted. Now, I very often respond to differences of view by asking the other person to say more about how he came to his view, or to expand further on his view. (I am only starting to get to a second stage of stating my views so as to invite others to inquire into them as well.)

Though I am still a novice in the discipline of balancing inquiry and advocacy, the rewards have been gratifying. What has become obvious on repeated occasions is that, when there is inquiry *and* advocacy, creative outcomes are much more likely. In a sense, when two people operate in pure advocacy, the outcomes are predetermined. Either person A will win, or person B will win, or both will simply retain their views. When there is inquiry and advocacy, these limitations dissolve. Persons A and B, by being open to inquire into their own views, make possible discovering completely new views.

While mastering the discipline of balancing inquiry and advocacy, I've found that it helps to keep in mind the following guidelines:[16]

When advocating your view:
  • *Make* your own reasoning explicit (i.e., say how you arrived at your view and the "data" upon which it is based)

- *Encourage* others to explore your view (e.g., "Do you see gaps in my reasoning?")
- *Encourage* others to provide different views (i.e., "Do you have either different data or different conclusions, or both?")
- Actively *inquire* into others' views that differ from your own (i.e., "What are your views?" "How did you arrive at your view?" "Are you taking into account data that are different from what I have considered?")

When inquiring into others' views:
- If you are making assumptions about others' views, state your assumptions clearly and acknowledge that they are assumptions
- State the "data" upon which your assumptions are based
- Don't bother asking questions if you're not genuinely interested in the others' response (i.e., if you're only trying to be polite or to show the others up)

When you arrive at an impasse (others no longer appear to be open to inquiring into their own views):
- Ask what data or logic might change their views.
- Ask if there is any way you might together design an experiment (or some other inquiry) that might provide new information

When you or others are hesitant to express your views or to experiment with alternative ideas:
- Encourage them (or you) to think out loud about what might be making it difficult (i.e., "What is it about this situation, and about me or others, that is making open exchange difficult?")
- If there is mutual desire to do so, design with others ways of overcoming these barriers

The point is not to follow such guidelines slavishly, but to use them to keep in mind the spirit of balancing inquiry and advocacy. Like any "formula" for starting on one of the learning disciplines, they should be used as "training wheels" on your first bicycle. They help to get you started, and give you a feel for what it is like to "ride," to practice inquiry with advocacy. As you gain skill, they can and probably should be discarded. But it is also nice to be able to come back to them periodically when you encounter some rough terrain.

However, it is important to keep in mind that guidelines will be of little use if you are not genuinely curious and willing to change your mental model of a situation. In other words, practicing inquiry and advocacy means being willing to expose the limitations in your own thinking—the willingness to be wrong. Nothing less will make it safe for others to do likewise.

Espoused Theory versus Theory-in-Use. Learning eventually results in changes in action, not just taking in new information and forming new "ideas." That is why recognizing the gap between our espoused theories (what we say) and our "theories-in-use" (the theories that lay behind our actions) is vital. Otherwise, we may believe we've "learned" something just because we've got the new language or concepts to use, even though our behavior is completely unchanged.

For example, I may profess a view (an espoused theory) that people are basically trustworthy. But I never lend friends money and jealously guard all my possessions. Obviously, my theory-in-use, my deeper mental model, differs from my espoused theory.

While gaps between espoused theories and theories-in-use might be cause for discouragement, or even cynicism, they needn't be. Often they arise as a consequence of vision, not hypocrisy. For example, it may be truly part of my vision to trust people. Then, a gap between this aspect of my vision and my current behavior holds the potential for creative change. The problem lies not in the gap but, as was discussed in Chapter 9, "Personal Mastery," in failing to tell the truth about the gap. Until the gap between my espoused theory and my current behavior is recognized, no learning can occur.

So the first question to pose when facing a gap between espoused theory and a theory-in-use is "Do I really value the espoused theory?" "Is it really part of my vision?" If there is no commitment to the espoused theory, then the gap does not represent a tension between reality and my vision but between reality and a view I advance (perhaps because of how it will make me look to others).

Because it's so hard to see theories-in-use, you may need the help of another person—a "ruthlessly compassionate" partner. In the quest to develop skills in reflection, we are each others' greatest assets. As Hanover's Bill O'Brien says, "The eye cannot see itself."

MENTAL MODELS AND
THE FIFTH DISCIPLINE

I have come to believe that systems thinking without mental models is like the DC-3's radial air-cooled engine without wing flaps. Just as the Boeing 247's engineers had to downsize their engine because they lacked wing flaps, systems thinking without the discipline of mental models loses much of its power. This is why much of our current research at MIT focuses on helping managers to integrate mental modeling and systems thinking skills. The two disciplines go naturally together because one focuses on exposing hidden assumptions and the other focuses on how to restructure assumptions to reveal causes of significant problems.

As shown at the outset of the chapter, entrenched mental models will thwart changes that could come from systems thinking. Managers must learn to reflect on their current mental models—until prevailing assumptions are brought into the open, there is no reason to expect mental models to change, and there is little purpose in systems thinking. If managers "believe" their world views are facts rather than sets of assumptions, they will not be open to challenging those world views. If they lack skills in inquiring into their and others' ways of thinking, they will be limited in experimenting collaboratively with new ways of thinking. Moreover, if there is no established philosophy and understanding of mental models in the organization, people will misperceive the purpose of systems thinking as drawing diagrams building elaborate "models" of the world, not improving our mental models.

Systems thinking is equally important to working with mental models effectively. Contemporary research shows that most of our mental models are systematically flawed. They miss critical feedback relationships, misjudge time delays, and often focus on variables that are visible or salient, not necessarily high leverage. MIT's John Sterman has shown experimentally that players in the beer game, for example, consistently misjudge the delay in receiving orders once placed. Most players either don't see or don't take into account in their decision making the critical reinforcing feedbacks that develop when they panic (place more orders for beer, which wipes out their supplier's inventory, forcing them to lengthen shipping delays, which can lead to further panic). Sterman has shown similar flaws in mental models in a variety of experiments.[17]

Understanding these flaws can help to see where prevailing mental models will be weakest and where more than just "surfacing" managers' mental models will be required for effective decisions.

Eventually, what will accelerate mental models as a practical management discipline will be a *library of "generic structures"* used throughout an organization. These "structures" will be based on systems archetypes such as those presented in Chapter 6. But, they would be suited to the particulars of a given organization—its products, market, and technologies. For example, the particular "shifting the burden," and "limits to growth" structures for an oil company would differ from those for an insurance company, but the underlying archetypes would be the same. Such a library should be a natural by-product of practicing systems thinking within an organization.

Ultimately, the payoff from integrating systems thinking and mental models will be not only improving our mental models (what we think) but altering our ways of thinking: shifting from mental models dominated by events to mental models that recognize longer-term patterns of change and the underlying structures producing those patterns. For example, Shell's scenarios not only made the company's managers aware of changes, they shifted the way the managers thought about those changes. While most other oil companies saw the rise of OPEC as a onetime event, it signalled a shift in basic patterns of supply-demand interactions for Shell's managers—an era of seller's market, instability, high prices, and reduced demand growth. That gave those managers a longer-term perspective in which to consider their strategic options, and it led them to policies which could serve for the rest of the decade. In other words, scenarios helped Shell's managers take a first step up from the world of events—seeing patterns of change.

Just as "linear thinking" dominates most mental models used for critical decisions today, the learning organizations of the future will make key decisions based on shared understandings of interrelationships and patterns of change.

11

SHARED VISION

A COMMON CARING

You may remember the movie *Spartacus*, an adaptation of the story of a Roman gladiator/slave who led an army of slaves in an uprising in 71 B.C.[1] They defeated the Roman legions twice, but were finally conquered by the general Marcus Crassus after a long siege and battle. In the movie, Crassus tells the thousand survivors in Spartacus's army, "You have been slaves. You will be slaves again. But you will be spared your rightful punishment of crucifixion by the mercy of the Roman legions. All you need to do is turn over to me the slave Spartacus, because we do not know him by sight."

After a long pause, Spartacus (played by Kirk Douglas) stands up and says, "I am Spartacus." Then the man next to him stands up and says, "I am Spartacus." The next man stands up and also says, "No, I am Spartacus." Within a minute, everyone in the army is on his feet.

It does not matter whether this story is apocryphal or not; it demonstrates a deep truth. Each man, by standing up, chose death. But the loyalty of Spartacus's army was not to Spartacus the man. Their loyalty was to a shared vision which Spartacus had inspired—the idea that they could be free men. This vision was so compelling that no man could bear to give it up and return to slavery.

A shared vision is not an idea. It is not even an important idea such as freedom. It is, rather, a force in people's hearts, a force of impressive power. It may be inspired by an idea, but once it goes further—if it is compelling enough to acquire the support of more than one person—then it is no longer an abstraction. It is palpable. People begin to see it as if it exists. Few, if any, forces in human affairs are as powerful as shared vision.

At its simplest level, a shared vision is the answer to the question, "What do we want to create?" Just as personal visions are pictures or images people carry in their heads and hearts, so too are shared visions pictures that people throughout an organization carry. They create a sense of commonality that permeates the organization and gives coherence to diverse activities.

A vision is truly shared when you and I have a similar picture and are committed to one another having it, not just to each of us, individually, having it. When people truly share a vision they are connected, bound together by a common aspiration. Personal visions derive their power from an individual's deep caring for the vision. Shared visions derive their power from a common caring. In fact, we have to come to believe that one of the reasons people seek to build shared visions is their desire to be connected in an important undertaking.

Shared vision is vital for the learning organization because it provides the focus and energy for learning. While adaptive learning is possible without vision, generative learning occurs only when people are striving to accomplish something that matters deeply to them. In fact, the whole idea of generative learning—"expanding your ability to create"—will seem abstract and meaningless *until* people become excited about some vision they truly want to accomplish.

Today, "vision" is a familiar concept in corporate leadership. But when you look carefully you find that most "visions" are one person's (or one group's) vision imposed on an organization. Such visions, at best, command compliance—not commitment. A shared vision is a vision that many people are truly committed to, because it reflects their own personal vision.

WHY SHARED VISIONS MATTER

It is impossible to imagine the accomplishments of building AT&T, Ford, or Apple in the absence of shared vision. Theodore Vail had a vision of universal telephone service that would take fifty years to bring about. Henry Ford envisioned common people, not just the wealthy, owning their own automobiles. Steven Jobs, Steve Wozniak, and their Apple cofounders saw the power of the computer to empower people. It is equally impossible to imagine the rapid ascendancy of Japanese firms such as Komatsu (which grew from one third the size of Caterpillar to its equal in less than two decades), Canon (which went from nothing to matching Xerox's global market share in reprographics in the same time frame), or Honda had they not all been guided by visions of global success.[2] What is most important is that these individuals' visions became genuinely shared among people throughout all levels of their companies—focusing the energies of thousands and creating a common identity among enormously diverse people.

Many shared visions are extrinsic—that is, they focus on achieving something relative to an outsider, such as a competitor. Pepsi's vision is explicitly directed at beating Coca-Cola; Avis's vision at Hertz. Yet, a goal limited to defeating an opponent is transitory. Once the vision is achieved, it can easily migrate into a defensive posture of "protecting what we have, of not losing our number-one position." Such defensive goals rarely call forth the creativity and excitement of building something new. A master in the martial arts is probably not focused so much on "defeating all others" as on his own intrinsic inner standards of "excellence." This does not mean that visions must be either intrinsic *or* extrinsic. Both types of vision can coexist. But reliance on a vision that is solely predicated on defeating an adversary can weaken an organization long term.

Kazuo Inamori of Kyocera entreats employees "to look inward," to discover their own internal standards. He argues that, while striving to be number one in its field, a company can aim to be "better" than others or "best" in its field. But his vision is that Kyocera should always aim for "perfection" rather than just being "best." (Note Inamori's application of the principle of creative tension— "it's not what the vision is, but what it does . . .")[3]

A shared vision, especially one that is intrinsic, uplifts people's aspirations. Work becomes part of pursuing a larger purpose embodied in the organizations' products or services—accelerating learning through personal computers, bringing the world into communication through universal telephone service, or promoting freedom of movement through the personal automobile. The larger purpose can also be embodied in the style, climate, and spirit of the organization. Max de Pree, retired CEO of the Herman Miller furniture company said his vision for Herman Miller was "to be a gift to the human spirit" —by which he meant not only Herman Miller's products, but its people, its atmosphere, and its larger commitment to productive and aesthetic work environments.[4]

Visions are exhilarating. They create the spark, the excitement that lifts an organization out of the mundane. "No matter how problematic the competition or our internal troubles," wrote John Sculley about Apple's renowned visionary product, "my spirit rebounded when I strolled into the Macintosh Building. We knew we would soon bear witness to an event of historical proportions."[5]

In a corporation, a shared vision changes people's relationship with the company. It is no longer "their company;" it becomes "our company." A shared vision is the first step in allowing people who mistrusted each other to begin to work together. It creates a common identity. In fact, an organization's shared sense of purpose, vision, and operating values establish the most basic level of commonality. Late in his career, the psychologist Abraham Maslow studied high-performing teams. One of their most striking characteristics was shared vision and purpose. Maslow observed that in exceptional teams

> the task was no longer separate from the self . . . but rather he identified with this task so strongly that you couldn't define his real self without including that task.[6]

Shared visions compel courage so naturally that people don't even realize the extent of their courage. Courage is simply doing whatever is needed in pursuit of the vision. In 1961, John Kennedy articulated a vision that had been emerging for many years among leaders within America's space program: to have a man on the moon by the end of the decade.[7] This led to countless acts of courage and daring. A modern-day Spartacus story occurred in the mid-1960s at MIT's Draper Laboratories. The lab was the lead contractor with NASA for the inertial navigation and guidance system to guide the Apollo astronauts to the moon. Several years into the project, the lab directors became convinced that their original design specifications were wrong. This posed considerable potential embarrassment, since several million dollars had already been spent. Instead of trying to jerry-rig an expedient solution, they asked NASA to disband the project and start over again. They risked not just their contract but their reputation. But no other action was possible. Their entire reason for being was embodied in one simple vision—having a man on the moon by the end of the decade. They would do whatever it took to realize that vision.

Apple Computer during the mid-1980s, when the entire small computer industry rallied behind the IBM PC, persevered with its vision of a computer which people could understand intuitively, a computer which represented the freedom to think on one's own. Along the way, Apple not only refused the "sure thing" opportunity to be a leading PC "clone" manufacturer, but its leaders gave up an innovation which they had pioneered: open architecture, where people could add their own components. This did not fit with a computer that was easy to use. Strategically, the change paid off in a company profile and reputation which even the foremost "clone" makers, such as Compaq, have never been able to equal. Apple's Macintosh was not only easy to use, it became a new industry standard and made having fun a priority in personal computing.

You cannot have a learning organization without shared vision. Without a pull toward some goal which people truly want to achieve, the forces in support of the status quo can be overwhelming. Vision establishes an overarching goal. The loftiness of the target compels new ways of thinking and acting. A shared vision also provides a rudder to keep the learning process on course when stresses develop. Learning can be difficult, even painful. With a shared vision, we are more likely to expose our ways of thinking, give up deeply held views, and recognize personal and organizational shortcomings. All that trouble seems trivial compared with the importance of what we are trying to create. As Robert Fritz puts it, "In the presence of greatness, pettiness disappears." In the absence of a great dream, pettiness prevails.

Shared vision fosters risk taking and experimentation. "When you are immersed in a vision," says Herman Miller's president Ed Simon, "You know what needs to be done. But you often don't know how to do it. You run an experiment because you think it's going to get you there. It doesn't work. New input. New data. You change direction and run another experiment. Everything is an experiment, but there is no ambiguity at all. It's perfectly clear why you are doing it. People aren't saying, 'Give me a guarantee that it will work.' Everybody knows that there is no guarantee. But the people are committed nonetheless.''

Lastly, shared vision addresses one of the primary puzzles that has thwarted efforts to develop systems thinking in management: "How can a commitment to the long term be fostered?"

For years, systems thinkers have endeavored to persuade managers that, unless they maintained a long-term focus, they will be in big trouble. With great vigor we have proselytized the "better before worse" consequences of many interventions, and the "shifting the burden" dynamics that result from symptomatic fixes. Yet, I have witnessed few lasting shifts to longer term commitment and action. Personally, I have come to feel that our failure lies not in unpersuasiveness or lack of sufficiently compelling evidence. *It may simply not be possible to convince human beings rationally to take a long-term view.* People do not focus on the long term because they *have* to, but because they *want* to.

In every instance where one finds a long-term view actually operating in human affairs, there is a long-term vision at work. The cathedral builders of the Middle Ages labored a lifetime with the fruits of their labors still a hundred years in the future. The Japanese believe building a great organization is like growing a tree; it takes twenty-five to fifty years. Parents of young children try to lay a foundation of values and attitude that will serve an adult twenty years hence. In all of these cases, people hold a vision that can be realized only over the long term.

Strategic planning, which should be a bastion of long-term thinking in corporations, is very often reactive and short-term. According to two of the most articulate critics of contemporary strategic planning, Gary Hamel of the London Business School and C. K. Prahalad of the University of Michigan:

> Although strategic planning is billed as a way of becoming more future oriented, most managers, when pressed, will admit that their strategic plans reveal more about today's problems than tomorrow's opportunities.[8]

With its emphasis on extensive analysis of competitors' strengths and weaknesses, of market niches and firm resources, typical strategic planning fails to achieve the one accomplishment that would foster longer range actions—in Hamel's and Prahalad's terms, setting "a goal that is worthy of commitment."

With all the attention given to this component of corporate learning, however, vision is still often regarded as a mysterious, uncontrollable force. Leaders with vision are cult heroes. While it is true that there are no formulas for "how to find your vision," there are principles and guidelines for building shared vision. There is a discipline of building vision that is emerging, and practical tools for working with shared visions. This discipline extends principles and insights from personal mastery into the world of collective aspiration and shared commitment.

THE DISCIPLINE OF
BUILDING SHARED VISION

ENCOURAGING PERSONAL VISION

Shared visions emerge from personal visions. This is how they derive their energy and how they foster commitment. As Bill O'Brien of Hanover Insurance observes, "My vision is not what's important to you. The only vision that motivates you is your vision." It is not that people care only about their personal self-interest—in fact, people's personal visions usually include dimensions that concern family, organization, community, and even the world. Rather, O'Brien is stressing that caring is *personal*. It is rooted in an individual's own set of values, concerns, and aspirations. This is why genuine caring about a shared vision is rooted in personal visions. This simple truth is lost on many leaders, who decide that their organization must develop a vision by tomorrow!

Organizations intent on building shared visions continually encourage members to develop their personal visions. If people don't have their own vision, all they can do is "sign up" for someone else's. The result is compliance, never commitment. On the other hand, people with a strong sense of personal direction can join together to create a powerful synergy toward what I/we truly want.

Personal mastery is the bedrock for developing shared visions. This means not only personal vision, but commitment to the truth and creative tension—the hallmarks of personal mastery. Shared vision can generate levels of creative tension that go far beyond individuals' "comfort levels." Those who will contribute the most toward realizing a lofty vision will be those who can "hold" this creative tension: remain clear on the vision and continue to inquire into current reality. They will be the ones who believe deeply in their ability to create their future, because that is what they experience personally.

In encouraging personal vision, organizations must be careful not to infringe on individual freedoms. As was discussed in chapter 9, "Personal Mastery," no one can give another "his vision," nor even force him to develop a vision. However, there are positive actions that can be taken to create a climate that encourages personal vision. The most direct is for leaders who have a sense of vision to communicate that in such a way that others are encouraged to share their visions. This is the art of visionary leadership—how shared visions are built from personal visions.

FROM PERSONAL VISIONS TO SHARED VISIONS

How do individual visions join to create shared visions? A useful metaphor is the hologram, the three-dimensional image created by interacting light sources.

If you cut a photograph in half, each part shows only part of the whole image. But if you divide a hologram, each part shows the whole image intact. Similarly, as you continue to divide up the hologram, no matter how small the divisions, each piece still shows the whole image. Likewise, when a group of people come to share a vision for an organization, each person sees his own picture of the organization at its best. Each shares responsibility for the whole, not just for his piece. But the component "pieces" of the hologram are not identical. Each represents the whole image from a different point of view. It's as if you were to look through holes poked in a window shade; each hole would offer a unique angle for viewing the whole image. So, too, is each individual's vision of the whole unique. We each have our own way of seeing the larger vision.

When you add up the pieces of a hologram, the image of the whole does not change fundamentally. After all, it was there in each piece. Rather the image becomes more intense, more lifelike. When more people come to share a common vision, the vision may not change fundamentally. But it becomes more alive, more real in the sense of a mental reality that people can truly imagine achieving. They now have partners, "cocreators"; the vision no longer rests on their shoulders alone. Early on, when they are nurturing an individual vision, people may say it is "my vision." But as the shared vision develops, it becomes both "my vision" and "our vision."

The first step in mastering the discipline of building shared visions is to give up traditional notions that visions are always announced from "on high" or come from an organization's institutionalized planning processes.

In the traditional hierarchical organization, no one questioned that the vision emanated from the top. Often, the big picture guiding the firm wasn't even shared—all people needed to know were their "marching orders," so that they could carry out their tasks in support of the larger vision. Ed Simon of Herman Miller says, "If I was the president of a traditional authoritarian organization and I had a new vision, the task would be much simpler than we face today. Most people in the organization wouldn't need to understand the vision. People would simply need to know what was expected of them."

That traditional "top-down" vision is not much different from a process that has become popular in recent years. Top management goes off to write its "vision statement," often with the help of consultants. This may be done to solve the problem of low morale or lack of strategic direction. Sometimes the process is primarily reflective. Sometimes it incorporates extensive analysis of a firm's competitors, market setting, and organizational strengths and weaknesses. Regardless, the results are often disappointing for several reasons.

First, such a vision is often a "one-shot" vision, a single effort at providing overarching direction and meaning to the firm's strategy. Once it's written, management assumes that they have now discharged their visionary duties. Recently, one of my Innovation Associates colleagues was explaining to two managers how our group works with vision. Before he could get far, one of the managers interrupted. "We've done that," he said. "We've already written our vision statement." "That's very interesting," my colleague responded. "What did you come up with?" The one manager turned to the other and asked, "Joe, where is that vision statement anyhow?" Writing a vision statement can be a first step in building shared vision but, alone, it rarely makes a vision "come alive" within an organization.

The second problem with top management going off to write their vision statement is that the resulting vision does not build on people's personal visions. Often, personal visions are ignored altogether in the search for a "strategic vision." Or the "official vision" reflects only the personal vision of one or two people. There is little opportunity for inquiry and testing at every level so that people feel they understand and own the vision. As a result, the new official vision also fails to foster energy and commitment. It simply does not inspire people. In fact, sometimes, it even generates little passion among the top management team who created it.

Lastly, vision is not a "solution to a problem." If it is seen in that light, when the "problem" of low morale or unclear strategic direction goes away, the energy behind the vision will go away also. Building shared vision must be seen as a central element of the daily work of leaders. It is ongoing and never-ending. It is actually part of a larger leadership activity: designing and nurturing what Hanover's Bill O'Brien calls the "governing ideas" of the enterprise—not only its vision per se, but its purpose and core values as well. As O'Brien says, "The governing ideas are far more important and enduring than the reporting chart and the divisional structure that so often preoccupy CEOs."

Sometimes, managers expect shared visions to emerge from a firm's strategic planning process. But for all the same reasons that most "top-down" visioning processes fail, most strategic planning also fails to nurture genuine vision. According to Hamel and Prahalad:

> Creative strategies seldom emerge from the annual planning ritual. The starting point for next year's strategy is almost always this year's strategy. Improvements are incremental. The company sticks to the segments and territories it knows, even though the real opportunities may be elsewhere. The impetus for Canon's pioneering entry into the personal copier business came from an overseas sales subsidiary—not from planners in Japan.[9]

This is not to say that visions cannot emanate from the top. Often, they do. But sometimes they emanate from personal visions of individuals who are not in positions of authority. Sometimes they just "bubble up" from people interacting at many levels. The origin of the vision is much less important than the process whereby it comes to be shared. It is not truly a "shared vision" until it connects with the personal visions of people throughout the organization.

For those in leadership positions, what is most important is to remember that their visions are still personal visions. Just because they occupy a position of leadership does not mean that their personal visions are *automatically* "the organization's vision." When I hear leaders say "our vision" and I know they are really describing "my vision," I recall Mark Twain's words that the official "we" should be reserved for "kings and people with tapeworm."

Ultimately, leaders intent on building shared visions must be willing to continually share their personal visions. They must also be prepared to ask, "Will you follow me?" This can be difficult. For a person who has been setting goals all through his career and simply announcing them, asking for support can make him feel very vulnerable.

John Kryster was the president of a large division of a leading home products company who had a vision that his division should be preeminent in its industry. This vision required not only excellent products but that the company supply the product to their "customer" (retail grocers), in a more efficient and effective manner than anyone else. He envisioned a unique worldwide distribution system that would get product to the customer in half the time and with a fraction of the cost in wastage and reshipments. He began to talk with other managers, with production workers, with distribution people, with grocers. Everyone seemed enthusiastic, but pointed up that many of his ideas could not be achieved because they contradicted so many traditional policies of the corporate parent.

In particular, Kryster needed the support of the head of product distribution, Harriet Sullivan, who—while technically Kryster's peer in the firm's matrix organization—had fifteen years more experience. Kryster prepared an elaborate presentation for Sullivan to show her the merits of his new distribution ideas. But for every piece of supporting data he offered, Sullivan had a countering criticism. Kryster left the meeting thinking that the doubters were probably right.

Then he conceived of a way to test the new system out in only one geographic market. The risk would be less, and he could gain the support of the local grocery chain which had been especially enthusiastic about the concept. But what should he do about Harriet Sullivan? His instincts were just not to tell her. After all, he had the authority to undertake the experiment himself, using his own distribution people. Yet, he also valued Sullivan's experience and judgment.

After a week of mulling it over, Kryster went back to ask for Sullivan's support. This time, though, he left his charts and data at home. He just told her why he believed in the idea, how it could forge a new partnership with customers, and how its merits could be tested with low risk. To his surprise, the crusty distribution chief started to offer help in designing the experiment. "When you came to me last week," she said, "you were trying to convince me. Now, you're willing to test your idea. I still think it's wrongheaded, but I can see you care a great deal. So, who knows, maybe we'll learn something.''

That was five years ago. Today, John Kryster's innovative distribution system is used worldwide by almost all the corporation's divisions. It has significantly reduced costs and been part of broad strategic alliances the corporation is learning to forge with retail chains.

When visions start in the middle of an organization the process of sharing and listening is essentially the same as when they originate at the top. But it may take longer, especially if the vision has implications for the entire organization.

Bart Bolton was a middle manager in IS (Information Systems) at Digital Equipment Corporation when, back in 1981, he and a small group of colleagues began to form an idea of Digital as an interconnected organization. "A group of us had been together at a workshop, and when we came back we just started talking about how we were going to turn around IS. The fundamental problem as we all saw it was that there simply was no IS vision. Everyone argued about the 'how to's' but no one knew the 'what.' Yet, we felt we could see an end result that was really worth going for. We didn't know exactly what it would look like, but the idea of tying the organization together electronically just felt 'right.' Given our products and technology we could become one of the first, if not the first large corporation that was totally and completely electronically interconnected." The idea was so exciting that he couldn't sleep much for several days as he thought about the implications.

But in 1981, no one had any idea how this could be done. "It was simply beyond the realm of what was possible at that time. We could transfer files between computers, but we couldn't network. There was some networking software under development but there were lots of problems with it. Perhaps, if we worked really hard at it we could interconnect ten or twenty machines, but no one even dreamed of interconnecting a hundred machines, let alone thousands. Looking back, it was like they say about Kennedy when he announced the 'Man on the Moon' vision—we knew about 15 percent of what we needed to know to get there. But we knew it was right."

Bolton and his compatriots had no "authority" to pursue the idea, but they couldn't stop thinking about it. In November 1981, he wrote a short paper which he read to all the senior IS people at a staff meeting. In it he said that the organization of the future would involve new IS technologies, would see "data as a resource just like the organization of the past saw capital and people as resources,'' and that "networks would tie together all the functions.'' "When I finished, no one spoke. It was like being in church. I really thought I'd blown it. My boss, Al Crawford, the head of IS, suggested a ten-minute break. When people came back, all they wanted to know was, 'How do we promote it? How can we make it happen?' My only response was, 'This has got to be your vision not mine, or it will never happen.' "

"I knew the guys at the top had to be 'enrolled,' and my job was to help them lead. By enrolling others, they too would become messengers." An IS group prepared a 35-mm slide show to be used by Crawford throughout the organization. He came up with the image of "wiring up the corporation." "It became incredibly exciting," says Bolton, "to watch the vision build, each person adding something new, refining it and making it come alive. We literally began talking about the 'copper wires running around the world.' "

Crawford presented the slide show to all Digital's major functional staffs in 1982. The idea, "the what," started to take hold. Then the IS organization created five overlapping programs to tackle the "how to's": a network program, a data program, an office automation program, a facilities program, and an applications program. By 1985 the first network was in place. By 1987, over 10,000 computers were on line. Today, Digital has over 600 facilities in over 50 countries and they are all interconnected. There are over 43,000 computers interconnected. Digital is now seen by experts as one of the pioneer "networked organizations." Moreover, the "networked organization" is a dominant theme in Digital's marketing strategy and advertising.

Organizational consultant Charlie Kiefer says that, "Despite the excitement that a vision generates, the process of building shared vision is not always glamorous. Managers who are skilled at building shared visions talk about the process in ordinary terms. 'Talking about our vision' just gets woven into day-to-day life. Most artists don't get very excited about the *process of* creating art. They get excited about the results." Or, as Bill O'Brien puts it, "Being a visionary leader is not about giving speeches and inspiring the troops. How I spend my day is pretty much the same as how any executive spends his day. Being a visionary leader is about solving day-to-day problems with my vision in mind."

Visions that are truly shared take time to emerge. They grow as a by-product of interactions of individual visions. Experience suggests that visions that are genuinely shared require ongoing conversation where individuals not only feel free to express their dreams, but learn how to listen to each others' dreams. Out of this listening, new insights into what is possible gradually emerge.

Listening is often more difficult than talking, especially for strong-willed managers with definite ideas of what is needed. It requires extraordinary openness and willingness to entertain a diversity of ideas. This does not imply that we must sacrifice our vision "for the larger cause." Rather, we must allow multiple visions to coexist, listening for the right course of action that transcends and unifies all our individual visions. As one highly successful CEO expressed it: "My job, fundamentally, is listening to what the organization is trying to say, and them making sure that it is forcefully articulated."

SPREADING VISIONS:
ENROLLMENT, COMMITMENT, AND COMPLIANCE[10]

Few subjects are closer to the heart of contemporary managers than commitment. Prodded by studies showing that most American workers acknowledge low levels of commitment[11] and by tales of foreign competitors' committed work forces, managers have turned to "management by commitment," "high commitment work systems," and other approaches. Yet, real commitment is still rare in today's organizations. It is our experience that, 90 percent of the time, what passes for commitment is compliance.

Today, it is common to hear managers talk of getting people to "buy into" the vision. For many, I fear, this suggests a sales process, where I sell and you buy. Yet, there is a world of difference between "selling" and "enrolling." "Selling" generally means getting someone to do something that he might not do if they were in full possession of all the facts. "Enrolling," by contrast, literally means "placing one's name on the roll." Enrollment implies free choice, while "being sold" often does not.

"Enrollment is the process," in Kiefer's words, "of becoming part of something by choice." "Committed" describes a state of being not only enrolled but feeling fully responsible for making the vision happen. I can be thoroughly enrolled in your vision. I can genuinely want it to occur. Yet, it is still your vision. I will take actions as need arises, but I do not spend my waking hours looking for what to do next.

For example, people are often enrolled in social causes out of genuine desire, for example, to see particular inequities righted. Once a year they might make a donation to help in a fund-raising campaign. But when they are committed, the "cause" can count on them. They will do whatever it takes to make the vision real. The vision is pulling them to action. Some use the term "being source" to describe the unique energy that committed people bring toward creating a vision.

In most contemporary organizations, there are relatively few people enrolled—and even fewer committed. The great majority of people are in a state of "compliance." "Compliant" followers go along with a vision. They do what is expected of them. They support the vision, to some degree. But, they are not truly enrolled or committed.

Compliance is often confused with enrollment and commitment. In part, this occurs because compliance has prevailed for so long in most organizations, we don't know how to recognize real commitment. It is also because there are several levels of compliance, some of which lead to behavior that looks a great deal like enrollment and commitment:

POSSIBLE ATTITUDES TOWARD A VISION

Commitment: Wants it. Will make it happen. Creates whatever "laws" (structures) are needed.

Enrollment: Wants it. Will do whatever can be done within the "spirit of the law."

Genuine compliance: Sees the benefits of the vision. Does everything expected and more. Follows the "letter of the law." "Good soldiers."

Formal compliance: On the whole, sees the benefits of the vision. Does what's expected and no more. "Pretty good soldier."

Grudging compliance: Does not see the benefits of the vision. But, also, does not want to lose job. Does enough of what's expected because he has to, but also lets it be known that he is not really on board.

Noncompliance: Does not see benefits of vision and will not do what's expected. "I won't do it; you can't make me."

Apathy: Neither for nor against vision. No interest. No energy. "Is it five o'clock yet?"

The speed limit is fifty-five in most states in the United States today. A person who was genuinely compliant would never drive more than fifty-five. A person formally compliant could drive sixty to sixty-five because in most states you will not get a ticket so long as you are below sixty-five. Someone grudgingly compliant would stay below sixty-five and complain continually about it. A noncompliant driver would "floor it" and do everything possible to evade troopers. On the other hand, a person who was genuinely committed to a fifty-five mph speed limit would drive that speed even if it were not the legal limit.

In most organizations, most people are in states of formal or genuine compliance with respect to the organization's goals and ground rules. They go along with "the program," sincerely trying to contribute. On the other hand, people in noncompliance or grudging compliance usually stand out. They are opposed to the goals or ground rules and let their opposition be known, either through inaction or (if they are grudgingly compliant) through "malicious obedience"— "I'll do it just to prove that it won't work." They may not speak out publicly against the organization's goals, but their views are known nonetheless (They often reserve their truest sentiments for the rest room or the cocktail lounge.)

Differences between the varying states of compliance can be subtle. Most problematic is the state of genuine compliance, which is often mistaken for enrollment or commitment. The prototypical "good soldier" of genuine compliance will do whatever is expected of him, willingly. "I believe in the people behind the vision; I'll do whatever is needed, and more, to the fullest of my ability." In his own mind, the person operating in genuine compliance often thinks of himself as committed. He is, in fact, committed, but only to being "part of the team."

In fact, from his *behavior* on the job, it is often very difficult to distinguish someone who is genuinely compliant from someone who is enrolled or committed. An organization made up of genuinely compliant people would be light-years ahead of most organizations in productivity and cost effectiveness. People would not have to be told what to do more than once. They would be responsive. They would be upbeat and positive in their attitude and manner. They might also be a bit "drone-like," but not necessarily. If what was expected of high performers was to "take initiative" and be "proactive," they would exhibit those behaviors as well. In short, people in genuine compliance would do whatever they could to play by the "rules of the game," both the formal and subtle rules.

Yet, there *is* a world of difference between compliance and commitment. The committed person brings an energy, passion, and excitement that cannot be generated if you are only compliant, even genuinely compliant. The committed person doesn't play by the "rules of the game." He is responsible for the game. If the rules of the game stand in the way of achieving the vision, he will find ways to change the rules. A group of people truly committed to a common vision is an awesome force. They can accomplish the seemingly impossible.

Tracy Kidder, in his Pulitzer-prize-winning book *The Soul of a New Machine,* tells the story of a product development team at Data General, brought together by a talented team leader to create an ambitious new computer. Against a business atmosphere of urgency bordering on crisis, the team turned out a ground-breaking computer in remarkable time. Visiting with the team manager Tom West in the book, and team members several years later, I learned just how remarkable their feat was. They told me of a stage in their project where certain critical software was several months behind schedule. The three engineers responsible came into the office one evening and left the next morning. By all accounts they accomplished two to three months of work that evening—and no one could explain how. These are not the feats of compliance.

What then is the difference between being genuinely compliant and enrolled and committed? The answer is deceptively simple. People who are enrolled or committed truly *want* the vision. Genuinely compliant people accept the vision. They may want it in order to get something else—for example, to keep their job, or to make their boss happy, or to get a promotion. But they do not truly want the vision in and of itself. It is not their own vision (or, at least, they do not know that it is their own vision).

Highly desired, shared commitment to a vision can be an elusive goal. One executive VP at a consumer goods company deeply desired to turn the very traditional organization into a world-class competitor by developing shared commitment to a new business vision. But after a year's effort, people continued to follow orders and do what they were told.

At this point he began to see the depth of the problem. People in his organization had *never been asked to commit to anything in their careers*. All they had ever been asked to do was be compliant. That was all they knew how to do. That was their only mental model. No matter what he said about developing a real vision, about being truly committed, it didn't matter because they heard it within their model of compliance.

Once he grasped this, he shifted tactics. He asked, "What might people be able to commit to?" He initiated a "wellness program," reasoning if there was anything to which people might become committed, it would be their own health. Over time, some did. They began to see that true commitment was possible in the workplace, and a near "ear" for the vision was opened.

Traditional organizations did not care about enrollment and commitment. The command and control hierarchy required only compliance. Still, today, many managers are justifiably wary of whether the energy released through commitment can be controlled and directed. So, we settle for compliance and content ourselves with moving people up the compliance ladder.

GUIDELINES FOR ENROLLMENT AND COMMITMENT

Enrollment is a natural process that springs from your genuine enthusiasm for a vision and your willingness to let others come to their own choice.

- *Be enrolled yourself*. There is no point attempting to encourage another to be enrolled when you are not. That is "selling," not enrolling and will, at best, produce a form of superficial agreement and compliance. Worse, it will sow the seeds for future resentment.
- *Be on the level*. Don't inflate benefits or sweep problems under the rug. Describe the vision as simply and honestly as you can.
- *Let the other person choose*. You don't have to "convince" another of the benefits of a vision. In fact, efforts you might make

to persuade him to "become enrolled" will be seen as manipulative and actually preclude enrollment. The more willing you are for him to make a free choice, the freer he will feel. This can be especially difficult with subordinates, who are often conditioned to feel as though they must go along. But you can still help by creating the time and safety for them to develop their own sense of vision.

There are many times when managers need compliance. They may want enrollment or commitment, but cannot accept anything below formal compliance. If that is the case, I recommend that you be on the level about it: "I know you may not agree wholeheartedly with the new direction, but at this juncture it is where the management team is committed to heading. I need your support to help it happen." Being open about the need for compliance removes hypocrisy. It also makes it easier for people to come to their choices, which may, over time, include enrollment.

The hardest lesson for many managers to face is that, ultimately, *there is nothing you can do to get another person to enroll or commit*. Enrollment and commitment require freedom of choice. The guidelines above simply establish conditions most favorable to enrollment, but they do not *cause* enrollment. Commitment likewise is very personal; efforts to force it will, at best, foster compliance.

ANCHORING VISION IN A
SET OF GOVERNING IDEAS

Building shared vision is actually only one piece of a larger activity: developing the "governing ideas" for the enterprise, its vision, purpose or mission, and core values. A vision not consistent with values that people live by day by day will not only fail to inspire genuine enthusiasm, it will often foster outright cynicism.

These governing ideas answer three critical questions: "What?" "Why?" and "How?"

- Vision is the "What?"—the picture of the future we seek to create.
- Purpose (or "mission") is the "Why?" the organization's answer to the question, "Why do we exist?" Great organizations have a larger sense of purpose that transcends providing for the needs

of shareholders and employees. They seek to contribute to the world in some unique way, to add a distinctive source of value.

• Core values answer the question "How do we want to act, consistent with our mission, along the path toward achieving our vision? "A company's values might include integrity, openness, honesty, freedom, equal opportunity, leanness, merit, or loyalty. They describe how the company wants life to be on a day-to-day basis, while pursuing the vision.

Taken as a unit, all three governing ideas answer the question, "What do we believe in?" When Matsushita employees recite the company creed: "To recognize our responsibilities as industrialists, to foster progress, to promote the general welfare of society, and to devote ourselves to the further development of world culture," they're describing the company *purpose*. When they sing the company song, about "sending our goods to the people of the world, endlessly and continuously, like water gushing from a fountain," they're proclaiming the corporate *vision*. And when they go to in-house training programs that cover such topics as "fairness," "harmony and cooperation," "struggle for betterment," "courtesy and humility," and "gratitude," the employees are learning the company's deliberately constructed *values*. (Matsushita, in fact, calls them its "spiritual values.") [12]

At Hanover Insurance, articulating all three of these "governing ideas" made an enormous difference in the firm's revival from near bankruptcy to a leader in the property and liability industry. Hanover's experience also illustrates the interdependencies among vision, values, and purpose.

"Early on," says O'Brien, "we recognized that there is a burning need for people to feel part of an ennobling mission. If it is absent many will seek fulfillment only in outside interests instead of in their work.

"But we also discovered that stating a mission or purpose in words was not enough. It ends up sounding like 'apple pie and motherhood.' People need visions to make the purpose more concrete and tangible. We had to learn to 'paint pictures' of the type of organization we wanted to be. My simple vision for the company is 'unquestioned superiority.' This simple term has great meaning for me. It leads me to envision an organization that serves the customer in unique ways, maintains a reputation for quality and responsibility, and creates a unique environment for its employees.

"Core values are necessary to help people with day-to-day decision making. Purpose is very abstract. Vision is long term. People need 'guiding stars' to navigate and make decisions day to day. But core values are only helpful if they can be translated into concrete behaviors. For example, one of our core values is 'openness,' which we worked long and hard to understand—finally recognizing that it requires the skills of reflection and inquiry within an overall context of trusting and supporting one another."

POSITIVE VERSUS NEGATIVE VISION

"What do we want?" is different from "What do we want to avoid?" This seems obvious, but in fact negative visions are probably more common than positive visions. Many organizations truly pull together only when their survival is threatened. They focus on avoiding what people don't want—being taken over, going bankrupt, losing jobs, not losing market share, having no downturns in earnings, or "not letting our competitors beat us to market with our next new product." Negative visions are, if anything, even more common in public leadership, where societies are continually bombarded with visions of "anti-drugs," "anti-smoking," "anti-war," or "anti-nuclear energy."

Negative visions are limiting for three reasons. First, energy that could build something new is diverted to "preventing" something we don't want to happen. Second, negative visions carry a subtle yet unmistakable message of powerlessness: our people really don't care. They can pull together only when there is sufficient threat. Lastly, negative visions are inevitably short term. The organization is motivated so long as the threat persists. Once it leaves, so does the organization's vision and energy.

There are two fundamental sources of energy that can motivate organizations: fear and aspiration. The power of fear underlies negative visions. The power of aspiration drives positive visions. Fear can produce extraordinary changes in short periods, but aspiration endures as a continuing source of learning and growth.

CREATIVE TENSION AND
COMMITMENT TO THE TRUTH

In Chapter 9 ("Personal Mastery"), I argued that personal vision, by itself, is not the key to more effective creativity. The key is "creative tension," the tension between vision and reality. The most effective people are those who can "hold" their vision while remaining committed to seeing current reality clearly.

This principle is no less true for organizations. The hallmark of a learning organization is not lovely visions floating in space, but a relentless willingness to examine "what is" in light of our vision.

IBM in the early 1960s, for example, carried out an extraordinary series of experiments in pursuit of a daring vision, a single family of computers that would make virtually all its previous machines obsolete. In the words of a *Fortune* writer, IBM staked "its treasure, its reputation, and its position of leadership in the computer field" on a radical new concept: a series of compatible machines serving the broadest possible range of applications, from the most sophisticated scientific applications to the relatively small business needs.[13]

Jay Forrester once remarked that the hallmark of a great organization is "how quickly bad news travels upward." IBM's capacity to recognize and learn from its mistakes proved pivotal during this period. One of the most discouraging was an early attempt at a high-end machine called "Stretch," introduced in 1960. IBM CEO Tom Watson, Jr., effectively killed the project in May 1961, after only a few had been sold. (Watson cut Stretch's hefty $13.5 million price tag almost in half, thereby making it uneconomical to produce.) To him, there was little choice: the machine did not satisfy its customers, never achieving more than 70 percent of its promised specifications. A few days later, Watson spoke candidly to an industry group. "Our greatest mistake in Stretch," he said, "is that we walked up to the plate and pointed at the center field stands. When we swung, it was not a homer but a hard line drive to the outfield. We're going to be a good deal more careful about what we promise in the future."

Indeed they were. Under the direction of many of the same men who had learned from Stretch, IBM introduced the System 360 three years later, which proved to be the platform for its extraordinary growth over the next ten years.

SHARED VISION
AND THE FIFTH DISCIPLINE

WHY VISIONS DIE PREMATURELY

Many visions never take root and spread—despite having intrinsic merit. Several "limits to growth" structures can come into play to arrest the building of momentum behind a new vision. Understanding these structures can help considerably in sustaining the "visioning process."

Visions spread because of a reinforcing process of increasing clarity, enthusiasm, communication and commitment. As people talk, the vision grows clearer. As it gets clearer, enthusiasm for its benefits builds.

And soon, the vision starts to spread in a reinforcing spiral of communication and excitement. Enthusiasm can also be reinforced by early successes in pursuing the vision (another potential reinforcing process, not shown on this diagram).

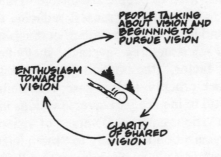

If the reinforcing process operated unfettered, it would lead to continuing growth in clarity and shared commitment toward the vision, among increasing numbers of people. But any of a variety of limiting factors can come into play to slow down this virtuous cycle.

The visioning process can wither if, as more people get involved, the diversity of views dissipates focus and generates unmanageable conflicts. People see different ideal futures. Must those who do not agree immediately with the emerging shared vision change their views? Do they conclude that the vision is "set in stone" and no longer influenceable? Do they feel that their own visions even matter? If the answer to any of these questions is "yes," the enrolling process can grind to a halt with a wave of increasing polarization.

This is a classic "limits to growth" structure, where the reinforcing process of growing enthusiasm for the vision interacts with a "balancing process" that limits the spread of the visions, due to increasing diversity and polarization:

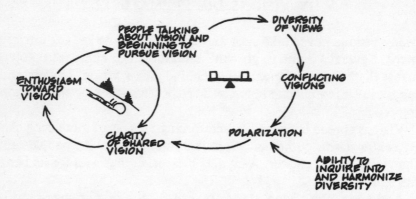

Reading clockwise around the balancing circle, from the top: As enthusiasm builds, more people are talking about the vision, the diversity of views increases, leading to people expressing potentially conflicting visions. If other people are unable to allow this diversity to be expressed, polarization increases, reducing the clarity of the shared visions, and limiting the growth of enthusiasm.

In limits to growth structures, leverage usually lies in understanding the "limiting factor," the implicit goal or norm that drives the balancing feedback process. In this case, that limiting factor is the ability (or inability) to inquire into diverse visions in such a way that deeper, common visions emerge. Diversity of visions will grow until it exceeds the organization's capacity to "harmonize" diversity.

The most important skills to circumvent this limit are the "reflection and inquiry" skills developed in Chapter 10, "Mental Models." In effect, the visioning process is a special type of inquiry process. It is an inquiry into the future we truly seek to create. If it becomes a pure advocacy process, it will result in compliance, at best, not commitment.

Approaching the visioning as an inquiry process does not mean that I have to give up my view. On the contrary, visions need strong advocates. But advocates who can also inquire into others' visions open the possibility for the vision to evolve, to become "larger" than our individual visions. *That* is the principle of the hologram.

Visions can also die because people become discouraged by the apparent difficulty in bringing the vision into reality. As clarity about the nature of the vision increases so does awareness of the gap between the vision and current reality. People become disheartened, uncertain, or even cyncial, leading to a decline in enthusiasm. The limits to growth structure for "organizational discouragement" looks like this:

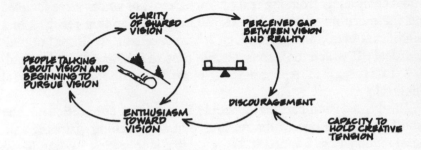

In this structure, the limiting factor is the capacity of people in the organization to "hold" creative tension, the central principle of personal mastery. This is why we say that personal mastery is the "bedrock" for developing shared vision—organizations that do not encourage personal mastery find it very difficult to foster sustained commitment to a lofty vision.

Emerging visions can also die because people get overwhelmed by the demands of current reality and lose their focus on the vision. The limiting factor becomes the time and energy to focus on a vision:

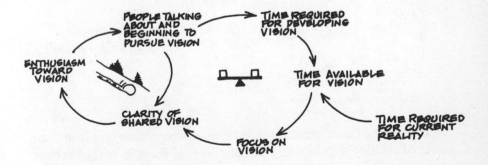

In this case, the leverage must lie in either in finding ways to focus less time and effort on fighting crises and managing current reality, or to break off those pursuing the new vision from those responsible for handling "current reality." In many ways, this is the strategy of "skunk works," small groups that quietly pursue new ideas out of the organizational mainstream. While this approach is often necessary, it is difficult to avoid fostering two polar extreme "camps" that no longer can support one another. For example, the group that developed the Macintosh computer in the early 1980s broke off almost completely from the rest of Apple, most of whom were focused on the more mundane Apple II. While the separation resulted in a significant breakthrough product, it also created a significant organizational rift which took considerable time to heal and led John Sculley to reorganize Apple into a more conventionally functional hierarchy.[14]

Lastly, a vision can die if people forget their connection to one another. This is one of the reasons that approaching visioning as a joint inquiry is so important. Once people stop asking "What do we really want to create?" and begin proselytizing the "official vision," the quality of ongoing conversation, and the quality of relationships nourished through that conversation, erodes. One of the deepest desires underlying shared vision is the desire to be connected, to a larger purpose *and* to one another. The spirit of connection is fragile. It is undermined whenever we lose our respect for one another and for each other's views. We then split into insiders and outsiders— those who are "true believers" in the vision and those who are not. When this happens, the "visioning" conversations no longer build genuine enthusiasms toward the vision:

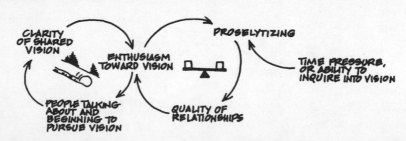

The limiting factor when people begin proselytizing and lose their sense of relationship can be time or skills. If there is great urgency to "sign up" for the new vision, people may just not perceive that there is time to really talk and listen to one another. This will be especially likely if people are also unskilled in how to have such a conversation, how to share their vision in such a way that they are not proselytizing, but are encouraging others to reflect on their own visions.

THE MISSING SYNERGY:
SHARED VISION AND SYSTEMS THINKING

I believe that the discipline of building shared vision lacks a critical underpinning if practiced without systems thinking. Vision paints the picture of what we want to create. Systems thinking reveals how we have created what we currently have.

In recent years, many leaders have jumped on to the vision band-wagon. They've developed corporate vision and mission statements. They've worked to enroll everyone in the vision. Yet, the expected surges in productivity and competitiveness often fail to arrive. This has led many to become disaffected with vision and visioning. The fad cycle has run its course, and the "baby" is about to be "thrown out with the bath water."

The problem lies not in shared visions themselves, so long as they are developed carefully. The problem lies in our reactive orientation toward current reality. Vision becomes a living force only when people truly believe they can shape their future. The simple fact is that most managers do not *experience* that they are contributing to creating their current reality. So they don't see how they can contribute toward changing that reality. Their problems are created by somebody "out there" or by "the system."

This attitude can be elusive to pin down because in many organizations the belief "We cannot create our future" is so threatening that it can never be acknowledged. There is a strong "espoused view" that being a good manager and leader means being "proactive," being in charge of your own destiny. A person who questions publicly that the organization can achieve what it has set out to do is quickly labeled as "not on board" and seen as a problem.

Yet, this "can do" optimism is a thin veneer over a fundamentally reactive view, because most organizations are dominated by linear thinking, not systems thinking. The dominance of the "event mentality" tells people that the name of the game is reacting to change, not generating change. An event orientation will eventually drive out real vision, leaving only hollow "vision statements," good ideas that are never taken to heart.

But as people in an organization begin to learn *how* existing policies and actions are creating their current reality, a new, more fertile soil for vision develops. A new source of confidence develops, rooted in deeper understanding of the forces shaping current reality and where there is leverage for influencing those forces. I'll always remember a manager emerging from an extended "microworld" session at one of the companies in our research program. When asked what he had learned, he replied: "I discovered that the reality we have is only one of several possible realities."

12

TEAM LEARNING

THE POTENTIAL WISDOM TEAMS

"By design and by talent," wrote basketball player Bill Russell of his team, the Boston Celtics, "[we] were a team of specialists, and like a team of specialists in any field, our performance depended both on individual excellence and on how well we worked together. None of us had to strain to understand that we had to complement each others' specialties; it was simply a fact, and we all tried to figure out ways to make our combination more effective. . . . Off the court, most of us were oddballs by society's standards—not the kind of people who blend in with others or who tailor their personalities to match what's expected of them." [1]

Russell is careful to tell us that it's not friendship, it's a different kind of team relationship that made his team's work special. That relationship, more than any individual triumph, gave him his greatest moments in the sport: "Every so often a Celtic game would heat up so that it became more than a physical or even mental game," he wrote, "and would be magical. The feeling is difficult to describe, and I certainly never talked about it when I was playing. When it happened I could feel my play rise to a new level . . . It would surround not only me and the other Celtics but also the players on the other team, and even the referees . . . At that special level, all sorts of odd things happened. The game would be in the white heat of competition, and yet I wouldn't feel competitive, which is a miracle in itself . . . The game would move so fast that every fake, cut, and pass would be surprising, and yet nothing could surprise me. It was almost as if we were playing in slow motion. During those spells, I could almost sense how the next play would develop and where the next shot would be taken . . . To me, the key was that *both* teams had to be playing at their peaks, and they had to be competitive. . . ."

Russell's Celtics (winner of eleven world championships in thirteen years) demonstrate a phenomenon we have come to call "alignment," when a group of people function as a whole. In most teams, the energies of individual members work at cross purposes. If we drew a picture of the team as a collection of individuals with different degrees of "personal power" (ability to accomplish intended results) headed in different directions in their lives, the picture might look something like this:[2]

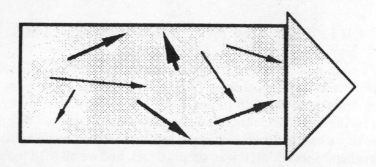

The fundamental characteristic of the relatively unaligned team is wasted energy. Individuals may work extraordinarily hard, but their efforts do not efficiently translate to team effort. By contrast, when a team becomes more aligned, a commonality of direction emerges, and individuals' energies harmonize. There is less wasted energy. In fact, a resonance or synergy develops, like the "coherent" light of a laser rather than the incoherent and scattered light of a light bulb. There is commonality of purpose, a shared vision, and understanding of how to complement one another's efforts. Individuals do not sac-

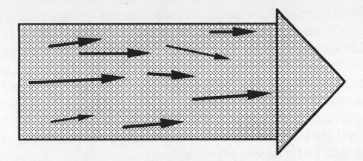

rifice their personal interests to the larger team vision; rather, the shared vision becomes an extension of their personal visions. In fact, alignment is the *necessary condition* before empowering the individual will empower the whole team. Empowering the individual when there is a relatively low level of alignment worsens the chaos and makes managing the team even more difficult:

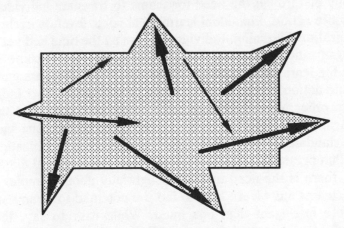

Jazz musicians know about alignment. There is a phrase in jazz, "being in the groove," that suggests the state when an ensemble "plays as one." These experiences are very difficult to put into words—jazz musicians talk about them in almost mystical terms: "the music flows through you rather than from you." But they are no less tangible for being hard to describe. I have spoken to many managers who have been members of teams that performed at similarly extraordinary levels. They will describe meetings that lasted for hours yet "flew by," not remembering "who said what, but knowing when we had really come to a shared understanding," of "never having to vote—we just got to a point of knowing what we needed to do."

Team learning is the process of aligning and developing the capacity of a team to create the results its members truly desire. It builds on the discipline of developing shared vision. It also builds on personal mastery, for talented teams are made up of talented individuals. But shared vision and talent are not enough. The world is full of teams of talented individuals who share a vision for a while, yet fail to learn. The great jazz ensemble has talent and a shared vision (even if they don't discuss it), but what really matters is that the musicians know how to *play* together.

There has never been a greater need for mastering team learning in organizations than there is today. Whether they are management teams or product development teams or cross-functional task forces —teams, "people who need one another to act," in the words of Arie de Geus, former coordinator of Group Planning at Royal Dutch/ Shell, are becoming the key learning unit in organizations. This is so because almost all important decisions are now made in teams, either directly or through the need for teams to translate individual decisions into action. Individual learning, at some level, is irrelevant for organizational learning. Individuals learn all the time and yet there is no organizational learning. But if teams learn, they become a microcosm for learning throughout the organization. Insights gained are put into action. Skills developed can propagate to other individuals and to other teams (although there is no guarantee that they will propagate). The team's accomplishments can set the tone and establish a standard for learning together for the larger organization.

Within organizations, team learning has three critical dimensions. First, there is the need to think insightfully about complex issues. Here, teams must learn how to tap the potential for many minds to be more intelligent than one mind. While easy to say, there are powerful forces at work in organizations that tend to make the intelligence of the team less than, not greater than, the intelligence of individual team members. Many of these forces are within the direct control of the team members.

Second, there is the need for innovative, coordinated action. The championship sports teams and great jazz ensembles provide metaphors for acting in spontaneous yet coordinated ways. Outstanding teams in organizations develop the same sort of relationship—an "operational trust," where each team member remains conscious of other team members and can be counted on to act in ways that complement each others' actions.

Third, there is the role of team members on other teams. For example, most of the actions of senior teams are actually carried out through other teams. Thus, a learning team continually fosters other learning teams through inculcating the practices and skills of team learning more broadly.

Though it involves individual skills and areas of understanding, team learning is a collective discipline. Thus, it is meaningless to say that "I," as an individual, am mastering the discipline of team learning, just as it would be meaningless to say that "I am mastering the practice of being a great jazz ensemble."

The discipline of team learning involves mastering the practices of dialogue and discussion, the two distinct ways that teams converse. In dialogue, there is the free and creative exploration of complex and subtle issues, a deep "listening" to one another and suspending of one's own views. By contrast, in discussion different views are presented and defended and there is a search for the best view to support decisions that must be made at this time. Dialogue and discussion are potentially complementary, but most teams lack the ability to distinguish between the two and to move consciously between them.

Team learning also involves learning how to deal creatively with the powerful forces opposing productive dialogue and discussion in working teams. Chief among these are what Chris Argyris calls "defensive routines," habitual ways of interacting that protect us and others from threat or embarrassment, but which also prevent us from learning. For example, faced with conflict, team members frequently either "smooth over" differences or "speak out" in a no-holds-barred, "winner take all" free-for-all of opinion—what my colleague Bill Isaacs calls "the abstraction wars." Yet, the very defensive routines that thwart learning also hold great potential for fostering learning, if we can only learn how to unlock the energy they contain. The inquiry and reflection skills introduced in Chapter 10 begin to release this energy, which can then be focused in dialogue and discussion.

Systems thinking is especially prone to evoking defensiveness because of its central message, that our actions create our reality. Thus, a team may resist seeing important problems more systemically. To do so would imply that the problems arise from our own policies and strategies—that is "from us"—rather than from forces outside our control. I have seen many situations where teams will say "we're already thinking systemically," or espouse a systems view, then do nothing to put it into practice, or simply hold steadfastly to the view that "there's nothing we can do except cope with these problems." All of these strategies succeed in avoiding serious examination of how their own actions may be creating the very problems with which they try so hard to cope. More than other analytic frameworks, systems thinking requires mature teams capable of inquiring into complex, conflictual issues.

Lastly, the discipline of team learning, like any discipline, requires practice. Yet, this is exactly what teams in modern organizations lack. Imagine trying to build a great theater ensemble or a great symphony orchestra without rehearsal. Imagine a championship sports team without practice. In fact, the process whereby such teams learn *is* through continual movement between practice and performance, practice, performance, practice again, perform again. We are at the very beginning of learning how to create analogous opportunities for practice in management teams—some examples are given below and in the chapter on Microworlds.

Despite its importance, team learning remains poorly understood. Until we can describe the phenomenon better, it will remain mysterious. Until we have some theory of what happens when teams learn (as opposed to individuals in teams learning), we will be unable to distinguish group intelligence from "groupthink," when individuals succumb to group pressures for conformity. Until there are reliable methods for building teams that can learn together, its occurrence will remain a product of happenstance. This is why mastering team learning will be a critical step in building learning organizations.

THE DISCIPLINE OF
TEAM LEARNING

DIALOGUE AND DISCUSSION[3]

In a remarkable book, *Physics and Beyond: Encounters and Conversations,* Werner Heisenberg (formulator of the famous "Uncertainty Principle" in modern physics) argues that "Science is rooted in conversations. The cooperation of different people may culminate in scientific results of the utmost importance." Heisenberg then recalls a lifetime of conversations with Pauli, Einstein, Bohr, and the other great figures who uprooted and reshaped traditional physics in the first half of this century. These conversations, which Heisenberg says "had a lasting effect on my thinking," literally gave birth to many of the theories for which these men eventually became famous. Heisenberg's conversations, recalled in vivid detail and emotion, illustrate the staggering potential of collaborative learning—that collectively, we can be more insightful, more intelligent than we can possibly be individually. The IQ of the team can, potentially, be much greater than the IQ of the individuals.

Given Heisenberg's reflections, it is perhaps not surprising that a significant contributor to the emerging discipline of team learning is a contemporary physicist, David Bohm. Bohm, a leading quantum theorist, is developing a theory and method of "dialogue," when a group "becomes open to the flow of a larger intelligence." Dialogue, it turns out, is a very old idea revered by the ancient Greeks and practiced by many "primitive" societies such as the American Indians. Yet, it is all but lost to the modern world. All of us have had some taste of dialogue—in special conversations that begin to have a "life of their own," taking us in directions we could never have imagined nor planned in advance. But these experiences come rarely, a product of circumstance rather than systematic effort and disciplined practice.

Bohm's recent work on the theory and practice of dialogue represents a unique synthesis of the two major intellectual currents underlying the disciplines discussed in the preceding chapters: the systems or holistic view of nature, and the interactions between our thinking and internal "models" and our perceptions and actions. "Quantum theory," says Bohm, "implies that the universe is basically an indivisible whole, even though on the larger scale level it may be represented approximately as divisible into separately existing parts. In particular, this means that, at a quantum theoretical level of accuracy, the observing instrument and the observed object participate in each other in an irreducible way. At this level perception and action therefore cannot be separated."

This is reminiscent of some of the key features of systems thinking, which calls attention to how what is happening is often the consequence of our own actions as guided by our perceptions. Similar questions are raised by the theory of relativity, as Bohm suggested in a 1965 book, *The Special Theory of Relativity*.[4] In this book, Bohm started to connect the systems perspective and mental models more explicitly. In particular, he argued that the purpose of science was not the "accumulation of knowledge" (since, after all, all scientific theories are eventually proved false) but rather the creation of "mental maps" that guide and shape our perception and action, bringing about a constant "mutual participation between nature and consciousness."

However, Bohm's most distinctive contribution, one which leads to unique insights into team learning, stems from seeing thought as "largely as collective phenomenon." Bohm became interested fairly early in the analogy between the collective properties of particles (for example, the system wide movements of an "electron sea") and the way in which our thought works. Later, he saw that this sort of analogy could throw an important light on the general "counterproductiveness of thought, as can be observed in almost every phase of life. "Our thought is incoherent," Bohm asserts, "and the resulting counterproductiveness lies at the root of the world's problems." But, Bohm asserts, since thought is to a large degree collective, we cannot just improve thought individually. "As with electrons, we must look on thought as a systemic phenomena arising from how we interact and discourse with one another."

There are two primary types of discourse, dialogue and discussion. Both are important to a team capable of continual generative learning, but their power lies in their synergy, which is not likely to be present when the distinctions between them are not appreciated.

Bohm points out that the word "discussion" has the same root as percussion and concussion. It suggests something like a "Ping-Pong game where we are hitting the ball back and forth between us." In such a game the subject of common interest may be analyzed and dissected from many points of view provided by those who take part. Clearly, this can be useful. Yet, the purpose of a game is normally "to win" and in this case winning means to have one's views accepted by the group. You might occasionally accept part of another person's view in order to strengthen your own, but you fundamentally want your view to prevail." A sustained emphasis on winning is not compatible, however, with giving first priority to coherence and truth. Bohm suggests that what is needed to bring about such a change of priorities is "dialogue," which is a different mode of communication.

By contrast with discussion, the word "dialogue" comes from the Greek *dialogos*. *Dia* means through. *Logos* means the word, or more broadly, the meaning. Bohm suggests that the original meaning of dialogue was the "meaning passing or moving through . . . a free flow of meaning between people, in the sense of a stream that flows between two banks."[5] In dialogue, Bohm contends, a group accesses a larger "pool of common meaning," which cannot be accessed individually. "The whole organizes the parts," rather than trying to pull the parts into a whole.

The purpose of a dialogue is to go beyond any one individual's understanding. "We are not trying to win in a dialogue. We all win if we are doing it right." In dialogue, individuals gain insights that simply could not be achieved individually. "A new kind of mind begins to come into being which is based on the development of a common meaning . . . People are no longer primarily in opposition, nor can they said to be interacting, rather they are participating in this pool of common meaning, which is capable of constant development and change."

In dialogue, a group explores complex difficult issues from many points of view. Individuals suspend their assumptions but they communicate their assumptions freely. The result is a free exploration that brings to the surface the full depth of people's experience and thought, and yet can move beyond their individual views.

"The purpose of dialogue," Bohm suggests, "is to reveal the incoherence in our thought." There are three types of incoherence. "Thought denies that it is participative." Thought stops tracking reality and "just goes, like a program." And thought establishes its own standard of reference for fixing problems, problems which it contributed to creating in the first place.

To illustrate, consider prejudice. Once a person begins to accept a stereotype of a particular group, that "thought" becomes an active agent, "participating" in shaping how he or she interacts with another person who falls into that stereotyped class. In turn, the tone of their interaction influences the other person's behavior. The prejudiced person can't see how his prejudice shapes what he "sees" and how he acts. In some sense, if he did, he would no longer be prejudiced. To operate, the "thought" of prejudice must remain hidden to its holder.

"Thought *presents* itself (stands in front) of us and pretends that it does not *represent*." We are like actors who forget they are playing a role. We become trapped in the theater of our thoughts (the words "theater" and "theory" have the same root—*theoria*—"to look at"). This is when thought starts, in Bohm's words, to become "incoherent." "Reality may change but the theater continues." We operate in the theater, defining problems, taking actions, "solving problems," losing touch with the larger reality from which the theater is generated.

Dialogue is a way of helping people to "see the representative and participatory nature of thought [and] . . . to become more sensitive to and make it safe to acknowledge the incoherence in our thought." *In dialogue people become observers of their own thinking.*

What they observe is that their thinking is active. For example, when a conflict surfaces in a dialogue people are likely to realize that there is a tension, but the tension arises, literally, from our thoughts. People will say, "It is our thoughts and the way we hold on to them that are in conflict, not us." Once people see the participatory nature of their thought, they begin to separate themselves from their thought. They begin to take a more creative, less reactive, stance toward their thought.

People in dialogue also begin to observe the collective nature of thought. Bohm says that "Most thought is collective in origin. Each individual does something with it," but originates collectively by and large. "Language, for example, is entirely collective," says Bohm. "And without language, thought as we know it couldn't be there." Most of the assumptions we hold were acquired from the pool of culturally acceptable assumptions. Few of us learn truly to "think for ourselves." He or she who does is sure, as Emerson said long ago, "to be misunderstood."

They also begin to observe the difference between "thinking" as an ongoing process as distinct from "thoughts," the results of that process. This is very important, according to Bohm, to begin correcting the incoherence in our thinking.

If collective thinking is an ongoing stream, "thoughts" are like leaves floating on the surface that wash up on the banks. We gather in the leaves, which we experience as "thoughts." We misperceive the thoughts as our own, because we fail to see the stream of collective thinking from which they arise.

In dialogue, people begin to see the stream that flows between the banks. They begin to "participate in this pool of common meaning, which is capable of constant development and change." Bohm believes that our normal processes of thought are like a "coarse net that gathers in only the coarsest elements of the stream. In dialogue, a "kind of sensitivity" develops that goes beyond what we normally recognize as thinking. This sensitivity is "a fine net" capable of gathering in the subtle meanings in the flow of thinking. Bohm believes this sensitivity lies at the root of real intelligence.

So, according to Bohm, collective learning is not only possible but vital to realize the potentials of human intelligence. "Through dialogue people can help each other to become aware of the incoherence in each other's thoughts, and in this way the collective thought becomes more and more coherent [from the Latin *cohaerere*— "hanging together"]. It is difficult to give a simple definition of coherence, beyond saying that one may sense it as order, consistency, beauty, or harmony.

The main point, however, is not to strive for some abstract ideal of coherence. It is rather for all the participants to work together to become sensitive to all the possible forms of *incoherence*. Incoherence may be indicated by contradictions and confusion but more basically it is seen by the fact that our thinking is producing consequences that we don't really want.

Bohm identifies three basic conditions that are necessary for dialogue:

1. all participants must "suspend" their assumptions, literally to hold them "as if suspended before us";
2. all participants must regard one another as colleagues;
3. there must be a "facilitator" who "holds the context" of dialogue.

These conditions contribute to allowing the "free flow of meaning" to pass through a group, by diminishing resistance to the flow. Just as resistance in an electrical circuit causes the flow of current to generate heat (wasted energy), so does the normal functioning of a group disspate energy. In dialogue there is "cool energy, like a superconductor." "Hot topics," subjects that would otherwise become sources of emotional discord and fractiousness become discussable. Even more, they become windows to deeper insights.

Suspending Assumptions. To "suspend" one's assumptions means to hold them, "as it were, 'hanging in front of you,' constantly accessible to questioning and observation." This does not mean throwing out our assumptions, suppressing them, or avoiding their expression. Nor, in any way, does it say that having opinions is "bad," or that we should eliminate subjectivism. Rather, it means being aware of our assumptions and holding them up for examination. This cannot be done if we are defending our opinions. Nor, can it be done if we are unaware of our assumptions, or unaware that our views are based on *assumptions,* rather than incontrovertible fact.

Bohm argues that once an individual "digs in his or her heels" and decides "this is the way it is," the flow of dialogue is blocked. This requires operating on the "knife edge," as Bohm puts it, because "the mind wants to keep moving away from suspending assumptions . . . to adopting non-negotiable and rigid opinions which we then feel compelled to defend."

For example, in a recent dialogue session involving a top management team of a highly successful technology company (reported in detail below), people perceived a deep "split" in the organization between R&D and everyone else, a split due to R&D's exalted role at the company. This split had its roots in the firm's history of a string of dramatic product innovations over the past thirty years, literally pioneering several dramatic new products that in turn became industry standards. Product innovation was the cornerstone of the firm's reputation in the marketplace. Thus, no one felt able to talk about the "split," even though it was creating many problems. To do so might have challenged the long-cherished value of technology leadership and of giving highly creative engineers the autonomy to pursue their product visions. Moreover, the number-two person in R&D was in the meeting.

When the condition of "suspending all assumptions" was discussed, the head of marketing asked, *"All* assumptions?" When he received an affirmative answer, he looked perplexed. Later, as the session continued, he acknowledged that he held the assumption that R&D saw itself as the "keeper of the flame" for the organization, and that he further assumed that this made them unapproachable regarding market information that might influence product development. This led to the R&D manager responding that he too assumed that others saw him in this light, and that, to everyone's surprise, he felt that this assumption limited his and the R&D organization's effectiveness. Both shared these assumptions *as assumptions,* not proven fact. As a result, the ensuing dialogue opened up into a dramatic exploration of views that was unprecedented in its candor and its strategy implications.

"Suspending assumptions" is a lot like seeing "leaps of abstraction" and "inquiring into the reasoning behind the abstraction," basic reflection and inquiry skills developed in Chapter 10, "Mental Models." But in dialogue, suspending assumptions must be done collectively. The team's discipline of holding assumptions "suspended" allowed the team members to see their own assumptions more clearly because they could be held up and contrasted with each others' assumptions. Suspending assumptions is difficult, Bohm maintains, because of "the very nature of thought. Thought continually deludes us into a view that 'this is the way it is.' " The team discipline of suspending assumptions is an antidote to that delusion.

Seeing Each Other as Colleagues. Dialogue can occur only when a group of people see each other as colleagues in mutual quest for deeper insight and clarity. Thinking of each other as colleagues is important because thought is participative. The conscious act of thinking of each other as colleagues contributes toward interacting as colleagues. This may sound simple, but it can make a profound difference.

Seeing each other as colleagues is critical to establish a positive tone and to offset the vulnerability that dialogue brings. In dialogue people actually feel as if they are building something, a new deeper understanding. Seeing each other as colleagues and friends, while it may sound simple, proves to be extremely important. We talk differently with friends from the way we do with people who are not friends. Interestingly, as dialogue develops, team members will find this feeling of friendship developing even towards others with whom they do not have much in common. What is necessary going in is the *willingness* to consider each other as colleagues. In addition, there is a certain vulnerability to holding assumptions in suspension. Treating each other as colleagues acknowledges the mutual risk and establishes the sense of safety in facing the risk.

Colleagueship does not mean that you need to agree or share the same views. On the contrary, the real power of seeing each other as colleagues comes into play when there are differences of view. It is easy to feel collegial when everyone agrees. When there are significant disagreements, it is more difficult. But the payoff is also much greater. Chosing to view "adversaries" as "colleagues with different views" has the greatest benefits.

Bohm has expressed doubts about the possiblity of dialogue in organizations because of the condition of colleagueship: "Hierarchy is antithetical to dialogue, and it is difficult to escape hiearchy in organizations." He asks: "Can those in authority really 'level' with those in subordinate positions?" Such questions have several operational implications for organizational teams. First, everyone involved must truly *want* the benefits of dialogue more than he wants to hold onto his privileges of rank. If one person is used to having his view prevail because he is the most senior person, then that privilege must be surrendered in dialogue. If one person is used to withholding his views because he is more junior, then that security of nondisclosure must also be surrendered. Fear and judgment must give way. Dialogue is "playful"; it requires the willingness to play with new ideas, to examine them and test them. As soon as we become overly concerned with "who said what," or "not saying something stupid," the playfulnes will evaporate.

These conditions cannot be taken lightly, but we have found many organizational teams consistently up to the challenge if everyone knows what will be expected of him in advance. Deep down, there is a longing for dialogue, especially when focused on issues of the utmost importance to us. But that doesn't mean dialogue is always possible in organizations. If all participants are not willing to live by the conditions of suspending assumptions and colleagueship, dialogue will not be possible.

A Facilitator Who "Holds the Context" of Dialogue. In the absence of a skilled faciltator, our habits of thought continually pull us toward discussion and away from dialogue. This is especially true in the early stages of developing dialogue as a team discipline. We take what "presents itself" in our thoughts as literal, rather than as a representation. We believe in our own views and want them to prevail. We are worried about suspending our assumptions publicly. We may even be uncertain if it is psychologically safe to suspend "all assumptions"—"After all, aren't there some assumptions that I must hold on to or lose my sense of identity?"

The facilitator of a dialogue session carries out many of the basic duties of a good "process facilitator." These functions include helping people maintain ownership of the process and the outcomes— we are responsible for what is happening. If people start to harbor reservations that "so and so" won't let us talk about this, that constitutes an assumption not held in suspension. The facilitator also must keep the dialogue moving. If any one individual should start to divert the process to a discussion when a discussion is not actually what is called for, this needs to be identified, and the group asked whether the conditions for dialogue are continuing to be met. The facilitator always walks a careful line between being knowledgeable and helpful in the process at hand, and yet not taking on the "expert" or "doctor" mantle that would shift attention away from the members of the team, and their own ideas and responsibility.[6]

But, in dialogue the facilitator also does something more. His understanding of dialogue allows him to influence the flow of development simply through participating. For example, after someone has made an observation, the facilitator may say, "But the opposite may also be true." Beyond such reminders of the conditions for dialogue, the facilitator's participation demonstrates dialogue. The artistry of dialogue lies in experiencing the flow of meaning and seeing the one thing that needs to be said now. Like the Quakers, who enjoin members to say not simply whatever pops into their heads but only those thoughts that are compelling (and which cause the speaker to *quake* from the need to speak them), the facilitator says only what is needed at each point in time. This deepens others' appreciation of dialogue more than any abstract explanation can ever do.

As teams develop experience and skill in dialogue, the role of the facilitator becomes less crucial and he or she can gradually become just one of the participants. Dialogue emerges from the "leaderless" group once the team members have developed their skill and understanding. In societies where dialogue is an ongoing discipline, there usually are no appointed facilitators. For example, many American Indian tribes cultivated dialogue to a high art without formal facilitators. Shamen and other wise men had special roles, but the group was capable of entering a dialogue on its own.

Balancing Dialogue and Discussion. In team learning, discussion is the necessary counterpart of dialogue. In a discussion, different views are presented and defended, and as explained earlier this may provide a useful analysis of the whole situation. In dialogue, different views are presented as a means toward discovering a new view. In a discussion, decisions are made. In a dialogue, complex issues are explored. When a team must reach agreement and decisions must be taken, some discussion is needed. On the basis of a commonly agreed analysis, alternative views need to be weighed and a preferred view selected (which may be one of the original alternatives or a new view that emerges from the discussion). When they are productive, discussions converge on a conclusion or course of action. On the other hand, dialogues are diverging; they do not seek agreement, but a richer grasp of complex issues. Both dialogue and discussion can lead to new courses of action; but actions are often the focus of discussion, whereas new actions emerge as a by-product of dialogue.

A learning team masters movement back and forth between dialogue and discussion. The ground rules are different. The goals are different. Failing to distinguish them, teams usually have neither dialogue nor productive discussions.

A unique relationship develops among team members who enter into dialogue regularly. They develop a deep trust that cannot help but carry over to discussions. They develop a richer understanding of the uniqueness of each person's point of view. Moreover, they experience how larger understandings emerge by holding one's own point of view "gently." They learn to master the art of holding a position, rather than being "held by their positions." When it is appropriate to defend a point of view, they do it more gracefully and with less rigidity, that is without putting "winning" as a first priority.

Moreover, to a large degree, the skills that allow dialogue are identical to the skills that can make discussions productive rather than destructive. These are the skills of inquiry and reflection, originally discussed in Chapter 10, "Mental Models." In fact, one of the reasons that dialogue is so important is that it offers a safe environment for honing these skills and for discovering the profound group learning that they can lead to.

Reflection, Inquiry, and Dialogue. In David Bohm's thinking we hear deep echoes of the "action science" approach discussed in Chapter 10—the importance of making one's views open to influence; and the problem of confusing our mental models with reality. What makes Bohm's work distinctive is that he is articulating a "new" vision of what can happen in a group that transcends the disabilities identified by the action scientists. Moreover, Bohm's dialogue is a *team discipline*. It cannot be achieved individually.

Part of the vision of dialogue is the assumption of a "larger pool of meaning" accessible only to a group. This idea, while it may appear radical at first, has deep intuitive appeal to managers who have long cultivated the subtler aspects of collective inquiry and consensus building.

Such managers learn early on to distinguish two types of consensus: a "focusing down" type of consensus that seeks the common denominator in multiple individual views, and an "opening up" type of consensus that seeks a picture larger than any one person's point of view. The first type of consensus builds from the "content" of our individual views—discovering what part of my view is shared by you and the others. This is our "common ground," upon which we can all agree.

The second type of consensus builds more from the idea that we each have a "view," a way of looking at reality. Each person's view is a unique perspective on a larger reality. If I can "look out" through your view and you through mine, we will each see something we might not have seen alone.

If dialogue articulates a unique vision of team learning, reflection and inquiry skills may prove essential to realizing that vision. Just as personal vision provides a foundation for building shared vision, so too do reflection and inquiry skills provide a foundation for dialogue and discussion. Dialogue that is *grounded in* reflection and inquiry skills is likely to be more reliable and less dependent on particulars of circumstance, such as the chemistry among team members.

DEALING WITH "CURRENT REALITY": CONFLICT AND DEFENSIVE ROUTINES

Contrary to popular myth, great teams are not characterized by an absence of conflict. On the contrary, in my experience, one of the most reliable indicators of a team that is continually learning is the visible conflict of ideas. In great teams conflict becomes productive. There may, and often will, be conflict around the vision. In fact, the essence of the "visioning" process lies in the gradual emergence of a shared vision from different personal visions. Even when people share a common vision, they may have many different ideas about how to achieve that vision. The loftier the vision, the more uncertain we are how it is to be achieved. The free flow of conflicting ideas is critical for creative thinking, for discovering new solutions no one individual would have come to on his own. Conflict becomes, in effect, part of the ongoing dialogue.

On the other hand, in mediocre teams, one of two conditions usually surround conflict. Either, there is an appearance of no conflict on the surface, or there is rigid polarization. In the "smooth surface" teams, members believe that they must suppress their conflicting views in order to maintain the team—if each person spoke her or his mind, the team would be torn apart by irreconcilable differences. The polarized team is one where managers "speak out," but conflicting views are deeply entrenched. Everyone knows where everyone else stands, and there is little movement.

For more than twenty-five years, Chris Argyris and his colleagues have studied the dilemma of why bright, capable managers often fail to learn effectively in management teams. Their work suggests that the difference between great teams and mediocre teams lies in how they face conflict and deal with the defensiveness that invariably surrounds conflict. "We are programmed to create defensive routines," says Argyris, "and cover them up with further defensive routines . . . This programming occurs early in life."[7]

Defensive routines, as noted in Chapter 10, "Mental Models," are entrenched habits we use to protect ourselves from the embarrassment and threat that come with exposing our thinking. Defensive routines form a sort of protective shell around our deepest assumptions, defending us against pain, but also keeping us from learning about the causes of the pain. The source of defensive routines, according to Argyris, is not belief in our views or desire to preserve social relations, as we might tell ourselves, but fear of exposing the thinking that lies behind our views. "Defensive reasoning," says Argyris ". . . protects us from learning about the validity of our reasoning."[8] For most of us, exposing our reasoning is threatening because we are afraid that people will find errors in it. The perceived threat from exposing our thinking starts early in life and, for most of us, is steadily reinforced in school—remember the trauma of being called on and not having the "right answer"—and later in work.

Defensive routines are so diverse and so commonplace, they usually go unnoticed. We say, "That's a very interesting idea," when we have no intention of taking the idea seriously. We deliberately confront someone to squash an idea, to avoid having to consider it. Or, in the guise of being helpful, we shelter someone from criticism, but also shelter ourselves from engaging difficult issues. When a difficult issue comes up, we change the subject—ostensibly out of respect for the "manners" of good behavior.

One forceful CEO recently lamented to me about the absence of "real leaders" in his organization. He felt his company was full of compliant people, not committed visionaries. This was especially frustrating to a man who regards himself as a skilled communicator and risk taker. In fact, he *is* so brilliant at articulating *his* vision that he intimidates everyone around him. Consequently, his view rarely get challenged publicly. People have learned not to express their own views and visions around him. While he would not see his own forcefulness as a defensive strategy, if he looked carefully, he would see that it functions in exactly that way.

The most effective defensive routines, like that of the forceful CEO, are those we cannot see. Ostensibly, the CEO hoped to provoke others into expressing their thoughts. But his overbearing behavior reliably prevented them from doing so, thereby protecting his own views from challenge. If expressed as a conscious strategy, the defensiveness is transparent: "Keep people on the defensive through intimidation, so they won't confront my thinking." If the CEO saw his strategy presented in such bald terms, he would almost certainly disavow it. The fact that it remains hidden to him keeps it operative.

Problems caused by defensive routines compound in organizations where to have incomplete or faulty understanding is a sign of weakness or, worse, incompetence. Deep within the mental models of managers in many organizations is the belief that managers must know what's going on. It is simply unacceptable for managers to act as though they do not know what is causing a problem. Those that reach senior positions are masters at appearing to know what is going on, and those intent on reaching such positions learn early on to develop an air of confident knowledge.

Managers who internalize this mental model find themselves in one of two binds. Some actually internalize this air of confidence and simply believe that they know the answers to most important problems. But, to protect their belief, they must close themselves to alternative views and make themselves uninfluenceable. Their bind is that to remain confident they must remain rigid. Others believe they are expected to know what is causing important problems but, deep down, recognize the uncertainty in their solutions. Their bind is that to maintain a facade of confidence they must obscure their ignorance. Whichever bind they find themselves in, managers who take on the burden of having to know the answers become highly skillful in defensive routines that preserve their aura as capable decision makers by not revealing the thinking behind their decisions.

Such defensiveness becomes an accepted part of organizational culture. Argyris says, "Whenever I ask individuals . . . what leads them to play political games in organizations? They respond that that's human nature and the nature of organizations. . . . We are the carriers of defensive routines, and organizations are the hosts. Once organizations have been infected, they too become carriers."[9]

Teams are microcosms of the larger organization, so it is not surprising that the defensive patterns characteristic of the larger organization become embedded in the team. In effect, defensive routines block the flow of energy in a team that might otherwise contribute toward a common vision. To the members of a team caught in their defensive routines, they feel very much like walls—blocks and traps that prevent collective learning.

To see how subtle team defensive routines become, consider the case of ATP products: a young division of an innovative, highly decentralized corporation. (The company and individual names are disguised.) Jim Tabor, the thirty-three-year-old division president, was deeply committed to the corporate values of freedom and local autonomy. He believed strongly in ATP's products, which were

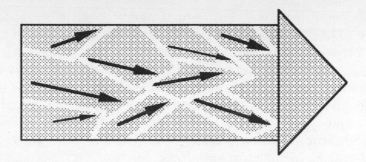

based on a new printed circuit board technology. He was tremendously enthusiastic, a natural cheerleader for his people. In turn, the members of his management team worked long hours and shared his enthusiasm for their prospects.

Their efforts were rewarded with several years of rapid (30 to 50 percent per year) growth in bookings, reaching $20 million in sales in 1984. However, 1985 witnessed a disastrous collapse in bookings.[10] Two major minicomputer manufacturers had become so convinced of ATP's technology that they had designed the ATP circuit boards into new lines of hardware. But when the 1985 downturn in the minicomputer industry hit, the manufacturers suspended work on the new lines, leaving ATP with a 50 percent shortfall on projected bookings. The business did not bounce back in 1986. Jim Tabor was eventually removed as division president, although he stayed on as engineering manager.

What went wrong at ATP? Through their enthusiasm, the ATP management had locked itself into a strategy that was internally inconsistent. The team had set aggressive growth targets, in part to please the corporate management, but also because of belief in their product. Meeting these targets had created strong pressures on the sales force, to which they had responded by building major business relationships with a few key customers, customers upon whom ATP had become highly dependent. When some of those customers ran into their own business troubles, ATP was doomed.

Why had ATP's management team sanctioned a strategy that left the division so vulnerable? Why did the corporate leadership not intervene to insist that the young division managers diversify their customer base? At the heart of their problem was a set of defensive routines, embedded in a "shifting the burden" structure.

As Argyris says, defensive routines are a response to a problem; here, the problem is a need to learn, arising from a "learning gap"

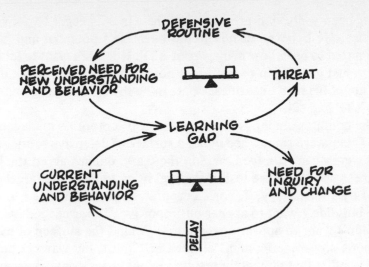

between what is known and what needs to be known. The "fundamental solution" is inquiry that results eventually in new understanding and new behavior—that is, learning. But the need for learning also creates a threat. Individuals and teams respond defensively to the threat. This leads to the "symptomatic solution": defensive routines that eliminate the learning gap by reducing the *perceived need* for learning.

All the key players at ATP were caught in their own particular defensive routines. Several of ATP's managers had expressed concern about their reliance on a narrow customer base. When the issue was raised in team meetings, everyone agreed it was a problem. But no one did anything about it because everyone was too busy. Driven by their challenging growth targets, ATP's managers had expanded capacity aggressively and created powerful pressures for new order bookings, regardless of where they came from.

The corporate managers to whom Tabor reported were caught in a similar bind. Here too there was concern about ATP's narrow customer base. Privately, some of the corporate managers had questions regarding Tabor's ability to build for long-term growth. But these same executives also believed strongly in a corporate philosophy of not undermining division presidents' authority to run their own businesses. They were uncertain how to raise their qualms without seeming unsupportive of Tabor's leadership, so they made only oblique comments or kept quiet.

On the other side of the table, Jim Tabor had questions himself, which he was reticent to raise in meetings with his superiors. He had never been a division president before. He was eager to prove his abilities. He believed deeply in the business's potential and he felt committed to his fellow managers at ATP. He didn't want to let them down, just as he didn't want to let down his superiors. So he didn't talk about his own uneasiness concerning the aggressive growth targets ATP had set.

The conflicts among ATP's management, corporate management, and Tabor were submerged under a surface of defensive routines and thus were never resolved. Within the team, qualms about the basic business strategy were lost in the pressures to meet the targets dictated by the strategy. Tabor's corporate superiors wanted to offer help but didn't want to appear unsupportive. Tabor needed help but he didn't want to appear unconfident. Behind the surface of mutual support, camaraderie, and "all for one" spirit, lay ways of dealing with conflict that ultimately resulted in outcomes contrary to everyone's intentions.

The more effective defensive routines are, the more effectively they cover up underlying problems, the less effectively these problems are faced, and the worse the problems tend to become. The real need to learn didn't go away at ATP. By avoiding the real problems —how to build up a broad customer base—they allowed the problems to get worse. As in all shifting the burden structures, the more teams turn to defensive routines, the more they come to rely on them. "The paradox," writes Argyris, "is that when [defensive routines] succeed in preventing immediate pain they also prevent us from learning how to reduce what causes the pain in the first place." [11]

As Argyris also says, defensive routines are "self-sealing"—they obscure their own existence. This comes in large measure because we have society-wide norms that say that we *should* be open and that defensiveness is bad. This makes it difficult to acknowledge defensive routines, even if we know that we are being defensive. If Tabor's corporate superiors had stated their strategy explicitly, it would have sounded something like the following: "We are avoiding questioning Jim's abilities, to avoid having to face the conflict that would ensue and to maintain an appearance of support." If such a strategy were stated, they would surely have eschewed it. Likewise, if Tabor had said, "I am avoiding expressing my doubts about how we are managing because I am afraid that it will make me look weak or incompetent," his defensive strategy would have been unsustainable. But no one voiced these feelings because of the same basic fears that made everyone take up the defensive routines in the first place.

If you can't easily state defensive routines, where is the leverage for reducing them? In most shifting the burden structures, there are two possible areas of leverage: (1) weaken the symptomatic solution and (2) strengthen the fundamental solution. One way of weakening the symptomatic solution is diminishing the emotional threat that prompts the defensive response in the first place. For example, if Tabor had felt comfortable about acknowledging his own uncertainty in front of his corporate superiors, or if they had felt comfortable raising their questions, each would have been less inclined to avoiding fundamental questioning of ATP's strategy.[12] Learning how to deal with defensive routines when they arise would also weaken the symptomatic solution. To retain their power, defensive routines *must remain undiscussable*. Teams stay stuck in their defensive routines only when they pretend that they don't have any defensive routines, that everything is all right, and that they can say "anything."

But how to make them discussable is a challenge. Trying to "fix" another person's defensive routine is almost guaranteed to backfire. For example, try asking someone why he has been behaving defensively. Universally, the first response is a protest: "Me? I'm not behaving defensively!" By focusing attention on the other person, the "confronter" has taken no responsibility for the situation. It *always* takes two (or more) to dance. If we perceive a defensive routine operating, it is a good bet that we are part of it. Skillful managers learn to confront defensiveness without producing more defensiveness.

They do so by self-disclosure and by inquiring into the causes of their own defensiveness. For example, they might say something such as, "I notice that I am feeling threatened by this new proposal. You may be also. Could you help me in seeing where this uneasiness is coming from?" Or, "Is what I am saying making sense? I think that the way I am communicating makes me seem closed and adamant on this point. But I'd like to hear your view so that we can get a more objective picture." (Obviously, it is the spirit of the statements not their specifics that matter.) Both of these statements acknowledge the speaker's experience of uneasiness and invite a joint inquiry into its causes.

The skills for defusing defensive routines are essentially the same skills for strengthening the "fundamental solution" in the shifting the burden structure—the skills of reflection and mutual inquiry. By inquiring effectively into the causes of the problems at hand—that is, by inquiring in such a way as to reveal your own assumptions and reasoning, make them open to influence, and encourage others to do likewise—defensive routines are less likely to come into play.[13]

While defensive routines can become especially pernicious in a team, on other hand, teams have unique capabilities for transcending defensiveness—if there is genuine commitment to learning. What is required, not surprisingly, is a vision of what we really want, both in terms of business results and how we want to work together, and a ruthless commitment to telling the truth about our "current reality." In this sense, team learning and building shared vision are sister disciplines. They naturally go together to build "creative tension" in a team.

In the presence of a genuinely shared vision, defensive routines become just another aspect of "current reality." Like the "structural conflicts" discussed in the chapter on personal mastery, they derive their power from being unrecognized. A team committed to the truth has unique powers to surface and acknowledge their own defensiveness. Then the defensive routines can actually become a source of energy rather than inertia.

Defensive routines can become a surprising ally toward building a learning team by providing a signal when learning is not occurring. Most of us know when we are being defensive, even if we cannot fully identify the source or pattern of our defensiveness. If you think about it, one of the most useful skills of a learning team would be the ability to recognize when people are *not* reflecting on their own assumptions, when they are *not* inquiring into each other's thinking, when they are *not* exposing their thinking in a way that encourages others to inquire into it. When we are feeling defensive, seeking to avoid an issue, thinking we need to protect someone else or ourselves—these are tangible signals that can be used to reestablish a climate of learning. But we must learn to recognize the signals and learn how to acknowledge the defensiveness without provoking more defensiveness.

Defensive routines may signal especially difficult and especially important issues. Often, the stronger the defensiveness, the more important the issue around which people are defending or protecting their views. If these views can be brought out productively, they may provide windows onto each other's thinking. When defensiveness is met by self-disclosure and inquiry balanced with advocacy, team members begin to see more of each other's thinking.

Lastly, as team members learn how to work with rather than against their defensive routines, they build confidence that "we are senior to our defensiveness." Defensive routines pull down team members. They drain energy and sap people's spirit. When a team sees itself transcend blocks that have been preventing learning, blocks which many felt were inevitable—as Argyris observed, "the nature of organizations"—they gain tangible experience that there may be many aspects of their reality that they have the power to change.

In medieval times, alchemy was a symbol for transformation of what is most common (lead) into what is most precious (gold). So, too, do learning teams practice a special form of alchemy, the transformation of potentially divisive conflict and defensiveness into learning. They do this through their vision and skill. Through dialogue, team members gain tangible experience of the larger intelligence that can operate. This experience strengthens the team members' vision of how they might operate. But unless the team also builds the skills for seeing rather than obscuring current reality, their capacity for learning will be unreliable. Without reflection and inquiry skills, they will get thrown off course when defensiveness arises—their learning will depend on circumstances.

It is not the absence of defensiveness that characterizes learning teams but the way defensiveness is faced. A team committed to learning must be committed not only to telling the truth about what's going on "out there," in their business reality, but also about what's going on "in here," within the team itself. To see reality more clearly, we must also see our strategies for obscuring reality.

The power and insight that start to emerge when this happens are considerable. In effect, defensive routines are like safes within which we "lock up" energy that could be directed toward collective learning. As defensiveness becomes "unlocked," that insight and energy are released, becoming available for building shared understanding and advancing toward what the team members truly want to create.

THE MISSING LINK: PRACTICE

It cannot be stressed too much that team learning is a *team skill*. A group of talented individual learners will not necessarily produce a learning team, any more than a group of talented athletes will produce a great sports team. Learning teams learn how to learn together.

If anything, team skills are *more* challenging to develop than individual skills. This is why learning teams need "practice fields," ways to practice together so that they can develop their collective learning skills. The almost total absence of meaningful "practice" or "rehearsal" is probably the predominant factor that keeps most management teams from being effective learning units.

What exactly is "practice"? Donald Schon, in his book *The Reflective Practitioner,* identifies the essential principles of practice as experimentation in a *"virtual world."* A virtual world is a "constructed representative of the real world." It can be as simple as the architects' sketchpad:

> Here they can draw and talk their moves in a spatial-action language, leaving traces which represent the forms of buildings on the site. Because the drawing reveals qualities and relations unimagined beforehand, moves can function as experiments . . . [discovering] that building shapes do not fit the slope and that . . . classrooms are too small in scale.[14]

The essence of a virtual world is the freedom it allows for experimentation. The pace of action can be slowed down or speeded up. Phenomena that occur very rapidly can be stretched out over time to study more carefully. Phenomena that stretch out over very long periods can be speeded up to see more clearly the consequences of particular actions. No move is irreversible. Actions that cannot be reversed or taken back and redone in the real setting can be redone countless times. Changes in the environment can be eliminated, either completely or partially. Complexity can be simplified by uncoupling variables that are interlocked in reality.

The manipulations that Schon describes in virtual worlds of the architects and other professionals match precisely what happens when the basketball team or the symphony orchestra practices. They vary the pace of the action—by slowing down the music, by running plays in slow motion. They isolate components and simplify the complexity—by playing individual sections, by running plays without a competitor. They reverse what is, in the real performance, irreversible—they replay the same section over and over, they rerun the play over and over.

Interestingly, the few examples in business of teams which learn consistently over a long period of time seem to be exactly those settings where effective virtual worlds operate. For instance, modern advertising practice is based on the concept of a creative team, where an account supervisor, art director, and copywriter work closely together, often for years. So close are these teams that team-mates often switch agencies together, rather than break apart. What makes advertising teams special is that they practice together, as consistently and intensively as the members of a basketball team do. They brainstorm ideas, and then experiment with them, testing them in storyboards or mock-ups, and eventually presenting them—first to higher-ups in the agency, then to the client.

Team learning requires that type of regular practice. But management teams, by and large, are bereft of it. True, they have the abstract, intellectual debates of ideas, and many team members come to learn each others' intellectual opinions, often only too well. But there is nothing akin to a storyboard or a rehearsal. The main product of the team's work is decisions about specific situations, often debated and decided under great time pressure, and each decision is final as soon as it is made. There is no experimentation with decisions; worse still, there is little opportunity to form reasoned assessments of the wisdom of different decisions, and there is no opportunity to step back, as a team, and reflect on how we might arrive at better decisions together.

LEARNING HOW "TO PRACTICE"

Today, the discipline of team learning is, I believe, poised for a breakthrough because we are gradually learning how "to practice." In particular, two distinct "practice fields" are developing. The first involves practicing dialogue, so that a team can begin to develop its *joint skill* in fostering a team IQ that exceeds individual IQs. The second involves creating "learning laboratories" and "micro-worlds," (Chapter 17), computer-supported environments where team learning confronts the dynamics of complex business realities.

Dialogue sessions allow a team to come together to "practice" dialogue and develop the skills it demands. The basic conditions for such a session include:

1. having all members of the "team" (those who need one another to act) together
2. explaining the ground rules of dialogue
3. enforcing those ground rules so that if anyone finds himself unable to "suspend" his assumptions, the team acknowledges that it is now "discussing" not "dialoguing"

4. making possible, indeed encouraging, team members to raise the most difficult, subtle, and conflictual issues essential to the team's work

We think of dialogue sessions as "practice" because they are designed to foster team skills. Yet, the practical results of such sessions can be significant.

Recently, the management team at DataQuest Drives, a leading manufacturer of disk drives and related computer peripherals held such a session.[15] As mentioned earlier, DataQuest is a firm with a well-established market image for technological innovation. In addition to being dominated internally by R&D, DataQuest's charismatic founder recently retired after shepherding the firm's successful growth for more than thirty years. After a year of spotty business success with the new management in place, things were rocky. DataQuest's new president, John MacCarthy, faced the daunting challenge of filling the shoes of a legend, facing more difficult business conditions than the legend ever had to worry about (the entire market was overbuilt), and with a team of strong players who had not yet begun to work as a whole.

On the heals of a tumultuous reorganization, MacCarthy's management team came together for two days with the following invitation from the president:

MEMO TO:

FROM John MacCarthy
SUBJECT *Special Meeting*

As you are well aware, we are accelerating change and I need your input prior to finalizing our strategies and implementation plans. I believe there is opportunity for us to improve our understanding and the way we implement change.

The session is intended to be the first in a series of dialogues to help us clarify the assumptions, programs, and responsibilities underlying the implementation of our key strategies. We have the view that only through the input from a larger group can we execute our changes and programs in a coherent and unambiguous way. The purpose of this two-day session is to gain understanding of each other's view by thinking through the major issues facing us at this time.

This session is not an attempt to make decisions as much as a setting to examine directions and the assumptions underlying them.

We have a second goal. This is to be together as colleagues, leaving all our roles and positions at the door. In this dialogue we should consider ourselves equals who still have substantive knowledge of the situations we are considering.

We see this meeting as the first step toward establishing ongoing substantive dialogue among us. Our experience begins to show that to engage in dialogue takes practice, and we should expect to be learning how to do this in this session. Several ground rules are helpful and we invite you to participate by following these as much as you can.

Suggested Ground Rules

1. Suspension of assumptions. Typically people take a position and defend it, holding to it. Others take up opposite positions and polarization results. In this session, we would like to examine some of our assumptions underlying our direction and strategy and not seek to defend them.
2. Acting as colleagues. We are asking everyone to leave his or her position at the door. There will be no particular hierarchy in this meeting, except for the facilitator, who will, hopefully, keep us on track.
3. Spirit of inquiry. We would like to have people being to explore the thinking behind their views, the deeper assumptions they may hold, and the evidence they have that leads them to these views. So it will be fair to begin to ask other questions such as "What leads you to say or believe this?" or "What makes you ask about this?"

Over the two days, many previously closed subjects became open, blocks to communication came down, and rifts were healed. None was more important for the organization than that between R&D and marketing and sales.

Joe Grauweiler, the head of R&D, and Charlie Smyth, the head of Marketing and Sales have had a friendly albeit distant relationship for over ten years. Both are deeply proud of what DataQuest has achieved. Both believe deeply in its commitment to "participative management" and its related ideals about people and the organization. Yet, both are caught in a conflict that epitomizes the forces that are restraining DataQuest Drives' continuing growth. R&D is viewed as artists, designers, creators. Marketing sees itself, and is seen by others, as "the great unwashed," dealing in the messy world of sleazy dealers' bargain making (who have no particular loyalty to DataQuest), price discounting, and irate customers.

The "two cultures" of R&D and Marketing are reflected in numerous organizational conflicts. For example, both Grauweiler and Smyth have their own product budgets. Grauweiler's is for new development. Smyth's is for acquisitions, buying smaller companies whose products round out DataQuest's and make the firm, in Smyth's eyes, more competitive in the marketplace. There is no integrated product plan uniting the two. Marketing felt compelled to this "end run" because they saw R&D as being unresponsive to the full range of customer needs. R&D, it turns out, saw itself being cut out of important product decisions. As the dialogue unfolded, Grauweiler expressed a level of concern that came as a surprise, because people assumed that R&D valued its autonomy:

> GRAUWEILER: Let me offer a way to look at the issue of product strategy, which I submit today is being viewed as sort of an arm wrestle. We have, in effect, amassed a two pronged product strategy. We've not been overt or clear about it. My evidence is that we've not really brought the full competencies of the organization together to understand what amounts really to Data Quest's make/buy decision on product. That being the case, we have one group of people spending money on some product programs with a certain level of confidence and another group of people spending money on product programs with a different view. And "never the twain shall meet." That's just insane to me. There should be a singular, overriding product strategy that supports R&D and marketing. And, beneath that, come any number of make/buy decisions . . ."
>
> MACCARTHY: I think we all fundamentally agree with that.
>
> GRAUWEILER: Could I submit that we are telegraphing the opposite.
>
> OTHERS: Yes.
>
> GRAUWEILER: It's more acute than just not doing it well. We're being perceived as doing the opposite.

SMYTH: I was trying to get back and think of the rationale for why the make versus buy decision is a different and separated decision. At this point, it appears disjointed . . . One is, in my view, problem-solving, research-driven focus. The DataQuest label . . . On the other hand, in other products that DataQuest has not directed resources to, we are doing that through "buy." We're acquiring the access to that in a way other than Data-Quest's research . . . because it is more market reactive than fundamental problem-solution driven. And we don't want to pollute, you might say, the purity of what it is we want to do with research. . . .

PHILLIPS (HUMAN RESOURCE VP): I think that has put us in conflict.

GRAUWEILER: Absolutely! That's the problem. That's the prejudgment that I don't tolerate. How about the people who you're depending upon having some say in it? And don't protect my purity for me.

SMYTH: Well . . . I'm not uncomfortable with the rationale for what we have done. There may be a better way to do it. But I do think that, at some point in our history here, we decided not to invest in vertical storage disk files . . . just conventional junk that the market will buy that's not innovative. It's not interesting . . . And we wanted to allocate our finite resources and talent to what DataQuest's image is, which is research, innovative, product-driven . . . So we went out and acquired the more pedestrian stuff.

PHILLIPS: If we are just blue-skying it today, let me tell you what has always confused me. And I'm laying that on both marketing and R&D. "Research-driven product company" is how we've always talked about ourselves. And when we talk that way, it kind of puts us to say that any product that doesn't have the DataQuest investment in innovative research is outside Data-Quest. Somehow or another, we've structured ourselves that way and become in competition . . .

MACCARTHY: That's one definition of research-based. Do you know the other definition? The other definition is that nobody else in DataQuest does any research and development if it's not on a new product.

GRAUWEILER: I don't like that one either.

PHILLIPS: You hit point number two, because I was saying to myself . . . if you take the overriding direction statement as it is on the board, whether or not your decision is to make or buy, it still has to be research- and development-driven. It's got to be innovative . . .

MACCARTHY: I think we're onto something here. What we're saying is that the company in the past has been locked in. The only thing that made us great was product research and development. So we're having this incredible tension here. I would suggest that we bought subsidiaries to launch us . . . I think the dilemma that you're [Grauweiler] helping us to see is that . . . we should be offering whatever products the customer fundamentally needs. But then there's the other side that says, "But if it come out of DataQuest's research, it has to carry a DataQuest label." What you're saying is that's not true. That [what label to put on] ought to be a marketing decision based on what positioning you're trying to do. That's very helpful . . . because most of us have felt that if a product is not going to have a DataQuest label on it, you won't develop it in the first place.

HADLY (MANUFACTURING VP): But that's also making a statement that the entire company is research-driven, not just R&D, that other innovative ideas including product can come from other sides of the company. It doesn't all have to funnel through R&D.

GRAUWEILER: That's fine, but I don't know why that needs to be said. I'm not challenging you at all. But I think there's an inference here again that troubles me. I feel saddled representing the R&D legacy of the past, which I don't buy into. And I find it ironic that the more I work desperately to move our organization forward to the new reality, the more you're convinced to hold us back where we used to be! And I find that a strange dilemma.

HADLY: And conversely, there's a feeling here that that's the same on the other side.

ALL: Yes.

HADLY: We try to move the organization forward . . . we seem to be held back because you can't be research-driven and innovative unless it comes through R&D.

GRAUWEILER: I never said that! . . . Now, could I play it a different way? I think the statement of a research-driven product company is a correct statement. I firmly believe that the company's success will, in part . . . always be governed by our prowess with products. Anything that I see that starts to erode

that orientation scares me to death. You have to have good stuff
. . . good services and good products. I don't say that implies
how you get them. Or that there's only one way to get good
product . . . We don't have a very concerted or collaborative
process in place to get that, but I know we have to.

MACCARTHY: Now the other side would be this—I believe some
of the work that Charlie [Smyth] has done in marketing and in
distribution [developing a new network of exclusive DataQuest
dealers] is as much "R&D effort" as what goes on in R&D.

GRAUWEILER: I totally believe that.

MACCARTHY: And yet we suffer that, if the investment made there
doesn't become instantaneously converted into a return, there's
an incredible criticism of the organization.

GRAUWEILER: Welcome to the world of R&D.

SMYTH: There are two points I want to make from this. It looks to
me like your efforts could be put to developing a product that
could be manufactured outside . . . it looks to me that we've
thrown away some development efforts that could have been
licensed to other companies even . . . I've always thought it
was crazy that, in order to get a product out of R&D, you had
to put a DataQuest label on it.

GRAUWEILER: That's been a constraint on our program . . .

SMYTH: Now, the other thing is that we're not communicating in
any kind of rich way between marketing and R&D. As a matter
of fact, it's getting more separate . . . If we're going to work on
the total needs of the customer . . . there has to be a way that
that's seen in a lot of different places in the company.

HADLY: You started off by asking why is there this tension between R&D and marketing. You also have the tension between
manufacturing and finance. . . . To me it comes down to two
words: "Empowerment versus Control." We tend to be a very
control-oriented organization overall . . . Because they've got
control and won't let me in, I'm going to go over here and do
my own thing because I feel powerless to affect that at all.
That's where I think some of it comes in—not by anything we
necessarily want to have happen, but it's happening all over the
company.

The results of this dialogue were nothing short of remarkable for
DataQuest. First, a thirty-year rift between R&D and marketing
started to be healed. Second, the "end run" that marketing had been

doing to augment product lines was no longer necessary. R&D was interested and wanted to participate in studying acquisitions as well as developing products that could be marketed under other labels, as part of one coordinated product plan. The sacrosanct DataQuest label was not limited to products developed by DataQuest's own R&D but should be used based on "market considerations." The R&D head made it clear that he did not want to be fit into an old stereotype that R&D alone was responsible for innovation. The other functions, in his view, were equal partners in innovation, by innovating in processes, in understanding customer needs, and in business management. Moreover the R&D head was angry that he was even being saddled with an old stereotype.

TEAM LEARNING
AND THE FIFTH DISCIPLINE

Both the perspective and the tools of systems thinking figure centrally in team learning.

David Bohm's work on dialogue is informed throughout by a systemic perspective. In fact, an integrating thread throughout Bohm's work has been to continue to advance the perspective of "wholeness" in physics. Bohm's primary critique of contemporary thought, the "pollution" in the stream of collective thinking, is "fragmentation," the "tendency of thought to break things apart."

Likewise, the approach taken by learning teams to defensive routines is intrinsically systemic. Rather than seeing the defensiveness in terms of others' behavior, the leverage lies in recognizing defensive routines as joint creations and to find our own role in creating and sustaining them. If we only look for defensive routines "out there," and fail to see them "in here" our efforts to deal with them just increase the defensiveness.

The tools of systems thinking are also important because virtually all the prime tasks of management teams—developing strategy, shaping visions, designing policy and organizational structures—involve wrestling with enormous complexity. Furthermore, this complexity does not "stay put." Each situation is in a continual state of flux.

Perhaps the single greatest liability of management teams is that they confront these complex, dynamic realities with a language designed for simple, static problems. Management consultant Charles

Kiefer says it this way: "Reality is composed of multiple-simultaneous, interdependent cause-effect-cause relationships. From this reality, normal verbal language extracts simple, linear cause-effort chains. This accounts for a great deal of why managers are so drawn to low leverage interventions." For example, if the problem is long product development times we hire more engineers to reduce times; if the problem is low profits we cut costs; if the problem is falling market share we cut price to boost share.

Because we see the world in simple obvious terms, we come to believe in simple, obvious solutions. This leads to the frenzied search for simple "fixes," a task that preoccupies the time of many managers. John Manoogian, director of Ford's "Project Alpha," says, "The find and fix mentality results in an endless stream of short-term fixes, which appear to make problems go away, except they keep returning. So, then, we go off and fix them again. The find and fix experts will go on forever."

The problems compound in a diverse, cross-functional team such as a management team. Each team member carries his or her own, predominantly linear mental models. Each person's mental model focuses on different parts of the system. Each emphasizes different cause-effect chains. This makes it virtually impossible for a shared picture of the system as a whole to emerge in normal conversation. Is it any wonder that the strategies that emerge often represent watered-down compromises based on murky assumptions, full of internal contradictions, which the rest of the organization can't understand, let alone implement? The team members genuinely resemble the proverbial blind men and the elephant—each knows the part of the elephant within his grasp, each believes the whole must look like the piece he holds, and each feels that his understanding is the correct one.

This situation is unlikely to improve until teams share a new language for describing complexity. Today, the only universal language of business is financial accounting. But accounting deals with detail complexity not dynamic complexity. It offers "snapshots" of the financial conditions of a business, but it does not describe how those conditions were created. Today, there are several tools and frameworks that provide alternatives to traditional accounting as a business language. These include competitive analysis, "Total Quality," and, though much less widely used, scenario methods such as those developed at Shell.[16] But none of these tools deals with dynamic complexity very well or at all.

The systems archetypes offer a potentially powerful basis for a language by which management teams can deal productively with complexity. As teams such as the one at ATP master the basic archetypes, their conversations will naturally become more and more conversations about underlying structures and leverage and less and less predominated by crises and short-term "fixes."

If the ATP management team had been fluent in the language of the systems archetypes, the implications of their narrow-minded focus on meeting monthly and quarterly sales targets would have been inescapable. In particular, they would have realized that *when they increased pressures to meet sales targets,* they communicated very clearly to the salesforce the message: "When push comes to shove, it's better to pursue the low-risk additional sale to a current customer than the high-risk effort to create a new customer." This "shifted the burden" from building their customer base to making more sales to existing customers, thereby making them more dependent on a few key customers.

If the corporate managers had likewise been able to see and discuss this structure, they would have been able to surface their concerns about Jim Tabor's management more effectively. Rather than wrestling with how they could raise issues that might appear critical of Tabor's management skills and unsupportive, they could have simply laid out the two feedback processes and inquired into how *any of them* could be more confident that the fundamental solution of broadening the customer base was receiving adequate attention.

When the systems archetypes are used in conversations about complex and potentially conflictual management issues, reliably, they "objectify" the conversation. The conversation becomes about "the structure," the systemic forces at play, not about personalities and leadership styles. Difficult questions can be raised in a way that does not carry innuendos of management incompetence or implied criticism. Rather, people are asking, "Is the burden shifting to selling to current customers versus broadening our customer base?" "How would we know if it was?" This, of course, is precisely the benefit of a *language for complexity*—it makes it easier to discuss complex issues objectively and dispassionately.

Without a shared language for dealing with complexity, team learning is limited. If one member of a team sees a problem more systemically than others, that person's insight will get reliably discounted—if for no other reason than the intrinsic biases toward linear views in our normal everyday language. On the other hand, the benefits of teams developing fluency in the language of the systems archetypes are enormous, *and* the difficulties of mastering the language are actually reduced in a team. As David Bohm says, language *is* collective. Learning a new language, by definition, means learning how to converse with one another in the language. There is simply no more effective way to learn a language than through use, which is exactly what happens when a team starts to learn the language of systems thinking.

PART IV

Prototypes

The Wright Brothers flew at Kitty Hawk in 1903—but only for 12 seconds and 120 feet. Between 1903 and 1935, when the DC-3 was introduced, there were many would-be commercial aircraft, but none succeeded in opening up commercial air travel as a significant industry. Nonetheless, they played an important part in the evolution of air travel. Prototypes are essential to discovering and solving the key problems that stand between an idea and its full and successful implementation. Significant innovation cannot be achieved by talking about new ideas; you must build and test prototypes.

In the evolution of the learning organization, we are today somewhere on the path from invention to innovation. Whether we are closer to 1910 or 1930, no one can say, but we are in the midst of the "prototyping era."

The prototyping era for any significant new innovation is a time of searching for synergy, for pulling together diverse elements into a new whole. The DC-3 brought together diverse technologies that complemented and enhanced one another. The variable-pitch propeller made the air-cooled engine more powerful at all speeds, just as retractable landing gear and the wing flaps gave the aerodynamics and the monocoque body the strength to take advantage of greater propulsion.

The search for synergy is inevitably perilous. Having a few elements of a new ensemble of technologies can be more dangerous than having none at all—similar to having a powerful engine without the capability to control it. Just as many of the most "learningful" aircraft prototypes crashed, so will many of the most daring and important organizational prototypes fail, with painful consequences for everyone involved. Yet, these are often the experiments (as with People Express Airlines) from which the most is learned. This is what makes learning about fundamental innovation very different from surveying "best practice." The people in many of the organizations discussed in this book, even the highly successful ones, would be uncomfortable to have their companies held up as "models" for others to emulate. Rather, they are "experimental laboratories," where important questions are being addressed and new insights are forming.

Whether or not the five disciplines discussed in this book prove sufficient will depend on whether, in concert, they can resolve the practical problems and issues faced by prototype learning organizations. These issues include:

How can the internal politics and game playing that dominate traditional organizations be transcended? (Chapter 13, "Openness")

How can an organization distribute business responsibility widely and still retain coordination and control? (Chapter 14, "Localness")

How do managers create the time for learning? (Chapter 15, "A Manager's Time")

How can personal mastery and learning flourish at both work and home? (Chapter 16, "Ending the War Between Work and Family")

How can we learn from experience when we cannot experience the consequences of our most important decisions (Chapter 17, "Microworlds")

What is the nature of the commitment and skills required to lead learning organizations? (Chapter 18, "The Leader's New Work")

These are difficult questions. The chapters in Part 4 show how the learning disciplines are contributing ideas and tools toward their resolution. But, in no cases are the questions fully resolved. This is what makes them powerful. The questions represent the learning that we need to do to build learning organizations.

13

OPENNESS

HOW CAN THE INTERNAL POLITICS AND GAME PLAYING THAT DOMINATE TRADITIONAL ORGANIZATIONS BE TRANSCENDED?

"I moved to a town with a paper mill once," says Hanover's Bill O'Brien, "and when we drove into town we almost drove right out again. Two weeks later, we had all gotten used to the smell and didn't notice it. Organizational politics is such a perversion of truth and honesty that most organizations reek with its odor. Yet, most of us so take it for granted that we don't even notice it."

A "political environment" is one in which "who" is more important than "what."[1] If the boss proposes an idea, the idea gets taken seriously. If someone else proposes a new idea, it is ignored. There are always "winners" and "losers," people who are building their power and people who are losing power. Power is concentrated and it is wielded arbitrarily. One person can determine another's fate, and there is no recourse to that determination. The wielding of arbitrary power over others is the essence of authoritarianism—so, in this sense, a political environment is an authoritarian environment, even if those possessing the power are not in the official positions of authority.

For most people in most organizations, this isn't even worth dwelling on because there's absolutely nothing that can be done about it. "So long as there are organizations there will be politics." Yet, very few people truly want to live in organizations corrupted by internal politics and game playing. This is why internal politics is the first of many organizational "givens" challenged by prototype learning organizations.

Challenging the grip of internal politics and game playing starts with building shared vision. Without a genuine sense of common vision and values there is nothing to motivate people beyond self-interest. But we can start building an organizational climate dominated by "merit" rather than politics—where doing *what is right* predominates over *who wants what done*. But a nonpolitical climate also demands "openness"—both the norm of speaking openly and honestly about important issues *and* the capacity continually to challenge one's own thinking. The first might be called participative openness, the second reflective openness. Without openness it is generally impossible to break down the game playing that is deeply embedded in most organizations. Together vision and openness are the antidotes to internal politics and game playing.

SHARED VISION:
BUILDING AN ENVIRONMENT WHERE
SELF-INTEREST IS NOT PARAMOUNT

In their book, *Leadership and the Quest for Integrity*,[2] Badaracco and Ellsworth write that "practitioners [of political leadership] believe that people are motivated by self-interest and by a search for power and wealth." As with many assumptions, this one can be self-fulfilling. If people are assumed to be motivated only by self-interest, then an organization automatically develops a highly political style, with the result that people must continually look out for their self-interest in order to survive.

An alternative assumption is that, over and above self-interest, people truly want to be part of something larger than themselves.

They want to contribute toward building something important. And they value doing it with others. You may recall that a cornerstone of the discipline of personal mastery (Chapter 9) is that people have an innate sense of purpose and that, when people reflect on what they truly want, most discover that aspects of their vision concern their families, their communities, their organizations, and for some their world. These are still "personal visions" in the sense that they emanate from an individual, but they reach far beyond the individual's self-interest in the narrow sense.

When organizations foster shared visions, they draw forth this broader commitment and concern. Building shared vision, as discussed in Chapter 11, leads people to acknowledge their own larger dreams and to hear each other's dreams. When managed with sensitivity and persistence, building shared vision begins to establish a sense of trust that comes naturally with self-disclosure and honestly sharing our highest aspirations. Getting started is as simple as sitting people in small circles and asking them to talk about "what's really important" to them. Invariably, people comment, "I never knew this about Joe, and we've been working together for five years," or "Knowing what I now know about you, my attitude toward working together is completely changed." When people begin to state and hear each other's visions, the foundation of the political environment begins to crumble—the belief that all we care about is self-interest. Organizations that fail to foster genuinely shared visions, or that foist unilateral visions on their members and pretend that they are shared, fail to tap this broader commitment. Though they may decry internal politics, they do nothing to nurture a nonpolitical environment.

As a part of building shared vision, the process of committing to live by certain basic values also undermines internal politics. Once, as part of a three-day visioning session for the management team of a Boston area technology firm, the question of honesty came up. The group had casually identified "honesty and forthrightness in all communications" as one of their operating ground rules. The management team had developed a vision they were beginning to get really excited about, when one of the senior salespeople commented offhandedly, "Of course, we don't mean that we will be honest to our customers."

The entire process ground to a halt. The group reconsidered what they meant by "commitment to honesty and forthrightness in all communications." The president broke the silence by stating, "Yes. For me, this means being completely honest with our customers."

The salesman responded, "If we do we'll lose 30 percent of our booking next month. In this business none of our competitors are honest when they tell a customer when a new computer system will arrive. If we tell the truth, our delivery times will be 50 percent longer than what customers believe they will get from competitors."

"I don't care," was the president's response. "I simply don't want to be part of an organization that sanctions lying, to our customers, our vendors, or anyone else. Moreover, I believe that, over time, we'll establish a reputation for reliability with our customers that will win us more customers than we'll lose."

The exchange continued for more than an hour. At the end, the group was together in support of telling the truth. The salesperson knew that if bookings dropped off in the next month or two, the other members of the team would not come screaming for his head. And he and the rest had begun to develop a vision of building a new reputation for honesty and reliability among their customers. This session took place six years ago. In the intervening period, the firm has prospered and established a preeminent position in its niche market.

Once a shared vision starts to take root, you might think that game playing and politics would take care of themselves, dissolved by the mutual commitment behind the vision. Sadly, this view often turns out to be naive. No matter how committed people are to a shared vision, they still are steeped in the habits of game playing and still are immersed in a highly politicized organizational climate. (Just because a few people start to build a shared vision, the larger organization does not immediately change.) If a vision is put into a highly political environment it can easily get ground up into a political objective: "Whose vision is this anyhow?" becomes more important than the intrinsic merit of a vision. Openness is needed to "unlearn" the habits of game playing that perpetuates internal politics.

But openness is a complex and subtle concept, which can be understood only in light of the disciplines of working with mental models and team learning.

PARTICIPATIVE OPENNESS AND REFLECTIVE OPENNESS

Many managers and organizations pride themselves on "being open," when in fact they are simply playing a new, more advanced

game. This is because there are two different aspects of openness—
participative and reflective. Unless the two are integrated, the behavior of "being open" will not produce real openness.

Participative openness, the freedom to speak one's mind, is the
most commonly recognized aspect of openness. This is because the
philosophy of "participative management," involving people more
in decision making, is widely espoused. In some organizations it is
almost a religion; they become "participative management" companies. It becomes a norm that everyone gets to state his view. Many
even institutionalize formal procedures for "open communication." [3]
I state my view. You state your view. We all *appear* to be contributing to collaborative learning—yet, little real learning takes place.
Why?

For one thing, people only feel safe sharing their views to a degree.
As O'Brien says, "How many managers describe an issue the same
way at a work team meeting at 10 A.M. as they do when they are
home or having a drink with friends that same evening?"

Secondly, on a deeper level, no one's view is changing or being
affected. After stating our opinions, if we don't agree, we simply
conclude that "people are different" and go our separate ways. If
one decision representing the group must be made, it either represents a watered-down "consensus" or the preference of the one or
two whose opinion counts most. Participative openness may lead to
more "buy-in" on certain decisions, but by itself it will rarely lead
to better quality decisions because it does not influence the thinking
behind people's positions. In the terms of personal mastery, it focuses purely on the "means" or process of interacting, not on the
"results" of that interaction. For example, people might say, "That
was a great meeting. Everybody got to express his views," instead
of judging the quality of decisions and actions taken over time. This
is why many managers find participative management wanting. As
one disgruntled executive in a "participative management" company told me recently, "The implicit assumption around here is that
the solution to all problems is sharing our views."

While participative openness leads to people speaking out, "reflective openness" leads to people looking inward. Reflective openness starts with the willingness to challenge our own thinking, to
recognize that any certainty we ever have is, at best, a hypothesis
about the world. No matter how compelling it may be, no matter
how fond we are of "our idea," it is always subject to test and
improvement. Reflective openness lives in the attitude, "I may be

wrong and the other person may be right." It involves not just examining our own ideas, but mutually examining others' thinking.

Reflective openness is based on skills, not just good intentions. There are the skills of reflection and inquiry, first presented in the mental models chapter. These include recognizing "leaps of abstraction," distinguishing espoused theory from theory-in-use, and becoming more aware of and responsible for what we are thinking and not saying. There are also the skills of dialogue and dealing with defensive routines, discussed in the team learning chapter. Organizations that are serious about openness support their members in developing these learning skills.

But these skills take time and persistence to develop, and most managers are completely unaware of them. Thus a "shifting the burden" structure often develops. We feel a need to be more open, to which we respond with the behaviors of participative openness—expressing our views more forthrightly, soliciting others' inputs, and talking more with everyone about our problems. When this happens, participative openness can become a "symptomatic solution." Then it shifts the burden away from the "fundamental solution"—reflective openness: developing the skills of inquiry, reflection, and dialogue.

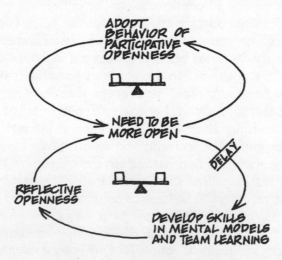

The insidiousness of the shifting the burden structure, as always, stems from the way the symptomatic solution weakens the fundamental solution. The more we talk to one another, the more we encourage workers to express their views, the more we may feel that we have dealt with the need to be more open. We never know the extent to which we are undermining any movement toward a deeper type of openness. The end result is the curious phenomenon of "open closedness," when everyone feels he has a right to air his views, yet no one really listens and reflects. "Talking at" one another substitutes for genuine communication and dialogue.

On the other hand, there also can be a positive synergy between participative and reflective openness. When this synergy develops it is a powerful force to undermine politics and game playing. The key, in my experience, is both making it safe to speak openly *and* developing the skills to productively challenge one's own and others' thinking.

To see how this can work, consider the case of a member of a senior team in a company noted for its "openness." The officer found himself, over time, being more and more criticized for specific decisions he made. But no one ever mentioned that a more general opinion was forming about his attitude. To the other managers, he was a "free spender" who "cared more about looking good and about his function than about the corporation as a whole." Behind his back, people discussed their opinion of him, but no one brought it up publicly. They felt that such "personal" views were inappropriate for business meetings. No one asked him directly about it. Instead, they continued to be "open" and forthright, bluntly criticizing his individual decisions. But, they never shared the reasoning behind their views.

The manager felt himself slipping into a position which the others all privately called "being in the barrel." It was a general ostracism which others had endured in the past. Moreover, he had no idea why he was in the barrel. Feeling isolated and attacked, he spent more and more time explaining and justifying each individual action— which in turn was seen as further evidence that he cared only about his own department. In fact, he was in a "no win" bind. Whether he vigorously defended his views, or kept silent, it mattered not. Both reinforced the other managers' negative impression of him.

Why didn't the other officers tell this person how they felt about him? It wasn't because of personal antipathy. Most said that they were his friends. But they were afraid of creating an upsetting argument (or, more charitably, they didn't see how to communicate their view constructively). There was also a more subtle reason, one which gets to the heart of reflective openness. Most of the other executives never saw the point of bringing the matter up. They had concluded that their mental model of this man was true—he *did* care more about looking good and making his function look good than about the corporation. They never thought to question it. It was a given.

Meanwhile, the "manager in the barrel" also never probed more deeply; he never asked, in a meeting, "Wait a minute. Is there a pattern here?" Despite the purported "openness" at every meeting, that would have felt inappropriate. In effect, both sides were still playing games; he was playing "Defend that decision," and they were playing, "Name that fault." The games blocked any efforts they might have made to probe the causes of his decisions, or the causes of their perception of him.

In other words, the managers formed a generalization based on specific observations, but they had never tested it. The more they talked to others behind his back about the generalization, the more they validated it in their own minds. It was a classic "leap of abstraction," as described in Chapter 10. This "vicious circle" might have gone on forever had not some of the managers (with a consultant's help) finally realized what they were doing. They sat down at a meeting with the "man in the barrel" and cited the specific things he had said and done that had prompted their generalizations. "It's led us to wonder whether you cared more about your domain or about the corporation."

He protested that he did, at least in his own mind, care a great deal about the corporation. Yes, he was prone to boasting. Yes, he did feel free to spend money for the programs he believed in. Yes, when a program was threatened he felt compelled to jump to its defense. But did that make him a traitor to the entire organization?

Once a few people at that meeting were willing to break the vicious circle, things began to change. The officer saw more deeply the nature of his colleagues' concerns. They, in turn, saw that they had misinterpreted his actions. Eventually, more and more of the mutual game playing began to wind down. The team had realized how subtle openness could be, and how they had inadvertently created new games in the name of "being open." They saw the tragic consequences of putting one of their members "in the barrel," and resolved that it would never happen again. They had learned a powerful lesson about the distinction between speaking out and real openness.

In my experience, a breakthrough of sorts often happens when managers realize that reflective openness is based in skills, not just good intentions. For example, being able to distinguish "facts" (direct observations) from generalizations based on those facts would have helped the executives with the "officer in the barrel." Such leaps of abstraction are particularly dangerous in seemingly "open" organizations, where people discuss their views freely and opinions can gain agreement rapidly, thereby quickly assuming the status of unassailable fact.

OPENNESS AND COMPLEXITY

Nothing undermines openness more surely than certainty. Once we feel as if we have "the answer," all motivation to question our thinking disappears. But the discipline of systems thinking shows that there simply is "no right answer" when dealing with complexity. For this reason, openness and systems thinking are closely linked.

A simple exercise we have used in our leadership workshops for many years gets at the central point.[4] We cover a large wall with blank paper, and then ask the group to work together to map out all the feedback relationships in a particular problem with which they are wrestling. "For instance," we might say, "let's create a systems diagram to figure out how to balance our work and family responsibilities." We usually start by identifying key variables and writing them on different parts of the large paper: time pressures; expectations of oneself; responsibilities; personal interests; career goals; distance between work and home; and so on. Then we begin suggesting feedback links: expectations influence career goals; distance between work and home influences time available for family; personal income influences independence, as well as budget. Within a half hour, we've covered the wall with circles and arrows. Everyone in the room feels overwhelmed, and yet we know that we've just begun to show the hundreds of interrelationships that exist in the real system. People gradually come to realize that no one could possibly come to figure out all these interactions.

This realization has a remarkable impact on people. Some try to rationalize it away: "Well, this is so obvious it's meaningless," they say. "What's the point?" Others insist that, given enough time, they could eventually figure it out. Some diehards keep trying to add links and loops. But those who can face the "un-figure-out-able-ness" of it all will often sit back in their chairs, laugh, and realize some spring has sprung.

The first time I saw the "Wall," it emerged accidentally. In the late 1970s, Donella Meadows led a three-hour workshop on Third World malnutrition with respected international experts, trying to build a comprehensive model, based on all their knowledge, of the causes of global hunger. Before long, the chart included everything from economic factors to politics to cultural values to international trade. In the audience, an experienced lobbyist on food and peace issues began moaning and shaking her head. Finally, Donella stopped the session to ask if she was ill. "My God," said the lobbyist. "All my life, I assumed that somebody, somewhere, knew the answer to this problem. I thought politicians knew what had to be done, but refused to do it out of politics and greed. But now I realize that nobody knows the answer. Not us, not them, not anybody."

The "Wall" reveals some fascinating insights into the roots of authoritarianism in our own thinking. Most people have grown up in an authoritarian environment. As children, their parents had "the answers." As students, their teachers had the answers. Naturally, when they enter organizations, they assume that "the boss" must have the answers. They are convinced deep down that people above them know what is going on, or at least they ought to know if they are competent. This mentality weakens them as individuals, and the organization as a whole. At some level it absolves them of responsibility in the organization's learning. It also predisposes them to cynicism when events eventually reveal that the people at the top did not have all the answers.

Conversely, when people in an organization come collectively to recognize that nobody has the answers, it liberates the organization in a remarkable way. I heard the reason articulated soon after we incorporated the "Wall" exercise into the workshop. One participant was a vice president of a Boston-based high-tech company. He had studied Zen Buddhism for ten years and was a very successful and creative engineer. After the exercise he remarked, "Many people will say that once you recognize that you can never figure life out, you have denied rationality. But that's not true. You have simply recontextualized rationality. To search for understanding, knowing that there is no ultimate answer, becomes a creative process— one which involves rationality but also something more."

This, of course, is the state of being open. You realize, as the "Wall" experience shows, that any "answer" you have is at best an approximation—always subject to improvement, never final. You may hone your rational ability to solve problems, and use that ability as best you can, all the while recognizing that it will never be enough. Then curiosity, previously buried under the belief that "I know the answer," is free to surface. The fear that "I don't know, but perhaps he or she does," or, "I don't know but I should," dissolves. We come to peace with knowing that we do not know, or as Einstein said, that "the most beautiful thing we can experience is the mysterious. It is the source of all true art and science."[5]

Unfortunately, the way knowledge is organized and structured in contemporary society destroys this sense of mystery. The "compartmentalization of knowledge" creates a false sense of confidence. For example, the traditional disciplines that influence management —such disciplines as economics, accounting, marketing, and psychology—divide the world into neat subdivisions within which one can often say, "This is the problem and here is its solution." But the boundaries that make the subdivisions are fundamentally arbitrary —as any manager finds out who attempts to treat an important problem as if it is purely "an economic problem," or "an accounting problem," or "a personnel problem." Life comes to us whole. It is only the analytic lens we impose that makes it seem as if problems can be isolated and solved. When we forget that it is "only a lens," we lose the spirit of openness.

This does not mean that all problems are unsolvable. Some problems *do* have "correct solutions," such as finding the best sitings for oil refineries *once* production and final distribution points, volume of demand, and costs of transport have been identified; or determining the optimal mix of debt and equity financing *once* a new investment project has been chosen and interest and dividend rates are established. These are problems where nearly all the dynamic complexity can be ignored with minimal side effects. Unfortunately, these are often not the most important problems that managers confront.

The British economist E. F. Schumacher, best known for writing *Small is Beautiful,* argued (in his book *A Guide for the Perplexed*) that there are two fundamentally different types of problems: "convergent problems" and "divergent problems."[6] Convergent problems have *a* solution: "the more intelligently you study them, the more the answers *converge.*" Divergent problems have no "correct" solution. The more they are studied by people with knowledge and intelligence the more they "come up with answers which contradict one another." The difficulty lies not with the experts, but in the nature of the problem itself. If you are in Boston and want to travel by car to Albany, there is a right answer to the question, "What is the fastest route to Albany?" But there is no right answer to the question, "Why do you want to go to Albany?" Schumacher's favorite example of a classic divergent problem is: "How do you most effectively educate children?" Different people of integrity and intellect will, inevitably, come to very different conclusions.

It is important to realize that divergent problems are not convergent problems that have not yet been solved. Rather, they are problems for which there is no single, best solution. As Schumacher says, "divergent problems offend the logical mind, which wishes to remove tension by coming down on one side or the other."

"How to best develop our people?" "What new products to invest in?" "How can we best satisfy our customers?"—these are divergent problems. Only genuine openness allows people to deal productively with them.

THE SPIRIT OF OPENNESS

While reflective openness benefits significantly from reflection and inquiry skills, and from systems thinking knowledge and skills, openness is more than a set of skills. As O'Brien says, "We should be careful not to prescribe a clinical treatment of a spiritual subject. Openness goes beyond a personal quality. It's a relationship you have with others. It is a change in spirit, as well as a set of skills and practices."

It is most accurate to think of openness as a characteristic of relationships, not of individuals. At some level, it makes no sense to say, "I am an open person." The same person will experience genuine openness with some people and not with others. In this sense, like David Bohm's concept of *dialogue,* openness emerges when two or more individuals become willing to suspend their certainty in each other's presence. They become willing to share their thinking and susceptible to having their thinking influenced by one another. And, as Bohm points out, in a state of openness, they gain access to depths of understanding not accessible otherwise.

If openness is a quality of relationships, then building relationships characterized by openness may be one of the most high-leverage actions to build organizations characterized by openness. This is precisely what I and many of my colleagues have observed time and again—that "learningful" relationships among key members of the organization have an extraordinary impact on the larger organization. When small groups of people (as few as two or three) become deeply committed and open they create a microcosm of a learning organization. This microcosm not only teaches them the skills they need but becomes a model for others.

The impulse toward openness, as O'Brien says, "is the spirit of love." Love is, of course, a difficult word to use in the context of business and management. But O'Brien does not mean romantic love. In fact, the type of love that underlies openness, what the Greeks called *agape,* has little to do with emotions.[7] It has everything to do with intentions—commitment to serve one another, and willingness to be vulnerable in the context of that service. The best definition of the love that underlies openness is the full and unconditional commitment to another's "completion," to another being all that she or he can and wants to be.

"I can practice all the analytical steps in the world toward openness," O'Brien says, "and it is not enough. If you have the fundamental spiritual disposition, without the skill you'll be ineffective. But, on the other hand, if you develop the skill without the spiritual disposition, that won't work fully either."

This is a tough, challenging notion of love (sometimes characterized by the phrase "ruthless compassion") which brooks no compromise in both sharing one's feelings and views and being open to having those views change.

FREEDOM

When most people say, "I am free to do what I want," what they mean is: "I have freedom of action. No one is telling me what to do; no one is keeping me from acting as I wish."

But "freedom," in the sense of being free from external constraints, can be a hollow prize. For example, in the beer game described in Chapter 3, people can run their local operation any way they want. Yet, ironically, the results they produce, in almost all cases, are contrary to what they intend. Because of this, they often feel helpless, trapped within a set of forces they cannot control, despite being free to make their own decisions. Moreover, they have the power to produce much more successful results—if they'd change their ways of thinking and acting. This is the great irony of freedom of action; by itself, it can result in helplessness, in feeling trapped and impotent.

"People think they are free because of the absence of external controls," says O'Brien. "But, in fact, they are prisoners of a deeper and more insidious form of bondage—they only have one way of looking at the world."

"Freedom to" (rather than "freedom from") is the freedom to create the results we truly desire. It is the freedom that people who pursue personal mastery seek. It is the heart of the learning organization, because the impulse to generative learning is the desire to create something new, something that has value and meaning to people.

14

LOCALNESS

HOW DO YOU ACHIEVE
CONTROL WITHOUT CONTROLLING?

People learn most rapidly when they have a genuine sense of responsibility for their actions. Helplessness, the belief that we cannot influence the circumstances under which we live, undermines the incentive to learn, as does the belief that someone somewhere else dictates our actions. Conversely, if we know our fate is in our own hands, our learning matters.

This is why learning organizations will, increasingly, be "localized" organizations, extending the maximum degree of authority and power as far from the "top" or corporate center as possible. Localness means moving decisions down the organizational hierarchy; designing business units where, to the greatest degree possible, local decision makers confront the full range of issues and dilemmas intrinsic in growing and sustaining any business enterprise. Localness means unleashing people's commitment by giving them the freedom to act, to try out their own ideas and be responsible for producing results. Or, as Ray Stata, CEO of Analog Devices, Inc., says, "In the traditional hierarchical organization, the top thinks and the local acts. In a learning organization, you have to merge thinking and acting in every individual."

Localness is especially vital in times of rapid change. Local actors often have more current information on customer preferences, competitor actions, and market trends; they are in a better position to manage the continuous adaptation that change demands.

In the Royal Dutch/Shell study on corporate longevity (cited at the beginning of Chapter 2), the long-term survivors, according to Shell Planning Coordinator Arie de Geus, were the ones with "the ability to continually run 'experiments in the margin,' to continually explore new business possibilities." The experiments usually originated locally. Localness is a cornerstone in designing learning organizations.[1]

But localness also means unique new challenges, unmet and unsolved in traditional hierarchical organizations. Two in particular stand out in organizations I have seen that struggle with localness. The first concerns the conflicts which many managers, especially senior managers, experience in giving up "being in control," giving over decision-making authority to local managers. The second concerns how to make local control work.

The ambivalence of many senior managers to giving over greater authority and control of decision making is, in part, rooted in fear of loss. Will senior or corporate management become unneeded or somehow less important—mere window dressing in the locally controlled organization? This fear is unfortunate because it keeps many senior managers from discovering their new role in a locally controlled organization: responsibility for continually enhancing the organization's capacity for learning. One of the big problems plaguing organizations that are becoming more localized is that corporate management, paralyzed by the fear of what they might lose, are neglecting this very important new role.

The ambivalence of many managers to localness is also rooted in legitimate questions: how can locally controlled organizations achieve coordination, synergy between business units, and collaborative efforts toward common corporate-wide objectives? In other words, how can the organization achieve "control" if local managers are not being controlled? How can the locally controlled organization be something other than simply a "holding company," where corporate headquarters imposes financial standards and otherwise leaves local operations completely alone?

The steady trend toward increasing localness over the past thirty years or so is making these questions increasingly important. The trend is led by many of the most respected corporations today, such as Royal Dutch/Shell, Johnson & Johnson, 3M, and Citicorp. It is abundantly clear that rigid authoritarian hierarchies thwart learning, failing both to harness the spirit, enthusiasm, and knowledge of people throughout the organization and to be responsive to shifting business conditions. Yet, the alternatives to authoritarian hierarchies are less than clear.[2]

Failure to resolve the dilemmas and puzzles inherent in localness has caused some of the most daring prototype learning organizations to fail. Some have failed because, despite strong feelings for values such as freedom and individual responsibility, senior managers could not bring themselves to give up the control that traditionally comes with their office. Others have failed because they *did* give up the control, and then found that enthusiastic committed local decision makers did not necessarily make good decision makers. Still others made attempts at involving people more in decision making, but failed to go far enough in letting people develop their own visions, design their own strategies and structures, and assume responsibility for their own learning.

The disciplines of the learning organization can help in making localness work. For example, learning how to work with managers' mental models can help in coordinating locally controlled companies. It is no coincidence that the organizations leading in the development of the discipline of mental models for example, such as Royal Dutch/Shell and Hanover Insurance, have a high degree of local control. The combination of mental models and the other disciplines paints a new picture of how a locally controlled organization can function—"control through learning."

While traditional organizations require management systems that control people's behavior, learning organizations invest in improving the quality of thinking, the capacity for reflection and team learning, and the ability to develop shared visions and shared understandings of complex business issues. It is these capabilities that will allow learning organizations to be both more locally controlled *and* more well coordinated than their hierarchical predecessors.

THE ILLUSION OF
"BEING IN CONTROL"

The first core challenge posed by localness is not so much an intellectual or even rational challenge so much as it is an emotional one. Robert Swiggett, retired CEO of the Kollmorgen Corporation, put it bluntly: "In moving from the traditional authoritarian, hierarchical organization to a locally controlled organization, the single greatest issue is control. Beyond money, beyond fame, what drives most executives of traditional organizations is power, the desire to be in control. Most would rather give up anything than control."

Yet, the perception that someone "up there" is in control is based on an illusion—the illusion that anyone could master the dynamic and detailed complexity of an organization from the top.

A simple illustration, which I learned many years ago from managers at Kollmorgen, demonstrates the point. Imagine that you have two roller skates, attached to one another by a spring. You use the first roller skate to control the motion of the second. Its a bit tricky, but doable. Now, add a third roller skate, attached with another spring—and, moreover, give that new spring a different "spring constant" (i.e., make it either easier or more difficult to extend than the first spring). Now, try to control the third roller skate by moving only the first. It's much trickier. Keep adding roller skates, each attached by springs with different spring constants. It doesn't take long to give up any hope of controlling the roller skate at the far end of the line. Organizations are infinitely more complex than this simple line of roller skates and springs. You can begin to see why one person dictating orders from "one end of the line" cannot possibly control what happens in a complex organization.

The illusion of being in control can appear quite real. In hierarchical organizations, leaders give orders and others follow. But giving orders is not the same as being in control. Power may be concentrated at the top but having the power of unilateral decision making is not the same as being able to achieve one's objectives. Authority figures may be treated deferentially, lavished with the highest salaries and other privileges of rank, but that does not mean that they actually exercise control commensurate with their apparent importance.

Because of the lingering belief that you can control decisions from the top, many corporations vacillate between localizing and centralizing. When business goes well, decisions are made more and more locally. When business begins to founder, the first instincts are to return control to central management. This "on again/off again" pattern of decision making testifies to the deep lack of confidence which senior managers have in local decision makers. Moreover, this centralizing/localizing cycle is a "shifting the burden" structure. At any hint of a crisis, the company shifts the burden of decision making back to the central staffs. Local decision-making skills atrophy and the infrastructure never develops which would help people experiment, coordinate, and learn on the local level.

Understanding that it is usually impossible to control a complex organization from the top can help senior managers begin to give up the need to feel "in control." But, for many, it is not enough. The emotional hold of being in control will relax only if localness is *what they truly want*. Unless they believe that the quality of learning, the ability to adapt, the excitement and enthusiasm, and the human growth fostered by localness are worth the risk, they are unlikely ever to *choose* to build a locally controlled organization. This is why localness is unlikely to endure unless it is an aspect of the organization's vision. This means that it must be an aspect of people's personal visions. Managers in positions of traditional authority must truly *want* a more locally controlled organization. Enough people in local operations must truly *want* the responsibility and freedom of greater local autonomy. Otherwise, no lasting movement will occur.

By contrast, today many organizations are cutting management levels and becoming more locally controlled because of expediency, driven by pressures to cut costs. Such moves to localness are not likely to lead to lasting, significant redistribution of decision-making authority; as soon as a recession comes, corporate managers will "pull in the reins" and once again increase management controls in the name of "weathering the storm."

Illustrative of the type of commitment required for localness to work is the following statement from Hanover's Bill O'Brien:

We are living in a time when people believe they can have less and less influence on events . . . In nearly all companies people learn to accept the world on its own terms and deal with it the way it comes. At Hanover, an essential part of our beliefs is that we *can* change our part of the world, that we as individuals *do* matter, and that we can have an effect on our environment, our growth, and our results. This is why localness is one of our core values.[3]

In 1988, former Johnson & Johnson CEO James Burke similarly expressed his commitment to localness, along with a reminder of its implications for top management.

We have 166 affiliate companies in 59 countries and an accelerating growth rate. Our commitment to decentralization demands a flexible organization permitting rapid decision making.[4]

That same year, *Fortune* quoted him on the subject:

Those of us in top management often say to each other that we had more fun running a J&J company than anything since. If you are having as much fun running a big corporation as you did running a piece of it, then you are probably interfering too much with the people who really make it happen."[5]

But there is no guarantee that energetic, committed local decision makers will be wise decision makers. Local decision makers can be myopic, failing to appreciate the impacts of decisions on the larger systems in which they operate. It can fail to take in the benefits of experience. It can be short term. The quality of local decision making is the second core in localness: "How can organizations achieve control without controlling?"

CONTROL WITHOUT "CONTROLLING"

Just because no one is "in control" does not mean that there is no "control." In fact, all healthy organisms have processes of control. However, they are distributed processes, not concentrated in any one authoritarian decision maker. As my MIT colleague Dan Kim suggests, imagine what would happen if the immune system had to wait for approval before releasing antibodies to fight an infection. You might imagine the conversation:

LOCAL AGENT: We've got a nasty-looking infection starting here.
CENTRAL AUTHORITY: Keep a close eye on it. Let me know if it looks like it's getting out of control.

By the time the central authority finally grants permission to act, the infection has overrun the whole system. The essence of organic control is the capacity to maintain internal balances critical to stability and to growth. In the human body, temperature is controlled, as is blood pressure, heartbeat, oxygen levels, physical balance, and the spread of diseases through myriad control processes.

Many writers on organizational theory have used the metaphor of "organization as organism" to suggest an entirely different image for organizational control from that of the traditional authoritarian hierarchy.[6] It is the image of local control—countless local decision-making processes that continually respond to changes, so as to maintain healthy conditions for stability and growth.[7]

For implementing in organizations this type of control that is found in nature, the learning disciplines are invaluable. The essence of the discipline of shared vision, for example, lies in bringing individual visions into harmony with a larger vision. If the organization's vision is imposed on local units, it will, at best, result in compliance not commitment. If there is an ongoing "visioning" process, local visions and organizational visions will continually interact with and enrich one another. The combination of mission, vision, and values creates the common identity that can connect thousands of people within a large organization. One of the chief tasks of leaders, at both the corporate and local level, is fostering this common identity. An observer of Johnson & Johnson's Burke cited "his greatest strength . . . [is his] day-to-day, layer-by-layer involvement in recognizing, prioritizing, and articulating Johnson & Johnson's ethical values."[8]

The discipline of managing mental models has already been shown to be vital for managing a locally controlled organization. Royal Dutch/Shell is one of the most localized large corporations in the world, with more than one hundred individual operating companies run highly autonomously. Shell evolved its "planning as learning" and emphasis on mental models precisely because it needed a way of assisting and coordinating this far-reaching network of businesses without infringing on their local autonomy. "Strategies are the product of a world view," said former Shell planner Pierre Wack. "When the world changes, managers need to share some common view of the new world. Otherwise, decentralized strategic decisions will result in management anarchy.[9]

The disciplines of team learning and personal mastery are also important. Team learning skills help, both within local management teams and in the interactions between local and corporate management, which is also a "team," albeit usually an unofficial team. At both levels, the capacity to blend dialogue and discussion and to deal productively with defensive routines is important. Personal mastery is vital because localness places enormous demands on an organization's leadership resources. Local business managers must be leaders as well as competent managers.

Lastly, in the absence of systems thinking, local decision making can become myopic and short-term. This happens because local decision makers fail to see the interdependencies by which their actions affect others outside their local sphere.

There is a particular systems archetype, first identified by ecologist Garrett Hardin and called "The Tragedy of the Commons," which is especially relevant for making localness work.[10] It describes situations where what's right for each part is wrong for the whole. The archetype is useful for dealing directly with problems where apparently logical local decision making can become completely illogical for the larger system.

For example, the Sahel region in sub-Saharan Africa was once a fertile pastureland. In the middle of this century, it supported over a hundred thousand herdsmen and over a half million head of grazing cattle (called "zebu"). Today, it is barren desert, yielding a small fraction of the vegetation it produced before. The people left there scratch out a meager existence under continual threat of drought and starvation.

The tragedy of the Sahel was rooted in steady growth of population and herd sizes from the 1920s to the 1970s. The growth accelerated from 1955 to 1965 due to unusually heavy rainfalls and assistance from international aid organizations who financed numerous deep wells. Each herdsman on the Sahel had incentives to expand his herd of zebu, both for economic gain and social status. As long as the common grazing lands were large enough to support these new, larger herds, there were no problems. But in the early 1960s, overgrazing began to occur. Eventually rangeland vegetation grew sparser. The sparser the vegetation, the more overgrazing, until it got to the point where the cattle consumed more foliage than the ranges could generate. The desertification reinforced itself as decreases in plant cover allowed wind and rain to erode the soil. Less vegetation was produced, which got overgrazed more severely to support the herds, leading to further desertification. The vicious spiral continued until disaster struck in the form of a series of droughts in the 1960s and 1970s. By the early 1970s, 50 to 80 percent of the livestock was dead and much of the population of the Sahel was destitute.[11]

Similar "Tragedies of the Commons" take place all over the world —in the world's fisheries, in farmlands in developing countries, in the Brazilian rain forests, and with acid rain and greenhouse-effect gases. At one time, the grass on the Boston Common could hardly be seen for the profusion of woolly backs of sheep. In all these situations, the logic of local decision making leads inexorably to collective disaster. Hardin first coined the term to describe situations where two conditions are met: (1) there exists a "commons," a resource shared among a group of people, and (2) individual decision makers, free to dictate their own actions, achieve short-term gains from exploiting the resource but do not pay, and are often unaware of, the cost of that exploitation—except in the long run.

The generic form of this archetype is:

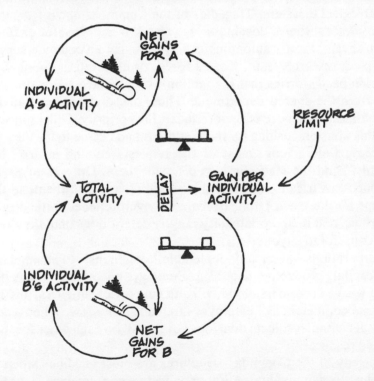

Each individual (here labeled as "A" and "B") focuses only on his own needs, not on the needs of the whole. In the short run, individuals gain by acting selfishly. This selfishness leads to success, which reinforces the actions that led to the success. (These are the two reinforcing processes at the top and bottom of the diagram.) The herdsmen add more cattle, which enriches their wealth and encourages them to add still more cattle. But, the sum total of all the individuals acting in their self-interest (the diagram shows two reinforcing loops for two individuals—in reality there may be hundreds or thousands of individual local decision makers) add up to a "total activity" with a life of its own. Eventually (the delay may be several years), the unsustainable "gain per individual activity" (profit per zebu) begins to decline, and the benefit to each individual begins to reverse. By the time they realize the import of that common error, it's too late to save the whole, and all the individuals fall with it. It's not enough for one individual to see the problem; the problem cannot be solved until most decision makers act together for the good of the whole.

Don't think that the Tragedy of the Commons structure is limited to ecological disasters. Tragedies of the Commons occur frequently in businesses where "localness" is valued. It happens, for example, when several locally autonomous divisions share a common support group—a research team, a sales force, or a secretarial pool. Each division head worries that his section won't receive adequate attention from the shared department. Thus, one division head advises his staff to make more of their requests high priority. Other divisions see this division pushing for more support and decide to try the same strategy. Before long, most of the requests coming in are "high priority" and the staff starts to discount them. Or, worse yet, the support staff tries to accomplish everything asked of them, so they accept all the extra requests, become overburdened with juggling priorities, and their work quality rapidly deteriorates until they're no longer useful to anyone.

Corporations have many depletable "commons" to share: financial capital, productive capital, technology, community reputation, good will of customers, good will and support of suppliers, and morale and competence of employees to name just a few. When a company decentralizes, local divisions compete with each other for those limited resources.

Tragedy of the Commons structures are most insidious when the coupling from individual action to collective consequence is weak in the short run, yet strong in the long run. When this happens, the "commons" usually go unrecognized. Local managers see their actions as independent, they don't realize how they may be jeopardizing their and others' future. They fail to see how their individual "activity" will eventually reduce everyone's "gain per activity."

The "commons" can be as simple, and subtle, as the limited time and attention of customers. "Our strong, long-standing, almost fanatical commitment to decentralization," lamented a CEO recently, "has resulted in different divisions with related products competing for the customer's time and attention. We have created a host of forces working against systemic understandings, and a spirit of 'all for one' with no corresponding 'one for all.' "

Herman Miller president Ed Simon argues that the rewards and pressures on local decision makers often jeopardize "commons," by intensifying short-term thinking. (The "commons" affected might include the organization's reputation, its financial vitality, or its morale.) "On the surface," says Simon, "breaking businesses into smaller pieces is supposed to encourage local initiative and risk taking. In fact, it does just the opposite. Divisionalization and autonomy has created more short-term oriented managers, managers who are more driven by the bottom line, than ever before. The reason is simple. These aggressive division presidents are accountable for their own profits, they are measured by their quarterly and yearly results, and they expect to stay in that position for two to four years. That produces a system designed to be driven by the short term. We can always tell when we are selling office furniture to a highly decentralized company. They are virtually always 'price buyers.' They make decisions based almost solely on price because only price will affect their bottom line in the short term."

To recognize Tragedy of the Commons structures in organizations two questions must be kept in mind: (1) what are our current and potential "commons" that could be depleted through overly aggressive local managers? and (2) what specific actions would lead to depleting or overrunning these "commons"?

Once a Tragedy of the Commons structure is identified, the organization faces a clear but challenging issue: *who will manage the "commons"?* There are two general options. The first is to set up manager of the "commons"—someone or some group who can influence the actions of local units that put the "commons" at risk. For example, the morale, skills, and alignment of an organization's people is one of its most valuable "commons." Talented corporate human resource managers work with live managers and staff throughout the organization to effectively manage this commons, just as systems-oriented sales managers might represent the voice of the customer throughout the organization. Being the manager of a commons can be thankless and counterproductive, unless there is a broad-based understanding throughout the organization—of why the resource is a commons, and why depleting it will work to *everyone's* disadvantage.

The second approach to managing a commons is to establish signals, perhaps coupled to rewards and costs, that alert local actors that a "commons" is in danger. This second approach puts the onus on local managers to practice self-restraint. For example, if customers' adverse reactions to multiple contacts from competing local units were immediately made known to all local units, pressure to limit or coordinate such contacts would be felt. Similar pressures would be generated if suppliers who were aggrieved by the ordering habits of one local unit had their complaints immediately known throughout the organization.

Bill Gore, founder of W. L. Gore and Associates, highly profitable maker of Gore-tex and other synthetic fiber products, had a lovely metaphor to instill in all employees an appreciation for the principle of the "commons." He called it the "water-line" principle. He continually encouraged all "associates" at W. L. Gore to venture out and take risks. But he said it was each associate's responsibility to know where the "water line" was. "If you make a mistake above the water line, it will not sink the ship. But if you are trying something which, if it failed, might be 'below the water line,' it could affect all of us." Below-the-water-line risks—actions which might jeopardize important "commons"—should be undertaken only after careful consultation with representatives of all other parties who might be affected.

Still, my experience is that recognizing Tragedy of the Commons structures will sometimes be difficult for local managers—because the key interdependencies may cut across the boundaries from one local unit to another. Thus, responsibility for identifying important "commons" and for determining how they should be managed should be vested in corporate or central management. Such responsibility becomes one element of the new, evolving role for central management in a locally controlled organization—responsibility for the organization's capacity for learning.

THE NEW ROLE
OF CENTRAL MANAGEMENT

The shift to locally controlled organizations will not be complete until the new roles of corporate or central managers become clear.

As local managers increasingly take on responsibility for growing and running local business units, what is left for the senior managers who formerly shared or owned outright those responsibilities? As noted above, one element of the role involves stewardship for the organization, "guiding ideas," its core values and mission, and its continually evolving visions. But there are additional elements that are not yet recognized.

As Ed Simon puts it, "The first important discovery [in building learning organizations] is that there is different work to be done by executives. We are dedicating ourselves to spend a certain amount of time on this "new work," even though we don't know exactly what it is all about. But we do know that it will have something to do with a new generation of 'organizational architects.' " This view is consistent with the observation of Hanover's Bill O'Brien, quoted earlier on how "managing, organizing, and controlling"—are giving way to "a new 'dogma' [of] vision, values, and mental models."

The essence of the new role, I believe, will be what we might call *manager as researcher and designer*. What does she or he research? Understanding the organization as a system and understanding the internal and external forces driving change. What does she or he design? The learning processes whereby managers throughout the organization come to understand these trends and forces.

To illustrate, one of the most important new tools for accelerating learning and for fostering shared mental models of the larger system among local decision makers is microworlds. These are microcosms of real business settings where teams of managers together learn by conducting experiments that are difficult or impossible to conduct in real business. (Chapter 17 describes microworlds in depth.) Developing a microworld involves research to understand the systemic structures underlying particular business issues, then developing a learning process for managers who work and live with these issues day by day. The research and design of microworlds will, I believe, come to be a primary task of central management in learning organizations of the future.

In many ways the role of "manager as researcher" is already starting to be practiced. For example, in firms that are seriously practicing total quality, local managers join with workers in the continual analysis and improvement of work processes.

This does not mean that central or corporate managers no longer participate in decision making. On the contrary, they will be involved in many important decisions, often in conjunction with other corporate and local managers. But, designing the organization's learning processes is a unique role which cannot be delegated. It cannot be done by local managers because local managers are too involved running their businesses and because local managers generally have less breadth of perspective to see the major, long-term issues and forces that will shape how the business evolves. The job of managers as designers is developed further in Chapter 18 ("The Leader's New Work"). If it is not seen as the responsibility of corporate management, including the most senior managers, it will not be done, or it will not be done well. The fact that few of those presently in such positions recognize this role is one of the main reasons that learning organizations are still rare.

FORGIVENESS

To be effective, localness must encourage risk taking among local managers. But to encourage risk taking is to practice forgiveness. Real forgiveness includes "forgive" and "forget." Sometimes, organizations will "forgive" in the sense of not firing someone if he makes a mistake, but the screw up will always be hanging over the offender's head. Real forgiveness includes "reconciliation," mending the relationships that may have been hurt by the mistake.

James Burke illustrates how he learned about forgiveness at Johnson & Johnson, during his first months as head of a new-products division. One day he was summoned to the office of Chairman General Robert Wood Johnson. One of Burke's first product ideas, a children's chest rub, had failed dismally. When Burke walked in Johnson asked, "Are you the one who just cost us all that money?" Burke nodded. The general said, "Well, I just want to congratulate you. If you are making mistakes, that means you are making decisions and taking risks. And we won't grow unless you take risks." [12]

Then there is the legend of Captain Kohei Asoh, who, in 1968, landed his Japan Air Lines DC-8 jetliner two and a half miles short of the runway, out in the waters of San Francisco Bay. The craft made a perfect three-point touchdown. Fortunately, the bay is only about ten feet deep at that point. The crew remained composed. The ninety-six passengers exited in an orderly fashion into the escape rafts which the crew prepared for them. There was not even much damage to the craft.

Soon afterward, the National Transportation Safety Board held an inquiry. Captain Asoh was summoned as the first witness. The chief investigator asked for his excuses, presumably expecting the usual chastened rationalizations or finger pointing. "Captain Asoh, in your own words, can you tell us how you managed to land that DC-8 stretch jet two and a half miles out in San Francisco Bay in perfect compass line with the runway?" Asoh's response, though never recorded in the official NTSB minutes, has gone down in airline folklore: "As you Americans say, Asoh fuck up." The captain took full responsibility for the error. His crew, bound by the orders of Japanese decorum that prohibit criticizing a superior, had sat silently as Asoh landed. Since there was nothing more to investigate, the investigators concluded the inquiry in record time, and let him return to Japan, where they probably expected he would be stripped of his command and demoted.

But Captain Asoh was allowed to continue his career. After a series of meetings with Japan Air Lines officials and a medical checkup, he returned to the cockpit. He flew continuously until his retirement in the late 1980s.[13]

Learning organizations practice forgiveness because, as Cray Research's CEO John Rollwagen says, "Making the mistake is punishment enough."

15

A MANAGER'S TIME

HOW DO MANAGERS CREATE THE TIME FOR LEARNING?

At one of our recent Leadership and Mastery programs, I talked to a manager who was born and raised in India, and who has worked in both United States and Japanese firms. She said that when a person in a Japanese firm sits quietly, no one will come and interrupt. It is assumed that the person is thinking. On the other hand, when the person is up and moving about, coworkers feel free to interrupt.

"Isn't it interesting," she said, "that it is exactly the opposite in American firms? In America, we assume that when a person is sitting quietly they aren't doing anything very important."

How can we expect people to learn when they have little time to think and reflect, individually and collaboratively? I know of few managers who do not complain of not having enough time. Indeed, most of the managers with whom I have worked struggle unceasingly to get the time for quiet reflection. Could this be a cultural norm that we take for granted—the incessant "busyness" of our daily lives?

Donald Schon, in his book *The Reflective Practitioner*, points out that the drive for instant action appears to come from public school classroom learning, where teachers are bound by a bureaucratic organization that discourages time to reflect. "If the teacher must somehow manage the work of thirty students in a classroom, how can she really listen to any one of them?" Thus, in the schoolroom, learning becomes synonymous with absorbing information dished out by an "expert," and everyone, both student and teacher, moves as quickly as possible so as to absorb as much as possible.[1]

In an organization, the manager is the "expert." If there is no authority figure to turn to, then successful professionals (according to Schon) must develop the capacity to work in continuous cycles of pausing to develop hypotheses, acting, and pausing to reflect on the results. Schon calls this "reflection-in-action" and talks about it as a characteristic of professionals who are successful learners. "Phrases like 'thinking on your feet,' 'keeping your wits about you,' and 'learning by doing,' " he wrote, "suggest not only that we can think about doing but that we can think about doing something while doing it."

But many American managers are too busy running to "think on their feet." For most of us our internal pictures about the nature of our work say that activity is good, that a manager's job is to keep things moving. Hanover's Bill O'Brien calls this the "chain gang" model of management: "Most managers seem to think of themselves like the boss of the chain gang: 'the speed of the boss sets the speed of the gang.' "

It is easy to blame this incessant activity and lack of time for reflection on organizational pressures but research is beginning to suggest otherwise. We have conducted numerous experiments, as part of research in developing managerial microworlds (Chapter 17), to study managers' learning habits. Surprisingly, these experiments show that *even* when there is ample time for reflection and the facility for retrieving all manner of relevant information (in the form of a computer-based simulation, in which the managers play out their real-life roles), most managers do *not* reflect carefully on their actions. Typically, managers in the experiments adopt a strategy, then as soon as the strategy starts to run into problems, they switch to another strategy, then to another and another. In a simulated four-year exercise, managers may run through three to six different strategies, without *once* examining why a strategy seems to be failing or articulating specifically what they hope to accomplish through a change in strategy.² Apparently, the "ready, fire, aim" atmosphere of American corporations has been fully assimilated and internalized by those who live in that atmosphere.

Learning takes time. When an individual is managing mental models, for example, it takes considerable time to surface assumptions, examine their consistency and accuracy, and see how different models can be knit together into more systemic perspectives on important problems.

The management of time and attention is an area where top management has a significant influence, not by edict but by example. For instance, O'Brien simply doesn't schedule short meetings. "If it isn't a subject that is worthy of an hour, it shouldn't be on my calendar." In a well-designed organization, the *only* issues that should reach a senior manager's attention should be complex, dilemma-like "divergent" issues. These are the issues that require the thought and experience of the most senior people, in addition to the input of less experienced people. If top managers are handling twenty problems in a workday, either they are spending too much time on "convergent" problems that should be dealt with more locally in the organization, or they are giving insufficient time to complex problems. Either way, it is a sign that management work is being handled poorly. "It's a big year for me," O'Brien adds, "if I make twelve decisions. I may pick someone to report directly to me. I may set a direction. But my job is not consumed with making many decisions. It is consumed with identifying important issues the organization must address in the future, helping others sort through decisions they must make, and the overarching tasks of organizational design" (see Chapter 18 on the design functions of leadership).

The principle is simple to say and understand, but it's not the way most organizations operate. Instead, people at the top continually make decisions on issues such as how to run a promotion—as opposed to why they need to run promotions at all. Or they discuss how to make a sale to a particular customer—instead of inquiring about how their products serve the customers' expressed and latent needs in general.

On the other hand, as the basic learning disciplines start to become assimilated into an organization, a different view of managerial work will develop. Action will still be critical, but incisive action will not be confused with incessant activity. There will be time for reflection, conceptualizing, and examining complex issues.

No one knows how much time managers in future organizations

will spend reflecting, modeling, and designing learner processes. But it will be a great deal more than was spent in the past. Ed Simon at Herman Miller has asked his management team to commit 25 percent of their work time to what he calls "learning the work of organizational architects." During the past year, the team has devoted itself to mastering the "reflection and inquiry" skills integral to the discipline of "mental models," and applying these skills to their most strategic issues. He said that this time commitment is necessary because although there is much to be learned about the "new work" of managers and leaders, "We know enough that we can get started."

One useful starting point for all managers is to look at their time for thinking. If it isn't adequate, why not? Are work pressures keeping us from taking the time, or, to some degree, are we doing it to ourselves? Either way, where is the leverage for change? For some people, it may involve changing personal habits. Others may need to soften or deflect the organization's demands for incessant "busyness." The way each of us and each of our close colleagues go about managing our own time will say a good deal about our commitment to learning.

16

ENDING THE WAR
BETWEEN WORK AND
FAMILY

HOW CAN PERSONAL MASTERY
AND LEARNING FLOURISH AT
WORK *AND* AT HOME?

In 1990 a *Fortune* magazine cover story, titled "Why Grade A Executives Get an F as Parents," observed that children of successful executives are more likely to suffer a range of emotional and health problems than children of "less successful" parents.[1] For example, one Ann Arbor Michigan study found that 36 percent of the children of executives undergo treatment for psychiatric or drug abuse each year, vs. 15 percent of children of non-executives in the same companies. The author went on to cite the executives' long hours and personal characteristics (perfectionism, impatience, and efficiency) as the chief culprits and counseled that high-powered managers need to learn how to boost their children's "self esteem." What was most interesting about the article, however, was what it didn't say. Nothing was mentioned about how the executives' organizations contributed to their problems as parents or what they might do to improve matters. It seems that the author, like most of the rest of us, simply accepts the fact that work inevitably conflicts with family life, and that the organization has no part to play in improving imbalances between work and family.

In recent years, I have noticed a considerable increase in concern over the work-family issue among participants in our Leadership and Mastery programs. Today, "finding balance between my work and my family" is cited as a number-one priority by more attendees than any other single issue.

Traditional organizations undeniably foster conflict between work and family. Sometimes, this is done consciously—through the simple threat that, "If you want to get ahead here, you must be willing to make sacrifices." More often, it is done inadvertently, by simply creating a set of demands and pressures on the individual that inevitably conflict with family and personal time. These demands include travel, dinner meetings, the increasingly common breakfast meetings, weekend retreats, and just plain old long hours at the shop. The pressures arise primarily from the narrow focus on organizational goals and objectives to the exclusion of personal goals and objectives. In other words, if all that matters is the organization's goals, there is simply "no space" for weighing the cost of those goals for an individual or the individual's family.

The disciplines of the learning organization will, I believe, end the taboo that has surrounded the topic of balancing work and family, and has kept it off the corporate agenda. The learning organization cannot support personal mastery without supporting personal mastery in all aspects of life. It cannot foster shared vision without calling forth personal visions, and personal visions are always multifaceted—they always include deeply felt desires for our personal, professional, organizational, and family lives. Lastly, the artificial boundary between work and family is anathema to systems thinking. There is a natural connection between a person's work life and all other aspects of life. We live only one life, but for a long time our organizations have operated as if this simple fact could be ignored, as if we had two separate lives.

THE STRUCTURE OF WORK/FAMILY IMBALANCE

There is a systems archetype underlying the work-family imbalance. This archetype is called "Success to the Successful" because it consists of two reinforcing growth processes, each of which tend to fuel increasing levels of success—albeit to competing activities. This archetype underlies a wide variety of situations where individuals, groups, or organizations compete for a limited resource. The success of one means that it tends to get more of the resource, which then reduces the success of the others. The resource could be limited dollars to invest in competing divisions of a business. It could be limited praise of a teacher in a crowded classroom. Or it could be the limited time of a busy manager:

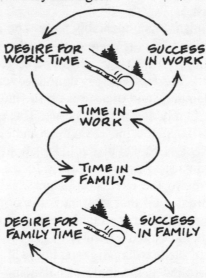

At the top of the diagram, there is the reinforcing (amplifying) growth of time and commitment in one's work: more time leads to greater success, which leads to more and more interesting opportunities and more desire for time at work, which leads to still more time at work. At the bottom of the diagram is a similar reinforcing growth of time and commitment at home: more time at home leads to more "success" (satisfying family relationships, healthy kids, family fun) at home, which leads to the desire for still more time at home. The two reinforcing processes are connected because if time at work goes up there is less time available for home, and vice versa.[2]

Like other structures dominated by reinforcing feedback (recall the "escalation structure" underlying the arms race), the "Success to the Successful" archetype is intrinsically unstable. Once it starts to drift one way or another, it will tend to continue to drift. And there are several reasons why it tends to drift toward more and more time at work. First, there is the matter of income. If time at work falls too far, income falls and creates pressure for more time at work.

(This could be drawn as a balancing process controlling time at work but is omitted from the diagram for simplicity.) Secondly, the reinforcing "time at home" process tends to be especially strong in the negative, "vicious spiral" direction. If you find yourself in a situation where less time at home is leading to poorer family relationships, there can be strong psychological pressures to avoid family problems still further. "Pushing ahead" with one's work becomes a convenient excuse for avoiding the anguish of going home to an unhappy spouse and troubled children. As you spend less time at home, "success in family" diminishes further, leading to still less desire for family time. Thirdly, for most highly successful professionals, there are more "external" pressures for time at work than for time at home: norms of twelve- to fifteen-hour days for high performers, new opportunities that require more travel, subtle peer pressure from colleagues with their own family problems.

Because of the dominant reinforcing feedback in "Success to the Successful," the imbalances are not self-correcting. Indeed, they grow worse and worse over time. This is why work-family issues are so vexing.

For several years, we have worked with this archetype in training programs. It has been fascinating to see how frequently people realize the futility of trying to manage their lives from within this structure. Any one-time improvement in, say, success in family tends to get overwhelmed by the continually escalating pressures for more and more time in work. Eventually, people realize that the structure itself must be changed—you cannot cope successfully within it if you want to achieve a balance between work and family because it will always be driving you toward imbalance.

THE INDIVIDUAL'S ROLE

The first task is stepping outside the structure—asking yourself if, given your ambitions, it is really your *vision* to have a balance between work and family. How serious are you? This is not a trivial question. If it were simple to achieve this balance, more people would do it. Many people lament the problem, but few have made a conscious choice to achieve the balance they espouse.

Making a conscious choice will entail setting clear personal goals for time at home. For example, when will you be home at night? What about dinner meetings? What about weekends? The *Fortune* article described several executives who committed themselves to being home for dinner so many nights a week, gave up weekend golf, and reduced evening business meetings. These may seem like modest steps but they are exactly the types of steps required to translate a vision of balance into tangible goals. Just setting goals without a genuine vision will likely lead to backsliding when the goals prove difficult to realize.

In some organizations, managers may pay a price in their career opportunities if they take a stand for a vision of balance between work and family. Very often, the person who takes such a stand will command the respect of their peers—many of whom may wish that they too could make a similar commitment. Nonetheless, such a stand can also generate conflicts, especially between managers who are committed to balance between work and family and those who are not. I know of no simple advice to offer in such circumstances except for these principles of personal mastery and enrollment:

- Identify what is truly important to you
- Make a choice (commitment)
- Be truthful with those around you regarding your choice
- Do not try to manipulate them into agreement or superficial support

Ultimately, the consequences of individuals' choices regarding work and family will depend, to a degree, on the overall organizational climate.

THE ORGANIZATION'S ROLE

Ironically, conflicts between work and family may be one of the primary ways through which traditional organizations limit their effectiveness and ability to learn. By fostering such conflict, they distract and unempower their members—often to a far greater degree than they realize. Moreover, they fail to exploit a potential synergy that can exist between learning organizations, learning individuals, and learning families.

"It's ironic," says Hanover's Bill O'Brien, "that we spend so much time and money trying to devise clever programs for developing leadership in our organizations and ignore a structure that already exists, and which is ideal for the job. The more I understand the real skills of leadership in a learning organization, the more I become convinced that these are the skills of effective parenting.

Leading in a learning organization involves supporting people in clarifying and pursuing their own visions, 'moral suasion,' helping people discover underlying causes of problems, and empowering them to make choices. What could be a better description of effective parenting? The fact that many parents don't succeed especially well simply shows that we haven't created the learning environment for parenting, just as we've not created the learning environment for developing leaders.''

O'Brien's reflections open up what I suspect will become an increasingly important topic in coming years: looking for the synergy between productive family life and productive work life. The old world of sharp boundaries between work and family is falling away. A new world of blurred boundaries is here, and it is a world that only a few organizations are facing up to.

In that old world, the man worked and the woman stayed at home to raise the children. Today, in families with children where at least one member holds a management position, only 51.5 percent have a stay-at-home spouse—in 28 percent either both spouses are at work or it is a single-parent family.[3] And the percentage of families with no spouse at home is continuing to rise.[4] One of the implications of this dramatic change is that family issues spill over much more into the managers' lives simply because there is no one else at home to whom the problem can be delegated. It also means that there are, by and large, more family issues.

In the old world, people's personal interests were their own concern. The corporation wanted only "an honest day's work for an honest day's pay." In the learning organization, the boundaries between what is personal and what is organizational are intentionally blurred. Learning organizations enter into a new compact, or "covenant" as Max de Pree puts it, with their members. The essence of this compact is the organization's commitment to support the full development of each employee, and the person's reciprocal commitment to the organization.[5] Intentional or inadvertent pressures that make success at work and success at home an "either/or" proposition violate this compact.

I believe these changes will lead more organizations to recognize what is long overdue—that organizations must undo the divisive pressures and demands that make balancing work and family so burdensome today. This is necessary because of their commitment to their members. But it is also necessary to developing the organization's capabilities.

There are many specific steps that organizations can take to begin contributing to more balance between work and family. Some steps, such as providing day care for single parents, have already been taken in many firms. But there are a broader and more challenging set of steps ahead. For example:

- Support personal mastery as a part of the organization's philosophy and strategy (Chapter 9 discusses the "how to's" and pitfalls in making such support effective).
- Make it acceptable for people to acknowledge family issues as well as business issues and to interject these into pertinent discussions, especially discussions involving time commitments.
- Where needed, help people obtain counseling and guidance for how to make effective use of their family time (many of the difficult problems in parenting and family relationships do not arise solely from inadequate time but from not knowing *how* to handle the issues effectively).

There are, undoubtedly, many other concrete steps that can be taken. But the most important step is the first step—acknowledging that one cannot build a learning organization on a foundation of broken homes and strained personal relationships.

The conflict between work and home is not just a conflict over time, but over values. All the habits that an executive learns in an authoritarian organization are exactly the habits, as *Fortune*'s article showed, that make them unsuccessful parents. How can an executive build up a child's self-esteem at home when he or she is accustomed to tearing down other people's self-esteem at the office? The values and habits learned by practicing the five disciplines of a learning organization serve to nurture the family as well as the business. It's a virtuous circle: not only is being a good parent a training ground for being a learningful manager, but being a learningful manager is also good preparation for parenting. The conflict between work and home diminishes dramatically when the organization fosters values in alignment with people's own core, values that have equal meaning at work and at home. Only then will it be possible for managers to stop living by two codes of behavior, and start being one person.

17

MICROWORLDS:
THE TECHNOLOGY
OF THE LEARNING
ORGANIZATION

HOW CAN WE REDISCOVER THE
CHILD LEARNER WITHIN US?

Human beings learn best through firsthand experience. We learn to walk, ride a bicycle, drive an automobile, and play the piano by trial and error: we act, observe the consequences of our action and adjust. But "learning by doing" only works so long as the feedback from our actions is rapid and unambiguous. When we act in a complex system the consequences of our actions are neither immediate nor unambiguous. Often, they are far removed from us in time and space. This leads to the "dilemma of learning from experience," one of the learning disabilities described in Chapter 2: we learn best from experience, but we never experience the consequences of our most important decisions. How, then, can we learn?

Microworlds enable managers and management teams to begin "learning through doing" about their most important systemic issues. In particular, microworlds "compress time and space" so that it becomes possible to experiment and to learn when the consequences of our decisions are in the future and in distant parts of the organization. While the computer-based microworlds described below are new, the principle of learning through microworlds is actually familiar to us all.

When they play with dolls, children rehearse ways of interacting with people. When they play with blocks, they teach themselves basic principles of spatial geometry and mechanics. Later in life they will learn the general properties of the pendulum through swinging on a swing and all about levers through the playground teeter-totter. The doll, the blocks, the swing, and teeter-totter are what educational theorists call "transitional objects"; the playroom or the playground is a microworld, a microcosm of reality where it is safe to play. Through experimentation with transitional objects in microworlds, children discover principles and develop skills that are relevant in reality beyond play.[1]

They also achieve a rate of learning that is truly astounding. By the age of three or four, children have learned basic principles of geometry and mechanics; they have mastered natural language, a feat which artificial intelligence researchers admit is still on the distant horizon for machines; and they have learned all about the "social systems" of home life such as "If I don't clean my room, my mother will." All without ever being "taught."

Learning through transitional objects and microworlds is not limited to children. The aeronautical engineer's model in a wind tunnel is a transitional object in a microworld, as is the naval designer's model ship in a "wave tank." Managers too have transitional objects and microworlds. When a work team goes white-water rafting or engages in some other outdoor team-building exercise, they are creating a microworld to reflect on and improve the way they work together. When personnel staff create a role-playing exercise to be used in supervisory training they are creating a microworld. Many team retreats serve as microworlds, as illustrated by the "dialogue" practice sessions discussed in the Team Learning chapter. Consultants often serve as a transitional object of sorts—a safe sounding board for exploring new and different business ideas without the risks of directly putting those ideas into practice.

But existing microworlds for managers are limited. For example, team-building exercises can produce powerful insights into learning processes, but they usually do not lead to new insights regarding strategic business issues. Role-playing exercises can help develop interpersonal management skills, but they do not show us whether our personnel policies are aligned with our manufacturing and marketing policies. Perhaps most importantly, few existing microworlds develop individual or team capacities to deal productively with complexity. Few capture the dynamic complexity that confronts the management team when it seeks to craft new strategies, design new structures and operating policies, or plan significant organizational change.

Now a new type of microworld is emerging. Personal computers are making it possible to integrate learning about complex team interactions with learning about complex business interactions. These new microworlds allow groups to reflect on, expose, test, and improve the mental models upon which they rely in facing difficult problems. They are settings for both crafting visions and experimenting with a broad range of strategies and policies for achieving those visions. Gradually, they are becoming a new type of "practice field" for management teams, places where teams will learn how to learn together while engaging their most important business issues.

Microworlds will, I believe, prove to be a critical technology for implementing the disciplines of the learning organization. And they will accomplish this by helping us rediscover the power of learning through play. Shell's Arie de Geus says that organizational learning occurs in three ways: through teaching, through "changing the rules of the game" (such as through openness and localness), and through play. Play is the most rare, and potentially the most powerful. Microworlds are places for "relevant play." There the issues and dynamics of complex business situations can be explored through trying out new strategies and policies and seeing what might happen. Costs of failed experiments disappear. Organizational sanctions against experimentation, either implicit or explicit, are nonexistent. Reflecting on our own and our team's learning skills can be enlightening and "lightening" (as in "lightening up") because this reflection can be separated from the risks and pressures of real decision making.

Today, microworlds for managers are exploring diverse issues from managing growth to product development and improving quality in both service and manufacturing businesses. These experiments build on and incorporate insights about system archetypes, team learning, and working with mental models. We still have a long way to go before "practice fields for management teams" are a way of life in learning organizations. But important principles and tools are emerging that are pointing the way.

What follows are descriptions of three different microworlds taken from three very different business settings. They illustrate the range of strategic and operational issues that microworlds can illuminate:

1. *Future Learning:* in which a management team discovers internal contradictions in a strategy that is only just being put into place;
2. *Seeing Hidden Strategic Opportunities:* in which a team experiments with its members' mental models, and discovers that the assumptions team members hold can shape their customers' preferences;
3. *Discovering Untapped Leverage:* in which we invite you to imagine playing out the roles of local managers in an insurance company in order to see how deceptively easy it is to "look good without being good," to mismanage workload in such a way that quality erodes and potential leverage for improving customer service and profitability is lost.

M i c r o w o r l d 1

FUTURE LEARNING: DISCOVERING INTERNAL CONTRADICTIONS IN A STRATEGY

Lying behind all strategies are assumptions, which often remain implicit and untested. Frequently, these assumptions have internal contradictions. When they do, the strategy also has internal contradictions, which will prove to make it difficult or impossible to implement. One benefit of microworlds is bringing these assumptions into the open and discovering these inconsistencies.

One such case occurred at a highly successful manufacturer of microcomputers (here called the "Index Computer Company").[2] The top management team had introduced a microworld as a part of a two-day planning retreat. They had taken on a strategic goal four months earlier: to reach $2 billion in sales in four years. They were all committed to the goal, from Index's President Tom Jamison on down. And everyone seemed happy with the progress so far.

That's why the vice president of Sales, James Sawyer, felt so uneasy. It was difficult enough to keep and train his present sales force—how did they expect him to double it? He had shared his qualms with other top managers, but they had only responded with platitudes: "You'll work it out. After all, you'll have the budget for it." Now he was in a bind. He didn't want his fellow executives to think he lacked their commitment to that magic $2 billion figure. He didn't want to get the reputation of a "nay sayer." And he certainly didn't want to let on that he thought he might not rise to the occasion, especially since he had a reputation as a "fixer" who could solve any problem. But every time he thought about the future, an involuntary shudder of pain ran through his stomach.

Soon the executives split into three-person microworld teams to play out the consequences of the sales plan. Their first task was to construct an explicit model on the computer of the assumptions behind the plan.[3] The plan called for a 20 percent annual sales growth, a continuation of the growth rate of the past ten years. And it also called for 20 percent more salespeople each year. As they looked at simulated sales figures for the next four years, it didn't take them long to recognize that the official plan implicitly assumed that the productivity of salespeople would hold steady as the sales force expanded. Hire 20 percent more salespeople, you make 20 percent more sales.

Making the assumption explicit prompted Sawyer to say, "Well, wait a minute. Not all salespeople are equal. There is so much they have to learn—about office automation, software, training, accounting, engineering, consulting, and manufacturing—before they can place a single system. Much of our historic growth," he continued, "came from hiring experienced salespeople whom we lured away from our competitors. We could do that as long as we were small. But now the numbers of new hires we need to sustain our 20 percent growth are getting much larger. We will not be able to get this many people by hiring away from our competitors. We'll be hiring many more inexperienced salespeople in the future."

Sawyer's comment sparked a lively debate about the differences in productivity between experienced and inexperienced salespeople. All agreed that it was necessary to distinguish new, inexperienced salespeople from veterans. When they split back into teams, each team modified their models to make more realistic assumptions. Sawyer's team, for instance, assumed that veterans would be four times as productive as rookies. Some groups assumed less, some groups assumed more, but everyone assumed that training and developing an experienced salesperson required two to four years.

Now, however, none of the models reached that $2 billion sales goal. Sawyer's model projected sales under $1.5 billion.

The problem came from the average productivity of the growing sales force. As the computer simulated the consequences of the projected hiring, it showed more and more rookies, because the rate of new hires exceeded the rate at which rookies became veterans. Although they hired enough total salespeople to meet their plan, the mix of inexperienced and veteran salespeople shifted progressively toward the inexperienced, pulling down average productivity. (The effects of rapid growth on the mix of experienced personnel, you may recall, was also an important dynamic at People Express Airlines in Chapter 8.)

The different work teams tried furiously to find a set of assumptions they could believe which would produce $2 billion in sales in four years. No one could do it. To see just how extreme the problems might become, one group asked the question, "How many salespeople *would* we have to hire if we simply kept hiring until our sales targets were met?" They found that, "We'd end up almost *doubling* the sales force in the fourth year alone, if we doggedly kept adding bodies until our sales target was reached." All knew that this magnitude of personnel growth would wreak havoc on the sales organization, not to mention the overall personnel budget.

After an hour, the president stood up and asked, "Is there anyone here who still believes that our strategic plan is internally consistent?" No one responded.

The managers had known both halves of the contradiction: that novices are less productive salespeople, and that the new sales goals would require them to hire more novices. But the assumptions came together only when they were put into a microworld that simulated their interaction over time. Now that everyone could see the internal inconsistency, Sawyer found himself able to articulate, for the first time, his general reservations.

"I've felt for some time that executing the new strategic plan will cause problems," he told the group. "And the problems might be even worse than even these simulations suggest. We have a tradition of not revising our business goals once we've announced them publicly. So, not only would we be likely to hire a lot more new salespeople than our official plan projects, but there will be a lot more pressure on our veterans. Couple that with the distractions and frustrations for our veterans who have to help all these new people get up to speed and I wouldn't be surprised if we end up with more veterans leaving and lower productivity from those who stay. We could get into a really vicious cycle. Many of our veterans came to us in the first place to escape this kind of situation somewhere else."

The other managers sensed that Sawyer's fears might well materialize. "Perhaps," said the president, "it's time to step back and consider some of the challenges we face." He had hardly finished his sentence before Susan Willis, the vice president of Human Resources, had motioned for the floor.

"This is crucial," said Willis. "Our people have some problems with the sales managers that I'd like to get onto the table." Willis then talked about the strained relationship between Human Resources and Sales. The sales managers, she said, especially resisted any call to invest their time in training and developing new salespeople. Why, she asked Sawyer, were they so reluctant?

"Well, we grew our sales organization by attracting the most aggressive people, the kind of people who spend all their time out in the field," said Sawyer. "They don't want to mentor any new hires. They thrive on closing a sale. That's not just where they get their kicks, it's where they make their money. Thanks to our strong incentives, the sales managers with high quotas are among the best-paid people at Index. There are no comparable incentives for helping newcomers; our organization is a lot stronger at rewarding individual accomplishment."

Then Sawyer added that the new strategic plan would simply reinforce this problem. "You must keep in mind that our whole sales organization is geared to meet aggressive targets," he said. "Give them a tougher target, and they'll respond by selling harder. I'll have a very tough time getting them to think about taking time in developing new hires. I understand Susan's problems. I have the same problems."

The microworld had brought to the surface a set of frustrations which had been brewing for some time. Moreover, it focused those frustrations on critical changes which needed to occur if the organization hoped to sustain past success. Most important, the declining sales productivity had failed to galvanize action to date, because it *had not yet taken place in the real world*. The microworld gave them a unique window on the future.

As their strategy retreat continued, the management team saw the core issue as either lowering their growth targets or transforming their sales organization. They concluded that the growth target was realizable *if* new sales people could be trained much more quickly. This presented a significant challenge, because it meant that veteran salespeople would need to be more committed to mentoring inexperienced colleagues. There would need to be new rewards for sales managers to develop their staffs. More support to help senior sales-people in mentoring and training would be needed. And they'd need to look more carefully for new hires who wanted to work in a collaborative team environment, where people helped one another become more effective. The changes were significant but achievable.

One tool for change would be another microworld—this one designed for sales managers, in which they could learn to balance, week by week, their time allocation between direct sales efforts, recruitment, training, and management. The salespeople could then discover the long-term benefits of allocating time to personnel development rather than to direct sales efforts.

Predictions such as those achieved at Index are different from normal business forecasts. As former Shell planner Pierre Wack observed: "Suppose heavy monsoon rains hit the upper part of the Ganges River basin. With little doubt you know that something extraordinary will happen within two days at Rishikesh at the foothills of the Himalayas; in Allahabad, three or four days later; and at Benares, two days after that."[4] This is a prediction, not a forecast. It is something you can say with confidence about the future, because it depends not on projecting historical data into the future, but on understanding the dynamics of an underlying system. By analogy, some of the most interesting learnings that come out of microworlds come from discovering implications for the future, when decisions play out in what had been unrecognized organizational systems.

Microworld 2

SEEING HIDDEN STRATEGIC OPPORTUNITIES: HOW OUR BELIEFS INFLUENCE OUR CUSTOMERS' PREFERENCES

Some of the most important microworlds help teams mired in conflicting views of complex issues. Here, microworlds can be crucial in surfacing different assumptions and discovering how they can be interrelated in a larger understanding. Often, our linear language and defensive ways of presenting our thinking lead to perceiving false dichotomies and irreconcilable differences. When in fact, as did the proverbial "blind men," different managers with different types of business experience are merely seeing "different parts of the elephant." Sometimes, the microworld allows them to "see the elephant" for the first time.

Bill Seaver and John Henry are president and VP for marketing, respectively, of the highly successful Meadowlands shelving company.[5] (As in the first story, some of the specifics here have been changed, but this is a true story.) Seaver and Henry had come to a basic impasse in the way they saw their customers and their market. Seaver believed that the key to success in the marketplace lay in having good products priced competitively. Henry agreed but also felt that service quality could play a big part in whether or not customers chose Meadowlands. He believed that the company should invest in upgrading its service through training Meadowlands dealers in performing a wide range of services from better account management to office design and troubleshooting for all manner of problems that Meadowlands customers might encounter. Seaver thought these were good ideas but would not support spending significantly more on dealer support than they were already because he was convinced that they would not have significant impact on Meadowlands' sales. "People expect decent service in our business," he said. "They will not pay extra for it."

Seaver appeared to have plenty of evidence on his side. For one, salespeople continually returned to the home office with stories of how difficult it was to make sales unless they could increase discounts. "Our competitors are discounting like mad and we can only hold our own if we match or better them," was the typical refrain. When the officers talked to customers, Henry had to admit, customers rarely asked for better or more diverse types of service. Even when Henry would pursue the point more forcefully, customers would usually respond, "That sounds nice but what would really make a difference to us would be another 5 percent off on the big order we've been discussing with your sales reps." He had to admit that he was the only one on the top team who took the service idea very seriously, and even he had to wonder sometimes.

Still, Henry held to his belief that there must be a way to gain competitive advantage through better service. Unable to resolve their differences, the two agreed to try experimenting with alternative strategies in a microworld the team designed on the basis of assumptions that they did share in common—the distinction between major purchases (e.g., when customers build a new facility) and minor purchases (e.g., replacing old shelving in an existing space), how long customers waited between major purchases, the value attached by customers to quality of design and manufacture, the effect of price on purchases, and the volume of current spending on dealer support. In the microworld, Seaver and Henry were joined by two other members of the Meadowlands management team: Jim Cortland and Tony Jaynes, the VPs of sales and distribution, respectively.

The four men split into two pairs of partners. Seaver and Henry teamed up as corporate management, deciding, jointly, how much to invest to help Meadowlands' local dealers build the infrastructure to provide customer service. Cortland and Jaynes became the Meadowlands sales department, deciding whether and how much to discount prices each quarter in order to reach sales targets. As in real life, these two decisions were made separately. There was, however, a common goal: the highest possible profits for the firm, over a five-year time span.

At the outset of the simulation, a temporary recession caused an early decline in new orders. Cortland and Jaynes, hoping to maintain market share, responded by increasing the discount percentage. Market share held relatively steady but there was a decline in profit margins, which meant that Seaver and Henry had to reduce their dealer support investment. Through their combined efforts market share held steady and margins declined only slightly over the first year.

Unfortunately, the quiet was short-lived. Over the next two years, Cortland and Jaynes found it necessary to gradually but steadily increase discounts. To compensate for the ever-declining profits, Seaver and Henry gave less and less support to dealers. By the end of three years, price discounts had risen 25 percent and margins had fallen 20 percent relative to the start. Although market share had been preserved, the team members felt little satisfaction with their business performance.

In the discussion that followed, Cortland and Jaynes said that the simulation confirmed their assumption that competitive pricing is critical. "As we kept going," said Cortland, "it seemed to me that customers wanted even *more* discounts than they did at the outset. When we tried to hold discounts fixed that last year, volume dropped dramatically"—far more rapidly, he said, than it had when they fixed discounts early in the game. Seaver said that the experiment had certainly done nothing to change his mind that pricing was much more critical than service; he and Henry had found that short-term boosts in dealer support appeared to have little impact on customer orders, while cutting dealer support had little apparent adverse affect on demand. But the overall decline in profitability disturbed him, especially since it matched what actually had been happening in Meadowlands' industry in recent years.

Bill Henry was quiet, apparently deep in thought. Finally, he suggested that they try another experiment. "Why don't we see what happens if, rather than boosting discounts, we increase dealer support and maintain prices. We've got nothing to lose. It's only a game." The others didn't see the point, but they didn't see any reason to refuse, either.

At first, their fears were realized. Customer orders fell off and profits were depressed, both by the reduction in revenues and by increases in dealer support. By the end of the second year, volume was still down five percent and margins were down 12 percent. Cortland and Jaynes asked if they really had to stay with the "no discounting" policy. Henry pointed out that orders were no longer falling, and that they should be patient. In the third year, a turnaround began. Volume started increasing, as did margins. They kept playing. By the fifth year, volume and margins were both well above their initial levels. The team members were surprised and a little incredulous.

When they examined more closely what had happened in the two simulations, the management team discovered a reinforcing process built into the structure of the model. The process tended to reinforce the starting assumptions. In the first simulation, their lower prices led to lower profits, which in turn led to less investment and lower service quality. This produced disgruntled customers, who in turn clamored for more price cuts. Late-in-the-game efforts to attract them with better service quality lacked credibility, because they had experienced poor service for so long. This put even further pressure on the company to lower prices, which started the cycle all over again.

Conversely, in the second simulation, the vicious spiral became a virtuous spiral. Following Bill Henry's assumption that service mattered to customers, they invested in dealer support, and service quality gradually improved. This made no difference in the short run because customers have to experience improved service before they take it seriously. The benefits of investing in service took several years to harvest because the repurchasing delay in the shelving industry is two to four years. That repurchase delay had never been seen as an important factor before.

Yet, it turned out to be critical to seeing that *both* Henry and Seaver were right. Seaver was right when he maintained that service doesn't matter as much as price. This is true in the short run, especially given that none of Meadowlands' competitors offer any but the most perfunctory services (such as sorting out misshipments) and these are provided halfheartedly. Consequently, customers don't expect service and don't ask for it. If a manufacturer offers to provide a higher standard of service, customers, understandably, respond skeptically. On the other hand, Henry was also right. Potentially, according to the model used in the microworld, service could be a competitive weapon.[6] The key lay in understanding that customers first had to experience the benefits of better service before they would value service. This meant that any service-oriented strategy had to be a long-term strategy.

Moreover, the process of managing in the microworld had revealed some fascinating patterns in how the team and other Meadowlands managers interacted. In the first play, before they had adopted Henry's alternative strategy, the two teams of decision makers had quickly formed into tight units and set about making decisions in ways that, in retrospect, seemed all too familiar at Meadowlands. The corporate people (Seaver and Henry) operated in a separate world from the local salespeople (Cortland and Jaynes). The two teams started strategizing and acting almost as if they were each other's adversaries. "We'd be making money if it weren't for you"; "You guys are giving away the store!" said Seaver and Henry, respectively, as Cortland and Jaynes kept increasing discounts to hold sales volume (which of course is how Meadowlands' sales force is measured). After a brief exchange in an effort to coordinate, Cortland said, "Let's do it the 'Meadowlands way'; you do it your way and we'll do it ours." A little later, Seaver cried out, "Leave it alone," as Cortland and Jaynes prepared to raise discounts one more time.

Afterward, the entire group read over transcripts of the actual exchange, which everyone found hilarious. As they chuckled, Henry offered the simple explanation, "This is why we sell shelving." Reflecting on the transcript, the team identified several themes which they felt often characterized how Meadowlands' management teams worked:

- Act as if your dimension of the system is the most important
- Hold others responsible for negative effects of the policies as I define negative
- Advocate your view, and do not inquire into your own or your partner's or other's reasoning

The microworld experiment at Meadowlands not only revealed an important strategic insight, but it had also begun to reveal, in a nonthreatening way, the need for individual- and team-learning skills. The team realized that its ways of interacting kept them from resolving important issues such as those between Henry and Seaver. They would remain "blind men" so long as they perpetuated the "Meadowlands way."

M i c r o w o r l d   3

DISCOVERING UNTAPPED LEVERAGE: THE DRIFT TO LOW QUALITY IN SERVICE BUSINESSES

The microworlds described thus far were used in the context of one- and two-day management meetings to surface implicit assumptions and catalyze rethinking of important issues. Yet, these represent only glimpses of the "practice fields of the future," where management teams will return regularly to craft strategy, debate critical issues as they arise, and continually extend their business understanding and learning skills. The following case is drawn from a continuing research project with Hanover Insurance, intended to create a "learning laboratory" that will become an ongoing feature of managerial work at Hanover. This learning laboratory illustrates the type of in-depth inquiry and testing of ideas that is sorely missing from today's organizations, and which microworlds are uniquely qualified to enable.

The issues brought out in the Hanover learning lab are not just about insurance. Underlying the specifics of managing claims adjusting is a generic set of dynamics that recur in diverse service organizations, from banking to overnight delivery service, from hospitals and universities to hotels. In all of these settings, there are systemic forces that work against sustaining high quality. It is very easy to think you are doing a good job when, in fact, you aren't. It is easy to "manage by the numbers" and end up with chronic "undercapacity"—overworked employees and unsatisfied customers. It is extremely easy to be modestly profitable and completely miss opportunities for significant increases in quality and profitability. In other words, in all of these service businesses, it is easy to miss the leverage for real success.

THE CLAIMS LEARNING LABORATORY

Managers come to the Claims Learning Laboratory to develop a more systemic understanding of cost and quality—subjects that have never been more crucial, both within the insurance industry and among its many customers. Escalating insurance costs are reaching crisis proportions. Physicians are giving up their practices in many states because they cannot afford malpractice insurance. The costs of worker's compensation and health insurance are becoming a competitive millstone to many U.S. businesses—for example, comprising upward of 20 percent of the total wage bill of Detroit auto makers, as opposed to 8 percent for their Japanese counterparts. Many firms can no longer afford to insure themselves against many important risks—such as toxic waste—and are turning to forms of self-insurance. As the 1980s drew to an end, a nationwide consumer backlash against rising automobile insurance premiums was brewing, led by a referendum in California to cap premiums regardless of the impact on insurance company profits.

For their part, reacting to the rising tide of criticism, insurers have blamed everything from avaricious lawyers and outdated government regulations to lax public morality and the "litigious society." Against this array of "external forces" they have increased lobbying, bolstered legal staffs, and cut costs. Few, however, have looked seriously at how their own practices could be contributing to the crisis. Yet, as you will discover shortly, practices held in good stead are perfectly capable of causing rising costs and falling quality—without any help from outside forces.

Imagine, then, that you are the manager of a claims adjusting office, sitting with your partner, another claims office manager, in front of a personal computer screen displaying the status of the "claims game."[7] You're in your second day of a three-day workshop back at the main office. Yesterday, you shared concerns and frustrations with fifteen other local managers—the difficulties in keeping good people (turnover rates among adjusters are typically 30 to 50 percent per year), the struggle to continually keep up with the workload, the dilemmas of improving quality while keeping a firm rein on costs. You also talked about your visions for your local office and for the company. Later in the day, you spent time learning about systems thinking, and you now have an intellectual grasp of the basics, and a sense of how it might affect your day-to-day work. But today, when you sat down for the first time at the computer screen representing a typical adjusting office, you realized that you still didn't have a gut feel for it. The screen before you didn't make it seem any easier: it was like the cockpit of a jet airplane:

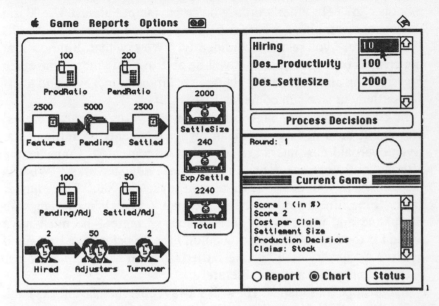

It didn't take long to become familiar with the layout—after all, all the jargon came right out of your daily office—which was fortunate, because an all-too-familiar crisis hit in month three. Without warning, incoming claims ("Features") jumped 20 percent. Your backlog of unsettled claims ("Pending") rose alarmingly. Your understaffed office was unable to keep pace and complaints from angry customers waiting to have their claims settled shot up. Fortunately, you and your partner, Rosabeth Harrold from the Schenectady office, had lived through many a similar real-life crisis and you reacted quickly. You raised production targets ("Desired Productivity")— in effect saying, "We'll ask each adjuster to settle 15 percent more cases per month for a while." You also hired a few more people. And you waited. Sure enough, by the eighth or ninth month, your policies had taken hold. Now, at the tenth month backlogs are back to normal even though new incoming claims remain high, customer complaints are down, and you and Rosabeth lean back in your chairs.

"I think we're in pretty good shape now," you say. "We weathered *that* crisis. Our problems are behind us."

At that moment, Bob Bergin, a senior claims manager and co-leader of the workshop, steps up behind you and looks over your shoulders. "Have both of you noticed," asks Bergin, "that your average settlement size is almost 10 percent higher than it was nine months ago?" (In other words, you're paying out almost $2,500, on the average, per claim, whereas before you were paying out $2,240.)

"Oh, sure," you respond confidently. "We saw that. But now that the crisis is over, our adjusters will be able to put in more time again investigating and negotiating claims. Quality will improve, and average settlement size will come back down."

In claims adjusting, high quality service, from the customers' viewpoint, does not merely mean higher payments on settlements. Even overpaid customers are often left discontented. Consider the aftermath of a car accident. The insurance adjuster asks, "What is the damage to your car?" The claimant says, "$3,000." The adjuster says, "Fine, the check will be in the mail." The claimant hangs up the phone and immediately feels a stab of regret—he must have asked for too little. Otherwise, wouldn't the adjuster have bargained harder? A "quality case" is one settled fairly, in which the customer is treated promptly and considerately.

Bergin appears satisfied. He walks away; but when he checks back a few "months" later, the settlement size has fallen nary a bit. "We're not happy about it," you say, "but it doesn't seem like there's much we can do about it."

"Well," says Bergin, "let's backtrack and see what's causing these problems." He reaches over and calls forth a historical chart of your progress so far.

You discover, to your chagrin, that the settlement size rose sharply during the first several months and never fell significantly thereafter. You and Rosabeth had set your target settlement size ("Des SettleSize" on the game screen), at the original $2,000 settlement size, but your office's performance had never achieved your standard. Not even for one month.

"I don't get it," you say. "Sure, for a while quality may have eroded a little. That always happens when there's a crisis—our people were under immense time pressure. But the time pressure eased off." They should have been able, then, to put that time back into their work—to improve quality and reduce overpayments. However, the quality never rebounded to its original level once the time pressure settled back to normal. But why should it have? Suddenly, you and Rosabeth realize that the time pressure was restored to normal by lowering quality! As an inadvertent consequence of your requests for higher productivity, adjusters now spend, on average, 7 percent less time investigating and settling each claim than they had before. You had tried to mandate excellence by fiat—but the rest of your decisions promoted mediocrity. By pushing to get claims settled, your adjusters did the only thing they could—they took less time per claim. Once the crisis was past, the lower quality became the new norm—after all, newly hired adjusters (remember the 50 percent turnover) had never been in an office that operated by any other norm. In effect, you paid for lowering the backlog and reducing time pressure through less time per claim and higher average settlement size.

Why couldn't you see this? In part, because your attention was fixed elsewhere: on the backlog of cases. Those statistics, easy to measure and compare, are the most common measurement of success in claims management. They demonstrate efficiency; and, since each office's figures are known by other offices, there's plenty of competition to keep the "production measures" (backlogs, claims settled per month, how long customers wait to get claims settled) in line. You and Rosabeth could have said, "We'll hire and train more people, keep our quality as high as ever, and if we can do that, it doesn't matter if our backlog slips for a few months. We'll recoup it later and then some." But it literally did not occur to either of you to try it.

At this point, Bergin and the other coleader, Geraldine Prusko, reconvene the entire group around the table. It turns out that most all the managers experienced the same outcomes as Rosabeth and you. Having all gone through the microworld simulation, the group begins to talk about mediocre quality, a subject you would never have felt comfortable discussing before—if you all hadn't generated that very problem as a result of your own decision making in the game.

Some of the managers talk about their tight budget pressures, how that makes them reluctant to hire and train as many new adjusters as they'd like. Suddenly, there is a wave of realization through the room: *If it weren't for all those overpriced claims settlements, we'd all have more money to build our departments to what they really need to be!*

At this point, Rosabeth says, "Given what we learned yesterday, it feels to me like there's a 'shifting the burden' structure operating. I'm not sure I can draw it, but look at the symptoms. We experience stress, in the form of time pressure, more work to do than we can get done. The 'fundamental solution' is to build adjuster capacity. But we 'cover up' the stress by telling our adjusters to work harder, to which they respond by lowering quality, getting the claims settled, and the stress goes away.''

One of the other managers picks up on her thread of thinking. ''But settlement size goes up,'' he says, ''which we either ignore or attribute to something else—like factors truly out of control, such as hurricanes or bad winters. The higher settlement size means higher total costs, and more pressures to control costs—which means controlling staff costs, leading to less adjusting capacity and eventually to more crises, more time pressure, and more decline in quality.'' After some discussion, the group puts together the following shifting the burden diagram summarizing their insights:

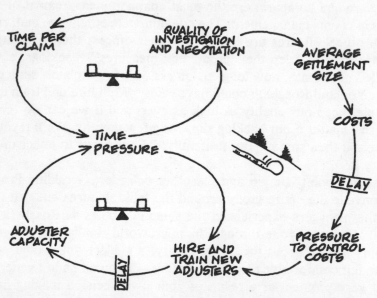

You're starting to realize that the problem goes beyond the policies of any one company; it stems from the cultural biases of an entire industry that has chronic undercapacity and doesn't know it. ''In my thirty years in the business,'' Bergin tells the group, ''I have seen a steady decline in the pay and status of insurance adjusting. Once it was a respected profession. Today, most adjusters are young college graduates with no aspirations to a career in adjusting. Our management practices both react to and reinforce this attitude.''

No wonder it's so difficult to keep experienced adjusters, you realize—and, of course, the more turnover, the harder it is to meet the already tough demands of that backlog.

"So what if we went back to the microworld," suggests Geraldine Prusko, "and tried out some other possible strategies?"

Now the computer game comes into its own. Rosabeth says, "Let's see if we can improve quality. Since we made it worse last time, maybe we can reverse our actions and make it better." This seems like a worthwhile experiment, so you set a target for improved quality of adjusting (you do this in the game much the same way it is often done in a real claims office—by setting a lower target settlement size). "This will send a clear signal to our staff," you say, "that we mean business regarding quality."

The signal may be clear but, it turns out, the results are anything but what you hoped for. After fifteen months, settlement size is even worse than before (almost $2,500) and things are quickly getting worse still. Chagrined, the two of you start to quit the simulation when Prusko stops by and asks, "I see you've tried to improve quality. Doesn't quite come out the way you expected. Have you figured out why?"

"It seems like the adjusters are ignoring our signal," you offer meekly, knowing that this doesn't really explain why the quality campaign backfired. But then you recall, "We tried something like this back in '86 in our region and it, too, backfired. After six months, the adjusters were so exasperated, we gave up on the quality campaign."

"See if you two can figure out what is going wrong," says Prusko, "so you can explain it to the rest of us when we reconvene the entire group."

It takes about a half hour, but you and Rosabeth eventually piece together an interesting explanation. "Quality campaigns increase time pressure on already beleaguered adjusters," you tell the group. "This leads to several reinforcing spirals that get things out of control in a hurry." You show the group how time pressure, which started to go up almost immediately with the quality campaign, kept on rising.

"We're falling behind the 'power curve,' " you offer, using an old flying metaphor. "When adjusters start trying to do a better job in order to achieve lower settlement sizes," you say, "they fall behind in their overall volume of claims, and backlogs grow. Customers get angry. And, as we all know, angry customers are difficult customers. They call frequently to check on their claims. They complain. They take up even more time. Less and less adjusters' time gets spent on adjusting, pushing them still further behind. We've all lived through this 'vicious spiral.' "

"And there's another vicious spiral," Rosabeth adds. "Once the pending backlog and time pressure get out of control, work stress goes through the roof. More adjusters leave and the people remaining have even more work, and even more time pressure—leading to even more turnover. That's why we all try so hard to control our pending backlogs. And it's why improving quality is so difficult."

MANAGING FOR QUALITY IN
SERVICE BUSINESSES

Those difficulties are hardly unique to claims management, or even to the insurance business.[8] In fact, the dynamics of managing quality and capacity do not differ fundamentally in a wide variety of service businesses.

Several years ago, after a presentation of the basic theory and a preliminary version of the claims management microworld to a group of visitors at MIT, an executive from the Internal Revenue Service came up to me and asked if I would consider making the same presentation in Washington. "Although insurance adjusting and tax auditing are very different professions," he said, "the system pressures toward undercapacity and mediocre quality you have described exist in spades at the IRS. I have felt for several years that we may have only a fraction of the tax investigators we should have to do a quality job and that the additional people would easily pay for themselves in additional tax revenues generated."

The simple fact is that most of our service businesses don't serve very well. Airlines which overbook as a matter of course, restaurants which provide no training to serving people, nurses who are too overworked to provide compassionate care, auto repair shops whose employees are rude and where you are overcharged—these are but a few of the regular service abuses which are so commonplace they go almost unnoticed. In "survey after survey," as Lynn Shostack wrote in the *Harvard Business Review*, "services top the list in terms of consumer dissatisfaction."[9]

Managing for quality in a service business is inherently challenging. First, service businesses do not produce a "thing" whose quality can be measured, weighed, and tested. Quality is determined in individual transactions between "servers" and customers, occurring literally thousands of times each day in a large organization. Service quality is inherently subjective and personal. It depends upon rapport between server and customer. It depends on how happy the server is and on whether he or she experiences the job as satisfying. It depends on the customer's expectations being met, expectations that might be neither clear nor mutually appreciated by both server and customer.

Because service quality is intangible, there is a strong tendency to manage service businesses by focusing on what is most tangible: such as numbers of customers served, costs of providing the service, and revenues generated. But focusing on what's easily measured leads to "looking good without being good"—to having measurable performance indicators that are acceptable yet not providing quality service. Work gets done but at a steadily poorer standard of quality, by servers who are increasingly overworked, underpaid, and underappreciated.

Entire industries are actually more vulnerable to this drift to mediocrity than individual firms. For one firm in a competitive industry, eroding quality will be corrected relatively quickly through loss of customers. But if there is no other place for customers to turn, the feedback signal from the market may be weak or nonexistent. Moreover, expectations adjust to past experience. After a while, customers give up asking for better service. Firms set their standards by looking at each other. If quality erodes industry-wide, firms come to accept low standards without ever questioning them.

Oftentimes, the only way this "trance of mediocrity" gets broken is when a completely new firm enters the market—for example, a foreign competitor—who has not been a victim of the trance. This rude awakening came to many U.S. manufacturing firms in the 1970s and 1980s, when they suddenly discovered their levels of quality were noncompetitive in a global marketplace. U.S. service firms have been sheltered from foreign competition, but that is starting to change—not through the invasion of foreign imports but through foreign purchase of U.S. firms. Foreign owners eventually bring in foreign managers, who in turn transplant foreign management practices and standards.[10] Increasing foreign competition in services promises to become one of the significant business trends of the 1990s.

Microworlds like that at Hanover offer a unique way to break out of the trance imposed by unquestioned industry standards. They do so by helping managers develop a "theory" of business operations and the strategic implications of basic changes in operating policies. This theory is based on applying systems principles and tools like the archetypes to the particulars of a given business.

As the workshop continues, the claims managers begin to ponder some important managerial lessons. It is now clear that the backlog of unsettled "pending" claims can be extremely misleading. In particular, it *never* tells you whether or not your capacity is adequate. If there is more work to do than can be done at the current standard, servers can always adjust the time they spend with each customer. If they come under pressure, they simply do the job more quickly and often more poorly. *It is simply not possible to assess capacity separately from quality in a service business.* If we cannot assess quality reliably, we cannot assess capacity reliably. This is why so many service businesses have chronic undercapacity.

To put your new insights to a test, you and Rosabeth experiment with some further strategies. You learn that what is required is more than just hiring people. When you "throw more bodies at the problem," hiring large numbers of new adjusters, it produces only modest gains in quality; the newcomers quickly adopt the mediocre standards of the rest of the office. You must develop a balanced strategy of aggressive hires and steadily elevating quality standards. The result, over the long run, is steady improvement in quality *and* cost.

By the third day, most of the managers are learning that successful strategies depend on no single factor, but upon *coordination*. You hire and train people at a steady rate, you reduce staff turnover, you let backlog slip somewhat at first, and you strengthen the quality target steadily. You pay close attention to the intangibles of quality and adjuster effectiveness. This strategy takes some patience, but after five "years" of it, you're shocked by how lucrative your on-screen business has become. Even more interesting, it is still improving. Total costs (settlement costs plus expense costs) are still falling as your expanded, more experienced and skillful adjuster force continues to improve quality.

The claims game was not designed for forecasting; and only time will tell what you, and the other claims managers, are able to achieve "back at the ranch." But the learning lab has given you some fascinating insights into what might be possible. It has also shown some dangerous problems in conventional management practice, such as managing by the production measures. As Rosabeth puts it, "In my career, I have developed some 'feel' for how managing the work flow, time pressure, adjuster stress and turnover, and quality of adjusting and fairness of settlements all interrelate over my years as a manager. But here we have been able to observe variables that are almost impossible to measure in real life—see interactions that are all but invisible to us in our offices." You leave with a richer picture of the interdependencies within which you live every day and a belief that there is more leverage for improvement in your own and other claims managers' policies than you ever dreamed possible."

MICROWORLDS AND
ORGANIZATIONAL LEARNING

Today, we are at the very beginning of learning how microworlds can accelerate organizational learning. Below are some of the key issues that are being studied.

- *Integrating the microworld and the "real" world*
  The unique power of microworlds lies in surfacing hidden assumptions, especially those lying behind key policies and strategies, discovering their inconsistency and incompleteness, and developing new, more systemic hypotheses for improving the real system. How can such learning lead to more carefully designed "real life" experiments to test insights gained in microworlds, and will these experiments, in turn, allow managers to design better microworlds?
- *Speeding up and slowing down time*
  In microworlds, the pace of action can be slowed down or speeded up. Phenomena that stretch out over many years can be compressed to see more clearly the long-term consequences of decisions. We often also want to slow down the interactions among members of the team, so that they can see subtle ways in which they shut down inquiry or discourage testing of different views. Will repeated experiences in microworlds expand managers' perceptual "time window," making them both more perceptive of slow, gradual organizational and business changes and of very rapid interpersonal interactions and thought processes?
- *Compressing space*
  In microworlds, managers can learn about consequences of actions that occur in distant parts of the system from where actions

are taken. Will this help them recognize such consequences in real life and make "the systemic choice"?

• *Isolation of variables*

In laboratories, scientists can eliminate intruding outside variables and carefully simplify the complexity of real processes. The real world of management offers no such control; but a microworld is a controlled environment, in which experimenters can ask "What if?" questions about outside factors. Microworlds also let you bring in potential outside factors that have not yet taken place in reality—for example, "Suppose regulators forced us to put a ceiling on rates: what might happen to us?" Will microworlds help managers learn to disentangle complex interactions in real settings?

• *Experimental orientation*

Microworlds let teams experiment with new policies, strategies, and learning skills. Actions that cannot be reversed or taken back in real business can be redone countless times in the microworld. Over time, will microworld learning make management teams more open to consider and test wide ranges of hypotheses, and less likely to get "locked in" to particular ways of looking at problems?

• *Pauses for reflection*

Microworld experiments have revealed just how nonreflective most managers are. Despite the ready access to information and controlled experimentation in the computer environment, managers tend to jump from one strategy to another without ever stating clearly their assumptions and without ever analyzing why strategies produce disappointing results. Will learning to explicate assumptions and reflect on outcomes of experiments in microworlds inculcate habits that carry over to real life decision making?

• *"Theory-based strategy*

The business practices of most firms are firmly "anchored" to standard industry practices. By contrast, systems thinking and microworlds offer a potentially new basis for assessing policy and strategy. They lead to "theories" of critical business dynamics which can then clarify the implications of alternative policies and strategies. Midway through the year-long research that resulted in the Claims Learning Laboratory, the claims vice president observed, "I am beginning to conclude that we have half the adjuster capacity we need to achieve high quality and minimize total costs (settlement costs and staff costs). You have no idea what a crazy thing that is to say—we already have *higher* staff costs than most of our competitors. Without these models it would be impossible to even seriously consider such an idea." Will continued development of microworlds lead to a new approach to strategy development, that is less vulnerable to accepting implicit mediocre industry standards?

• *Institutional memory*

"Learning builds on past knowledge and experience—that is, on memory," wrote Ray Stata, CEO of Analog Devices, in 1989 in the *Sloan Management Review*. "Organizational memory must depend on institutional mechanisms," rather than on individuals, Stata says, or else you risk "losing hard-won lessons and experiences as people migrate from one job to another." Will continued research on microworlds and "generic structure" theories of business dynamics—such as the theory of quality-cost-capability interactions underlying the "claims game"—lead to a "library of microworlds"? And will such a library, when tailored to the needs of a particular firm, create a significant new form of organizational memory?

The microworlds of today are rough precursors of what microworlds of the future will be like. All the examples cited above would have been impossible only four or five years ago, before the current generation of personal computers with advanced graphics capabilities. The coming years will see dramatic advances in both the availability and capabilities of microworlds for managers.

Beyond just advances in technology, future microworlds will be more sophisticated in fostering the multiple learning disciplines. For example, imagine a computer simulation that actively fosters reflection by looking at your decisions and saying, "Do you realize the patterns of the decisions you have made?" Future microworlds for teams will allow managers to play out their real-world roles and understand more deeply how those roles interact. This will help management teams hone their systems thinking and team learning skills simultaneously, while also analyzing how individual decisions interact to create important problems. (The "beer game" from Chapter 3 and the Meadowlands case above are actually simple examples of such microworlds.)

In the long run, microworlds will, I believe, have dramatic effects on both people and organizations. The computer is not yet an artifact of daily life. In the next generation it will be. To my eight-year-old son Nathan, the computer is not much more significant than his pencil. (His first was given as a present when he was four.) And he uses it just as readily. He will grow up seeing simulation as being just as commonplace as representation. As often as we ask "What is it?" he will ask "How do things work?" and "How might they work differently?" Representation is the tool for adaptation. Simulation is the tool for creating.

In the learning organization of the future, microworlds will be as common as business meetings are in today's organizations. And, just as business meetings reinforce today's focus on coping with present reality, microworlds will reinforce a focus on creating alternative future realities.

18

THE LEADER'S
NEW WORK

WHAT DOES IT TAKE TO
LEAD A LEARNING ORGANIZATION?

"I talk with people all over the country about learning organizations and 'metanoia,' and the response is always very positive," says Hanover's Bill O'Brien. "If this type of organization is so widely preferred, why don't people create such organizations? I think the answer is leadership. People have no real comprehension of the type of commitment it requires to build such an organization."

Learning organizations demand a new view of leadership. My colleague, organizational consultant Charles Kiefer, tells a story of working with a product development team whose members became committed to a shared vision of a dramatic new product, which they eventually brought to market in one third the normal time required. "Once the vision of the product and how they would develop it began to crystallize," says Kiefer, "the team began to work in an extraordinary way. The energy and enthusiasm were palpable. Each individual felt a genuine sense of responsibility for how the team as a

whole functioned, not just for 'doing his part.' Openness to new
ideas shifted dramatically and technical problems that had been
blocking their progress began to get solved.

"But a new problem emerged. The prevailing leadership style in
the organization was the traditional style—clear directions and well-
intentioned manipulation to get people to work together toward common goals. The team leader recognized that the skills and behaviors
that had made him an effective leader in the past would now be
counterproductive. People *with* a sense of their own vision and commitment would naturally reject efforts of a leader to 'get them committed.' He literally did not know what to do, now that he had a self-
directed team with a clear vision, that was learning how to learn
together."

Our traditional views of leaders—as special people who set the
direction, make the key decisions, and energize the troops—are
deeply rooted in an individualistic and nonsystemic worldview.
Especially in the West, leaders are *heroes*—great men (and occasionally women) who "rise to the fore" in times of crises. Our
prevailing leadership myths are still captured by the image of the
captain of the cavalry leading the charge to rescue the settlers from
the attacking Indians. So long as such myths prevail, they reinforce a focus on short-term events and charismatic heroes rather
than on systemic forces and collective learning. At its heart, the
traditional view of leadership is based on assumptions of people's
powerlessness, their lack of personal vision and inability to master
the forces of change, deficits which can be remedied only by a few
great leaders.

The new view of leadership in learning organizations centers on
subtler and more important tasks. In a learning organization, leaders
are designers, stewards, and teachers. They are responsible for
building organizations where people continually expand their capabilities to understand complexity, clarify vision, and improve shared
mental models—that is, they are responsible for learning.

This new view is vital. When all is said and done, learning organizations will remain a "good idea," an intriguing but distant vision
until people take a stand for building such organizations. Taking this
stand is the first leadership act, the start of *inspiring* (literally "to
breathe life into") the vision of learning organizations. In the absence of this stand, the learning disciplines remain mere collections
of tools and technique—means of solving problems rather than creating something genuinely new.

LEADER AS DESIGNER

Imagine that your organization is an ocean liner, and that you are "the leader." What is your role?

I have asked this question of groups of managers many times. The most common answer, not surprisingly, is "the captain." Others say, "The navigator, setting the direction." Still others say, "The helmsman, actually controlling the direction," or "the engineer down there stoking the fire, providing energy," or, "the social director, making sure everybody's enrolled, involved, and communicating." While these are legitimate leadership roles, there is another which, in many ways, eclipses them all in importance. Yet, rarely does anyone think of it.

The neglected leadership role is the *designer* of the ship. No one has a more sweeping influence than the designer. What good does it do for the captain to say, "Turn starboard thirty degrees," when the designer has built a rudder that will turn only to port, or which takes six hours to turn to starboard? It's fruitless to be the leader in an organization that is poorly designed. Isn't it interesting that so few managers think of the ship's designer when they think of the leader's role?

Although *"leader as designer"* is neglected today, it touches a chord that goes back thousands of years. To paraphrase Lao-tzu, the bad leader is he who the people despise. The good leader is he who the people praise. The great leader is he who the people say, "We did it ourselves."

Lao-tzu also illuminates part of the reason why design is a neglected dimension of leadership: little credit goes to the designer. The functions of design are rarely visible; they take place behind the scenes. The consequences that appear today are the result of work done long in the past, and work today will show its benefits far in the future. Those who aspire to lead out of a desire to control, or gain fame, or simply to be "at the center of the action" will find little to attract them to the quiet design work of leadership. Not that this type of leadership is without its rewards. Those who practice it find deep satisfaction in empowering others and being part of an organization capable of producing results that people truly care about. In fact, they find these rewards more enduring than the power and praise granted to traditional leaders.

For example, consider the role of systems thinking in a leader's work. Joanne, the president of a new division that is growing rapidly, recognizes a limits to growth structure that could undermine continuing growth: as the number of managers in the new division grows, the diversity of management styles will increase, undermining the coherence of vision and operating values that has made the division a success to date. The "limiting factor" will be the division's capacity to assimilate new managers. Rather than waiting for the problem to arise and then dealing with it, Joanne develops a selection and self-assessment process that helps new managers understand the current vision and values and see if their own style is compatible; and she allocates a significant portion of her own time to working with new managers. The result is continuing growth of the division. Given our normal "leader as hero" viewpoint, this is not leadership. There is no crisis—in fact, there isn't even a problem that gets solved. The "problem" of inconsistency in values and vision simply never develops; it wasn't "solved," it was "dissolved." This is the hallmark of effective design.

As this story illustrates, the design work of leaders includes designing an organization's policies, strategies, and "systems." But it goes beyond that. Designing policies and strategies that no one can implement because they don't understand or agree with the thinking behind them has little effect. To appreciate the new view of "leader as designer," let's return to the DC-3.

The critical design function, without which the DC-3 would never have succeeded, involved *integrating the five component technologies*. For example, designing the engine specifications required understanding the effects of the variable pitch propellers, the wing flaps, the retractable landing gear, as well as the stress characteristics of the new monocoque body. So, too, did the wing and body design depend on the engine's thrust. The task of integrating the component technologies was more critical to the success of the DC-3 than the task of designing any single component.

Design is, by its nature, an integrative science because *design requires making something work in practice*. "We would not consider a car well designed," says Herman Miller's Ed Simon, "if it had the best transmission, the best seats, and the best engine, but was terrible to ride in and impossible to control on wet roads. The essence of design is seeing how the parts fit together to perform as a whole."

So too does the crucial design work for leaders of learning organizations concern integration. As background for this chapter I interviewed three leaders who have been part of our MIT research program for several years, Simon, Bill O'Brien of Hanover Insurance, and Ray Stata of Analog Devices. Each pointed to design as a critical function of leadership and each saw design as an integrative task. "The new job description of leaders," according to Stata, "will involve design of the organization and its policies. This will require seeing the company as a system in which the parts are not only internally connected, but also connected to the external environment, and clarifying how the whole system can work better." Or as Simon put it, "We need a new generation of organizational architects. But to get there we must first correct basic misunderstandings about the nature of business design. It's not just rearranging the organization structure. We have to get away from the P&L statement and design for the long term—based on understanding interdependencies. Most changes in organization structure are piecemeal reactions to problems. Real designers are continually trying to understand wholes."

Just as the DC-3 designers had to integrate the five component technologies, crucial design work for leaders of learning organization concerns integrating vision, values, and purpose, systems thinking, and mental models—or more broadly, integrating all the learning disciplines. It is the synergy of the disciplines that can propel an organization to major breakthroughs in learning. As best we can tell so far, *all* the disciplines are critical and must be developed. Leaders must guard against slipping into a comfortable "groove" of relying on particular disciplines, each of which, in isolation, will prove self-limiting. This is why organizations that get fired up by vision can become "vision junkies," just as organizations that come to "believe in" systems thinking as the answer to life's problems will reach diminishing returns in their ongoing systems analyses.

This does not mean that all the disciplines must be developed simultaneously. Though all are important, there are crucial questions concerning sequencing and interactions among the disciplines. What disciplines should be developed first? How can understanding in one area lead to mastery in another? How do we sustain movement along all critical dimensions and not become self-satisfied with our accomplishments in one area? These are the types of design questions that leaders must ponder.

Most of the leaders with whom I have worked agree that the first leadership design task concerns developing vision, values, and purpose or mission. "Organization design is widely misconstrued as moving around boxes and lines,'' says Bill O'Brien. ''The first task of organizational design concerns designing the governing ideas— the purpose, vision, and core values by which people will live.'' ''Designing the organization as a whole,'' says Stata, ''includes the intangibles of even the more subtle values that knit things together.''

Building shared vision is important early on because it fosters a longer-term orientation and an imperative for learning. Systems thinking is also important early on because managers are inherently pragmatic and need insights into ''current reality'' as well as a picture of the future toward which they are moving. Some understanding of mental models and the basics of bringing underlying assumptions to the surface is also important early on. Introducing conceptual tools such as systems thinking in isolation from learning how to work with mental models, both individually and in teams, often proves disappointing. Managers believe that the purpose is to figure out the ''system out there,'' not to discover inconsistencies in their own ways of thinking.

Personal mastery is often one of the later disciplines to emphasize because managers are often, justifiably, cautious in overemphasizing personal growth. Freedom of individual choice is critical in any organization effort to foster personal mastery. As already discussed, what matters most is the visible behavior of people in leadership positions in sharing their own personal visions and demonstrating their commitment to the truth.

These statements are broad guidelines at best. The art of leadership involves sizing up the players and needs in each situation and crafting strategies suitable to the time and setting. For example, some organizations have a high ethic of collaboration, which makes them especially receptive to team learning and shared vision. Yet, in the same organization, people might have difficulties with systems thinking, which they might see as confronting established mental models and operating policies. In a large organization, different combinations of learning disciplines will be developing in different operating units; and leadership is operating at many levels, from local leaders who are bringing the disciplines to bear on current problems, to central leaders who are addressing global issues and organization-wide learning processes.

Even the criteria that you'd bring to bear in making these choices are not yet certain. Do you start with the ''easiest disciplines,'' that is, the disciplines where there is the greatest readiness and least resistance? In general, I find people eager to master new learning disciplines so long as they can connect those skills to important problems and personal learning needs. But if there is resistance to certain disciplines, do you push or do you hold off until you have built up momentum in another area?

Generally, I would counsel against pushing. Usually it is more effective to look for the source of the resistance, either in perceived lack of relevance, fear of failure (i.e., "I won't be competent in the new discipline"—remember we were all schoolchildren once), or perceived threat to the status quo. The leaders who fare best are those who continually see themselves as designers not crusaders. Many of the best intentioned efforts to foster new learning disciplines founder because those leading the charge forget the first rule of learning: people learn what they need to learn, not what someone else thinks they need to learn.

In essence, the *leaders' task is designing the learning processes* whereby people throughout the organization can deal productively with the critical issues they face, and develop their mastery in the learning disciplines. This is new work for most experienced managers, many of whom rose to the top because of their decision-making and problem-solving skills, not their skills in mentoring, coaching, and helping others learn. But, as Ed Simon says, this is no reason to turn back: "There is much that we do not know about what will be required to build learning organizations, but one thing is certain—there is *new work* here, and we must be willing to abandon our whole paradigm of who we are as managers to master this new work."

LEADER AS STEWARD

The interviews that I conducted as background for this chapter led to what was, for me, a surprising discovery. Although the three leaders with whom I talked operate in completely different industries —a traditional service business, a traditional manufacturing business, and a high-tech manufacturing business—and although the specifics of their views differed substantially, they each appeared to draw their own inspiration from the same source. Each perceived a deep story and sense of purpose that lay behind his vision, what we have come to call the *purpose story*—a larger "pattern of becoming" that gives unique meaning to his personal aspirations and his hopes for their organization. For O'Brien the story has to do with "the ascent of man." For Ed Simon, it has to do with "living in a more creative orientation." For Ray Stata, it has to do "with integrating thinking and doing."

This realization came late one evening, after a very long day with the tape and transcript of one of the interviews. I began to see that these leaders were doing something different from just "story telling," in the sense of using stories to teach lessons or transmit bits of wisdom. They were relating *the* story—the overarching explanation of why they do what they do, how their organization needs to evolve, and how that evolution is part of something larger. As I reflected back on gifted leaders whom I have known, I realized that this "larger story" was common to them all, and conversely that many otherwise competent managers in leadership positions were not leaders of the same ilk precisely because they saw no larger story.

The leader's purpose story is both personal and universal. It defines her or his life's work. It enobles his efforts, yet leaves an abiding humility that keeps him from taking his own successes and failures too seriously. It brings a unique depth of meaning to his vision, a larger landscape upon which his personal dreams and goals stand out as landmarks on a longer journey. But what is most important, this story is central to his *ability to lead*. It places his organization's purpose, its reason for being, within a context of "where we've come from and where we're headed," where the "we" goes beyond the organization itself to humankind more broadly. In this sense, they naturally see their organization as a vehicle for bringing learning and change into society. This is the power of the purpose story—it provides a single integrating set of ideas that gives meaning to all aspects of the leader's work.

Out of this deeper story and sense of purpose or destiny, the leader develops a unique relationship to his or her own personal vision. He or she becomes a *steward* of the vision.

The best way to appreciate the "leader as steward" in the context of building learning organizations is to see the way individuals committed to such work describe their own sense of purpose. The following are excerpts from my interviews:

Bill O'Brien
President and CEO, Hanover Insurance

PMS: Bill, why are there such pressures for change in management today—is it primarily because of competitive pressures?

O'BRIEN: No. I think there is something beyond competitive pressures.

Our traditional organizations are designed to provide for the first three levels of Maslow's hierarchy of human needs: food, shelter, and belonging. Since these are now widely available to members of industrial society, our organizations do not provide significantly unique opportunities to command the loyalty and commitment of our people. The ferment in management will continue until organizations begin to address the higher order needs: self-respect and self-actualization.

This is the quest we at Hanover have been on for almost twenty years now—to discover the guiding principles, design, and tools needed to build organizations more consistent with human nature.

PMS: How did you get interested in "learning organizations."

O'BRIEN: We weren't focused on organization learning initially. We set out to identify and eliminate the diseases that afflict hierarchical organizations and make them inconsistent with the higher aspects of human nature.

All of this was based on certain beliefs about people, as are all forms of organization. If you believe that people are most concerned with getting along and putting together coalitions to wield power, that's a political environment. If you believe that once you're on top the secret is staying on top, that's a bureaucratic environment. If you believe, as we did, that there's an enormous reservoir of untapped potential in people that can be channeled more productively than it is, you try to build a value-based, vision-driven environment.

Now, I think that the human being has a deep drive to learning. So, as you create organizations that are more in line with human nature, you are building learning organizations. So, although we started in a different place, we ended up in the same place.

PMS: Why do you think that organizations more consistent with human nature are timely?

O'BRIEN: My personal view is that this has to do with the evolution of consciousness. Mankind's nature is to ascend to greater awareness of our place in the natural order—yet, everywhere we look we see society in a terrible mess of self-centeredness, greed, and nearsightedness. In modern society, business has the greatest potential to offer a different way of operating. The potential of business to contribute toward dealing with a broad range of society's problems is enormous. But we must show the way by example not by moralizing. We must learn how to harness the commitment of our people—then our commitment to building a better world will have some meaning.

Ed Simon
President and COO, Herman Miller

PMS: How does your interest in organizational learning relate to changes you see as important for Herman Miller?

SIMON: I believe that we must become a "vision-led" company. That means that our reference point, our anchor, is in the future. I see organizational learning as learning how to accept, embrace, and seek change.

Traditional organizations change by reacting to events. The reason for this, I think, is that the "reference points" for traditional organizations are external, outside ourselves. Usually these reference points are the way things were in the past. Sometimes, they include the way our competitors operate. Change means giving up these reference points. So, naturally, it is resisted.

To be vision-led means that our reference points are internal, the visions of the future we will create, not what we were in the past or what our competitors are doing. Only when it is vision-led, will an organization embrace change.

PMS: Why are more organizations not vision-led, oriented toward learning how to create what they want?

SIMON: I believe that human beings truly seek to live in a more creative orientation. But people don't realize the incredible extent to which traditional organizations are designed to keep people comfortable and to inhibit taking risks. The learning cycle is a continuous process of experimentation. You cannot experiment without taking risks. Despite rhetoric to the contrary, I believe most American businesses are engaged in building "no-risk" environments. Even when they break apart old functional bureaucracies, which clearly avoided risk taking, they create decentralized business units where managers stay in one position for two years. Clearly, their eye is on promotion and the only types of risks they will take are ones with a high probability of producing "success" during their tenure.

PMS: If we must give up some of the safety of a traditional organization, does that mean that a learning organization is in a constant state of turmoil?

SIMON: Our task is to find a new balance. Embracing change does not mean abandoning a core of values and precepts. We must balance our desire for continuity with our desire to be creative. We must learn how to not abandon that core, while simultaneously letting go of past ways of doing things. I think we have learned something about this at Herman Miller in our commitment to the creative process in research and design. Now that commitment to the creative process must be extended to the business as a whole. This requires a new paradigm, a new model of how organizations work—organizations that operate in a continual learning mode, creating change.

Ray Stata
President and CEO, Analog Devices, Inc.

PMS: How did you get interested in "organizational learning"?

STATA: Organizational learning as a concept is what emerged at the end of the process we've been going through. The starting point was back in the late '70s and early '80s, when it became increasingly clear that our company, as well as other companies in America, were coming under heavy pressure from Japan. I gradually became convinced that there was a crisis looming of enormous magnitude, a crisis that is still, in my estimation, looming, despite the progress we've made in recent years.

In response to this crisis, we began to get involved with the variety of improvement processes coming out of Japan. But, you quickly get lost with the "alphabet soup" of TQC, JIT, QFD, and all the consultants running around with today's newest acronym. Drawing on the thinking of Shell's Arie de Geus [another participant in the MIT research program], I began to see accelerating organizational learning as an integrating concept for a broad range of improvement tools and methods. Most importantly, as I tried to illustrate in an article for *Sloan Management Review,* I began to see that the rate at which organizations learn may become the only sustainable source of competitive advantage, especially in knowledge-intensive businesses.[1]

PMS: What do you see as the central challenges in building learning organizations?

STATA: The "scientific management" revolution of Frederick Taylor took the traditional division of labor, between workers and managers, and gave us the "thinkers" and the "doers." The doers were basically prohibited from thinking. I believe our fundamental challenge is tapping the intellectual capacity of people at all levels, both as individuals and as groups. To truly engage everyone—that's the untapped potential in modern corporations. This leads me to the notion of an organization as a learning organism.

That is easy to say, but I believe there are significant insights that will be required to make it real. One of the questions that interests me deeply is, "What are the rules of the cognitive processes by which valid learning takes place?" I believe we can use the term organizational learning very loosely and it will end up having little meaning. It will become just another fad.

PMS: How do you distinguish between valid learning and specious learning?

STATA: One of the fundamentals is that valid learning does not occur unless you continuously go back to reality. All knowledge is objective in the sense that there must be some correspondence to reality. That seems fairly obvious, but, as Ayn Rand observed, mankind tends to drift toward the primacy of consciousness and to the supremacy of thought, and it's only by discipline that you actually come to accept reality as a judge.

In response to this, the "pragmatists" of modern philosophy take the view that there is no point in worrying about general theory. You should do what works, and whatever works today may not work tomorrow. This view is strongly reinforced in contemporary management with its emphasis on solving problems. It's so easy to just go from one problem to the next, "from pillar to post," without ever seeing a larger pattern. Pragmatism denies any ability of the human mind to synthesize, to see a bigger picture.

Pragmatism has become dominant, in part, because of the previous dominance of elaborate theoretical systems that had no real correspondence to reality. The nineteenth century was a great time for this; and the obvious failure of these great systems of thought like Marx's world system has been one of the justifications for pragmatism.

Interestingly, just as local workers have gotten stuck as the "doers" in traditional organizations, managers have gotten stuck as "the thinkers." There is a tremendous tendency of people high in the organization to become remote from reality and the facts, to begin to hypothesize and conjecture without any formal grounding of their theories. The greatest manifestation of the fallacy of this dichotomy between the "thinkers" and the "doers" was the fad in the 60's to create strategic planning staffs separate from operational staffs. Once accepted, this further separated the world of thought from the world of reality.

I think, to some extent, we jump back and forth between these two extremes of over-conceptualization and pure pragmatism because we don't have the tools to connect them. The core challenge faced by the aspiring learning organization is to develop tools and processes for conceptualizing the big picture and testing ideas in practice. All in the organization must master the cycle of thinking, doing, evaluating, and reflecting. Without, there is no valid learning.

Crafting a larger story is one of the oldest domains of leadership. There is indeed a mythic quality about this type of leadership: "The real task of the knights [of the Round Table] now lies before them, wrote Heinrich Zimmer in his book about myth, *The King and the Corpse*. To Zimmer, Merlin was a master in the domain of the "purpose story," "first uniting the knights in the circle of the Round Table, and then scattering them forth again on the paths of their several transformations." Though the knights travel their separate paths, they are "united in a common bond, and their paths, though predestined for each one of them alone, will meet, cross, and intertwine . . ."[2]

The purpose stories of the three leaders above each describes a context of deep issues that transcend the problems of any one organization, implies a sense of urgency that makes action imperative, and illuminates their own personal vision. For each, the story involves a new type of organization emerging that is "more consistent with human nature" (O'Brien), enables people to balance "the desire for continuity with the desire to be creative" (Simon), and integrates "conceptualizing the big picture and testing ideas in practice" (Stata).

But the stories are also incomplete. They are evolving as they are being told—in fact, they are *as a result of being told*. This is the reason that their visions have such special significance to such leaders; the vision is a vehicle for advancing the larger story.

In a learning organization, leaders may start by pursuing their own vision, but as they learn to listen carefully to others' visions they begin to see that their own personal vision is part of something larger. This does not diminish any leader's sense of responsibility for the vision—if anything it deepens it. "The willingness to abandon your paradigm," says Simon, "comes from your stewardship for the vision."

Being the steward of a vision shifts a leader's relationship toward her or his personal vision. It ceases to be a possession, as in "this is *my* vision," and becomes a calling. You are "its" as much as it is yours. George Bernard Shaw expressed the relationship succinctly when he said:

> This is the true joy in life, the being used for a purpose recognized by yourself as a mighty one . . . the being a force of nature instead of a feverish, selfish little clod of ailments and grievances complaining that the world will not devote itself to making you happy.[3]

Slightly different in tone and focus, but no less evocative, is the characterization of Lebanese poet Kahlil Gibran, who, in speaking of parents and children, captured the special sense of *responsibility without possessiveness* felt by leaders toward their vision:

> *Your children are not your children.*
> *They are the sons and daughters of life's longing for itself.*
> *They come through you, not from you.*
> *And though they are with you, they belong not to you.*
> *You may give them your love but not your thoughts,*
> *For they have their own thoughts.*
> *You may house their bodies but not their souls,*
> *For their souls dwell in the house of tomorrow, which you cannot visit, not even in your dreams.*
> *You may strive to be like them, but strive not to make them like you.*
> *For life goes not backward nor tarries with yesterday.*
> *You are the bows from which your children as living arrows are sent forth.*
> *The archer sees the mark upon the path of the infinite, and he bends you with his might that the arrows may go swift and far.*
> *Let your bending in the archer's hand be for gladness;*
> *For even as he loves the arrow that flies, so he loves the bow that is stable.*[4]

LEADER AS TEACHER

The first responsibility of a leader," writes retired Herman Miller CEO Max de Pree, "is defining reality."[5] While it is clear that leaders draw their inspiration and spiritual reserves from their sense of stewardship, much of the leverage leaders can actually exert lies in helping people achieve more accurate, more insightful, and more *empowering* views of reality.

"Reality" as perceived by most people in most organizations means pressures that must be born, crises that must be reacted to, and limitations that must be accepted. Given such ways of defining reality, vision is an idle dream at best and a cynical delusion at worst —but not an achievable end. By contrast, for painters, composers, or sculptors, creating involves working within constraints—for example, the constraints imposed by their media. If one had but to snap one's fingers and the vision became reality, there would be no creative process. How, then, do leaders help people achieve a view of reality, such as the artist's, as a medium for creating rather than as a source of limitation? This is the task of the "leader as teacher."

Building on the hierarchy of explanation first introduced in Chapter 3, leaders can influence people to view reality at four distinct levels: events, patterns of behavior, systemic structures, and a "purpose story." The key question becomes *where predominantly do they focus their and their organization's attention?*

By and large, leaders of our current institutions focus their attention on events and patterns of behavior—and, under their influence, their organizations do likewise. That is why contemporary organizations are predominantly reactive, or at best responsive—rarely generative.

On the other hand, leaders in learning organizations pay attention to all four levels, but focus predominantly on purpose and systemic structure. Moreover, they "teach" people throughout the organization to do likewise.

Systemic structure is the domain of systems thinking and mental models. At this level, leaders are continually helping people see the big picture: how different parts of the organization interact, how different situations parallel one another because of common underlying structures, how local actions have longer-term and broader impacts than local actors often realize, and why certain operating policies are needed for the system as a whole. But, despite its importance, the level of systemic structure is not enough. By itself, it lacks a sense of purpose. It deals with the *how,* not the *why.*

By focusing on the "purpose story"—the larger explanation of why the organization exists and where it is trying to head—leaders add an additional dimension of meaning. They provide what philosophy calls a "teleological explanation" (from the Greek *telos,* meaning "end" or "purpose")—an understanding of what we are trying to become. When people throughout an organization come to share in a larger sense of purpose, they are united in a common destiny. They have a sense of continuity and identity not achievable in any other way.

Leaders talented at integrating story and systemic structure are rare in my experience. Undoubtedly, this is one of the main reasons that learning organizations are still rare.

One person who had the gift was Bill Gore, the founder and longtime CEO of W. L. Gore and Associates (makers of Gore-tex and other synthetic fiber products). Bill Gore was not an especially charismatic speaker. But he was adept at a particular story-telling art: stories that integrated the organization's core values and purpose and its operating policies and structures. Bill was very proud of his highly egalitarian organization, in which there were (and are still) no "employees," only "associates," all of whom own shares in the company and participate in its management. At one talk, he explained the company's policy of controlled growth:

> Our limitation is not financial resources. Our limitation is the rate at which we can bring in new associates. Our experience has been that if we try to bring in more than 25% per year increase, we begin to bog down. 25% per year growth is a real limitation; you can do much better than that with an authoritarian organization. However, one of the associates, Esther Baum, went home to her husband and reported the limitation to him. Well, Professor Baum was an astronomer and a mathematician; he worked at Lowell Observatory, and he said, "That is indeed a very interesting figure." He took out a pencil and paper and calculated and said, "Do you realize that in only 57½ years, everyone in the world will be working for Gore?"[6]

Through this simple story, Gore explains the rationale behind a key policy, limited growth rate, a policy that undoubtedly caused a lot of stress in the organization. He reaffirms the organization's commitment to creating a unique environment for its "associates" and illustrates the types of sacrifices that the firm is prepared to make in order to remain true to its vision: "You can do much better [in growth rate] than that with an authoritarian organization." (Recall that one of the failings of People Express was the very absence of policies that controlled growth to a rate commensurate with assimilating new people into *its* innovative work system.) The last part of the story shows that, despite the self-imposed limit, the company is still very much a "growth company," another aspect of its vision.

Unfortunately, much more common are leaders who have a sense of purpose and genuine vision but little ability to foster systemic understanding. Many great "charismatic" leaders, despite having a deep sense of purpose and vision, manage almost exclusively at the level of events. Such leaders deal in visions and crises, and little in between. They foster a lofty sense of purpose and mission. They create tremendous energy and enthusiasm. But, under their leadership, an organization caroms from crisis to crisis. Eventually, the worldview of people in the organization becomes dominated by events and reactiveness. People experience being jerked continually from one crisis to another; they have no control over their time, let alone their destiny. Eventually, this will breed deep cynicism about the vision, and about visions in general. The soil within which a vision must take root—the belief that we can influence our future—becomes poisoned.

Such "visionary crisis managers" often become tragic figures. Their tragedy stems from the depth and genuineness of their vision. They often are truly committed to noble aspirations. But noble aspirations are not enough to overcome systemic forces contrary to the vision. As the ecologists say, "Nature bats last." Systemic forces will win out over the most noble vision if we do not learn how to recognize, work with, and gently mold those forces.

Similar problems arise with the "visionary strategist," the leader with a sense of vision who operates at the levels of patterns of change as well as events. This leader is better prepared to manage change, but still teaches people only to see trends not underlying structures. He imparts a responsive orientation, not a generative orientation. Ironically, leaders with a sense of vision and an understanding of major business trends are often held out as models of effective leadership. This is because they are so much more effective than leaders with no vision whatsoever, or leaders who deal only with vision and events.

But leaders of learning organizations must do more than just formulate strategies to exploit emerging trends. They must be able to help people understand the systemic forces that shape change. It is not enough to intuitively grasp these forces. Many "visionary strategists" have rich intuitions about the causes of change, intuitions that they cannot explain. They end up being authoritarian leaders, imposing their strategies and policies or continually intervening in decisions. They fall into this fate even if their values are contrary to authoritarian leadership—because *only* they see the decisions that need to be made. Leaders in learning organizations have the ability to conceptualize their strategic insights so that they become public knowledge, open to challenge and further improvement.

"Leader as teacher" is not about "teaching" people how to achieve their vision. It is about fostering learning, for everyone. Such leaders help people throughout the organization develop systemic understandings. Accepting this responsibility is the antidote to one of the most common downfalls of otherwise gifted leaders— losing their commitment to the truth.

When Lyndon Johnson first became President, his "Great Society" inspired full-hearted support throughout the country, despite the tragedy which brought him into office. Johnson was a master enroller, with the patience to take Congress through his proposed legislation one bill at a time, with stunning results; out of ninety-one proposals, Congress only rejected two. His enrollment of the public was no less stunning: "His goals had been the country's goals," wrote historian William Manchester. But the results of Johnson's leadership eventually proved disappointing, in part, because Johnson could not keep his commitment to the truth. When he was told that the United States could not afford the Great Society and the Vietnam War at the same time, he began systematically lying about the costs of the war. "If I [tell Congress] about the cost of the war," he told his advisers, according to Manchester, "old [Senator] Wilbur Mills will sit down there and he'll thank me kindly and send me back my Great Society." Gradually Johnson began to isolate himself from criticism, even from his advisers; soon, many of the members of his Cabinet resigned. Eventually, Johnson's chain of lies found its way to public attention and became the "credibility gap"—so christened by the *New York Herald Tribune* in 1965. His leadership was effectively over—to the point where he could not run for reelection in 1968.[7]

History, mythology, and business lore abound with examples, from Oedipus to present times, of leaders who fail because they lack commitment to the truth.

As my colleague, organization consultant Bryan Smith puts it, "I have met many leaders who have been destroyed by their vision." This happens, almost always, because the leaders lose their capacity to see current reality. They collude in their and their organization's desire to assuage uneasiness and avoid uncertainty by pretending everything is going fine. They become speech makers rather than leaders. They become "true believers" rather than learners.

CREATIVE TENSION

Leaders who are designers, stewards, and teachers come to see their core task very simply. "Just as Socrates felt that it was necessary to create a tension in the mind," said Martin Luther King, Jr., "so that individuals could rise from the bondage of myths and half truths . . . so must we . . . create the kind of tension in society that will help men rise from the dark depths of prejudice and racism."[8] The tension of which King spoke is the *creative tension* of personal mastery. This tension is generated by holding a vision and concurrently telling the truth about current reality relative to that vision—"to dramatize the issue so that it can no longer be ignored," as King put it.

The leader's creative tension is not anxiety: that is psychological tension. A leader's story, sense of purpose, values and vision establish the direction and target. His relentless commitment to the truth and to inquiry into the forces underlying current reality continually highlight the gaps between reality and the vision. Leaders generate and manage this creative tension—not just in themselves but in an entire organization. This is how they energize an organization. That is their basic job. That is why they exist.

Mastering creative tension throughout an organization leads to a profoundly different view of reality. People literally start to see more and more aspects of reality as something they, collectively, can influence. This is no hollow "belief," which people say in an effort to convince themselves that they are powerful. It is a quiet realization, rooted in understanding that *all* aspects of current reality—the events, the patterns of change, and even the systemic structures themselves—are subject to being influenced through creative tension. This shift of view, or metanoia, was expressed beautifully by the Hebrew existentialist philosopher Martin Buber:[9]

Our thinking of today has established a more tenacious and oppressive belief in fate than has ever before existed. No matter how much is said about the laws we hold to be true of life . . . at the basis of them all lies possession by process, that is by unlimited causality. But the dogma of process leaves no room for freedom, whose calm strength changes the face of the earth. This dogma does not know the man who surmounts the universal struggle, tears to pieces the web of habitual instincts, and stirs, rejuvenates and transforms the stable structures of history.

The only thing that can become fate for man is belief in fate. The free man is he who wills without arbitrary self-will. He believes in destiny, and believes that it stands in need of him. It does not keep him in leading strings, it awaits him, he must go to it, yet does not know where it is to be found. But he knows that he must go out with his whole being. The matter will not turn out according to his decision; but what is to come will come only when he decides on what he is able to will. He must sacrifice his puny, unfree will, that is controlled by things and instincts, to his grand will, which quits defined for destined being.

Then, he intervenes no more, but at the same time he does not let things merely happen. He listens to what is emerging from himself, to the course of being in the world; not in order to be supported by it but to bring it to reality as it desires.

HOW CAN SUCH LEADERS
BE DEVELOPED?

In February 1990, when President De Klerk of South Africa announced the lifting of bans on black political groups and the freeing of political prisoners, I was in the country as part of an initiative to foster a cadre of black and white leaders capable of building learning organizations and learning communities. With the impending release of Nelson Mandela (which came one week later), we shared the following statement from Corazon Aquino of the Philippines. When her husband, Benigno Aquino, left prison, she said:

It seemed clear to those who knew him that much had changed in him. The superb political animal—shrewd, fast, eloquent, and brave—who had placed his immense talents in the service of the Republic in the hope of public honors had evolved into a man for whom love of country was only the other face of his love for God. And I think this is the truest and best kind of patriotism. It is only

on this plane that patriotism ceases to be, as they say, the refuge
of scoundrels and becomes, instead, the obligation of a Christian . . .

We cannot, of course, just place an order for such men and
women to be or to lead the opposition. Such people are not made
to order. They make themselves that way.

If you share, therefore, my growing conviction that it is only by
such people that the changes we want will be brought about, then
you must also share the conclusion I have come to: the changes
will come and victory will be attained—a victory that will mean
more than a change of faces—only when there are enough of us
who have become like that.[10]

One of the most striking aspects of this statement is that "such
people are not made to order. They make themselves that way."
Most of the outstanding leaders I have worked with are neither tall
nor especially handsome; they are often mediocre public speakers;
they do not stand out in a crowd; and they do not mesmerize an
attending audience with their brilliance or eloquence. Rather, what
distinguishes them is the clarity and persuasiveness of their ideas,
the depth of their commitment, and their openness to continually
learning more. They do not "have the answer." But they do instill
confidence in those around them that, together, "we can learn whatever we need to learn in order to achieve the results we truly desire."

The ability of such people to be natural leaders, as near as I can
tell, is the by-product of a lifetime of effort—effort to develop conceptual and communication skills, to reflect on personal values and
to align personal behavior with values, to learn how to listen and to
appreciate others and others' ideas. In the absence of such effort,
personal charisma is style without substance. It leaves those affected
less able to think for themselves and less able to make wise choices.
It can devastate an organization or a society.

That is why the five learning disciplines developed in Parts II and
III are so important to those who would lead. They provide a framework for focusing the effort to develop the capacity to lead. Systems
thinking, personal mastery, mental models, building shared vision,
and team learning—these might just as well be called the *leadership
disciplines* as the learning disciplines. Those who excel in these areas
will be the natural leaders of learning organizations.

In our own work to help people develop their leadership capacities, we stress the "individual disciplines" of systems thinking,

working with mental and personal mastery. These disciplines span the range of conceptual, interpersonal, and creative capacities vital to leadership. But most of all, they underscore the deeply personal nature of leadership. It is impossible to reduce natural leadership to a set of skills or competencies. Ultimately, people follow people who believe in something and have the abilities to achieve results in the service of those beliefs. Or, to put it another way, who are the natural leaders of learning organizations? They are the learners.

TIME TO CHOOSE

One of the paradoxes of leadership in learning organizations is that it is both collective and highly individual. Although the responsibilities of leadership are diffused among men and women throughout the organization, the responsibilities come only as a result of individual choice.

Choice is different from desire. Try an experiment. Say, "I want." Now, say, "I choose." What is the difference? For most people, "I want" is passive; "I choose" is active. For most, wanting is a state of deficiency—we want what we do not have. Choosing is a state of sufficiency—electing to have what we truly want. For most of us, as we look back over our life, we can see that certain choices we made played a pivotal role in how our life developed. So, too, will the choices we make in the future be pivotal.

The choice to be part of a learning organization is no different. Whether it is an "organization" of three or three thousand matters not. Only through choice does an individual come to be the steward of a larger vision. Only through choice does an individual come to practice the learning disciplines. Being in a supportive environment can help, but it does not obviate the need for choice. Learning organizations can be built only by individuals who put their life spirit into the task. It is our choices that focus that spirit.

It is not the purpose of this book to convince people that they *should* choose to build learning organizations. Rather, I have tried to paint the picture of what such an organization would be like and how it might be built—so that people can see the choice that exists. The choice, as is always the case, is yours.

PART V

Coda

19

A SIXTH DISCIPLINE?

The DC-3 revolutionized commercial air travel, but the airline industry didn't become a major industry until the widespread use of two additional technologies more than ten years later—the jet engine and radar. Interestingly, radar was a by-product of the war effort, not "aircraft" research.

The five disciplines now converging appear to comprise a critical mass. They make building learning organizations a systematic undertaking, rather than a matter of happenstance. But there will be other innovations in the future. If the airline analogy is apt, perhaps one or two developments emerging in seemingly unlikely places, will lead to a wholly new discipline that we cannot even grasp today.

The jet engine and radar fostered a burgeoning infrastructure of airports, pilots and mechanics, aircraft manufacture, and commercial airlines. This was the foundation upon which the modern airline industry was built. Likewise, the immediate task is to master the possibilities presented by the present learning disciplines, to establish a foundation for the future.

20

REWRITING
THE CODE[1]

Systems thinking teaches that there are two types of complexity—the "detail complexity" of many variables and the "dynamic complexity" when "cause and effect" are not close in time and space and obvious interventions do not produce expected outcomes.

The tools for systems thinking introduced in this book are especially designed for understanding dynamic complexity. They help in seeing underlying structures and patterns of behavior that are obscured in the fury of daily events and the incessant activity that characterizes the manager's life. They help in understanding why conventional solutions are failing and where higher leverage actions may be found.

But what about detail complexity? What about the hundreds, perhaps thousands, of feedback processes in any real managerial situation, all operating simultaneously? How can we possibly cope with such complexity? What good is systems thinking, anyhow, if it only teaches us to identify a few feedback processes amid this welter of activity?

In Chapter 13, I suggested that one of the subtler lessons of the systems perspective is that this enormous detail complexity renders all rational explanations inherently incomplete. Human systems are infinitely complex. "You can never figure it out," I suggested—because it's "un-figure-out-able." Nonetheless, we *can* enhance our mastery of complexity.

Evidence is overwhelming that human beings have "cognitive limitations." Cognitive scientists have shown that we can deal only with a very small number of separate variables simultaneously. Our conscious information processing circuits get easily overloaded by detail complexity, forcing us to invoke simplifying heuristics to figure things out.

But then how can we explain driving an automobile at sixty miles per hour in heavy traffic—or playing tennis, or playing a Mozart sonata? All of these tasks are enormously complex, involving hundreds of variables and rapid changes that must be recognized and responded to immediately. Moreover, to the extent that we are masterful in these tasks, they are accomplished with little or no "conscious attention." We drive through traffic while carrying on a conversation with the person next to us. The tennis professional focuses entirely on the strategy of the match and the point being played. The concert pianist thinks only of the aesthetics of the performance, not the mechanics.

Clearly there is an aspect of our minds that deals quite well with detail complexity—in fact, which is designed for the task. In the chapter on personal mastery, we called this "the subconscious" to suggest an aspect of mind that lies "below" or "behind" our normal conscious mental processes. Other labels are possible, such as automatic mind or "tacit knowledge," but the label is unimportant.[2] What is important is recognizing that we have enormous capacities to deal with detail complexity at the subconscious level that we do not have at the conscious level.

It is also important to recognize that the subconscious can be "trained." In fact, all learning involves an interplay of the conscious mind and the subconscious that results in training the subconscious. We did not start off driving in heavy traffic; we practiced driving very slowly in a parking lot or on a quiet street because the subconscious was not yet trained to the task of driving. Gradually, more and more of the task is "taken over" by the subconscious—shifting gears becomes "automatic," "natural." This frees our conscious mind (with its limited information processing ability) to focus on the next stage of learning.[3]

There are many ways by which the subconscious gets programmed. Cultures program the subconscious. If you grow up in a society that discriminates sharply between certain races or castes, you will literally see and interact with people differently from the way you will if you grow up in a culture that is less race or caste-conscious. Beliefs also program the subconscious. It is well established, for example, that beliefs affect perception: if you believe that people are untrustworthy, you will continually "see" double-dealing and chicanery that others without this belief would not see.

Perhaps most subtly, language programs the subconscious. The effects of language are especially subtle because language appears not so much to affect the *content* of the subconscious but the way the subconscious *organizes and structures* the content it holds. If this is true, how, then, have we been teaching the subconscious to organize information?

As shown in Chapter 5, it is extremely awkward in normal verbal language to describe circular feedback processes. So, by and large, we give up and just say, in effect, "A caused B, which caused C." But this convenient shorthand suggests to the subconscious mind that "A *did* cause B." Subconsciously, we tend to forget that "B also caused A." If all we have is linear language, then we think in linear ways, and we perceive the world linearly—that is, as a chain of events. It is impossible for us to grasp the scope of the consequences, but we know they are sweeping.

However, if we begin to master a systemic language, all this starts to change. The subconscious is subtly retrained to structure data in circles instead of straight lines. We find that we "see" feedback processes and systems archetypes everywhere. A new framework for thinking becomes embedded. A switch is thrown, much like what happens in mastering a foreign language. We begin to dream in the new language, or to think spontaneously in its terms and constructs. When this happens with systems thinking, we become, as one manager puts it, "looped for life."

As organizational theorist Charles Kiefer puts it, "When this switch is thrown subconsciously, you become a systems thinker ever thereafter. Reality is automatically seen systemically as well as linearly (there still are lots of problems for which a linear perspective is perfectly adequate). Alternatives that are impossible to see linearly are surfaced by the subconscious as proposed solutions. Solutions that were outside of our 'feasible set' become part of our feasible set. 'Systemic' becomes a way of thinking (almost a way of being) and not just a problem solving methodology."

The subconscious is not limited by the number of feedback processes it can consider. Just as it deals with far more details than our conscious mind, it can also deal with far more intricate dynamic complexity. Significantly, as it assimilates hundreds of feedback relationships simultaneously, it integrates detail and dynamic complexity together.

This is why practice is so important. For any meaningful interplay of conscious and subconscious, practice is essential. Conceptual learning is not enough, any more than it would be for learning a foreign language or for learning to ride a bicycle. In this context, tools like microworlds come into their own—as cultural media, as places to practice thinking and acting systemically.

The value of systems thinking also goes beyond that derived by any institution. To explain, let me take a step back.

There is a certain irony to mankind's present situation, viewed from an evolutionary perspective. The human being is exquisitely adapted to recognize and respond to threats to survival that come in the form of sudden, dramatic events. Clap your hands and people jump, calling forth some genetically encoded memory of saber-toothed tigers springing from the bush.

Yet today the primary threats to our collective survival are slow, gradual developments arising from processes that are complex both in detail and in dynamics. The spread of nuclear arms is not an event, nor is the "greenhouse effect," the depletion of the ozone layer, malnutrition and underdevelopment in the Third World, the economic cycles that determine our quality of life, and most of the other large-scale problems in our world.

Learning organizations themselves may be a form of leverage on the complex system of human endeavors. Building learning organizations involves developing people who learn to see as systems thinkers see, who develop their own personal mastery, and who learn how to surface and restructure mental models, collaboratively. Given the influence of organizations in today's world, this may be one of the most powerful steps toward helping us "rewrite the code," altering not just what we think but our predominant *ways of thinking*. In this sense, learning organizations may be a tool not just for the evolution of organizations, but for the evolution of intelligence.

21

THE INDIVISIBLE
WHOLE

When I was young I always wanted to be an astronaut. I even studied aeronautics and astronautics in college to prepare. But then I got hooked on "systems theory" and a new, earthbound career was born.

But I still remained deeply fascinated with the *experience* of being in space, a fascination that was heightened by the first Apollo pictures of the earth. So it was with great interest that I finally had an opportunity to get to know astronaut Rusty Schweickart who attended one of our leadership programs several years ago.

I learned from Rusty that many of the astronauts struggle when they return to earth, trying to put into words their feelings of what it meant to them to hover above their home planet. Rusty struggled for five years (he flew on Apollo 9, which tested the lunar module in earth orbit in March 1969) before words adequate to the task began to form.

In the summer of 1974, he had been invited to speak to a gathering on "planetary culture" at Lindisfarne, a spiritual community on Long Island. After considering and discarding many ways of sharing his experience he realized that he couldn't tell it as *his* story. Because it was *our* story. He realized that he and the other astronauts represented an "extension of the sensory apparatus of the human species. Yes, I was looking out from my eyes and feeling with my senses but it was also our eyes and our senses. We who were the first to leave and look back at the earth were looking back for all of humankind. Though there were only a few of us, it was our responsibility to report back what we experienced." Realizing this, he decided simply to describe what it was like—as if you and I, the listeners, were there as well.[1]

Up there you go around every hour and a half, time after time after time. You wake up usually in the mornings. And just the way that the track of your orbits go, you wake up over the Mideast, over North Africa. As you eat breakfast you look out the window as you're going past and there's the Mediterranean area, and Greece, and Rome, and North Africa, and the Sinai, the whole area. And you realize in one glance that what you're seeing is what was the whole history of man for years—the cradle of civilization. And you think of all the history you can imagine looking at that scene.

And you go around down across North Africa and out over the Indian Ocean, and look up at that great sub-continent of India pointed down toward you as you go past it. And Ceylon off to the side, Burma, Southeast Asia, out over the Philippines, and up across that monstrous Pacific Ocean, vast body of water—you've never realized how big that is before. And you finally come up across the coast of California and look for those friendly things: Los Angeles, and Phoenix, and on across El Paso and there's Houston, there's home, and you look and sure enough there's the Astrodome. And you identify with that, you know—it's an attachment.

And down across New Orleans and then looking down to the south and there's the whole peninsula of Florida laid out. And all the hundreds of hours you spent flying across that route, down in the atmosphere, all that is friendly again. And you go out across the Atlantic Ocean and back across Africa.

And that identity—that you identify with Houston, and then you identify with Los Angeles and Phoenix and New Orleans and everything. And the next thing you recognize in yourself, is you're identifying with North Africa. You look forward to that, you anticipate it. And there it is. That whole process begins to shift what it is you identify with. When you go around it in an hour and a half you begin to recognize that your identity is with the whole thing. And that makes a change.

You look down there and you can't imagine how many borders and boundaries you crossed again and again and again. And you don't even see 'em. At that wake-up scene—the Mideast—you know there are hundreds of people killing each other over some imaginary line that you can't see. From where you see it, the thing is a whole, and it's so beautiful. And you wish you could take one from each side in hand and say, "Look at it from this perspective. Look at that. What's important?"

And so a little later on, your friend, again those same neighbors, the person next to you goes to the moon. And now he looks back and sees the Earth not as something big where he can see the beautiful details, but he sees the Earth as a small thing out there. And now that contrast between the bright blue and white Christmas tree ornament and that black sky, that infinite universe, really comes through.

The size of it, the significance of it—it becomes both things, it becomes so small and so fragile, and such a precious little spot in the universe, that you can block it out with your thumb, and you realize that on that small spot, that little blue and white thing is everything that means anything to you. All of history and music, and poetry and art and war and death and birth and love, tears, joy, games, all of it is on that little spot out there that you can cover with your thumb.

And you realize that that perspective . . . that you've changed, that there's something new there. That relationship is no longer what it was. And then you look back on the time when you were outside on the EVA [extravehicular activity] and those few moments that you had the time because the camera malfunctioned, that you had the time to think about what was happening. And you recall staring out there at the spectacle that went before your eyes. Because now you're no longer inside something with a window looking out at the picture, but now you're out there and what you've got around your head is a goldfish bowl and there are no boundaries. There are no frames, there are no boundaries.

Floating in space, Rusty discovered the first principles of systems thinking. But he discovered them in a way that few of us ever do—not at a rational or intellectual level but at a level of *direct experi-*

ence. The earth is an indivisible whole, just as each of us is an indivisible whole. Nature (and that includes us) is not made up of parts within wholes. It is made up of wholes within wholes. All boundaries, national boundaries included, are fundamentally arbitrary. We invent them and then, ironically, we find ourselves trapped within them.

But there was something more. In the years following that first talk at Lindisfarne, Rusty found himself drawn into a whole new series of insights and personal changes. He found himself drawn into new work, leaving his post as commissioner of the California Energy Commission and becoming more active in joint projects involving U.S. astronauts and Soviet cosmonauts.[2] He listened and learned about others' experience. He began to involve himself in activities that seemed congruent with his new understandings.

One that had a special impact was learning about the "Gaia" hypothesis—the theory that the biosphere, all life on earth, is itself a living organism.[3] This idea, which has deep roots in many preindustrial cultures, such as American Indian cultures, "struck a deep chord in me," says Rusty. "For the first time it gave the scientist in me a way to talk about aspects of my experience in space that I couldn't even articulate to myself. I had experienced the earth in a way that I had no way to describe. I had experienced the *aliveness* of it—of it all."

At the conclusion of the leadership workshop, someone asked spontaneously, "Rusty, tell us what it was like up there?" He paused for a long time. When he finally spoke, he said only one thing. "It was like seeing a baby about to be born."

Something new is happening. And it has to do with *it all*—the whole.

APPENDIX 1:
THE LEARNING
DISCIPLINES

Each of the five learning disciplines can be thought of on three distinct levels:

- practices: what you do
- principles: guiding ideas and insights
- essences: the state of being of those with high levels of mastery in the discipline

The practices are activities upon which practitioners of the discipline focus their time and energy. For example, systems thinking entails using the "systems archetypes" in order to perceive underlying structures in complex situations. Personal mastery entails "clarifying personal vision," and "holding creative tension," simultaneously focusing on the vision and current reality and allowing the tension between the two to generate energy toward achieving the vision. Working with mental models involves distinguishing the direct "data" of experience from the generalizations or abstractions that we form based on the data.

The practices are the most evident aspect of any discipline. They are also the primary focus of individuals or groups when they begin to follow a discipline. For the beginner, they require "discipline" in the sense of conscious and consistent effort because following the practices is not yet second nature. In a heated debate, the novice at working with mental models will have to make an effort to identify the assumptions he is making and why. Often the beginner's efforts in a discipline are characterized by time displacement: only *after* the debate, does one see one's assumptions clearly and distinguish them from the "data" and reasoning upon which they are based. However, eventually, the practices of a discipline become more and more automatic and active in "real time." You find yourself spontaneously thinking of systems archetypes, re-creating (which is different from recalling) your vision, and recognizing your assumptions as they come into play, while confronting pressing problems.

Equally central to any discipline are the underlying principles. These represent the theory that lies behind the practices of the disciplines. For example, "structure influences behavior" is a central principle underlying systems thinking, as is "policy resistance," the tendency of complex systems to resist efforts to change their behavior. The former implies that the ability to influence reality comes from seeing structures that are controlling behavior and events. The latter implies that efforts to manipulate behavior, for example through well-intentioned programs such as building new houses for disadvantaged urban dwellers, will generally improve matters only in the short run and often lead to still more problems in the long run. Similarly, the power of vision is a principle of personal mastery, as is the distinction between "creative tension" and "emotional tension."

The principles behind a discipline are important to the beginner as well as to the master. For the beginner, they help him in understanding the rationale behind the discipline and in making sense of the practices of the discipline. For the master, they are points of reference which aid in continually refining the practice of the discipline and in explaining it to others.

It is important to recognize that mastering any of the disciplines requires effort on both the levels of understanding the principles *and* following the practices. It is tempting to think that just because one understands certain principles one has "learned" about the discipline. This is the familiar trap of confusing intellectual understanding with learning. Learning always involves new understandings and new behaviors, "thinking" and "doing." This is the reason for distinguishing principles from practices. Both are vital.

The third level, the "essences" of the disciplines, is different. There is no point in focusing one's conscious attention and effort on these essences in learning a discipline, any more than it would make sense to *make an effort* to experience love or joy or tranquillity. The essences of the disciplines are the *state of being* that comes to be experienced naturally by individuals or groups with high levels of mastery in the disciplines. While these are difficult to express in words, they are vital to grasp fully the meaning and purpose of each discipline. Each of the disciplines alters its practitioner in certain very basic ways. This is why we refer to them as *personal* disciplines, even those that must be practiced collaboratively.

For example, systems thinking leads to experiencing more and more of the interconnectedness of life and to seeing wholes rather than parts. Whenever there are problems, in a family or in an organization, a master of systems thinking automatically sees them as arising from underlying structures rather than from individual mistakes or ill will. Likewise, personal mastery leads to an increased sense of "beingness," awareness of the present moment, both what is happening within us and outside of us, and to heightened experience of "generativeness," of being part of the creative forces shaping one's life.

At the level of essences, the disciplines start to converge. There is a common sensibility uniting the disciplines—the sensibility of being learners in an intrinsically interdependent world. Yet, there are still differences between the disciplines. But the differences become increasingly subtle. For example, "interconnectedness" (systems thinking) and "connectedness" (personal mastery) are subtle distinctions. The former has to do with awareness of how things interrelate to one another; the latter with awareness of being part of rather than apart from the world. So, too, is the distinction between "commonality of purpose" (shared vision) and "alignment" (team learning) a fine one. While the former has to do with a common direction and reason for being, the latter has to do with "functioning as a whole" when we actually work together. Though subtle, these distinctions are important. Just as the connoisseur of fine wines makes distinctions that the novice would not, so do individuals and groups who develop high levels of mastery in the disciplines see distinctions that might be obscure to beginners.

Lastly, the disciplines of building shared vision and team learning differ from the other three in that they are inherently collective in nature. The practices are activities engaged in by groups. The principles must be understood by groups. And the essences are states of being experienced collectively.

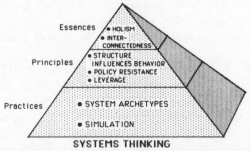

SYSTEMS THINKING

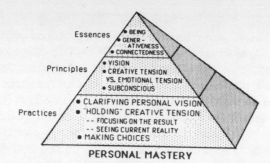

PERSONAL MASTERY

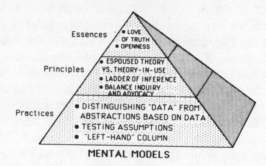

MENTAL MODELS

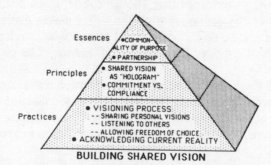

BUILDING SHARED VISION

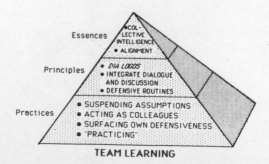

TEAM LEARNING

One does not master a discipline all at once. There are distinct stages of learning that we all go through. Diana Smith has devised a three-stage continuum for developing new capacities that is helpful in approaching all the learning disciplines:

New Values and Assumptions	**Stage Three: Values and Operating Assumptions** People can string together rules that reflect new action values and operating assumptions. They can enact these rules under stress and ambiguity, continuing to aid their own and others' learning. By this stage, people will have adapted the rules into their own particular model, speaking in their own voice.
New Action Rules	**Stage Two: New Action Rules** As old assumptions "loosen" in response to the cognitive insights of Stage One, people begin to experiment with action rules based on new assumptions so they can see what they yield. They may need to rely on the new language to produce new actions, and they will find it difficult to access or string together new rules when under stress.
New Cognitive, Linguistic Capacities	**Stage One: New Cognitive Capacities** People see new things and can speak a new language. This allows them to see more clearly their own and others' assumptions, actions, and consequences of both. Typically, they find it hard to translate these new cognitive and linguistic competencies into fundamentally new actions. They may begin to behave differently, but the basic rules, assumptions, and values are the same.

APPENDIX 2: SYSTEMS ARCHETYPES[1]

BALANCING PROCESS
WITH DELAY

Structure:

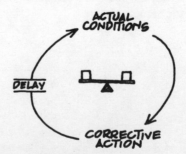

Description: A person, a group, or an organization, acting toward a goal, adjusts their behavior in response to delayed feedback. If they are not conscious of the delay, they end up taking more corrective action than needed, or (sometimes) just giving up because they cannot see that any progress is being made.

Early Warning Symptom: "We thought we were in balance, but then we overshot the mark." (Later, you may overshoot in the other direction again.)

Management Principle: In a sluggish system, aggressiveness produces instability. Either be patient or make the system more responsive.

Business Story: Real estate developers keep building new properties until the market has gone soft—but, by then, there are already enough additional properties still under construction to guarantee a glut.

Other Examples: A shower where the hot water responds sluggishly to changes in the faucet positions; production/distribution glut and shortage cycles (such as that of the beer game); cycles in production rates and in-process inventory due to long manufacturing cycle times; the Tiananmen Square massacre, in which the government delayed its reaction to protest, and then cracked down unexpectedly hard; sudden, excessive stock market soars and crashes.

LIMITS TO GROWTH

Structure:

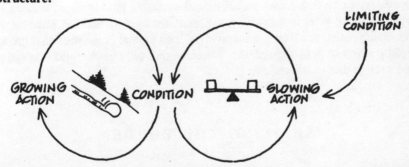

Description: A process feeds on itself to produce a period of accelerating growth or expansion. Then the growth begins to slow (often inexplicably to the participants in the system) and eventually comes to a halt, and may even reverse itself and begin an accelerating collapse.

The growth phase is caused by a reinforcing feedback process (or by several reinforcing feedback processes). The slowing arises due to a balancing process brought into play as a "limit" is approached. The limit can be a resource constraint, or an external or internal response to growth. The accelerating collapse (when it occurs) arises from the reinforcing process operating in reverse, to generate more and more contraction.

Early Warning Symptom: "Why should we worry about problems we don't have? We're growing tremendously." (A little later, "Sure there are some problems, but all we have to do is go back to what was working before." Still later, "The harder we run, the more we seem to stay in the same place.")

Management Principle: Don't push on the reinforcing (growth) process, remove (or weaken) the source of limitation.

Business Story: A company instituted an affirmative action program, which grew in support and activity as well-qualified minority employees were successfully introduced into work teams throughout the company. But eventually resistance emerged; the new staffers were perceived as not having "earned" their positions over other qualified aspirants. The harder individual teams were pressured to accept the new members, the more they resisted.

Other Examples: Learning a new skill, such as tennis, you make rapid progress early on as your competence and confidence builds, but then you begin to encounter limits to your natural abilities that can be overcome only by learning new techniques that may come "less naturally" at first.

A new startup that grows rapidly until it reaches a size that requires more professional management skills and formal organization; a new product team that works beautifully until its success causes it to bring in too many new members who neither share the work style nor values of the founding members; a city that grows steadily until available land is filled, leading to rising housing prices; a social movement that grows until it encounters increasing resistance from "nonconverts"; an animal population that grows rapidly when its natural predators are removed, only to overgraze its range and decline due to starvation.

SHIFTING THE BURDEN

Structure:

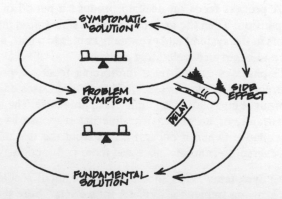

Description: A short-term "solution" is used to correct a problem, with seemingly positive immediate results. As this correction is used more and more, more fundamental long-term corrective measures are used less and less. Over time, the capabilities for the fundamental solution may atrophy or become disabled, leading to even greater reliance on the symptomatic solution.

Early Warning Symptom: "Look here, this solution has worked so far! What do you mean, there's trouble down that road?"

Management Principle: Focus on the fundamental solution. If symptomatic solution is imperative (because of delays in fundamental solution), use it to gain time while working on the fundamental solution.

Business Story: A dramatic new circuit board technology can be used to develop unique functionality and cost savings in a great many new product applications, but it can also be substituted for existing boards in current products. Salespeople can try to sell to "specialty customers" who appreciate the special properties of the technology and will eventually design new products which exploit it fully (the "fundamental solution") or sell to "commodity customers" who do not care about its special properties and will simply substitute it for other boards (the "symptomatic solution"). Given management pressures to meet quarterly sales targets, salespeople sell to whoever is ready to buy, which usually will be commodity customers since there are more of them and delays in the selling cycle are shorter. Over time, the dramatic new technology fails to develop a loyal customer base and becomes subject to the price and margin pressures that characterize commodity products.

Other Examples: Selling more to existing customers rather than broadening the customer base (The "ATP case" from Chapter 12); paying bills by borrowing, instead of going through the discipline of budgeting; using alcohol, drugs, or even something as benign as exercise to relieve work stress and thereby not facing the need to control the workload itself; and any addiction, anywhere, to anything.

SPECIAL CASE:
SHIFTING THE BURDEN TO THE INTERVENOR

Structure:

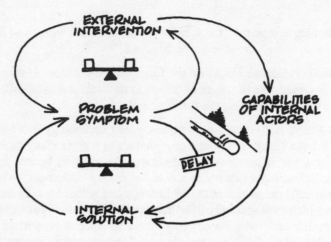

One area where shifting the burden structures are so common and so pernicious that it warrants special notice is when outside "intervenors" try to help solve problems. The intervention attempts to ameliorate obvious problem symptoms, and does so so successfully that the people within the system never learn how to deal with the problems themselves.

Management Principle: "Teach people to fish, rather than giving them fish." Focus on enhancing the capabilities of the "host system" to solve its own problems. If outside help is needed, "helpers" should be strictly limited to a one-time intervention (and everyone knows this in advance) or be able to help people develop their own skills, resources, and infrastructure to be more capable in the future.

Business Story: An innovative insurance company was committed to the concept of independent local offices that would call on headquarters staff only for occasional help. Initially the concept worked well, until the industry went through a crisis. Facing sudden severe losses, the local offices called in the more experienced central management for help in rewriting rate structures—a process which took months. Meanwhile, the local managers focused their attention on managing the crisis. The crisis was resolved, but the next time rate structures were called into question, the local offices had lost some of their confidence. They called in the central managers as "insurance." After several years of this behavior, the local offices found themselves without underwriters who could manage rate structure changes independently.

Other Examples: Dependence on outside contractors instead of training your own people. Numerous forms of government aid that attempt to solve pressing problems only to foster dependency and need for increasing aid: welfare systems that foster single-family households; housing or job training programs that attract the needy to cities with the best programs; food aid to developing countries which lowers deaths and increases population growth; social security systems that reduce personal savings and encourage the breakup of the extended family.

ERODING GOALS

Structure:

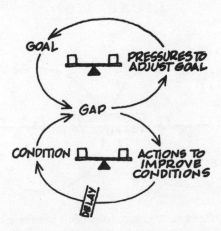

Description: A shifting the burden type of structure in which the short-term solution involves letting a long-term, fundamental goal decline.

Early Warning Symptom: "It's okay if our performance standards slide a little, just until the crisis is over."

Management Principle: Hold the vision.

Business Story: A high-tech manufacturer finds itself losing market share, despite a terrific product and ongoing improvements. But the firm, oriented toward its design "geniuses," had never gotten production scheduling under control. An outside investigator discovered that customers were increasingly dissatisfied with late schedules, and were turning to competitors instead. The company stood on its record: "We've maintained a consistent 90 percent success in meeting the delivery time quoted to the customer." It therefore looked elsewhere for the problem. However, every time the company begin to slip its schedules, it responded by making the quoted delivery time a little longer. Thus, the quoted delivery time to customers was getting lengthier, and lengthier, and lengthier . . .

Other Examples: Successful people who lower their own expectations for themselves and gradually become less successful. Firms that tacitly lower their quality standards by cutting budgets rather than investing in developing new higher quality (and perhaps lower cost) ways of doing things, all the while proclaiming their continued commitment to quality. Lowered government targets for "full employment" or balancing the federal deficit. Sliding targets for controlling dangerous pollutants or protecting endangered species.

ESCALATION

Structure:[2]

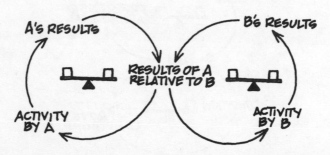

Description: Two people or organizations each see their welfare as depending on a relative advantage over the other. Whenever one side gets ahead, the other is more threatened, leading it to act more aggressively to reestablish its advantage, which threatens the first, increasing its aggressiveness, and so on. Often each side sees its own aggressive behavior as a defensive response to the other's aggression; but each side acting "in defense" results in a buildup that goes far beyond either side's desires.

Early Warning Symptom: "If our opponent would only slow down, then we could stop fighting this battle and get some other things done."

Management Principle: Look for a way for both sides to "win," or to achieve their objectives. In many instances, one side can unilaterally reverse the vicious spiral by taking overtly aggressive "peaceful" actions that cause the other to feel less threatened.

Business Story: A company developed an ingenious design for a stroller, which carried three toddlers at once, yet was light and convenient for travel. It was an immediate hit with families with several young children. Almost simultaneously, a competitor emerged with a similar product. After several years, jealous of the other company's share of the market, the first company lowered its price by 20 percent. The second company felt a decline in sales, and lowered its price too. Then the first company, still committed to boosting share, lowered its prices still further. The second company reluctantly did the same, even though its profits were beginning to suffer. Several years later, both companies were barely breaking even, and survival of the triple carriage was in doubt.

Other Examples: Advertising wars. Increasing reliance on lawyers to settle disputes. Gang warfare. The breakup of a marriage. Inflating budget estimates: as some groups inflate their estimates, others find themselves doing likewise in order to get "their piece of the pie," which leads to everyone inflating his estimates still further. Battle for the "ear" of the president of a company. And, of course, the arms race.

SUCCESS TO THE SUCCESSFUL

Structure:

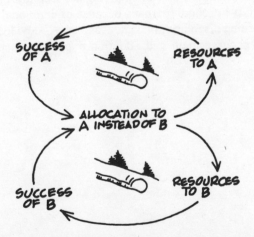

Description: Two activities compete for limited support or resources. The more successful one becomes, the more support it gains, thereby starving the other.

Early Warning Symptom: One of the two interrelated activities, groups, or individuals is beginning to do very well and the other is struggling.

Management Principle: Look for the overarching goal for balanced achievement of both choices. In some cases, break or weaken the coupling between the two, so that they do not compete for the same limited resource (this is desirable in cases where the coupling is inadvertent and creates an unhealthy competition for resources).

Business Story: A manager has two protégés, and wishes to bring both along equally in the firm. However, one of the two ends up getting preferential treatment because the other is out sick for a week. When the second protégé returns to work, the manager feels guilty, and avoids the person, thereby giving still more opportunity to the first protégé. The first protégé, feeling the approval, flourishes, and therefore gets more opportunity. The second protégé, feeling insecure, does less effective work and receives even fewer opportunities, although the two people had equal ability in the beginning. Eventually, the second protégé leaves the firm.

Other examples: Balancing home and work life, in which a worker gets caught working overtime so much that relationships at home deteriorate and it gets more and more "painful" to go home, which, of course, makes the worker even more likely to neglect home life in the future. Two products compete for limited financial and managerial resources within a firm; one is an immediate hit in the marketplace and receives more investment, which depletes the resources available to the other, setting in motion a reinforcing spiral fueling growth of the first and starving the second. A shy student gets off to a poor start in school (perhaps because of emotional problems or an undetected learning disability), becomes labeled a "slow learner," and gets less and less encouragement and attention than his or her more outgoing peers.

TRAGEDY OF THE COMMONS

Structure:

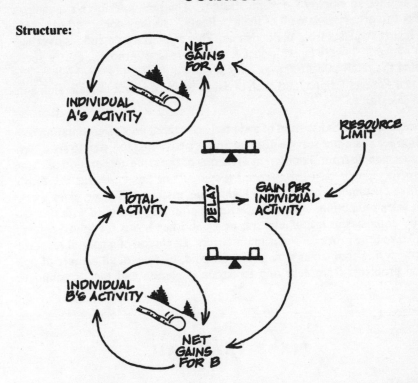

Description: Individuals use a commonly available but limited resource solely on the basis of individual need. At first they are rewarded for using it; eventually, they get diminishing returns, which causes them to intensify their efforts. Eventually, the resource is either significantly depleted, eroded, or entirely used up.

Early Warning Symptom: "There used to be plenty for everyone. Now things are getting tough. If I'm going to get any profit out of it this year, I'll have to work harder."

Management Principle: Manage the "commons," either through educating everyone and creating forms of self-regulation and peer pressure, or through an official regulating mechanism, ideally designed by participants.

Business Story: Several divisions of a company agreed to share a retail salesforce. Each district manager was initially concerned that the shared salesforce wouldn't give enough attention to his or her particular business, and that volume would decline. One particularly aggressive manager advised all his account managers to set higher sales targets than were truly needed, so that the salesforce would at least give them the minimum support they needed. The other divisions saw this division pushing for extra work, and decided to employ the same strategy. The new salesforce's managers wanted to accommodate all of their "clients," so they continued to accept the higher requests from the divisions. This created a tremendous overburden of work, lowered performance, and increased turnover. Pretty soon, joining the retail salesforce was only slightly more popular than joining the French Foreign Legion, and each division had to go back to maintaining its own salesforce.

Other Examples: Exhaustion of a shared secretarial pool. Deteriorating reputation for customer service after customers have had to listen to six different salespeople from six different divisions of the same corporation pitching competing products. (The "shared resource" in this case was the firm's positive customer reputation.) A highly successful retail chain gives up on joint sales promotions with manufacturers after being deluged with proposals by enthusiastic manufacturers, or establishes terms for joint ventures that leave little profit for the manufacturers. Depletion of a natural resource by competing companies which mine it. And, of course, all manner of pollution problems from acid rain to ozone depletion and the "greenhouse effect."

FIXES THAT FAIL

Structure:

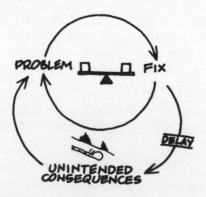

Description: A fix, effective in the short term, has unforeseen long-term consequences which may require even more use of the same fix.

Early Warning Symptom: "It always seemed to work before; why isn't it working now?"

Management Principle: Maintain focus on the long term. Disregard short-term "fix," if feasible, or use it only to "buy time" while working on long-term remedy.

Business Story: A manufacturing company launched a new set of high-performance parts, which were wildly successful at first. However, the CEO was driven by maximizing his ROI, so he deferred ordering expensive, new production machines. Manufacturing quality suffered, which led to a reputation for low quality. Customer demand fell off dramatically over the ensuing year, which depressed returns and made the CEO even more unwilling to invest in new production equipment.

Other Examples: People and organizations who borrow to pay interest on other loans, thereby ensuring that they will have to pay even more interest later. Cutting back maintenance schedules to save costs, which eventually leads to more breakdowns and higher costs, creating still more cost-cutting pressures.

GROWTH AND
UNDERINVESTMENT

Structure:

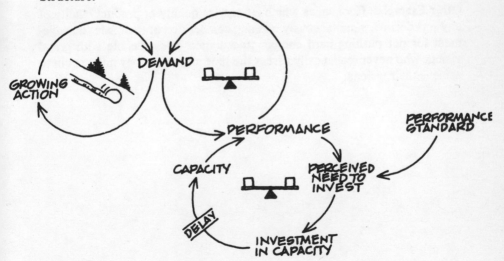

Description: Growth approaches a limit which can be eliminated or pushed into the future if the firm, or individual, invests in additional "capacity." But the investment must be aggressive and sufficiently rapid to forestall reduced growth, or else it will never get made. Oftentimes, key goals or performance standards are lowered to justify underinvestment. When this happens, there is a self-fulfilling prophecy where lower goals lead to lower expectations, which are then borne out by poor performance caused by underinvestment. (This is the Wondertech structure described in Chapter 7.)

Early Warning Symptom: "Well, we used to be the best, and we'll be the best again, but right now we have to conserve our resources and not over-invest."

Management Principle: If there is a genuine potential for growth, build capacity in advance of demand, as a strategy for creating demand. Hold the vision, especially as regards assessing key performance standards and evaluating whether capacity to meet potential demand is adequate.

Business Story: As described in Chapter 8, the People Express Airlines, found itself unable to build service capacity to keep pace with exploding demand. Rather than putting more resources into training or growing more slowly (for example, through raising prices somewhat), the firm tried to "outgrow" its problems. The result was deteriorating service quality and increased competition, while morale deteriorated. In order to keep up with the continued stress, the company relied more and more on the "solution" of underinvesting in service capacity, until customers no longer found flying People Express attractive.

Other Examples: Companies which let service quality or product quality of any sort decline, simultaneously blaming competition or their sales management for not pushing hard enough to maintain sales. People with grand visions who never realistically assess the time and effort they must put in to achieve their visions.

NOTES

CHAPTER 1
"GIVE ME A LEVER LONG ENOUGH...AND SINGLE-HANDED I CAN MOVE THE WORLD"

1. Daniel Yankelovich, *New Rules: Searching for Self-fulfillment in a World Turned Upside Down* (New York: Random House), 1981.
2. I am indebted to my MIT colleague Alan Graham for the insight that basic innovation occurs through the integration of diverse technologies into a new ensemble. See A. K. Graham, "Software Design: Breaking the Bottleneck," *IEEE Spectrum* (March 1982): 43–50; A. K. Graham and P. Senge, "A Long-Wave Hypothesis of Innovation," *Technological Forecasting and Social Change* (1980): 283–311.
3. Arie de Geus, "Planning as Learning," *Harvard Business Review* (March/April 1988): 70–74.

CHAPTER 2
DOES YOUR ORGANIZATION HAVE A LEARNING DISABILITY?

1. Arie de Geus, "Planning as Learning," *Harvard Business Review* (March/April 1988): 70–74.

2. These figures come from the United States Department of Commerce, *U.S. Industrial Outlook*, in 1962 (pp. 58–59), 1970 (p. 355), 1975 (p. 355), 1979 (p. 287), 1981 (p. 320), and 1989 (pp. 34–35), and U.S. Congress Office of Technology Assessment, *Technology and the American Economic Transition: Choices for the Future Washington:* (U.S. Government Printing Office), 1988 (p. 326).

3. Draper Kauffman, Jr. *Systems 1: An Introduction to Systems Thinking* (Minneapolis: Future Systems Inc.), 1980 (available through Innovation Associates, P.O. Box 2008, Framingham, MA 01701).

4. Chris Argyris, *Overcoming Organizational Defenses* (New York: Prentice-Hall), 1990.

5. Barbara Tuchman, *The March of Folly: From Troy to Vietnam* (New York: Knopf), 1984.

6. Ibid.

CHAPTER 3
PRISONERS OF THE SYSTEM, OR PRISONERS OF OUR OWN THINKING?

1. Directions for the interactive game can be obtained from the System Dynamics Group at MIT Sloan School of Management, Cambridge MA 02139. Complete sets of materials and directions are available from Innovation Associates, P.O. Box 2008, Framingham, MA 02139.

2. In the actual decision-making simulation there are four positions, one of which (a distributor) is omitted to simplify the story—which is complicated enough as it is.

3. But, of course, any simulation is a simplification. You might wonder if changing any of the details of the game would change the results. Wondering the same thing, we've tinkered often over the years. Sometimes, as in the story told here, there are three players. Usually, we play with four. We've varied the penalties imposed for excess inventory and for backlogs. Sometimes we use a computer simulation to make the calculations; most times we set up a big board game on long tables, moving pennies from square to square to represent beer deliveries. Players have been given different amounts of advance information about the range of consumer demands that retailers can expect. Different patterns of consumer demand have been tried. Some of these variations make the crisis slightly more extreme; some make it slightly milder. But none affect the overall pattern of crises.

4. U.S. Congress Office of Technology Assessment: *Technology and the American Economic Transition: Choices for the Future* (Washington: U.S. Government Printing Office), 1988, 324.

5. Steven Burke, "Chip Manufacturers Find a Pot of Gold in DRAM

Shortage," *PC Week*, May 31, 1988, 107; Steven Burke and Ken Sieg-mann, "Memory-Board Prices Surging in the Wake of Growing Chip Shortage," *PC Week*, March 1, 1988, 1.

6. J. Rhea "Profits Peak as Semiconductor Sales Boom," *Electronic News* 18:1 (August 6, 1973); "Boom Times Again for Semiconductors," *Business Weekly*, April 20, 1974, 65–68; "Semiconductors Take a Sudden Plunge," *Business Week*, November 16, 1974, 64–65; F. Pollare, "Inventory Buildup: Semiconductor Distress Sales Emerge," *Electronic News* 20:45 (February 10, 1975).

7. Joseph B. White and Bradley A. Stertz, "Auto Industry Battens Down for a Slump," *Wall Street Journal*, May 30, 1989, sec. A.

8. "MacNeil-Lehrer Newshour," video documentary on the beer game and business cycles (interview with John Sterman at MIT), aired November 1989, Public Broadcasting System.

9. Donella H. Meadows, "Whole Earth Models and Systems," *Co-Evolution Quarterly* (Summer 1982): 98–108.

10. Leo Tolstoy, *War and Peace* (Constance Garnett translation).

11. Ibid.

12. Janice T. Gibson and Mika Haritos-Fatouros, "The Education of a Torturer," *Psychology Today*, November 1986, 50. Also: "The Mind is a Formidable Liar: A Pirandellian Prison," *New York Times Magazine*, April 8, 1973.

13. Similar amplification is characteristic of real business cycles, where raw material producing industries typically fluctuate far more than retail and service industries. See Gottfried Haberler, *Prosperity and Depression* (London: Allen & Unwin), 1964; Alvin H. Hansen, *Business Cycles and National Income* (New York: Norton), 1951.

14. John Sterman, "Modeling Managerial Behavior: Misperceptions of Feedback in a Dynamic Decisionmaking Experiment," *Management Science*, vol. 35, no. 3 (March 1989): 335.

15. When simulated by computer, the results for the "no strategy" strategy show that the retailer has the worst backlogs because he only starts receiving full shipments once the supplier's backlogs are eliminated. This means that retailers would be especially vulnerable under this strategy—which is precisely why most retailers place larger orders in the real world.

16. In the simulation game, total costs are computed by assessing $1.00 cost for each backlog unit (each week) and $0.50 for each inventory unit (each week), and by summing the resulting costs of each position to calculate a total team cost. An average cost for a four-stage game of thirty-five weeks is $2,028 (Sterman, "Modeling Managerial Behavior"), 331–39, corresponding to a cost of about $1,270 for thirty weeks in a three-stage game. The total team cost for the "do nothing" strategy is about $825.

17. Potentially, the players could learn from their experience in the game, in ways that players in real production-distribution systems cannot learn —if they were able to play the game repeatedly and to understand, collaboratively, how their decisions interact in the larger system. The beer game would then be a "microworld." See Chapter 17.

18. Because the game is usually not played with the different positions in regular contact, there is little opportunity to observe how the players fare in face-to-face interactions. Nonetheless, as the teams currently operate, most team members become consumed in blaming one another for their problems. Other decision-making simulations are designed to deal more directly with the dynamics of team learning.

19. A common example of seeing patterns of behavior in business is "trend analysis," so that a firm can best *respond* to shifting demographic trends or changing customer preferences.

20. William Manchester, *The Glory and the Dream* (Boston: Little, Brown), 1974, 80–81.

21. It is also possible to redesign the physical structure of the game, although this was not an option for the players when the game was first played. For example, you could redesign the information system so that wholesalers and breweries, as well as retailers, had current information on retail sales. Or, you could eliminate the middlemen entirely and have breweries supply retailers directly. Redesigning the physical system (physical flows of goods, people, and materials; information; rewards and other factors outside the individual decision makers' immediate control) is an important leadership function in real life. But success depends on leaders' systemic understanding, just as changing individual ways of placing orders depends on systemic understanding. Thus, achieving systemic understanding is the primary task, from which redesigning physical systems, as well as operating policies, can follow.

CHAPTER 4
THE LAWS OF THE
FIFTH DISCIPLINE

1. These laws are distilled from the works of many writers in the systems field: Garrett Hardin, *Nature and Man's Fate* (New York: New American Library), 1961; Jay Forrester, *Urban Dynamics*, Chapter 6 (Cambridge, Mass.: MIT Press), 1969; Jay Forrester, "The Counterintuitive Behavior of Social Systems," *Technology Review* (January 1971, pp. 52–68; Donella H. Meadows "Whole Earth Models and Systems," *Co-Evolution Quarterly* (Summer 1982): 98–108; Draper Kauffman, Jr., *Systems 1: An Introduction to Systems Thinking,* (Minneapolis: Future Systems Inc.), 1980 (available through Innovation Associates, P.O. Box 2008, Framingham, MA 01701.

2. This and many other Sufi tales can be found in the books of Idries Shah, eg., *Tales of the Dervishes* (New York: Dutton), 1970, and *World Tales* (New York: Harcourt Brace Jovanovich), 1979.
3. George Orwell, *Animal Farm* (New York: Harcourt Brace), 1954.
4. D. H. Meadows, "Whole Earth Models and Systems."
5. Lewis Thomas, *The Medusa and the Snail* (New York: Bantam Books), 1980.
6. Charles Hampden Turner, *Charting The Corporate Mind: Graphic Solutions to Business Conflicts* (New York: Free Press), 1990.

CHAPTER 5
A SHIFT OF MIND

1. A comprehensive summary of the "cybernetic" and "servo-mechanism" schools of thought in the social sciences can be found in George Richardson, *Feedback Thought in Social Science and Systems Theory* (Philadelphia: University of Pennsylvania Press), 1990.
2. There are probably more self-described "systems analysts" in the U.S. Department of Defense, National Security Agency, and CIA than in all other branches of government. For their part, the Soviets have pioneered in systems theory; for the past forty years, probably more theoretical contributions have come from Soviet mathematicians than from those of any other country. In part, the Soviet government sponsored systems research because of the great dream to use sophisticated computer tools for state control of the national economy.
3. It is ironic that the Soviets should initiate a true systems approach to the arms race, because they, even more than the U.S., have suffered severely from the allure of fighting complexity with complexity. The state-controlled economy failed abysmally because, in part, it turned out to be impossible to control centrally the dynamics and vast "detail complexity" of a national economy. This, plus the economic drain of continuing the arms race, has forced fundamental rethinking, *Perestroika* and *glasnost*—the great new dream for the Soviets—are literally born out of the ashes of the great old dream of the state-controlled economy. So, in effect, the dynamic complexity view of the arms race is now emerging precisely because the detail complexity view has failed, both for controlling the arms race and more broadly.
4. See Nancy Roberts, "Teaching Dynamic Feedback Systems Thinking: An Elementary View," *Management Science* (April 1978), 836–843; and Nancy Roberts, "Testing the World with Simulations," *Classroom Computer News*, January/February 1983, 28.
5. The principles and tools of systems thinking have emerged from diverse roots in physics, engineering, biology, and mathematics. The particular tools presented in this chapter come from the "system dynamics" ap-

proach pioneered by Jay Forrester at MIT. See, for example, *Industrial Dynamics* (Cambridge, Mass.: MIT Press), 1961; *Urban Dynamics* (Cambridge, Mass.: MIT Press), 1969; and "The Counterintuitive Behavior of Social Systems," *Technology Review* (January 1971), 52–68. This particular section owes a special debt to Donella Meadows, whose earlier article "Whole Earth Models and Systems," *Co-Evolution Quarterly* (Summer 1982), 98–108 provided the model and the inspiration for its development.

6. By contrast, many "Eastern" languages such as Chinese and Japanese do not build up from subject-verb-object linear sequences. David Crystal, *The Cambridge Encyclopedia of Language* (New York: Cambridge University Press), 1987.

7. The *Bhagavad-Gita,* or "The Lord's Song," translated by Annie Besant, reprinted in Robert O. Ballou, *The Bible of the World* (New York: Viking), 1939.

8. Robert K. Merton, "The Self-Fulfilling Prophecy," in Robert K. Merton, editor, *Social Theory and Social Structure* (New York: Free Press), 1968.

9. R. Rosenthal, "Teacher Expectation and Pupil Learning"; and R. D. Strom, editor, *Teachers and the Learning Process* (Englewood Cliffs, N.J.: Prentice-Hall); R. Rosenthal, "The Pygmalion Effect Lives," *Psychology Today,* September 1973.

10. This does not suggest that free-market forces are sufficient for all forms of balance and control needed in modern societies—delays, inadequate information, unrealistic expectations, and distortions such as monopoly power also reduce efficiency of "free markets."

CHAPTER 6
NATURE'S TEMPLATES: IDENTIFYING THE
PATTERNS THAT CONTROL EVENTS

1. Two are presented in detail below, and eight altogether are used in this book. This is roughly half the archetypes that professional systems thinkers "carry in their heads."

2. Initial curricula building on generic structures have been developed. See Mark Paich, "Generic Structures," in *System Dynamics Review,* vol. 1, no. 1 (Summer 1985): 126–32; Alan Graham, "Generic Models as a Basis for Computer-Based Case Studies" (Cambridge, Mass.: System Dynamics Group Working Paper D-3947), 1988; Barry Richmond *et al., An Academic User's Guide to STELLA,* Chapters 8, 9 (Lyme, N.H.: High Performance Systems), 1987. David Kreutzer, "Introduction to Systems Thinking and Computer Simulation," *Lesley College Graduate Course Comp 6100,* 1987.

3. In this case, the balancing feedback process goes around the outside of

the figure: from R&D budget, to increasing management complexity, longer product development times, reduced rate of new product introductions, and, eventually, back to smaller R&D budgets.

4. To my knowledge, Barry Richmond was the first to analyze this structure, which we have since found to be virtually endemic in management consulting firms, not to mention academic departments that grow rapidly, then become top heavy with tenured faculty.

5. For a discussion on the failures of Quality Circles and suggestions on taking a systems perspective, see Gordon Meyer and Randall Stott, "Quality Circles: Panacea or Pandora's Box?", *Organizational Dynamics*, Spring 1986, 34–50. See also Edward Lawler III and Susan Mohrman, "Quality Circles: After the Honeymoon," *Organizational Dynamics*, Spring 1987, 42–54.

6. *Facts on File 1990* (New York: Facts on File).

7. Ibid.

8. This and the other "systems archetype" templates are reproduced with the permission of Innovation Associates, where they are used in the *Leadership and Mastery* and *Business Thinking: A Systems Approach* workshops.

9. Information on Alcoholics Anonymous can be found in the following books: *Alcoholics Anonymous*, 1976; *Living Sober*, 1975; *Twelve Steps and Twelve Traditions*, 1953; all published by Alcoholics Anonymous World Services, Inc., P.O. Box 459, Grand Central Station, New York, NY 10163.

CHAPTER 7
THE PRINCIPLE OF LEVERAGE

1. The model developed below derives from Jay Forrester's original studies of corporate growth: (Jay W. Forrester, "Modeling the Dynamic Processes of Corporate Growth," IBM Scientific Computing Symposium on Simulation Models and Gaming (December 1964), and J. W. Forrester, "Market Growth as Influenced by Capital Investment," *Industrial Management Review*, 1968, 83–105.

2. David Birch, *Job Creation in America* (New York: The Free Press), 1987, 18.

3. This figure is produced by computer simulation of the interrelationships of the WonderTech structure with a fixed delivery time standard. The simulation incorporates a simplifying assumption of an unlimited potential market, which was essentially true in WonderTech's early years. Even with realistic limits on the potential market, however, there is a dramatic improvement in behavior when the delivery time standard is held fixed.

The simulation is done with STELLA, a systems thinking model building and simulation program available from High Performance Systems. The actual simulation model used is presented in Jay Forrester, 1968, and in P. Senge, "Systems Principles for Leadership," in *Transforming Leadership,* J. Adams, editor (Alexandria, Va.: Miles River Press), 1984.

CHAPTER 8
THE ART OF SEEING THE
FOREST *AND* THE TREES

1. *Facts on File 1990* (New York: Facts on File), 1990.
2. The following analysis is based on John Sterman's study of People Express Airlines, "Strategy Dynamics: The Rise and Fall of People Express," Lecture notes (Cambridge, Mass.: MIT System Dynamics Group Working Paper D-3959/3967), March 1988. Also see D. Whitstone, "People Express (A)," Harvard Business School case study, 1983, doc. 483-103.
3. Whitstone, "People Express (A)."
4. Ibid.
5. Ibid.
6. These charts are produced by the simulation model developed by John Sterman (explained in the "People Express Management Flight Simulator" (Cambridge, Mass.: MIT Sloan School of Management), 1988, based on the interactions shown in the diagram on page 133. The model reproduces historical behavior patterns at People Express quite accurately, even without any of the external events (such as the American Airlines Sabre reservation system) or changes in industry conditions that occurred during People Express's history. This suggests that the basic "overshoot and collapse" pattern of behavior was due to systemic interactions and not to external factors outside People Express's control.
7. In fact, the growth and underinvestment dynamics at People Express were much more complicated than suggested by the structure above. There were several reinforcing "engines of growth," including expansion of fleet and routes, advertising, and positive "word of mouth" among People's initially satisfied customers. There was also a reinforcing spiral involving employee morale and profitability and stock price: rapid growth and high stock prices contributed to high morale and excellent customer service; when the stock price was falling, morale was lower and it affected service adversely. Customer demand at People Express responded to service quality *and* relative price. People Express's success prompted strong competitive response; for example, price competition from American and the other major carriers. This competitor price created an additional balancing process. Service capac-

ity involved hiring and training service personnel with varying levels of experience, and turnover. People Express's financial performance was tied to its passengers and revenues; to fleet, marketing, and personnel costs; to equity and debt costs; and, in turn, affected its investments in fleet and personnel and its stock price. All of these interactions are captured in Sterman's model, as described in the "People Express Management Flight Simulator" (ibid.), but the basic structure of the model fits the growth and underinvestment form.

CHAPTER 9
PERSONAL MASTERY

1. K. Inamori, "The Perfect Company: Goal for Productivity." Speech given at Case Western Reserve University, June 5, 1985.
2. H. Ford, *Detroit News*, February 7, 1926.
3. R. Fritz, *The Path of Least Resistance* (New York: Fawcett-Columbine), 1989.
4. B. O'Brien, "Advanced Maturity." Available from Hanover Insurance, 100 North Parkway, Worcester, MA 01605.
5. Daniel Yankelovich, *New Rules: Searching for Self-Fulfillment in a World Turned Upside Down* (New York: Random House), 1981.
6. M. dePree, *Leadership is an Art* (New York: Doubleday), 1989.
7. George Bernard Shaw, *Man and Superman*, Preface (Penguin, 1950).
8. Pierre Wack, "Scenarios: Uncharted Ahead," *Harvard Business Review* (September/October 1985): 73–89.
9. Bill Russell and Taylor Branch, *Second Wind: The Memoirs of an Opinionated Man* (New York: Random House), 1979.
10. Fritz's *Path of Least Resistance* delves into the reasons behind this habit.
11. Ibid.
12. Ibid.
13. David Kantor and William Lehr, *Inside the Family: Toward a Theory of Family Process* (San Francisco: Jossey-Bass), 1975.
14. The term "subconscious" has been used by many others, such as Freud and Jung, to represent phenomena somewhat different from those discussed here.
15. W. Timothy Gallwey's *The Inner Game of Tennis* (New York: Bantam Books), 1979, focuses specifically on conscious-subconscious interaction in learning, showing that if the conscious mind can be kept in a quiet nonjudgmental "state of observation" and playfulness, the subconscious picks up new capabilities most rapidly.
16. The following brief discussion borrows from many spiritual traditions, from developmental Christianity to Zen, but owes a special debt to the

work of Robert Fritz (see note 3). Useful readings from these different traditions include, *Finding Grace at the Center,* editor Thomas Keating et al. (Still River, Mass.: St. Bede Publications), 1978; and Shunryu Suzuki Roshi, *Zen Mind, Beginner's Mind.* (New York and Tokyo: Weatherhill), 1975.

17. Quoted in Fritz, *The Path of Least Resistance.*
18. Weston Agor, *Intuitive Management:* Integrating Left and Right Brain Management Skills (Englewood Cliffs, N.J.: Prentice-Hall), 1984; Henry Mintzberg, "Planning on the Left Side and Managing on the Right," *Harvard Business Review* (July/August 1976): 49–58; Daniel Isenberg, "How Top Managers Think" *Harvard Business Review* (July/August 1976): 49.
19. The cases described in the "Microworlds" chapter illustrate developing systemic explanations to explain previously inexplicable intuitions.
20. Karen Cook, "Scenario for a New Age; Can American Industry Find Renewal in Management Theories Born of Counterculture?" *New York Times Magazine,* September 25, 1988; Robert Lindsey, "Gurus Hired to Motivate Workers are Raising Fears of Mind Control," *New York Times,* April 17, 1987.

CHAPTER 10
MENTAL MODELS

1. H. Gardner, *The Mind's New Science* (New York: Basic Books), 1984, 1985.
2. C. Argyris, *Reasoning, Learning and Action: Individual and Organizational* (San Francisco: Jossey-Bass), 1982.
3. Thomas S. Kuhn, *The Structure of Scientific Revolutions* (Chicago: University of Chicago Press), 1962, 1970.
4. U.S. Department of Commerce, Bureau of Economic Analysis, "National Income and Product Accounts," *Survey of Current Business,* vol. 67, no. 6 (July 1987), Table 1.17. Cited in Office of Technology Assessment, *Technology and the American Economic Transition: Choices for the Future,* (U.S. Government Printing Office), 1988.
5. Ian Mitroff, *Break-Away Thinking,* (New York: John Wiley), 1988.
6. The Detroit example also suggests that entire industries can develop mental models chronically out of touch with reality. In some ways, industries are especially vulnerable because all the individual members of the industry look to each other for standards of best practice. It may take someone from "outside the system," such as foreign competitors, with different mental models, to finally break the spell.
7. Pierre Wack, "Scenarios: Uncharted Waters Ahead," *Harvard Business Review* (September/October 1985), 72; and "Scenarios: Shooting

the Rapids," *Harvard Business Review* (November/December 1985), 139.

8. "After the Middle East and the North African nations asserted themselves and took control of the oil in their lands, Shell's position was enhanced. . . . It enjoyed an edge that has enabled it to come close to [its founder] Deterding's goal: eclipse Exxon as the world's largest oil company."—Milton Moskowitz in *The Global Marketplace* (New York: Macmillan), 1987.

9. The core values at Hanover, in addition to openness and merit, include "localness" (no decision should ever be made higher up than is absolutely necessary), and leanness (continually increasing the capacity to produce more, higher quality results with less resources).

10. C. Argyris and D. Schon, *Organizational Learning: A Theory of Action Perspective* (Reading, Mass.: Addison-Wesley), 1978; C. Argyris, R. Putnam, and D. Smith, *Action Science* (San Francisco: Jossey-Bass), 1985; C. Argyris, *Strategy, Change, and Defensive Routines* (Boston: Pitman), 1985.

11. For example, see Peter Checkland, *Systems Thinking, Systems Practice* (New York: John Wiley), 1981, and Colin Eden, *Management Decision and Decision Analysis* (New York: John Wiley), 1975.

12. A. de Geus, quoted in Art Kleiner, "Consequential Heresies," 1990; unpublished manuscript.

13. Donald Schon, *The Reflective Practitioner: How Professionals Think in Action* (New York: Basic Books), 1983.

14. G. A. Miller, "The magical number seven plus or minus two: Some limits on our capacity for processing information," *Psychological Review*, vol. 63, 1956, 81–97.

15. Stuart Gannes, "Sun's Sizzling Race to the Top," *Fortune*, August 17, 1987, 88: the analysis of Sun and Apple owes much to the insight of Alan K. Graham.

16. I am indebted to Diana Smith for allowing me to reproduce these guidelines.

17. John Sterman, "Misperceptions of Feedback in Dynamic Decisionmaking," Cambridge, Mass.: MIT Sloan School of Management Working Paper WP-1933-87, 1987.

CHAPTER 11
SHARED VISION

1. Some facts about the man Spartacus come from Arthur Koestler's postscript to his novel *The Gladiator*, translated by Edith Simon (New York: Macmillan), 1939.

2. These cases of corporate vision have been analyzed by G. Hamel and

C. K. Prahalad in "Strategic Intent," *Harvard Business Review*, May–June, 1989.

3. Kazuo Inamori, "The Perfect Company: Goal for Productivity," speech given at Case Western Reserve University, Cleveland, Ohio, June 5, 1985.

4. Max de Pree, *Leadership is an Art* (New York: Doubleday/ Currency), 1989.

5. John Sculley with John A. Byrne, *Odyssey: Pepsi to Apple* (New York: Harper and Row), 1987.

6. A. Maslow, *Eupsychian Management*, (Homewood, Ill.: Richard Irwin and Dorsey Press), 1965.

7. William Manchester, *The Glory and the Dream* (Boston: Little, Brown and Company), 1974.

8. G. Hamel and C. K. Prahalad, "Strategic Intent."

9. Ibid.

10. The ideas expressed in this section come from many hours of discussion with my colleagues at Innovation Associates, notably Charles Kiefer, Alain Gauthier, Charlotte Roberts, Rick Ross, and Bryan Smith.

11. For example the Daniel Yankelovich and John Immerwahr study in 1983, which found that only 25 percent of U.S. workers said they were working as hard as they could be. "Are U.S. workers lazy?" by Joani Nelson-Horchler, *Industry Week*, June 10, 1985, 47.

12. M. Moskowitz, The Global Marketplace (New York: Macmillan Publishing Company), 1987.

13. "IBM's $5,000,000,000 Gamble," *Fortune*, September 1966, and "The Rocky Road to the Marketplace," *Fortune*, October 1966 (two-part article).

14. Sculley with Byrne, *Odyssey*.

CHAPTER 12
TEAM LEARNING

1. W. Russell and T. Branch, *Second Wind: Memoirs of an Opinionated Man* (New York: Random House), 1979.

2. This diagram appeared originally in C. Kiefer and P. Stroh, "A New Paradigm for Developing Organizations," in J. Adams, editor, *Transforming Work* (Alexandria Va.: Miles Riler Press), 1984.

3. This section benefited especially from conversations with Bill Isaacs and with David Bohm, who was also very kind letting me reproduce many of his observations.

4. David Bohm, *The Special Theory of Relativity* (New York: W. A. Benjamin), 1965.

5. Many of David Bohm's statements contained here come from a series

of "dialogues" in which David has participated in Cambridge and elsewhere over the past year. I am deeply grateful for his permission to include them here, as well as excerpts from his forthcoming book, with coauthor Mark Edwards, provisionally entitled *Thought, the Hidden Challenge to Humanity* (San Francisco: Harper & Row). Other related books include *Wholeness and the Implicate Order* (New York: Ark Paperbacks), 1983; with F. D. Peat, *Science, Order, and Creativity* (New York: Bantam), 1987.

6. See, for example, E. Schein, *Process Consultation*, vol. 2 (Reading Mass.: Addison Wesley), 1987.
7. C. Argyris, *Strategy, Change, and Defensive Routines* (Boston: Pitman), 1985.
8. Ibid.
9. Ibid.
10. See, for example, D. C. Wise and G. C. Lewis, "A Fire Sale in Personal Computers," *Business Week*, March 25, 1985, 289, and "Rocky Times for Micros," *Marketing Media Decisions*, July 1985.
11. Argyris, *Strategy, Change, and Defensive Routines*.
12. Interestingly, reduced threat in talking about sensitive issues is exactly what happens in "dialogue sessions," where the ground rules are such that concern for "right" or "wrong" insights quickly disappears. As dialogue sessions become a regular part of how teams work together, such threats perceived by team members may well decline generally.
13. In order to move beyond defenses, it helps to create a learning environment—what we call a microworld—in which people can openly explore their hesitancies about moving toward more openness. When people surface their hesitancies in such a setting, it's possible to design mini-experiments that help them to incrementally try out new ways of acting in the face of their concerns.
14. Donald Schon, *The Reflective Practitioner: How Professionals Think in Action* (New York: Basic Books), 1983.
15. The names and other specifics of this story are fictitious but the dialogue itself, and the background organizational issues it addressed, are real. The dialogue is reproduced from transcripts of the actual meeting (which is a common feature of our research on team learning), which are only shortened, not edited, in an attempt to preserve the feeling of the dialogue itself. I am indebted to Bill Isaacs for his help in organizing this material.
16. Michael Porter, *Competitive Advantage: Creating and Sustaining Superior Performance* (New York: Free Press), 1985, and Michael Porter, *Competitive Strategy: Techniques for Analyzing Industries and Competitors* (New York: Free Press), 1980.

CHAPTER 13
OPENNESS

1. I am of course using the term "political" in the pejorative, as it is commonly used today. This is a far cry from its original meaning. In many ways, the spirit of openness, localness, and merit that must prevail in a learning organization recaptures much of the original Greek notion of *"polis"* as a place where governance was achieved through dialogue and advocacy balanced with inquiry. The heart of Aristotle's definition of *polis* is retained in our current use of the phrase "a circle of friends," which represents a "finite group of people united by acquaintance, common sentiments, and interests—in short an association." From Terence Dall, Political Theory and Praxis (Minneapolis: University of Minnesota Press), 1977.
2. Badaracco, Joseph L. Jr., and Richard R. Ellsworth, *Leadership and the Quest for Integrity* (Boston: Harvard Business School Press), 1989.
3. A well-known example of this is the "Scanlon" process for participative management, which typically involves weekly meetings where workers and management exchange views on whatever issues are most important. See Barrie T. Smith, "A Way to a Competitive Tomorrow," *Production Engineering,* February 1986, 28, and Kenneth O. Alexander, "Democracy in the Workplace," *Technology Review,* November/December 1983, 12.
4. The "Wall" exercise is part of the Leadership & Mastery seminars, Innovation Associates, Framingham, Massachusetts.
5. Albert Einstein, quoted in *Bartlett's Familiar Quotations,* 15th edition, Emily Morrison Beck, editor (Boston: Little, Brown & Company), 1980.
6. E. F. Schumacher, *A Guide for the Perplexed* (New York: Harper and Row), 1977.
7. The seventeenth-century translators of the King James version of the Bible had the same problem. They translated the word in Paul's Letters to the Corinthians as "charity."

CHAPTER 14
LOCALNESS

1. According to many organizational theorists, localness also means fundamental innovations in formal organizational structures: networks of highly autonomous business units, dozens perhaps hundreds of free-standing profit centers, radical changes in traditional corporate hierarchies. (Jay Forrester, "A New Corporate Design," *Sloan Management*

Review, 7, 1 (Fall 1965), and Russell Ackoff, *Creating the Corporate Future* (New York: Wiley), 1981.

2. A recent study by Michael Gold and Andrew Campbell of the London Business School (*Harvard Business Review,* November/December 1987, 70) found that different equally successful corporations balanced local and corporate control in different ways: some emphasized strong centralized strategy development with local freedom to implement strategies; others set financial standards at the corporate level and left business units to devise their own strategies and operational plans; others practiced a mix. All sought the benefits of local autonomy while not giving up corporate control.

3. The Hanover philosophy statement on localness can be obtained from Hanover Insurance National Office, 100 N. Parkway, Worcester, MA 01605.

4. Johnson & Johnson press release, October 24, 1988, on occasion of appointment of new CEO.

5. *Fortune,* June 6, 1988, 50.

6. See Gareth Morgan, *Images of Organizations* (Newbury Park, CA: Sage Publications), 1986, and Stafford Beer, *Brain of the Firm* New York: Herder and Herder), 1972.

7. Peter Lorange, M. F. Scott Morton, and S. Ghoshal, *Strategic Control Systems* (St. Paul, Minn.: West), 1986.

8. Anthony G. Miller, "Corporate Heirlooms: Productivity Tools of the Nineties," *Business Quarterly,* vol. 54 (4) (Summer 1989), 80–84.

9. Pierre Wack, "Scenarios: Uncharted Waters Ahead," *Harvard Business Review,* September/October 1985, 73–89.

10. Garrett Hardin, "The Tragedy of the Commons," *Science,* December 13, 1968; Dennis Soden, *The Tragedy of the Commons: Twenty Years of Policy Literature, 1968–1988* (Monticello, Illinois: Vance Bibliographies), 1988.

11. Lester R. Brown et al, *State of the World 1986: A Worldwatch Institute Report on Progress Toward a Sustainable Society* (New York: W. W. Norton and Company), 1986.

12. *Fortune,* June 6, 1988, 50.

13. Jerry B. Harvey, *The Abilene Paradox and other Meditations on Management* (Lexington, Mass.: Lexington Books), 1988.

CHAPTER 15
A MANAGER'S TIME

1. Donald Schon, *The Reflective Practitioner: How Professionals Think in Action* (New York: Basic Books), 1983.

2. Preliminary accounts of this research can be found in Daniel H. Kim,

"Designing a Reflective Learning Environment," and Peter Senge, "Organizational Learning: A New Challenge for System Dynamics," both in *Computer-Based Management of Complex Systems: Proceedings of the 1989 International Conference of the System Dynamics Society,* Stuttgart, July 10–14, 1989, Peter M. Milling and Erich O. K. Zahn, editors (Berlin: Springer-Verland), 1989.

CHAPTER 16
ENDING THE WAR BETWEEN
WORK AND FAMILY

1. Brian O'Reilly, *Fortune,* January 1, 1990, 36–46.
2. Technically, this third feedback process is also reinforcing, but it does not produce a runaway because there is a limit, the total time available (waking hours in a week).
3. U.S. Department of Commerce, Bureau of Census, *Statistical Abstract of the United States, 1982–1983;* and *1989* (Washington: U.S. Government Printing Office), 1983 and 1989.
4. *Technology and the American Economic Transition: Choices for the Future* (Washington: U.S. Congress Office of Technology Assessment), May 1988.
5. Max de Pree, *Leadership Is an Art,* (New York: Doubleday/Currency), 1989.

CHAPTER 17
MICROWORLDS: THE TECHNOLOGY
OF THE LEARNING ORGANIZATION

1. The term "microworld" was coined by educator and computer scientist Seymour Papert, developer of "Logo," the pioneering computer learning system for young children. Papert's microworlds are designed microcosms of reality within which children learn through experimentation with computer-based transitional objects, such as the famous "Logo turtle," with which children *discover* the principles of geometry by learning how to instruct the turtle to trace out squares, rectangles, triangles, and circles. See Seymour Papert, *Mindstorms: Children, Computers, and Powerful Ideas* (New York: Basic Books), 1980.
2. The name and specifics of the company are changed, but the insights are based on a real case involving my colleague Barry Richmond, of Dartmouth College and High Performance Systems.
3. The teams were using a software package called STELLA with which simulation models can be built at a screen of a personal computer with

advanced graphics capabilities (such as a Macintosh). STELLA is available from High Performance Systems, Inc., Lyme, N.H.

4. Pierre Wack, "Scenarios: Uncharted Waters Ahead," *Harvard Business Review*, September/October 1985.

5. This story is based on a case involving Jennifer Kemeny and myself. The names and specifics of the company have been changed.

6. The model incorporated assumptions regarding potential customer response to better service based on the firm's own market research. These assumptions were varied through several replays of the game to test the sensitivity to the *degree* of customer response to improved service. It was found that there was still potential leverage in investing more in service over a wide range of assumptions.

7. The game and underlying model were developed originally by Nathan B. Forrester and myself, with the assistance of Ernst Diehl. See P. Senge, "Catalyzing Systems Thinking in Organizations," in *Advances in Organization Development*, F. Masarik, editor (Norwood, N.J.: Ablex), 1990. For more detail on the learning process described below, see D. Kim, "Designing a Reflective Learning Environment," and P. Senge, "Organizational Learning: a New Challenge for System Dynamics," both in *Computer-Based Management of Complex Systems: Proceedings of the 1989 International Conference of the System Dynamics Society*, Stuttgart, July 10–14, 1989, Peter M. Milling and Erich O. K. Zahn, editors (Berlin: Springer-Verland), 1989.

8. Several underwriters have made a point of remarking how, as underwriters, they face similar dynamics.

9. G. Lynn Shostack, "Designing Services that Deliver," *Harvard Business Review*, January/February 1984.

10. Witness the trend toward foreign ownership of U.S. service firms. For example, in 1989, 25 percent of banking assets in California were controlled by Japanese-owned banks, up from less than 5 percent in 1980. *Fortune*, Fall 1989; and "How the Japanese Attract the California Depositor," *Euromoney*, June 1980.

11. In fact, the learning process described comes from the first series of Claims Learning Laboratory workshops. The Hanover managers are now planning the second stage of work focused on designing and carrying out experiments with the structures, reward systems, and operating practices of actual claims offices and regions. The important point is that lying behind these "real life" experiments will be shared understandings of the dynamics of the claims system and the objectives. Expected outcomes of the experiments will be formulated in advance through experimentation and discussion in the microworld.

CHAPTER 18
THE LEADER'S NEW WORK

1. Ray Stata, "Organizational Learning—The Key to Management Innovation," *Sloan Management Review*, Spring 1989, 63–64.
2. Heinrich Zimmer, *The King and the Corpse* (Princeton, New Jersey: Princeton University Press), 1948.
3. George Bernard Shaw, epistle dedicatory for *Man and Superman* (London), 1903.
4. Khalil Gibran, *The Prophet* (New York: Alfred A. Knopf), 1923.
5. Max de Pree, *Leadership Is an Art* (New York: Doubleday/Currency), 1989.
6. William F. Gore, "The Lattice Organization," speech given at Reinventing the Corporation Workshop (Washington, D.C.: The Naisbitt Group), 1985.
7. William Manchester, *The Glory and the Dream* (Boston: Little, Brown and Company), 1974.
8. Martin Luther King, Jr., "Letter from Birmingham Jail," *American Visions* (January/February 1986), 52–59.
9. Martin Buber, *I and Thou* (New York: Charles Scribner's Sons), 1970.
10. Corazon C. Aquino, speech delivered on March 10, 1984.

CHAPTER 20
REWRITING THE CODE

1. I am indebted to my longtime colleague Charlie Kiefer for suggesting the idea developed in this chapter.
2. The term "subconscious" has been used by many others, such as Freud and Jung, to represent phenomena somewhat different from those discussed here.
3. Many accelerated learning techniques such as "super-learning" or Tim Gallwey's "inner game of tennis" focus specifically on conscious-subconscious interaction in learning, showing that if the conscious mind can be kept in a quiet nonjudgmental "state of observation" and playfulness, the subconscious picks up new capabilities most rapidly. See Sheila Ostrander and Lynn Schroeder, *Superlearning* (New York: Laurel/Confucian Press Book), 1982; or W. Timothy Gallwey, *The Inner Game of Tennis* (New York, Bantam), 1979.

CHAPTER 21
THE INDIVISIBLE WHOLE

1. The following is reprinted with permission from "Whose Earth," by Russell Schweickart, in *The Next Whole Earth Catalog*, Stewart Brand, editor (New York: Point Foundation/Random House), 1980.
2. One recent product was the beautiful book *The Home Planet*, edited by Kevin Kelley, with photographs and reflections from many astronauts and cosmonauts. The book was released at Christmas 1988, the first book ever published simultaneously in the United States (Reading, Mass.: Addison-Wesley) and the U.S.S.R.
3. This hypothesis has been advanced by several scientists. For a good introduction to the idea and the supporting data, see J. Lovelock, *Gaia: A New View of Life on Earth* (New York: Oxford University Press), 1979.

APPENDIX 2
SYSTEMS ARCHETYPES

1. Many people in the system dynamics field have contributed to identifying and coding these archetypes, or (as they are often called), "generic structures." I would particularly like to thank Jennifer Kemeny, Michael Goodman, Ernst Diehl, Christian Kampmann, Dan Kim, Jack Nevison, and John Sterman for their contributions.

ACKNOWLEDGMENTS

In writing this book, I have often felt more like a reporter than an author. The work of so many people is treated, and the work of so many more lies behind the scenes, that my biggest fear is that I will forget someone who should be on these pages.

So I will proceed chronologically, in hope that this will be the most foolproof strategy. My introduction to systems thinking as a management and leadership discipline came from Jay W. Forrester, and he has been my mentor for some twenty years now. My debt to Jay is vast—obviously for his wisdom, less obviously for his enduring standards of excellence, most subtly for his commitment to always focus on the most important problems rather than the most tractable.

Harriet Rubin and Arie de Geus were instrumental in getting this project launched. Many thanks to Harriet for her belief (still to be proven out) in a first-time author. Her genuine enthusiasm for this project and uncanny intuitions were a continual delight. I learned to always listen to her comments, especially when my "academic mind" tried to intervene. Arie introduced me to the idea of learning organizations many years ago, then suggested that a book on the subject was in order over two years ago. Unfortunately, his duties at Shell precluded having as much of a role in producing the book as I would have liked. But his thinking and passion for the idea are evident nonetheless.

Many colleagues at MIT, Harvard, and Innovation Associates contributed significantly to particular aspects of the book: John Sterman, Jennifer Kemeny, and Dan Kim contributed to the systems thinking chapters; Bill Isaacs and Diana Smith helped enormously with the material on mental models and team learning; Charlie Kiefer, Charlotte Roberts, and Bryan Smith lent their considerable expertise in the areas of personal mastery and building shared vision. Alain Gauthier read the entire manuscript and offered many helpful suggestions. A special thanks to David Bohm and Chris Argyris for helping me to draw so extensively on their seminal works.

The practical experience and much of the inspiration lying behind this effort come from opportunities over the years to work with leaders who endeavor to live what is herein described—alas there are more of you than I could ever list. Especially helpful for this project have been my good friends Bill O'Brien of Hanover Insurance, Ed Simon of Herman Miller, and Ray Stata of Analog Devices. Each gave patiently of his time and generously of his spirit. Thank you also to Bart Bolton of Digital; and Geri Prusko, Bob Bergin, and Paul Stimson of Hanover for helping with specific applications discussions.

Don Ryan's artwork was critical to my concept of a book that would be more than a series of "linear" statements strung together. Thanks also to Janet Coleman of Doubleday for one thousand forms of assistance in "getting it done." Meanwhile, Janet Gould and Nan Lux kept our research center afloat while I disappeared; and Angela Lipinski, in addition to helping me, as always, with whatever needed to get done, simply handled the rest of my outside professional obligations through the duration of my hibernation. Robert Fritz's moral support meant a great deal because he too had learned to "book-write," becoming a remarkably good author remarkably quickly (as behooves someone whose expertise is creating). Michael Goodman's and Donella Meadows's support meant a great deal, just because it always does.

Three colleagues warrant special thanks. Bill Isaacs and Dan Kim helped with virtually all facets of the project, bringing to bear critical areas of expertise and helping to mold the overall product. Dan even took on the onerous task of completing all the notes and references (with assistance from researcher Judith Bruk). Without Art Kleiner, who served as writing coach, critic, editor, and for certain key sections (like the story of "Lover's Beer"), coauthor, this book would simply not be the same book. Last summer he asked me to describe my thesis for the book in a sentence—that was the beginning of a thorough refocusing and reorganizing (and eventual rewriting) of a manuscript I had been "puttering with" for over a year. I will never forget his patience, tireless (or near tireless) effort and unflagging spirit. But, I bet he and Faith will not miss my 3 A.M. calls.

Lastly, thank you to my son Nathan for being my daily teacher about the joys and sorrows of living life as a learner, and thanks beyond thanks to Diane. Just about the time I started to move into "high gear" to reshape the book, our newest son, Ian, arrived. Caring for both "projects" simultaneously was enough work for four parents. Thanks, Diane, for your patience and your perseverance. Most of all, thank you for sharing the vision. I always knew that you wouldn't let me settle for less than was possible.

INDEX